Forgotten Warriors

MODERN WAR STUDIES

Theodore A. Wilson
General Editor

Raymond A. Callahan
J. Garry Clifford
Jacob W. Kipp
Allan R. Millett
Carol Reardon
Dennis Showalter
David R. Stone
Series Editors

Forgotten Warriors

The 1st Provisional Marine
Brigade, the Corps Ethos,
and the Korean War

T. X. Hammes

University Press of Kansas

Published by the University Press of Kansas (Lawrence, Kansas 66045), which was
organized by the Kansas Board of Regents and is operated and funded by Emporia State
University, Fort Hays State University, Kansas State University, Pittsburg State
University, the University of Kansas, and Wichita State University

ISBN 978-0-7006-1732-6

Printed in the United States of America

To Janet for her patience and support while I pursued
this story of the U.S. Marine Corps
and
to the marines of Korea,
who added so much to our corps's legacy

Contents

(A photo section follows page 86)

Preface

In 1987 Clay Blair wrote a history of the Korean War titled *The Forgotten War: America in Korea, 1950–1953.* He noted that the war was long, difficult, bloody, and largely ignored by historians and the American public. Although Blair's contention that the conflict in Korea was a forgotten war was true at the time, since 1987 there has been a series of new works, including a rash of books, articles, and monographs published for the fiftieth anniversary of that war in 2000. Perhaps the Korean War can no longer claim to be a forgotten one. However, the early phase of the campaign, the long retreat down the peninsula and the defense of the Pusan Perimeter, remains overlooked even in the new literature. This critical phase is often dealt with in a single chapter. The two best-known commercial books written about the Pusan Perimeter vary greatly in quality. Edwin Hoyt's *The Pusan Perimeter* (1984) suffers from being based almost entirely on secondary sources that Hoyt apparently made little effort to verify. Fortunately, in 1996 Uzal W. Ent, a veteran of the 27th Infantry's actions in the perimeter, published a detailed history titled *Fighting on the Brink: Defense of the Pusan Perimeter,* based on extensive research and interviews with survivors. In 2000 Terry Addison published *The Battle for Pusan: A Memoir.* He wrote this account during the fall and winter of 1950–1951 while recovering from wounds received during his service as a forward observer with the 8th Artillery Battalion assigned to the 27th Infantry Regiment in the perimeter. Addison's account is an exceptional first-person account of the 1st Battalion, 27th Infantry's actions in the perimeter. The 27th Infantry is widely regarded as the most combat-effective U.S. Army unit in the perimeter.

Yet, despite the recent surge in interest in Korea, there are only two books that study the role of the 1st Provisional Marine Brigade in the fight for the Pusan Perimeter. The first, published in 1953, is the corps's official history, *U.S. Marine Operations in Korea, Volume 1: The Pusan Perimeter.* The second, *The Darkest Summer,* published in 2009, provides a "band of brothers" history of the fighting in the perimeter as well as in the Pusan-Seoul campaign. Although these histories cover the brigade's combat actions in detail, even they don't give full credit to its remarkable accomplishments or to the corps as a whole in maintaining combat readiness during the lean years of 1946–1950.

As its name implies, the brigade was not a standing organization. Over a week after the North Koreans invaded South Korea, the brigade was hastily assembled in California from the woefully understrength 1st Marine Division and 1st Marine Air Wing. Shipping out only six days after activation, the brigade entered combat four days after its arrival in Korea. Despite the hasty formation and long sea voyage, the brigade quickly defeated each North Korean attack it faced; for the first time in the perimeter, a U.S. unit drove the North Koreans back in disarray. What combination of factors allowed the brigade to succeed so dramatically despite the enormous obstacles it faced?

Over the years a number of authors have partially addressed this issue as part of longer works on the Korean War. Writing in 1982, Joseph C. Goulden noted the brigade's intensive training, unit cohesion, and physical fitness:

> The Marines had several inherent advantages over the army. They had been in combat training in the United States; they arrived in cohesive units in which officers and men had served together for months (not hours, as was the case with many jerry-built army "companies"); they insisted on controlling their own air support, in coordinated actions based upon years of experience. Further, given the corps's stress on arduous physical training for every man, regardless of his assignment, the Marines arrived in Korea in far better condition than their army counterparts.[1]

In 1985 Donald Knox compiled a wide range of individual oral histories. In analyzing the brigade, he noted the exceptional combat experience of the brigade's officers and noncommissioned officers (NCOs): "What the brigade lacked in numbers . . . it made up for in experience. Most of its officers and two out of three NCOs were veterans of the tough island fighting of the Second World War; company commanders and platoon leaders and squad leaders had been blooded at places like Peleliu, Guam, Bougainville, Iwo Jima and Okinawa."[2]

In his popular and highly regarded book on the marines in Korea, *The New Breed*, published in 1989, Andrew Geer wrote, "Ninety per cent of the officers of the new brigade had been in combat; sixty-five per cent of the senior NCO's had been in action against an enemy, but of the corporals and Pfc.'s [privates first class], only ten per cent had ever been under enemy fire."[3]

By 2000 the belief that the brigade had trained hard as a formed unit over the winter of 1949–1950 and been led almost exclusively by veterans of tough ground combat was firmly rooted in corps legend. In an article for *Leatherneck* magazine commemorating the fiftieth anniversary of the Korean War, Allan Bevilacqua, a retired marine major, wrote,

Save for those Marines hastily joined from posts and stations up and down the West Coast, the 5th Marines had been together at Camp Pendleton, Calif., for a year and more. . . . It may be that the Marine Corps never sent a better trained regiment to war. . . . Beyond that they had the added advantage of being led by officers and staff noncommissioned officers who were almost entirely veterans of the war against Japan—men who had fought battles as ferocious as anything on record in any war.[4]

In 2000 the History and Museums Division, Headquarters, U.S. Marine Corps, issued a series of monographs commemorating the war's fiftieth anniversary. The first, *Fire Brigade: U.S. Marines in the Pusan Perimeter*, provided a concise history of the formation of the brigade, its time in combat in the perimeter, and its reembarkation and deactivation on September 13, 1950. But even *Fire Brigade* authoritatively ascribed the combat success of the brigade to the extensive combat experience of its leaders, its intensive training the previous year, the cohesion of its units, and the physical fitness of its individual marines.[5]

None of the accounts of the brigade studied the period between the end of World War II and the beginning of the Korean War. None examined the impact of demobilization, integration, atomic weapons, plummeting budgets, dramatically decreased end strengths, and peacetime personnel policies on the Marine Corps of the late 1940s. Rather, each account simply starts with the North Korean invasion of South Korea. Despite the failure to examine the years that shaped the corps before the Korean War, these interpretations have become generally accepted. Within the Marine Corps, these beliefs have become part of the internal historical narrative that is reflected not only in the official histories but in the sea stories marines tell. These internal narratives are an essential element in the culture of every successful organization.

When I first joined the Marine Corps in 1975, there were still a few Korean War veterans on active duty. In keeping with marine tradition, they told stories to the junior marines, and their stories reflected the internal legends that had grown up since they had fought in Korea. The marines who told the stories pointed to several critical factors they felt had made the brigade successful. For example, they emphasized the point that the leaders of the brigade had almost all been World War II combat veterans. They said that, unlike the U.S. Army occupation troops in Japan, who were the first U.S. forces committed to ground combat in Korea, the marines had trained hard during the years before the war. Therefore, unlike their army counterparts, the marines had been very physically fit. Finally, every marine pointed to the corps's extensive experience using marine air in support of ground forces. They were proud to say the marines had pioneered close air support during the Banana Wars and had refined it to a high art during World War II. Our storytellers were convinced that the corps had drawn heavily on its World War II expertise to fight in Korea.

In these narratives, despite the fact that the brigade had had only six days to form, embark, and sail, the marines were able simply to reapply the skills they had used so effectively in World War II and practiced so intensely during peacetime. Obviously these accounts were a tribute to the high professional standards and intensive focus on readiness of the corps between 1946 and 1950. In 1975, with the corps recovering from the Vietnam War, the stories of the brigade stood in stark contrast to the high turnover of personnel, shortages of equipment and personnel, periodic reorganizations, and lack of training funds that marked our day-to-day lives in the operating forces.

Unfortunately, as we will see, these stories are mostly myths that have hidden the real accomplishments both of the men of the Provisional Brigade and of the U.S. Marine Corps as a whole between World War II and Korea. By attributing intensive training, unit cohesion, and physical fitness to the brigade, the myths minimize the exceptional courage and determination shown by these marines during the perimeter defense. They also denigrate the farsighted efforts of the corps's leadership and its exceptional efforts to maintain the corps's culture despite enormous pressures that included three efforts to do away with the corps altogether.

The purpose of this book is threefold. First, I hope to provide insights into how the corps's leaders maintained its culture and combat effectiveness during the extraordinarily tough period between World War II and Korea. Second, I want to dispel the myths concerning training, organization, and combat experience of the units that formed the brigade. Finally, I want to provide a detailed account of the brigade's frenetic embarkation process and its monthlong combat operations.

Obviously the first issue, how the corps maintained combat effectiveness between the wars, is not entirely new ground. A number of studies have examined what makes military organizations effective in combat. Probably the best known are Millett and Murray's three-volume work *Military Effectiveness, Volume 1: The First World War*, *Volume 2: The Interwar Period*, and *Volume 3: The Second World War*. Using a case-study method, the authors explore the reasons behind the successes and failures of the armed forces of six nations over this period. Though exceptional in their scholarship, these volumes measure effectiveness more than they explore the reasons for it. Their *Military Innovation in the Interwar Period* takes the studies a major step further by exploring the factors that either encouraged or inhibited innovation during this critical period. Unfortunately, they have not explored the period after World War II.

Stephen Biddle's *Military Power: Explaining Victory and Defeat in Modern Battle* measures effectiveness by how well a force can inflict damage on an enemy force while preserving its own, how well it takes and holds ground, and how quickly it can accomplish these two tasks.[6] He argues that effectiveness flows from a military's ability to use the modern system of force employment—essentially effective combined arms at the tactical and operational level. By Biddle's measures, the brigade was highly successful in using the modern system.

Although his measure is a very good one, it does not explain how a force becomes good at the modern system—particularly when facing the political and budgetary pressures the corps faced after World War II. In an effort to give both the brigade and the corps as a whole proper credit for the truly remarkable accomplishment of maintaining combat effectiveness, I will examine six aspects similar to those van Creveld labeled *Fighting Power* when he compared the U.S. and German armies in World War II.

Because the 1st Provisional Marine Brigade existed only from 7 June to 13 September 1950, I will examine the Marine Corps's culture, educational system, doctrine, organization, training, and leadership between Victory in Japan (VJ) Day (15 August 1945) and North Korea's invasion of South Korea (25 June 1950). Actions taken during those years set the conditions for the brigade. The combat accomplishments of the brigade are indisputable, but the incredible handicaps it had to overcome have not been properly appreciated. In particular the widely held beliefs that the brigade's units had trained together, were physically fit, and were led by officers and NCOs with extensive ground combat experience during World War II are all false.

This book will try to separate the myths from reality to determine the reasons for the brigade's truly remarkable record. This attempt at clarification is particularly important for marines, who draw much of their identity from a deep regard for their history. The men who set the conditions and the men who fought in Korea deserve to have their incredible accomplishments properly recorded—unclouded by the myths that have arisen since. Despite the enormous handicaps they faced, their actions upheld the standards of previous generations of marines and passed them along intact for generations of marines to come.

This book would not have been possible without the guidance and assistance of many people. Three historians in particular have spent a lifetime assisting others in research and writing and generously shared their time with me. I would particularly like to thank Professor Hew Strachan, who was willing to supervise a decidedly overage graduate student; Professor Allan R. Millett, who both introduced me to academic research at the Mershon Center for Strategic Studies long ago and shared his encyclopedic knowledge of the Corps and the Korean War to help me refine the various drafts of this book; and finally, Professor Kenneth Hamburger, who was kind enough to read the manuscript and recommend significant improvements in both content and presentation. All errors of both omission and commission belong solely to me.

Abbreviations Used in This Book

ALO	air liaison officer
ANGLICO	Air Naval Gunfire Liaison Company
ASCU	air support control unit
BAR	Browning automatic rifle
BLT	battalion landing team
CG	commanding general
CNO	chief of naval operations
CO	commanding officer
CP	command post
CPX	command post exercise
CVE	escort carrier
DASC	direct air support center
FAC	forward air controller
FDC	fire direction center
FEAF	Far East Air Force
FSCC	fire support coordination center
FMF	Fleet Marine Force
FMFLant	Fleet Marine Force Atlantic
FMFPac	Fleet Marine Force Pacific
H&S	Headquarters and Service
Hedron	Headquarters Squadron
HMX 1	Marine Helicopter Squadron 1
JCS	Joint Chiefs of Staff
KIA	killed in action
KMAG	Korea Military Advisory Group
LSD	landing ship dock
LST	landing ship tank

MACG	Marine Air/Aircraft Control Group
MAG	Marine Air Group
MAW	Marine Air/Aircraft Wing
MGCIS	Marine Ground Control Intercept Squadron
MIA	missing in action
MP	military police
MOS	military occupational specialty
MTACS	Marine Tactical Air Control Squadron
NCO	noncommissioned officer
NKPA	North Korean People's Army
Pfc	private first class
PHIB	amphibious
RCT	Regimental Combat Team
RLT	regimental landing team
ROK	Republic of Korea
SNCO	staff noncommissioned officer
T/Os	Tables of Organizations
TAC	tactical air controller
TACP	Tactical Air Control Party
TAD	temporary additional duty
TF	Task Force
TG	Task Group
VJ Day	Victory in Japan Day
VMF	Marine Fighter Squadron
VMF(N)	Marine All Weather Fighter Squadron
VMO	Marine Observation Squadron
VMP	Marine Photo Squadron
WIA	wounded in action
XO	executive officer

1

From "A Corps for the Next 500 Years" to a Fight for Existence

On the morning of 25 June 1950, the North Korean Army launched seven divisions, a tank brigade, and two independent regiments across the 38th parallel. Having failed to achieve peaceful political union, Kim Il Sung, North Korea's dictator, was gambling that he could unify Korea by force. Although both U.S. and South Korean military officials had been predicting an invasion, the ferocity and power of the actual attack stunned the ill-prepared, poorly trained, and under-equipped South Korean Army. While the conflict was obviously a serious matter, most Americans did not think it would affect them. The Truman administration had repeatedly stated that Korea was outside the area considered vital to the U.S. defense, strongly implying that the United States would not fight in Korea. Yet, within thirty-six hours of the North Korean invasion, U.S. forces were at war.

The sudden U.S. commitment to fight in Korea was more accidental than planned. It grew out of the postwar division of Korea, which itself had been an accidental result of World War II. At the Yalta Conference in February 1945, the United States had pressed the Soviet Union to enter the war against Japan upon the defeat of Germany. To entice the Soviets, the United States offered them limited territorial gains in postwar Manchuria. Despite this incentive, the Soviets did not declare war immediately after the Germans surrendered on 8 May 1945. Instead the Soviets waited until 8 August, after the atomic bombing of Hiroshima, to declare war and then used the declaration primarily as an opportunity to occupy Manchuria and parts of Korea. In contrast to this apparent Soviet planning for Korea, U.S. military planners remained focused on the invasion of the Japanese home islands—a campaign expected to take between one and two years. There was no apparent immediate need for the United States to finalize postwar political plans; in fact the United States had not even developed a plan for the postwar occupation of Korea. The sudden surrender of Japan on 15 August, following the

1

atomic bombing of Hiroshima and Nagasaki, genuinely surprised U.S. planners. With Soviet troops moving into Korea from the north, the allies needed an easily defined boundary to prevent accidental clashes as U.S. forces arrived in Korea. With virtually no planning or thought, the United States proposed the 38th parallel, and the Soviets accepted. Both agreed this was to be a temporary division for the purpose of accepting the surrender of Japanese troops.

The United States had hoped Korea could be an area of cooperation between China, the United States, and the Soviet Union. The Truman administration saw the division as a temporary expedient until an independent Korean government could be formed. This proved a false hope, and as the U.S. and Soviet postwar positions hardened, Korea remained divided. In the north the Soviets installed Kim Il Sung as the leader of a communist dictatorship. In the south, after years of indecision, the United States finally turned to Syngman Rhee to form a government. Neither man was willing to compromise to create a unified Korea. Instead each started a subversive campaign in an effort to overthrow the other and unify the Korean Peninsula under his rule.

Once the repatriation of Japanese forces was complete, the only remaining U.S. interest lay in establishing an independent Korea. Although remaining engaged in attempts to unify Korea under an interim government, the Truman administration clearly wanted to minimize the resources it expended in Korea. On 25 July 1947, the Joint Chiefs of Staff (JCS) made the following recommendation to Secretary of State George C. Marshall: "In light of the present state of severe shortage of military manpower, the corps of two divisions totaling some 45,000 men, now maintained in Korea, could well be used elsewhere. The withdrawal of these forces from Korea would not impair the military position of the Far East Command, unless in consequence, the Soviets establish military strength in South Korea capable of mounting an assault on Japan."[1]

In a follow-up memo dated 25 September 1947, Gen. Dwight D. Eisenhower, chairman of the JCS, confirmed the JCS position by writing, "Given America's limited resources, the United States has little strategic interest in keeping bases and troops in Korea."[2] Reflecting this assessment, the United States withdrew its last combat troops in March 1949. Despite its decision to withdraw, the administration remained concerned that the Soviets would read the withdrawal as an opportunity to step up subversive activities in South Korea. U.S. officials decided the best way to prevent such a misinterpretation was a rapid buildup of the South Korean Army to the point at which it could defend itself. For that purpose, the United States created the Korea Military Advisory Group (KMAG) on 1 July 1949. KMAG was tasked with raising and training a South Korean army of 100,000 soldiers as well as a small navy and air force. In theory, that force would be sufficient to defend South Korea from a North Korean invasion. Just as important from the U.S. point of view, the force would be insufficient to allow South Korean president Syngman Rhee to initiate an invasion of the north.[3] Although Kim's aggressive statements made the administration worry about a North Korean invasion, Rhee's equally shrill declarations raised concern that, if provided with an effective army, Rhee would attack the north. Thus, despite Rhee's repeated forceful requests for more military aid, the Truman administration limited military aid to $11 million for 1950 and focused more on the economic development of Korea. The administration planned to provide $300 million of economic aid over the next three years because it believed that a prosperous South Korea would evolve only after the national economy was developed.[4]

Budgetary limitations and the belief that Korea was not vital to U.S. strategy meant KMAG was assigned only 500 men and very limited resources. The advisory group was simply too small to overcome the numerous deficiencies of the South Korean Army. Despite KMAG's efforts over the winter of 1949–1950, South Korean troops still lacked training in the fundamentals, from combat skills to maintenance of weapons and equipment. The maintenance deficiencies provided an insight into the true state of South Korea's army. Vehicle readiness rates were less than 40 percent. In fact, South Korean army maintenance was so bad that after one inspection of the cavalry regiment's armored vehicles, KMAG seriously suggested converting the unit to horse cavalry.[5] Although equipped with some artillery, more vehicles, and additional weapons during the latter part of 1949 and early 1950, the South Korean Army remained essentially a constabulary force despite the fact that the South Koreans had been fighting the North Koreans in various ways almost since the separation had taken place in 1945. During the summer of 1949 alone, there were over 500 combat encounters between South Korean troops and insurgents across South Korea as well as frequent border incidents with North Korea.[6] Further, the South Korean Army predicted an invasion in 1950, perhaps as early as March. They knew the Soviets had built a real army for the North Koreans and that the North Koreans were preparing to use it.

On 12 January 1950 Secretary of State Dean Acheson gave a speech titled "Crisis in China—An Examination of United States Policy." In this now famous speech to the National Press Club, Acheson described the new U.S. defense perimeter in Asia as running "along the Aleutians to Japan and then . . . to the Ryukyus . . . to the Philippine Islands."[7] Both Korea and Taiwan were outside the perimeter. At the same time, no less an authority than Gen. Douglas MacArthur, commander of U.S. forces in the far east, assured the National Security Council that the South Korean army was trained and equipped well enough to defend itself without assistance from U.S. forces. Unfortunately, this statement was not true. As noted earlier, the South Korean Army suffered from major deficiencies and was no match for the North Korean Army the Soviets had trained and equipped. Yet despite the inferiority of South Korea's army, KMAG gave highly optimistic reports that supported MacArthur's position. On 8 March 1950 Brig. Gen. W. L. Roberts, chief of the U.S. Military Advisory Group to the Republic of Korea, wrote Maj. Gen. C. L. Bolts, G-3 of the army, stating that the North Korean Army was "an inferior ground force" compared to the South Korean Army. His only concern was that the North Koreans had an air force of 100 aircraft.[8] Based on these reports and in keeping with Secretary Acheson's statement, the administration continued its disengagement from the peninsula by reducing KMAG in the spring of 1950.

When almost eight North Korea divisions supported by a small air force invaded on Sunday, 25 June, they were faced by only four understrength South Korean divisions and one independent regiment. The North Korean divisions were larger, better equipped, and better trained than their South Korean counterparts. Each North Korean division had an artillery regiment and a self-propelled artillery battalion as well as antitank and reconnaissance battalions. The North Koreans also committed an armored brigade equipped with 150 T-34 tanks. In contrast, each South Korean division had only a single light artillery battalion (short 105mm howitzers), no armor, no recoilless rifles, and not even any antitank mines. Worse, the South Korean Army had only a few days' ammunition supply on hand. Because the South Korean Army was in peacetime status, only a single regiment from each division was occupying defensive positions along the border. The bulk of each division was in garrison fifteen to thirty miles to the rear. Further, the South Korean Army had a liberal weekend-pass policy, which meant many of its officers, including KMAG advisers, were not present with their units.

Despite the overwhelming surprise and weight of the attack, the South Koreans fought hard. The North Koreans took Seoul only after four days of tough fighting. It was two more days before the North Koreans drove the South Koreans south across the Han River. In those six days the South Korean Army lost 44,000 of its 98,000 men, almost all its artillery, and 70 percent of its individual weapons.[9]

Still confident in their prewar evaluations that the South Korean Army was a match for North Korean forces, U.S. decision-makers were slow to grasp the seriousness of the situation. Despite the confusion, on Monday, 26 June (U.S. time), President Harry Truman ordered U.S. air and naval forces to defend South Korea and protect Taiwan.[10] The same day Truman authorized MacArthur to send a survey party to Korea. Led by Brig. Gen. John H. Church, the survey was tasked to determine the logistical requirements of the Republic of Korea (ROK) forces. MacArthur still believed ROK forces could defeat the North Koreans without intervention by U.S. ground forces. It was not until MacArthur returned from his own brief visit to Korea on 29 June (Korea time) that he requested permission to commit U.S. ground forces in the defense of Korea. On 29 June (U.S. time) Truman authorized him to do so.[11] Despite a lack of preparedness, the U.S. armed forces found themselves at war.

In Korea ROK forces continued to fight delaying actions along all three invasion corridors but were unable to halt the North Korean advance. The North Koreans spent 30 June to 3 July getting three divisions (3rd, 4th, and 6th) across the Han River. By the morning of 4 July the North Korean 3rd and 4th Divisions were assembled south of the river and poised to continue the attack.

Within hours of Truman's authorization of ground forces on 29 June, the 8th

Army dispatched Task Force Smith, built around the badly understrength 1st Battalion, 21st Infantry Regiment, 24th Infantry Division under Lt. Col. Charles B. Smith, to Korea. Most Americans were convinced that once U.S. troops arrived, the North Korean attack would easily be defeated. First Lt. Phillip Day, who was typical of the survivors of Task Force Smith, commented, "We thought they would back off as soon as they saw American troops."[12] Instead the badly equipped and poorly supplied Task Force Smith met the onrushing North Koreans and was defeated and badly scattered in an eight-hour fight on 5 July.

This was only the first in a series of stinging defeats inflicted on U.S. Army units. From 5 to 12 July, successive U.S. battalions were committed to stop division-strength North Korean attacks, and each battalion was overwhelmed in turn. It was not until 13 July that the U.S. Army fought a higher-level action when it defended the Kum River line with the 19th and 34th Infantry Regiments. Driven back from that line on 16 July, the two regiments attempted another stand at Taejon and held this position from 19 to 20 July. The lack of training, equipment, and personnel combined with their piecemeal commitment doomed the U.S. units to one defeat after another.

As the U.S. Army fought in the main corridor between Seoul and Pusan, the ROK troops fought delaying actions of their own in the corridors that run down the east coast and center of Korea. Defending multiple axes, the U.S. and ROK armies bought time for U.S. reinforcements to arrive. The infantry regiments of the 24th Infantry Division closed on Korea by 5 July, the 25th Infantry Division by 15 July, and the 1st Cavalry Division by 22 July. The 8th Army fed these forces into the fight as it continued a fighting withdrawal south.

On 23 July 5th Air Force aerial reconnaissance confirmed reports that North Korean forces were moving to flank the 8th Army by moving down the west coast to Kwangju, then turning and advancing across the southern end of the Korean Peninsula. Gen. Walton "Bulldog" Walker, commander of the 8th U.S. Army (the senior ground headquarters in Korea), had no forces in place to meet this threat. He ordered the 24th Infantry Division to move south to defend a sixty-mile stretch of front from Chinju to Kumch'on.

On 1 August the 8th Army issued orders for all units to withdraw into the Pusan Perimeter. Anchored on the Sea of Japan, the perimeter ran west from the vicinity of Pohang to northwest of Taegu and then south along the Naktong River to the ocean. Roughly 50 miles across the top and 100 miles along the west side, the perimeter was much too long to establish a continuous defense line. Nonetheless, Walker declared that the allies could retreat no farther. His battered forces would have to hold this line to protect the port of Pusan. If the 8th Army lost Pusan, it lost Korea.

Thus, the situation at the end of July was grim. Walker had the remnants of four ROK and three U.S. divisions to hold more than 150 miles of front. The ROK army had sustained 70,000 casualties and U.S. forces just over 6,000. Walker's depleted forces were being pressed hard along four major axes by ten North

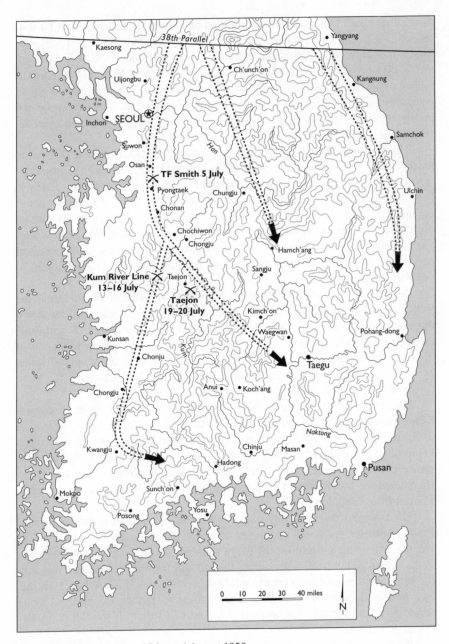

The North Korean invasion, 25 June–4 August 1950.

Korean infantry divisions, an armored division, an independent motorized regiment, and an independent infantry regiment. The only good news was that the North Korean People's Army (NKPA) had suffered an estimated 58,000 casualties during the thirty-six-day campaign.[13]

Even as the 8th Army withdrew into the Pusan Perimeter, major reinforcements were arriving. Between 31 July and 5 August the U.S. Army's 2nd Infantry Division and 5th Regimental Combat Team as well as the 1st Provisional Marine Brigade arrived in Pusan. Walker was gaining the strength necessary to hold his line just in time.

WHAT HAPPENED?

Americans were stunned by these early defeats. At the end of World War II, the United States had more than twelve million men in uniform, more than ninety well-equipped divisions, tens of thousands of aircraft, and more than a thousand combat ships. Yet by July 1950 the U.S. Army had been reduced to the point at which its forces were being overrun by troops from a nation most Americans could not find on a map. How did the U.S. military that had smashed both Germany and Japan less than five years before end up in this condition?

To understand what happened in Korea during the summer of 1950, we have to understand what happened to the U.S. armed forces between the end of World War II and the Korean invasion. Only by examining this period can we appreciate the challenges and triumphs of the forces fighting in Korea.

Quite simply, the United States had demobilized at an astonishing speed. Never a nation to maintain significant forces in peacetime, it traditionally counted on mobilizing its population and resources in times of crisis to win wars. Throughout U.S. history the regular army had been no more than a nucleus around which to form a wartime army of mobilized civilians. World War II had been no different. Thus, at the end of the war the vast majority of U.S. soldiers, sailors, and marines naturally expected to return immediately to their rudely interrupted civilian lives. Although career military personnel were concerned with maintaining U.S. military capabilities, demobilization was a politically driven priority that disregarded concerns about military readiness. After all, there were no more enemies left to fight, and if another appeared the people of the United States were confident they could once again mobilize to defeat it.

To appreciate the suddenness of the demobilization, it is necessary to remember that at the time of the Japanese surrender, U.S. officials believed it would take at least one and very possibly two more years to conquer Japan. At the beginning of August 1945 U.S. armed forces were making massive preparations to invade Japan. The vicious fighting and high casualties that had occurred on Iwo Jima and Okinawa indicated the invasion would be the bloodiest of the war. The navy, army, and army air forces were shifting resources from Europe to the Pacific in anticipation of a long, bloody campaign. They were not planning for any form of demobilization. Then the use of two atomic bombs brought a sudden halt to the war.

At the beginning of August 1945 the U.S. Army (including the army air forces) had 8,200,000 men on its rolls. By the end of 1945 it had cut that number in half. By 1947 the army, which still included the army air forces, was down to fewer than a million men. By the summer of 1950 it had only 591,000 men, and the now independent U.S. Air Force had only 411,000.[14] The navy fell from 3,380,000 on VJ Day to just 380,000 in June 1950.[15] Yet the American people were not concerned. Although slashed over 90 percent from the end of World War II, these forces were still four times their 1939 strength. In World War II, the Allies had defeated Germany and Japan despite starting with minuscule forces. The American people could see no justification for maintaining a large standing force.

U.S. MARINE CORPS, 1945–1949

Because the topic of this book is the U.S. Marine Corps, it is appropriate to examine more closely what happened to the corps during this vital period. Naturally it was not exempt from the pressures applied to the other services. It demobilized at the same frenetic pace—yet demobilization was not the worst of its problems. Without any time for planning, the corps was faced with six major tasks:

> To demobilize a Corps of five hundred thousand officers and men and "get the boys home" under pressure of a wave of home-town hysteria that temporarily crippled our foreign policy. . . .
>
> To maintain efficient occupation forces, two or three divisions strong in North China and Japan.
>
> To shape the organization and select the right people for a postwar regular Marine Corps about five times the size of the 1939 Corps (in 1945, Congress had established 107,000 officers and men as the authorized peacetime strength of the Corps).
>
> To confront ill-defined but disturbing pressures for extensive reorganization of the defense establishment, which boded nothing but trouble for the Marine Corps.
>
> To respond professionally to the chorus of doubts and unanswered questions inspired by the advent of the atomic bomb, especially prophesies that "there would never be another amphibious landing."[16]

Demobilization

The most politically charged issue facing the corps was managing the extremely rapid demobilization while still meeting its continuing operational missions and preparing for the next fight. Although the vast majority of marines were focused on a quick discharge and getting on with civilian life, those who were staying in the corps faced the immediate problem of maintaining operationally ready forces during this period of extreme turbulence. Thus, despite the push for demobilization, the quartermaster general of the Marine Corps, Maj. Gen. W. P. T. Hill, directed all marine units to recover as much material as possible for shipment back to the United States. Although rapid demobilization caused a shortage of skilled supply, maintenance, and aviation personnel, marines across the Pacific complied by packing up everything they could get their hands on (without being too fastidious about who actually owned the gear they were packing). The marines returned from the Pacific with huge stocks of equipment and even entire buildings (quonset huts). This material was moved to Marine Logistics Base in Barstow, California, for refurbishment and storage to be ready for the next fight.

This frugality was a hallmark of the corps and permeated the thinking of marines from the commandant to the privates. It reflected each marine's belief that his service would always be the last to be equipped, and therefore he must rely on "initiative" to ensure that he was properly equipped for a fight. Each marine believed he had a license to acquire government property at any time without observing the niceties of paperwork. This reallocation of government property was seen, at least by those marines staying in the corps, as an essential part of demobilization.

Occupation

Although demobilization was the political priority, the immediate operational issue was deploying the forces required for occupation duty. In the preparation for the invasion of Japan, the V Amphibious Corps had been focused on Hokkaido, the southernmost island of mainland Japan. The corps, consisting of the 2nd and 5th Marine Divisions and already assigned to 6th U.S. Army, was the logical choice for the marines' contribution to the occupation of Japan. Both divisions immediately deployed to Japan for occupation duty. The III Amphibious Corps, consisting of the 1st and 6th Marine Divisions, was assigned to the 8th U.S. Army, which had been preparing for the follow-up invasion of the Tokyo Plain on Honshu, the main island of Japan. Instead the III Amphibious Corps was detached from the 8th Army and sent to China to accept the surrender of Japanese troops stationed there.

Although the Marine Corps deployed these forces quickly and efficiently, maintaining them would have been impossible given the demands of demobilization. Fortunately, occupation duties in both countries proved much easier than anticipated and allowed for the rapid demobilization demanded by the American public. In November 1945 the 4th Marine Division was demobilized. In December the III Amphibious Corps headquarters, 3rd and 5th Marine Divisions, followed. In March 1946 it was the V Amphibious Corps's turn. At the same time the 6th Division was reduced to a single brigade. In June 1946 the 2nd Marine Division left Japan and sailed to Camp Lejeune, North Carolina, to become one of the two active marine divisions. The 1st Marine Division remained on occupation duty in China. It would not come home until 1948, but by June 1946 it was one of only two remaining marine divisions and was maintained overseas despite the reduced strength of the Marine Corps. The aviation and logistics elements of the corps demobilized just as rapidly.[17]

From 485,000 personnel on VJ Day, the corps was reduced to 155,000 in less than a year.[18] That still wasn't enough. In April 1946 Congress passed a naval strength bill that required the corps to be reduced to 7,000 officers and 100,000 enlisted men by August.[19] This would be the corps's authorized strength until the beginning of the Korean War. However, due to further budget cuts, the corps could not afford to fill its authorized strength. By June 1950 the entire Marine Corps comprised only 74,279 men.

Postwar Organization and New Realities

Despite the enormous problems presented by massive demobilization, the corps still had to shape its postwar organization. This proved difficult because first Congress and then the Pentagon kept reducing the corps's manpower. The corps had hoped to maintain a force of three division-wing teams. However, the cuts mandated by the April 1946 naval strength bill ensured that the corps could not maintain a force anywhere near this size.

Although struggling with the implications of the new strength limits, the corps also had to understand the impact that atomic bombs would have on amphibious warfare. In July 1946 Lt. Gen. Roy Geiger, USMC, observed the atomic bomb test at Bikini Atoll. He immediately wrote the commandant a letter stating, "It is trusted that Marine Corps Headquarters will consider this a very serious and urgent matter and will use its most competent officers in finding a solution to develop the technique of conducting amphibious operations in the Atomic Age."[20]

The commandant, Lt. Gen. Alexander A. Vandegrift, responded quickly by assigning Brig. Gens. Lemuel Shepherd, Oliver P. Smith, and Field Harris to a board to study the problem and make recommendations. On 16 December 1946, after several months of intensive study, the board made a series of recommendations:

- The existence of atomic weapons meant wide dispersion of forces was required with emphasis on the ship-to-shore movement phase.
- Radical changes in doctrine and equipment would be required for future amphibious operations.
- The Corps must explore a number of different possibilities to include helicopters, landing craft and large fixed wing sea planes.
- "Vertical envelopment" using the very recently developed helicopters could give new life to amphibious operations.[21]

Despite the fact that the best helicopter of the day could carry only the pilot and two passengers, the board specifically recommended the immediate formation of an experimental squadron of helicopters to serve as a platform for developing the concept.

A year later, on 1 December 1947, Marine Helicopter Squadron 1 (HMX 1) was established at Quantico, Virginia. Quantico was the logical location because the corps had already assigned dozens of top-notch combat veterans there to capture their wartime experiences while they were still fresh. The Advance Base Team had been reactivated and was drafting a series of slim blue volumes (known as the PHIB, a U.S. Navy abbreviation for "amphibious," series) to codify the amphibious techniques refined during the war. In addition, a navy-marine team had just completed a compilation of amphibious doctrine for the postwar naval forces, cryptically titled USF-63. In a single location, the corps was both recording its recent combat experience and experimenting with how to conduct amphibious operations in the presence of atomic weapons. In short, the aggressive, enterprising spirit that had driven the development of amphibious warfare concepts in 1933 returned to Quantico to prepare the corps for the next war.[22]

Thus while the corps's operating forces grappled with the problems of occupation, rapid demobilization, and drastic budget cuts, the marines at Quantico, under the direction of Headquarters Marine Corps, were developing the concepts and organizations that would prepare the corps for future battles to include the possible use of atomic weapons. Finally, headquarters was developing the personnel selection and retention policies that determined which officers and NCOs would be retained in the drawdown. Each of these difficult issues was being dealt with successfully.

By early 1947, in response to concerns about atomic weapons and demands for manpower reductions, the 1st and 2nd Marine Divisions were preparing to reorganize under the new J-Series Tables of Organizations (T/Os). This reorganization, which cut the strength of each division from 22,000 to only 10,500 men, is discussed in greater detail in Chapter 3.

Unification

Unification, the final postwar challenge to the corps's leadership, would consume enormous amounts of time and effort over the next seven years because it threatened the corps with extinction. The effort to do away with the corps surprised the marines. Because of the corps's exceptional wartime success, its leaders believed its future was secure. At Iwo Jima in February 1945, Secretary of the Navy James Forrestal had said that the "raising of that flag on Suribachi means there will be a Marine Corps for the next 500 years."[23] Fifteen months later the commandant was fighting for the corps's very existence.

The army began planning for unification in 1943. By 1945 the army staff had presented the Collins Plan to the Senate Military Affairs Committee. The plan proposed an independent air force, a Marine Corps reduced to a light infantry constabulary force, and a single chief of staff who would control the budget of the armed forces and act as the primary adviser to the president on military matters. The navy and Marine Corps, by appealing to Congress, turned back this effort in 1946. However the army, backed by President Truman, continued to push for unification. A struggle ensued, which, due to strenuous efforts on the part of Marine Corps headquarters, resulted in a compromise that became the National Security Act of 1947. Despite the apparent statutory protection provided by the act, the secretary of defense and the Joint Staff continued to cut marine end strength and to threaten the existence of the corps. Over the next three years the corps struggled through the roles and missions debate, modifications to the National Security Act of 1947, and steadily declining end strengths and budgets. Gen. Clifton B. Cates, who became commandant in 1948, noted that "the unification fight, you might say, was the top priority because they were trying to cut us to six BLTs [battalion landing teams] and six squadrons, which really would have just made us what President Truman said, a police force."[24] Obviously, with the focus on unification, Marine Corps headquarters had less time to assist the operational forces, which faced massive challenges of their own during the five years between World War II and Korea.

SUMMER 1949 TO SUMMER 1950: THE LAST YEAR OF PEACE

With Secretary of Defense Louis Johnson stating he would cut the corps's manpower authorization to 65,000 active-duty marines, the corps knew it could not maintain the eight battalion landing teams the J-Series T/Os called for. In addition, after two years of testing, the 1947 "atomic" T/Os had been found wanting. Thus, on 1 October 1949, the marine divisions reorganized under the K-Series T/Os.[25] Under this plan the strength of each marine division would consist of a single peacetime-strength infantry regiment supported by reduced artillery, armor, engineers, and other support elements. The division's other two regiments and their supporting elements would be activated only for wartime. The K-Series would allow the corps to meet the requirement to reduce personnel while maintaining the essential structure necessary to allow rapid mobilization of a full division in time of war. In October the eight existing battalion landing teams were disbanded to create six peacetime infantry battalions. These battalions were consolidated into two infantry regiments—the 5th and 6th Marines. The 5th Marines were assigned to the 1st Marine Division and the 6th Marines to the 2nd Marine Division.

The 6th Marines at Camp Lejeune, North Carolina, took command of its three battalions on 1 October 1949. The U.S. military envisioned the next war as being against the Soviet Union, so the 6th Marines was considered the regiment most likely to go to war. The 5th Marines at Camp Pendleton, California, did not receive its third infantry battalion until the Guam brigade was disbanded and its ground combat element returned to Camp Pendleton. The brigade's arrival at Pendleton stretched out over late February and early March 1950, and many key personnel who had been overseas for years were reassigned. During March and early April, as the old personnel were transferred and new members joined, the brigade's infantry battalion was redesignated as the 3rd Battalion, 5th Marines, and assigned to the 5th Marine Regiment. At the same time, the battalion reorganized under the new K-Series T/Os.

Even with the greatly reduced peacetime T/Os, Fleet Marine Force (FMF) units, the corps's combat forces, could not be brought up to strength. The Department of Defense's fiscal year 1950 budget reduced the corps's end strength from the congressionally authorized 100,000 to only 79,000. As a result, the corps was forced to drastically reduce the strength of the FMF. In addition, the corps had to plan for a further cut to 65,000 in fiscal year 1951. Thus, instead of the K-Series wartime organization of three rifle companies, a weapons company, and a headquarters and support company per infantry battalion, the battalions had been reduced to the K- Series peacetime organization of only two rifle companies. To save even more billets, each rifle company had only two rifle platoons and two-thirds of a weapons platoon. Thus, a battalion had only four rifle platoons instead of the normal nine, and for a variety of reasons inherent to most peacetime military organizations, even these few platoons were understrength. The battalion weapons and headquarters and service companies were similarly reduced.[26] The artillery suffered as well. Each division had a single artillery regiment, which was reduced to a single cannon battalion with only twelve 105mm howitzers in three four-gun batteries rather than the eighteen in three six-gun batteries called for in wartime battalion.

The corps's aviation elements were no better off. At the end of World War II the Marine Corps had 120 flying squadrons. Under the 1951 budget, the total would be reduced to 6 flying squadrons. Due to the ever-present budget shortages, the flying squadrons had severely reduced flight hours and suffered from continual parts shortages throughout the late 1940s. The other aviation squadrons— such as air traffic control, airfield operations, and engineering—faced the same problems in conducting the training required to be ready for war. In addition, both marine air wings were in the process of activating and training their first jet squadrons. And of course HMX 1, though not an operational squadron, was still consuming Marine Corps operational funds and personnel. Both the new jets and the new helicopters absorbed resources as the corps organized, trained, equipped, and experimented to determine how these new squadrons could best be employed in combat. Jets and helicopters represented the future of the corps, and these early efforts were invaluable. However, they naturally reduced the resources available to the World War II–era, prop-driven F4U Corsair squadrons. Unfortunately, in

1950 the Corsair squadrons were the backbone of the marine air forces. The one major advantage of these squadrons was the fact that every pilot had been flying Corsairs since World War II.

By late June 1950 the normal summer personnel rotation was taking place across the Marine Corps. This regular but necessary turbulence further reduced the FMF's readiness. After World War II the corps had generally established a program of one-year tours for most personnel in the operating forces. The thinking was that with so few units, the only way to maintain any level of individual training was to rotate individual marines through the units on short tours. Then, if war came, the corps could rapidly expand. Thus, many, if not most, of the officers and NCOs transferred every summer. All but two of the 1st Provisional Marine Brigade's regimental, group, battalion, and squadron commanders were in their first month in command on 25 June 1950; most were in their first week or took command after the war started. Further, key staff officers were just arriving at Camp Pendleton at the end of June. And, in keeping with personnel policies, all staffs were intentionally undermanned. For instance, none of the 5th Marines' infantry battalions was assigned executive officers in June 1950.

THE 1ST PROVISIONAL MARINE BRIGADE (REINFORCED)

When North Korea invaded on 25 June, it caught the U.S. Marine Corps at a bad time. In the middle of a seven-year battle for existence, struggling to deal with massive personnel and resources cuts and in the midst of summer rotations, the corps was a shadow of the force that had performed so well in World War II. Despite these issues, Fleet Marine Force Pacific (FMFPac) was given less than ten days to embark a brigade-sized air-ground team for Korea. In fact, when FMFPac received its warning order on 3 June, no such brigade existed. Thus, a brigade had to be formed, absorb over 50 percent new personnel just to reach *peacetime* strength, transfer hundreds of marines who could not deploy, field new equipment, and build new subordinate organizations. All this had to be accomplished while simultaneously embarking the units at ports more than 100 miles apart. The one factor the brigade leaders were told not to worry about was training. The plan was for the brigade to sail to Japan, disembark, and train for thirty days before being committed to the fight.

In fact, the ground elements of the brigade sailed right past Japan and unloaded in Pusan Harbor, South Korea. The air elements did unload in Japan, but only to immediately redistribute the squadrons to the ships and bases they would fight from. After almost three weeks at sea in extremely cramped transports, all air and ground elements entered combat within days of reaching pierside.

The day-fighter squadrons unloaded in Japan on 31 July, sorted themselves out, conducted refresher training, reembarked on two escort carriers, and started flying strikes on 3 August. The night-fighter squadron disembarked on 31 July and began flying night interdiction missions over Korea on 8 August. The observation squadron unloaded in Japan, flew its aircraft to Korea, found an operating base, and was flying in support of ground marines on 6 August. The ground-combat elements unloaded in Korea on 3 August and were in combat by the night of 6 August.

Yet, unlike every other U.S. unit committed to Korea, the brigade decisively defeated the North Koreans each time they met. In its first action the brigade not only stopped the North Korean attack; it also drove the 6th North Korean Division back twenty-six miles in four days, rendering that division combat-ineffective. Then, as it pursued the remnants of the 6th Division, the brigade was suddenly ordered to send a battalion twenty-nine miles to its rear to restore a breakthrough in the adjacent army unit's line. The next day, with two battalions attacking to the west to finish the destruction of the North Korean 6th Division and a third moving rapidly east to destroy the North Korean penetration, the brigade commander was ordered immediately to break contact, reassemble the entire force, return to reserve, and prepare to counterattack in a different sector. Within hours the marines successfully broke contact with the enemy and rapidly withdrew to a designated assembly area.

Despite the crisis, when the brigade arrived at the assembly area the 8th Army commander had not decided where to commit it, so he put the brigade in reserve. Making good use of the break in combat operations, the brigade replenished its depleted rifle platoons by assigning rear-echelon marines to the line units. There were no other replacements available, so the brigade was forced to test the corps creed that every marine is a rifleman. The brigade had only two days to integrate the new marines, attempt to replace damaged equipment, and grab a bit of rest. On 17 August the brigade launched a counterattack against a North Korean breakthrough on the Naktong River. In three days of fierce fighting, the brigade destroyed the North Korean 4th Division and drove the remnants back across the river. On orders from MacArthur's headquarters, the brigade turned the restored defensive line back over to the army and withdrew to prepare for the upcoming Inchon landing.

When the brigade reached the assembly area, 800 replacements arrived. The units immediately started an aggressive training program to integrate the new men while simultaneously trying to scrounge sufficient weapons to replace those worn out in the month of fighting. As the brigade prepared for embarkation, Col. Edward W. Snedecker, the brigade chief of staff, led a team of planners to Japan to confirm the myriad details necessary for the planned 15 September amphibious assault at Inchon. While integrating the new marines and planning for the assault, the units were sending their heavy equipment to the pier to embark for the landing. Time was critical. The brigade had less than three weeks to prepare for an exceedingly difficult, complex assault directly into the city of Inchon.

In the middle of these hectic preparations, the North Koreans launched a final all-out effort to destroy the Pusan Perimeter. Once again they broke through. The

U.S. 8th Army commander stated that without the brigade, the perimeter could not be held. Despite protests from the amphibious planners, MacArthur allowed the 8th Army to commit the brigade to the Naktong Bulge fight. From 3 to 5 September, the brigade drove the North Koreans back yet again. Finally, at midnight on 5 September, the brigade was ordered out of the line. After a day of movement back to Pusan, the brigade had only five days to absorb more replacements into its existing organizations, integrate the newly arrived third rifle companies, and again scrounge for replacement weapons and equipment, all while rapidly embarking upon amphibious shipping. On 12 September the brigade sailed out of Pusan Harbor, destined to be the assault wave at Inchon. On 13 September, somewhere in the South China Sea, the brigade ceased to exist. It was deactivated and its units reassigned to their parent organizations in the 1st Marine Division and 1st Marine Air Wing.

During its brief existence from 7 July to 13 September 1950, the brigade accomplished legendary feats. Given only six days from activation to sailing, the brigade had overcome enormous challenges just to get under way. The operating forces had been in the middle of the normal summer personnel rotations, which had completely changed the key leaders from FMPac down to the battalion level. Activated on 7 July, the brigade had to form a staff, assemble an air group, find personnel to bring the regiment up to peacetime strength (still a third below wartime strength), form a combat service element, absorb more than 50 percent new men, and move everything to two different ports—San Diego and Long Beach—for embarkation.

All this had to be accomplished after the Marine Corps had struggled through five years of precipitously declining budgets, personnel cuts exceeding 80 percent of the corps's strength, and desperate fights for its very existence. Despite the fact that the brigade had been literally thrown together, squeezed aboard ship, and delivered directly to the fight, it not only fought well but drove back three different North Korean offensives. The question this book will attempt to answer is: What combination of culture, education, doctrine, organization, training, and leadership allowed the corps to survive the enormous stresses imposed between 1945 and 1950 and still assemble a small brigade that not only stopped but drove back the North Koreans?

2

Marine Culture

> You cannot exaggerate about the Marines. They are convinced to the point of arrogance, that they are the most ferocious fighters on earth—and the amusing thing about it is that they are.
>
> —Father Kevin Keaney, chaplain, 1st Marine Division, Korean War

To understand why and how a military organization fights, it is essential first to understand the unique culture of that organization—how it views itself and what values, attitudes, and beliefs it passes on to its members. Once the culture is understood, then the student can examine how the organization perpetuates that culture through its education system. Only then can he or she understand how, and more importantly why, the organization employs its fighting doctrine. Obviously this is not a new approach to studying military organizations. John A. Lynn, author of *Battle: A History of Combat and Culture,* wrote, "The way militaries think is the most fundamental element of their effectiveness,"[1] and he went on to say that such thinking "encapsulate[s] ways in which different armed forces do things in different ways for reasons that are not simply dictated by reality."[2]

Terry Terriff, who has studied marine culture closely, noted, "Organizational culture can be broadly defined as the assumptions, ideas, and beliefs, expressed or reflected in organization symbols, rituals, and practices that give meaning to the activity of the organization. . . . [Understanding] military culture is very useful, for it provides a means for understanding how beliefs, or cultural characteristics, influence the self-identity, thinking and activities of an organization and its individual members."[3]

Thus, the first Marine Corps characteristic to examine is the unique military culture that defines what it is to be a marine. Gen. Anthony Zinni served forty years in the corps, capping his career with service as commander-in-chief, U.S. Central Command. Zinni, who joined the corps in 1961, was trained and shaped

by the veterans of World War II and Korea. In his book *Battle Ready* he captured
the culture of the corps in a precise series of paragraphs:

> The first thing Marines have to realize is that our service is not vital to the
> existence of the nation. The second thing we have to realize, however, is that
> we offer to the nation a service that has unique qualities—qualities and val-
> ues that the nation admires, respects, and can ill afford to lose. They
> include:
> One: Our first identity as Marines is to be a Marine. We are not primarily
> fighter pilots, scuba divers, tank drivers, computer operators, cooks, or what-
> ever. The proper designation for each Marine from privates to generals is
> "Marine."
> Two: Every Marine has to be qualified as a rifleman. Every Marine is a
> fighter. We have no rear area types. All of us are warriors.
> Three: We feel stronger about our traditions than any other service. We
> salute the past. This is not merely ritual or pageantry. It is part of the essence
> of the Marine Corps. One of the essential subjects every Marine has to know
> is his corps' history; he has to take that in and make it an essential part of
> himself.
> Four: We carry a sense of responsibility for those who went before us,
> which ends up meaning a lot to Marines who are in combat. We don't want to
> let our predecessors down or taint our magnificent heritage.[4]

Clearly Zinni's list focuses on marine identity and standards of behavior.
Identity and standards establish how marines see themselves and how, based on
that self-image, they act—particularly under the pressure of combat. It is essential to understand what impact these critical cultural standards had on the corps
between 1946 and 1950.

Zinni mentions marine identity as the first quality essential to the culture of
the Marine Corps. The corps strives to instill that identity in marines from their
first day in boot camp. Its remarkable success is reflected in the statements of marines who served with the 1st Provisional Marine Brigade. Almost every marine
used similar phrases to describe his feelings about being a marine—and almost all
of them emphasized that the feelings were rooted in the culture they had learned
before they went to war. Joseph A. Crivello Jr., a communicator with 1st Battalion, 11th Marines, remembered:

> During the first full week in boot camp, recruits study Marine Corps history.
> For me, that meant from Tun Tavern, Philadelphia, to the end of World War
> II. To the recruit now in boot camp, it probably covers Tun Tavern to Desert
> Storm. I sometimes think they are studying our exploits in Pusan, Seoul, and
> the Reservoir. So, we are the Marines they talk about. They will be the Ma-
> rines that future recruits will study. Each Marine—past, present, future—is
> and will be part of that heritage. Once a Marine, always a Marine.—Semper
> Fi, Brothers.[5]

Dean Servais, a tank crewman with Company A, wrote, "Once a Marine, Always a Marine. Ask any Marine, and no matter how long he was in or where he served, he feels that being a part of the greatest fighting machine there is was time well spent and they are damn proud of it."[6]

The similarity of their words makes them sound almost like a learned response rather than what the marines genuinely believe. Yet the same theme runs through personal narratives from World War I until today. Robert Leckie, a World War II marine and author of *Helmet for My Pillow,* read John W. Thomason's *Fix Bayonets* while Leckie was in the hospital in Australia. He felt Thomason's stories about marines in World War I and in China between the wars captured the corps he knew in World War II:

> Here in muscular, evocative prose and spare, stark pictures was the Marine Corps Family: cocksure colonels, swaggering captains, shy shavetails [second lieutenants], and, most vivid and lifelike of all, our senior NCOs—those grizzled gunnies and topkicks in whose weather-beaten faces every wrinkle is said to be a broken commandment, and under whose profane, brutal but sometimes tender tutelage we privates had learned the pride of being a Marine.[7]

In *With the Old Breed,* Eugene B. Sledge's account of his service as a marine infantryman in two of the corps's bloodiest campaigns, Peleliu and Okinawa, the author concluded the book by saying, "War is brutish, inglorious and a terrible waste. Combat leaves an indelible mark on those who are forced to endure it. The only redeeming factors were my comrades' incredible bravery and their devotion to each other. Marine Corps training taught us to kill efficiently and to try to survive. But it also taught us loyalty to each other and love. That esprit de corps sustained us."[8]

Twenty years later a Vietnam-era marine, Philip Caputo, wrote of his time at the Marine Corps's Officer Candidate School, "It was a society unto itself, demanding total commitment to its doctrines and values, rather like one of those quasi-religious military orders of ancient times, the Teutonic Knights or the Theban Band."[9]

This marine identity is not limited to wartime marines. In 1994, a period between wars, Corp. Jeff Sorni told the *Navy Times,* "I love the Marine Corps for those intangible possessions that cannot be issued: pride, honor, integrity, and being able to carry on the traditions for generations of warriors past."[10]

The remarkable consistency in how marines from World War I to today speak of their marine identity shows that *semper fidelis* (always faithful) is not just a short-term slogan that marines parrot when asked. Rather it is an integral part of the identity itself. Each of these men echoed Zinni's theme of identity established through teaching and enforcing the corps's history and standards. The identity was and continues to be strongly reinforced by Marine Corps policy that a recruit is not called "marine" until he officially graduates from boot camp. The memory of the day they earned the title is another constant woven through personal accounts, letters, articles, books, and official histories.

In its 14 August 1950 issue, *Time* magazine captured the importance of boot camp in instilling the marine identity:

> Explained one Marine officer: "A kid reports for boot camp and we challenge the s.o.b., we dare him to try and be a Marine. We give him so much of that in boot camp—and even flunk some of them out—that when he gets out, he's the proudest damn guy in the world, because he can call himself a United States Marine. He's nothing but a damn private but you'd think he's just made colonel."[11]

Boot camp establishes the identity, but it is reinforced daily wherever the marine is stationed. Reinforcement is both formal, in the ceremonies and traditions that are part of official Marine Corps duties, and (perhaps even more important) informal, in the stories the marines hear from other marines. Of course they hear these stories not just from their fellow active-duty marines but also from retired marines, often family members, who in an age-old tradition reminisce about their time "in the corps."

As Zinni noted, a second critical pillar of marine identity is the concept that every marine is a rifleman. Regardless of his actual military occupational specialty, each marine expects to fight. There are no "rear-area" marines who require protection from the enemy. Each must be prepared to fight as a rifleman in a line company. This theme emerged before World War I in the form of the famous "First to Fight" recruiting posters: "In 1907, when Army posters said, 'Join the Army and Learn a Trade,' and Navy posters said, 'Join the Navy and See the World,' the Marine posters came to the point with disarming simplicity, 'First to Fight.'"[12]

Before the Korean War every marine regular attended boot camp. (Due to budget constraints, reserves did not attend boot camp but were trained at their reserve unit home station, but the basic concept remained the same.) In describing his boot-camp training, Maurice J. Jacques, who enlisted in 1948, recalled:

> We were shown combat footage from World War II as a means of helping to strengthen the esprit de corps that is synonymous with the Marine Corps. Those unedited scenes of the horror, taken on the islands of Tarawa, Peleliu, Iwo Jima, and Okinawa, left little doubt in any of us as to what demands would be made on us, once called upon to fight. Watching those films helped build confidence while showing the realities of war.[13]

The warrior concept remains integral to the corps's identity even today. In 2005 David J. Danelo wrote about the marines who fought with him in Iraq: "The warrior religion, inculcated into every Marine for life, represents this same unflinching code of honor. The samurai called it Bushido, the way of the warrior. Although Marines venerate the history of many warrior cultures, the

Spartans—especially as described in Steven Pressfield's novel *Gates of Fire*—have had a profound effect in defining the Marine ideal of leadership, valor and citizenry."[14] One of the most important elements of that ideal is the belief that marines never leave another marine behind. Former marine and U.S. senator John Chafee named five basic principles in making marines: "Rigorous training. Strict discipline. The installation of pride, in himself and pride in the Corps. A sense of responsibility toward each other, officer for enlisted man and enlisted man for officer. Finally, determination to prevail, and not to let down our country, our Corps, or our fellow Marines."[15]

As well as discussing the discipline and pride that are instilled by marine training, Chafee emphasized the sense of responsibility and trust and the determination to never let down a fellow marine. A veteran of World War II and Korea, Chafee understood the intense bond between marines that allowed them to fight without concern that they would be abandoned by their comrades. Will Diaz, a member of the brigade, also emphasized the trust that provided comfort in combat:

> Korea was an experience where the young kids who had joined the Marines, myself included, grew up to be hardened and determined military combatants. Pride was evident throughout the troops and we felt that we were part of an organization that would not give up or give in, even when confronted with overwhelming forces. Trust between the men was so strong that it gave each Marine a comforting mental feeling that no matter what, the guy next to him was his guardian angel.[16]

Richard A. Olson, a young NCO who fought with the brigade, wrote, "It would take a book to give all the reasons why I think the training I received in boot camp served me well in Korea. In a nutshell, Marines back up Marines. As long as there were Marines on our left and Marines on our right, we didn't worry about the people on the flank bugging out. . . . Everything about boot camp reeked of cooperation and dependability."[17]

A fourth cultural pillar provides essential support to Marines in combat—the fear of letting down their predecessors. Gerald P. Averill, a World War II NCO who was granted a direct commission before Korea, captured the feeling that marines internalize about not disgracing the corps:

> To the Marine, the Corps is his religion, his reason for being. He cannot be committed up to a point. For him, involvement is total. He savors the traditions of his Corps and doubts not the veracity of them. He believes implicitly that he must live up to those epics of physical and moral courage established by those who preceded him. He believes that the Corps is truly unique—that it is the most elite military organization ever devised and that he, as an integral part of that organization, must never bring disgrace or dishonor upon it.[18]

Averill's words are echoed by Robert Speights, a combat engineer who served with the brigade in the perimeter. In an interview he said he really believed the "BS" he had learned. He was convinced that no one could beat U.S. marines. In particular, he said he could feel the presence of marines from the past every time he was in a fight, especially during the breakout from the Chosin.[19] Raymond E. Stevens expressed his feelings succinctly: "The fact that we had a tradition to live up to and were part of a famous battalion helped our resolve. We also felt that if we were hit, we would not be left behind."[20]

Another cultural factor drives the Marine Corps's performance in both peace and war. Terry Terriff noted that the Marine Corps has a "cultural attribute of organizational paranoia"[21] based on the belief that the Department of Defense (DOD) and the other services are determined to do away with it. This paranoia is not unfounded: "On the average of once every eleven years since 1829, the Marine Corps has faced a direct challenge to its existence. These challenge episodes have not been merely perfunctory threats by interservice rivals, presidents, budgeters, military and policy analysts, 'efficiency experts,' and the like. On the contrary, had any one of the challenges succeeded, the Marine Corps would have been eliminated as a separate organizational entity."[22]

This paranoia is reinforced within the corps. Zinni noted that "the first thing Marines have to realize is that our service is not vital to the existence of the nation."[23] Thus, there is a pervasive feeling in the corps that it can be done away with at any time. An old marine joke captures this paranoia. The scene is the birthplace of the corps, Tun Tavern, Philadelphia, 1775. The first two marines have just enlisted. The first marine turns to the second and says, "You know, they are out to get us." To marines and former marines, the basic message is darkly humorous and clear. Ever since the founding of the corps, it has been threatened with disbandment.

It is difficult to understand the genuine fear marines felt for their service's continued existence during the late 1940s and early 1950s unless one understands the intensity of the corps's seven-year struggle for statutory protection. From 1945 to 1952, the efforts by other institutions to minimize and eventually kill the corps shaped the attitudes of all marines. As early as 1943 General George C. Marshall, chairman of the JCS, put forward a JCS proposal favoring a single Department of Defense after the war. By 1945 this proposal had matured into the Collins Plan, presented by Lt. Gen. J. Lawton Collins to the Senate Military Affairs Committee.[24] It recommended the creation of a single DOD with much more centralized control of the military and the creation of an independent air force that would include all land-based air. In support of the Collins Plan, the Joint Staff developed a series of secret papers known as the JCS 1478 studies. In them Gen. Dwight D. Eisenhower, army chief of staff, and Gen. Carl W. Spaatz, the new chief of Army Air Forces, proposed that the Marine Corps be reduced to lightly armed regiments without aviation. In essence, they proposed reducing the

Marine Corps to a navy police force whose only functions would be rescuing U.S. citizens overseas and driving the amphibious landing craft the army would use to conduct amphibious operations.[25] Despite the fact that the 1478 papers directly addressed the future of the Marine Corps, they were classified top secret and were specifically withheld from the marines. Only when the Marine Corps obtained a copy of the papers through irregular channels did corps leaders even become aware of the seriousness of the threat. In December 1945, even as the corps's leadership was absorbing the implications of the 1478 papers, President Harry S. Truman came out strongly in favor of a single department run by a civilian secretary with one military commander in charge of all roles and missions.

The Marshall study and Collins Plan were the first steps in the process that led to the postwar reorganization of U.S. defense institutions. This long, convoluted, and highly political struggle became known simply as unification. By the time it was over, the old Departments of War and of the Navy were combined into the DOD with separate Departments of the Army, Navy, and Air Force. The U.S. Navy and the Marine Corps remained, as before, separate services in the Department of the Navy.

Unification was not a smooth process. Along with its proposed establishment as a separate service, the U.S. Army Air Forces sought control of all aviation—a stand the navy and Marine Corps resisted fiercely. Facing the inevitable postwar cuts, the army reasoned that a large Marine Corps would compete for resources dedicated to both land and air forces. Therefore, the army sought to return the corps to its pre–World War I role as a small naval expeditionary force without heavy weapons. Organized in units no larger than regiments, the corps would not compete with the army or the air force. The army justified its plan by stating that a large Marine Corps would simply duplicate tasks the army was more than capable of performing. After all, the army had made more amphibious landings during World War II than the Marine Corps, so why did the United States need a separate service specializing in amphibious assault?

With strong presidential backing, the Senate rapidly developed Senate Bill 2044 to unify the services into a single department run by the same Joint Staff that had recommended the corps's reduction. Without a marine representative on the JCS, the corps was unable to make its arguments for continued existence as a combined arms force heard within the executive branch. As it had in the past, the corps was forced to turn to Congress.

Once again Congress ensured that the corps had its say. In May 1946 marines and their allies instigated hearings on the proposed unification, which were conducted by the Senate Naval Affairs Committee. During the hearings the commandant of the Marine Corps, Lt. Gen. Alexander A. Vandegrift, laid out the logical arguments for the continued existence of the Marine Corps, with particular emphasis on the marines' readiness to fight. Despite the strong logic of his arguments, it was the emotional appeal of his closing remarks that turned the tide:

The Congress has always been the nation's traditional safeguard against any precipitate action calculated to lead the country into trouble. In its capacity as a balance wheel this Congress has on five occasions since the year 1829 reflected the voice of the people in examining and casting aside a motion which would damage or destroy the United States Marine Corps. In each instance, on the basis of its demonstrated value and usefulness alone, Congress has perpetuated the Marine Corps as a purely American investment in continued security. Now I believe that the cycle has again repeated itself, and that the fate of the Marine Corps lies solely and entirely with the Congress.

The Marine Corps, then, believes that it has earned this right—to have its future decided by the legislative body which created it—nothing more. Sentiment is not a valid consideration in determining questions of national security. We have pride in ourselves and in our past but we do not rest our case on any presumed gratitude owing us from the nation. The bended knee is not a tradition for our Corps. If the Marine as a fighting man has not made a case for himself after 170 years of service, he must go. But I think you will agree with me, he has earned the right to depart with dignity and honor, not by subjugation to the status of uselessness and servility planned for him by the War Department.[26]

This "no bended knee" speech was an all-or-nothing bet. Vandegrift essentially said, "Keep us as a combined arms team or not at all." His bet not only paid off by ensuring the continued existence of the Marine Corps but also reinforced in the public mind the concept of the corps as a "force in readiness."

By mid-May 1946 it was clear that Senate Bill 2044 could not pass Congress. However, the requirement for unification remained. In the fall President Truman directed Secretary of the Army Robert P. Patterson and Secretary of the Navy James V. Forrestal to work out the differences between the services and make a joint proposal.

Over the next few months the services negotiated among themselves to determine their future size, shape, and missions. The army position remained essentially unchanged: army officials were adamant that the nation needed a strong chief of staff, a single budget controlled by that chief, a separate air force that would own all aviation, and a Marine Corps reduced to a light infantry force with restrictions on its expansion during wartime. For its part, the navy sought to maintain its own organizational integrity (read: navy air), a collective strategy-making process rather than a single chief of staff, and civilian control of the budget. The navy did not have a strong position on the future of the Marine Corps, and the corps was not allowed to have its own representative at the talks. The navy leaders assured the corps that they would look out for marine interests. During the negotiations the situation became even more threatening for the corps when the navy replaced its negotiator on the subject, Vice Adm. Arthur W. Radford, a supporter of the marines, with Vice Adm. Forrest P. Sherman, a strong supporter of naval aviation. Many marines believed Sherman would trade away the corps to save navy air because navy air was an integral part of the navy's position, whereas the continued existence of the Marine Corps was not.

In January 1947 the army and navy sent a joint agreement to the president with proposed compromise positions on the critical issues. He endorsed it and sent it on to the 80th Congress. When Congress took up the subject of unification, the joint agreement was the starting point for what would become the National Security Act of 1947.

The commandant was surprised by the joint recommendations. Brig. Gen. Gerald C. Thomas, chief of staff Headquarters Marine Corps, noted that, based on its recent successes in combat, the corps was feeling

> well entrenched both politically and from the standpoint of public relations, but the fact of the matter was that the Marine Corps not only had no plan of action but did not even have a single influential congressman or senator who could be contacted at the time on a regular basis, and be relied on to act in the Marine Corps' behalf. Also, in spite of Truman's statements, the Marine Corps had no reliable major outlet to which it could break a news story. Consequently, the Marine Corps was as deficient in its ability to state its case in public as it was to protect itself through influential sponsors in the Congress.[27]

For once the corps's institutional paranoia had failed. Coming off a hugely successful campaign in the Pacific, the corps was focused on improving its operational capabilities in the midst of the DOD's budget cuts. The corps had to start from scratch to organize both a public relations campaign and a campaign in Congress to ensure that the unification legislation did not effectively destroy it. The effort was truly extraordinary but exceeds the scope of this chapter.[28] In short, the corps mobilized enough public and congressional support to protect the corps by inserting definitions of its roles and missions into the proposed law. This portion of the law was written largely by Lt. Col. James D. Hittle, USMC, who had been seconded to Representative Clare E. Hoffman's staff. On 24 June 1947 the Senate-House conference committee reported out a compromise bill with the Marine Corps's roles and mission intact. The National Security Act of 1947 was passed by Congress the next day.

When the act became law, the corps seemed to have secured legislative sanction for its role as a force in readiness, amphibious assault specialists, and a force "of combined arms, together with supporting air components."[29] The law required the Marine Corps to be "organized, trained and equipped to provide fleet Marine forces of combined arms, together with supporting air components, for service with the fleet."[30]

Despite the apparent protection of the new law, the marines could not relax. The corps was still operating on the slimmest of budgets while maintaining almost 50 percent of its battalions deployed overseas. In 1948 the Marine Corps

Board Report on the Organization of the Fleet Marine Force in War and Peace noted that in

> responding to JCS contingency plans and commitments, the Corps in early 1948 had only four BLTs not preassigned or deployed. Two BLTs were still in China, two were assigned on a rotating basis as the landing force of the 6th Fleet in the Mediterranean, two were assigned missions in the Persian Gulf, and another was stationed at Quantico to test new tactical concepts and equipment. Amphibious training in the United States and the Caribbean, plagued by personnel and equipment shortages, continued on a shoestring level despite Vandegrift's understanding that the Corps needed much more experience in antitank warfare, night operations, and fire support coordination.[31]

Shortly after becoming commandant in 1948, Clifton B. Cates, in an interview with Richard Tregaskis, stated, "My biggest worry is to keep the Marine Corps alive. . . . There are lots of people here in Washington who want to prevent that, who want to reduce us to the status of Navy policemen or get rid of us entirely."[32]

Cates was right to be worried. On 11 March the new secretary of defense, James V. Forrestal, called the JCS to a four-day conference in Key West, Florida. His intent was to settle the service arguments over roles and missions. Despite the fact that numerous issues of critical importance to the Marine Corps were to be discussed, the commandant was not invited, nor were any other marines present. Displaying remarkable speed for the Pentagon, Forrestal issued a paper titled "Functions of the Armed Forces and the Joint Chiefs of Staff" on 21 April 1948.[33] The paper established roles and missions for the JCS, the unified commanders, and the services. Three of its directives had critical implications for the corps. Their presence in the document fully justified the corps's institutional paranoia.

First, the conference put a four-division limit on the corps in any future mobilization. Second, the Marine Corps would never control units above corps level. Finally, the corps was specifically forbidden to form a second land army.[34] Clearly the army-dominated Joint Staff was determined that the corps would not consume critical resources during this period of austerity, nor expand greatly in time of war. The secretary of the army, Kenneth C. Royall, made this determination pointedly clear when he testified before a Senate committee in April 1949. He said the president should "make the Marines part of the Army, or the Army part of the Marines." When specifically asked if he was proposing to abolish the Marine Corps, Royall replied, "That is exactly what I am proposing."[35]

On 28 March 1949 President Truman dismissed Forrestal and replaced him with Louis A. Johnson, a prominent Democratic fund-raiser. Johnson quickly made clear his views on the value of the navy and Marine Corps in a lecture to Admiral R. L. Conolly: "Admiral, the Navy is on its way out. . . . There's no reason for having a Navy and Marine Corps. General Bradley tells me that amphibious operations are a thing of the past. We'll never have any more amphibious operations. That does away with the Marine Corps. And the Air Force can do anything the Navy can do nowadays, so that does away with the Navy."[36]

In keeping with his beliefs, Johnson cut the Fleet Marine Force from 35,000 to 31,000 during fiscal year 1949 (July 1948–June 1949). He announced that he planned to cut it further in fiscal year 1950, to only eight battalion landing teams and twelve squadrons.[37] His boldest assault on the corps came in mid-April 1949 when he announced to reporters that the papers directing transfer of marine aviation to the air force were on his desk. Fortunately for the corps, the secretary's action was perceived to be an encroachment on the powers of Congress. At the end of April, the chairman of the House Armed Services Committee, Carl Vinson, felt it necessary to call Johnson in to literally lay down the law. He told Johnson that marine aviation would neither be transferred nor abolished and that any further discussion of the subject must be referred to Congress before action was proposed. Johnson had to state publicly that there were no plans to do away with marine aviation. Yet again, Congress had come to the rescue.

After being turned back by Vinson, the secretary of defense, supported by the Joint Staff, attempted to use his control over the budget and end strength to eliminate the corps by reducing its budget to the point where it was no longer a combined arms force. These efforts succeeded in slowly reducing the corps's strength and capabilities. But the corps was not the only object of Secretary Johnson's cost-cutting decisions. In 1949 Johnson used his control of the budget to add funding for air force B-36 bombers while simultaneously canceling funding for the navy's supercarrier, USS *United States*. This action sparked "the revolt of the admirals" in which Secretary of the Navy John L. Sullivan resigned on 26 April 1949 in protest over the administration's policies.[38] This protest motivated the navy's supporters to get involved.

As a result, in June the House Armed Services Committee initiated hearings for "thorough studies and investigations relating to matters involving the B-36 bomber."[39] The corps took advantage of these congressional hearings to present its own concerns to the committee. The commandant chose to emphasize two areas — marine aviation and the corps's lack of representation in the JCS.[40] Given the congressional focus on reducing budgets, marine leaders noted that the "entire cost of Marine aviation in 1949 was $175,000,000 — less than one-third of what the most optimistic transfer-artists estimated the same force would cost if submerged in the Air Force."[41] Although this was, and remains, a solid argument, the corps's real focus was on limiting the power of the JCS by obtaining marine representation in that body. The corps's leadership was convinced that only the presence of the commandant as a member of the JCS could protect the corps's interests within the DOD, and it chose to appeal directly to Congress by noting that the secretary of defense was defying Congress's express intent, as written in the National Security Act of 1947. In his testimony, Vandegrift, by then retired, stated, "I note about the national capital the same signs and portents that were present here in 1946 and 1947 when the National Security Act was being enacted.

Its seems as though we have come full cycle and that we stand no closer today to deciding these vital matters than we stood in 1946."[42]

And Cates noted:

> During the past two years, the time, energy and attention of our leadership has been steadily consumed by the effort necessary to resist the inroads and incursions of those who appear unwilling to accept the verdict of Congress. ... I have to inform you that the Army General Staff group today stands within measurable distance of achieving each one of its three ends against the Marine Corps despite the provisions of the law.[43]

To the dismay of the corps's leaders, the 1949 hearings did not change this fact. Congress was tired of the controversy and feared that action would result in an increasing defense budget at a time when it was striving to reduce the federal budget. Thus, despite the controversy over the "admirals' revolt," the corps was unable to gain any further congressional protection. It was not until four months after the completion of the hearings that the committee even issued its report recommending that the navy and Marine Corps maintain their own air arms and that the commandant be made a member of the JCS. Secretary of Defense Johnson simply ignored the report. He had not even waited for it before firing Adm. Louis Denfeld, the chief of naval operations, for opposing his policies. On 2 November Johnson appointed Adm. Forrest Sherman as chief of naval operations (CNO).[44] Sherman, who had not opposed the secretary of defense on the carrier issue, was much less sympathetic to the corps than his predecessor. One of his first acts as CNO was to place a freeze on all marine amphibious training for the year. He did so by assigning all available amphibious ships to train army forces.[45] Clearly the CNO was supporting Johnson's efforts to prove that the corps was superfluous. Then, in an exceptionally petty move that reflected the atmosphere in Washington, the secretary ordered the commandant be removed from the list of officials authorized to use a limousine and driver.

In yet another decision aimed directly at the corps, Johnson prohibited the observance of 10 November as the Marine Corps's birthday. To marines, the birthday celebration is the most important act of remembrance of the year, combining both ceremonial and social events. Naturally marines perceived Johnson's decree as a direct assault on the history and identity of their corps and responded accordingly. Although the secretary could forbid official observances, he could not prohibit marines worldwide from hosting private parties on the date of their most cherished tradition. Refuting the spirit if not the letter of the secretary's directive, marines held private parties that included the traditional cake, toasts, and reading of the commandant's birthday message.[46]

Unchecked by Congress, Johnson pushed through a fiscal year 1950 budget that reduced the corps from eleven to eight infantry battalions and from twenty-three to twelve aviation squadrons.[47] And, when considering the budget for fiscal year 1951, Johnson threatened to cut the corps to just six battalion landing teams.

Cates responded strongly: "It is not merely to be a question of cuts in men and money—although they are serious enough. We are being told in detail—and told by the Department of Defense—where and how these cuts are to be made—by striking into our combat forces. . . . I cannot agree that a cut so pointedly directed at reducing the strength of the highly effective organization is an economy."[48]

Cates's plea had no effect. By June 1950 it appeared that the corps was doomed to be reduced to a police force for the navy.[49] However, this threat to the corps's existence was not entirely negative. Lt. Gen. Victor H. Krulak, who was a key player in turning back an effort to cripple the corps, noted that it drove marines to maintain high standards: "Beneficial or not, the continuous struggle for a viable existence fixed clearly one of the distinguishing characteristics of the corps—a sensitive paranoia, sometimes justified, sometimes not. It is in this atmosphere of institutional vigilance that the Marines have been nourished over the years. This instinctive personal concern of Marines as individuals for the survival of their corps has certainly been one of the principal factors in its preservation."[50]

This institutional paranoia, at its peak due to the unification conflict, clearly was a factor in the hard training the corps conducted over the winter of 1949–1950. All of the principal commanders on both the air and ground sides were acutely aware of the continuing threat to the corps's existence. The major amphibious demonstrations conducted by East Coast marines in 1948 and then by West Coast marines in 1950 were part of a corpswide effort to inform political and military decision-makers of the unique value of the corps. This paranoia obviously reinforced the drive each marine felt not to fail his predecessors, for failure would surely lead to the extinction of the corps.

Terriff, who made an extensive study of the culture of the Marine Corps and how it affects the corps's ability to innovate, believes that

> the organizational paranoia essentially manifests in three ways. First, the Corps is perennially wary of the implications for its organizational survival of external pressures for change. Second, it is perennially vigilant to the ramifications of change in the strategic, military environment, lest a failure to adjust make it appear effectively irrelevant as a distinct organization. And third, the Marine Corps is perennially concerned that in adjusting to environmental changes or to pressures to change, that it is not seen to be encroaching on the functions of the other US military services, or, worse, to be perceived as becoming little more than another version of another US military service, particularly the US Army, lest this create the perception that it provides a redundant military capability.[51]

Obviously, the leadership of the corps is acutely aware of this culture and strives to preserve and reinforce it. Every year on 10 November, every marine worldwide is tasked to celebrate the birthday of the corps. It does not matter if the celebration takes place at a fancy ball in a capital city or is simply the exchange of greetings between two marines sharing canned rations in the field. An essential element of the celebration is the reading of Maj. Gen. Commandant John A. Lejeune's 1921 birthday message to the marines of the corps. This ritual is a conscious effort to preserve the corps's heritage as a fighting force, to impress upon each marine that the reputation of the corps may well ride on his or her performance in combat. The commandant's message addressed and shaped those traits that Zinni identified and sums up the view marines have of their corps as a fighting organization:

On November 10, 1775, a Corps of Marines was created by a resolution of the Continental Congress. Since that date, many thousands of men have borne the name Marine. In memory of them, it is fitting that we who are Marines should commemorate the Birthday of our Corps by calling to mind the glories of its long and illustrious history.

The record of our Corps is one which will bear comparison with that of the most famous military organizations in the world's history. During 90 of the 146 years of its existence the Marine Corps has been in action against the nation's foes. From the battle of Trenton to the Argonne, Marines have won foremost honors in war, and in the long eras of tranquility at home. Generation after generation of Marines have grown gray in war in both hemispheres and in every corner of the seven seas that our country and its citizens might enjoy peace and security.

In every battle and skirmish since the birth of our Corps Marines have acquitted themselves with the greatest distinction, winning new honors on each occasion until the term Marine has come to signify all that is highest in military efficiency and soldierly virtue.

This high name of distinction and soldierly repute we who are Marines today have received from those who preceded us in the Corps. With it we also received from them the eternal spirit which has animated our Corps from generation to generation and has been the distinguishing mark of the Marines in every age. So long as that spirit continues to flourish Marines will be found equal to every emergency in the future as they have been in the past, and the men of our nation will regard us as worthy successors to the long line of illustrious men who have served as "Soldiers of the Sea" since the founding of the Corps.

3

Education: Reuniting the Air-Ground Team

At the end of World War II, Lt. Gen. Alexander A. Vandegrift, the commandant of the Marine Corps, understood that the pressures of wartime mobilization and combat had seriously eroded the corps's prewar concept that marines should always fight as an air-ground team. He attributed this erosion to two factors. First, the operational separation of the air and ground elements of the corps during the Pacific campaign had prevented marine air from supporting marine ground elements. Second, although the air-ground concept had been a cornerstone of corps doctrine and an integral part of marine education prior to the war, Vandegrift recognized that the war had disrupted the corps's philosophy that all marines share the same initial education and training to bind them as a team. The demands of the war had eliminated the opportunity for air and ground officers to start their careers in the same school, and the combination of separate training and combat service had greatly undercut the concept of a marine air-ground team. At an even more fundamental level, Vandegrift was concerned that the separation had eroded the feeling that every marine was a marine first. Vandegrift was also deeply concerned that wartime experience had created veterans highly expert in their own specialties but with little appreciation for the broader aspects of their profession.

Vandegrift understood that education must be a central element in rebuilding the prewar concept of the air-ground team, and he immediately set about restoring the corps's educational system. This restoration was critical because although the extensive combat experience of World War II had resulted in a generation of officers with invaluable knowledge, that knowledge was often limited to their specific combat specialties. It provided little understanding of the organization and functioning of the corps as a whole. More important, the common understanding of the corps's culture and mission had eroded badly. Before the war, all officers had trained together at the Basic School before reporting to the operating forces. In addition, all prewar officers had completed a college degree before entering the

Basic School. Wartime personnel requirements changed all that because the corps no longer had the luxury of time to bring all officers together for training. To meet urgent combat needs, aviation candidates trained separately. Immediately after their basic training, they went to flight school and from there directly to the operating forces. Because of rapid expansion, aviators were needed to fly immediately. There was no time to teach general administrative subjects about the Marine Corps or air-ground tactics. World War II also saw the direct commissioning of large numbers of enlisted personnel in order to meet the pressing requirement for ever-expanding numbers of company-grade officers. The NCOs who were commissioned had already demonstrated the practical knowledge necessary to lead in combat. However, once the war was over, their lack of formal education about the Marine Corps as a whole threatened to limit their future usefulness. There were also a large number of ground officers who had spent the entire war either at a marine barracks or aboard ship. They had learned nothing about ground combat and were now too senior to learn by working their way up through the ranks.

To remedy these deficiencies, Vandegrift placed an emphasis on education (which was continued by his successor, Clifton B. Cates) to ensure that every marine understood the corps as a whole and internalized its values and standards. Robert D. Heinl wrote, "The postwar pattern of officer schooling was rigorous and firmly enforced. Basic School was reestablished, but at Brown Field, Quantico's original though long superseded air facility. For company officers and junior field officers there was the Junior School, located at the newly constructed Geiger Hall; for the most senior field officers, the Senior Course held sway in Breckenridge Hall."[1]

Central to the commandant's concern was the growing split between the air and ground elements of the corps. Gen. Vernon E. Megee, who played a critical role in developing the tactics, techniques, and procedures necessary to employ close air support effectively, later wrote an article describing how the air-ground split had come about:

> In line with pre-war experience, each MAG (Marine Air Group) was made self-sustaining in shop maintenance equipment, airfield appurtenances, and heavy motor transport. As a result the maintenance element of the group required a formidable tonnage of scarce shipping for displacement to the forward areas, to the later despair of Transport Quartermasters and Amphibious Commanders alike. The inevitable solution was piecemeal deployment by squadrons. . . . Thus handicapped, Marine Aviation was left out of certain amphibious planning due to the impracticability of providing bottoms to haul ground equipment to forward operating bases. . . .
>
> [During the Guadalcanal campaign in late 1942] there had been no opportunity to practice and perfect our yet deficient technique of close air support. Our pilots had not the experience, nor the ground units the communication equipment, to permit the close-in air attack missions, which came to be

standard procedure later in the war. In short, Marine Aviation throughout the Guadalcanal campaign had necessarily functioned as a miniature land-based air force—strictly in "the wild blue yonder." The thrills of air combat and air attack on live maneuvering ships, for the pilots who flew the planes and for the air commanders who directed the missions, were calculated to downgrade the less spectacular—if equally dangerous—chore of planting the bombs in front of the troops. Possibly, too, the troops who had learned to rely on their own organic supporting weapons while the air war raged above them did not realize what they had missed. While in retrospect it appears certain that Guadalcanal brought participating ground and air personnel closer together as individuals than they had been since Nicaragua; yet it would appear also that here was the first shadow of that schism which was later to separate the elements of the Corps. . . .

[From 1943 to 1945] while the Marine air wings vegetated in SoPac [Southern Pacific Theater], the Marine Divisions were having their moments of glory in the grand-scale amphibious movement across the Central Pacific, supported, after a fashion, by Naval carrier-based aircraft. From Tarawa to Guam, the Marine ground forces fought their way across coral strands and bloody beaches without benefit of their own specially trained air arm. Action reports are replete with complaints as to the inadequacy of the substitute they were compelled to accept, although in fairness to the Navy fliers it must be noted that they did their best on secondary missions for which they were neither completely trained nor properly equipped.

In the Peleliu campaign there was a brief resurgence of the old air-ground teamwork when Marine fighter squadrons, operating from an airfield literally in the front lines, materially aided the 1st MarDiv Marines in blasting the tenacious Japanese defenders out of their coral caves. This performance was so spectacular as to arouse the admiration of certain Army Air Corps observers, whose enthusiastic report was not received favorably in Washington. Elsewhere, though, the Marine airmen did not arrive in time to be of much assistance to the landing forces.

Thus we found ground Marines of all ranks who completed an entire Pacific tour, during which they participated in one or more major amphibious operations, without ever having seen a Marine combat aircraft. Conversely, many Marine pilots came and went without ever seeing a Marine ground unit in action. From December, 1943, to April, 1945, with the token exceptions of Peleliu and Iwo Jima, the two elements of the Marine Corps were fighting separate wars in widely separate areas. All they had left in common was the Marine Corps emblem. This, then, was the great schism which led to much erosion of mutual amity for many years to come.[2]

Further aggravating the split between air and ground were the administrative policies that had accumulated over the years. Maj. Gen. Louis E. Woods informed the commandant that his junior aviators "have a feeling the Marine Corps is no longer interested in them. Orders come out to them from Headquarters and they are signed by the director of Aviation—they are not signed by the Commandant of the Marine Corps."[3] Given the speed with which the corps expanded in World War II, in particular the air arm, one has to assume that this practice was merely an administrative convenience based on perceived necessity rather than an intentional slight. However, it did not change the aviators' perception that they were being treated as second-class citizens and that their contributions to the war effort were not fully appreciated.

Edward C. Dyer, then a lieutenant colonel who would soon command HMX 1, noted that from an aviator's point of view, even those ground officers who appreciated air, such as Brig. Gen. Merrill B. Twining, wanted to limit its role: "Twining was in many ways fully appreciative of the value of aviation. He understood it and wanted to use it, and he didn't want to lose it. On the other hand, he didn't want any sass from it. He wanted Marine Aviation to stay strictly where it was, roughly like the artillery or signal people." Dyer noted that the rising feeling among aviators was "if Marine Aviation wasn't really wanted, if it wasn't really part of the team, then okay, let's go someplace where we are wanted."[4]

The Marine Corps's initial efforts to adapt to the atomic battlefield reinforced this perception. Ronald A. Salmon, a World War II marine aviator, remembered that Lt. Gen. Roy Geiger was deeply impressed when he observed the Bikini atoll test. Salmon recalled Geiger saying, "No longer should the Marine Corps concept be of divisions and regiments and RLTs [regimental landing teams]. We are going to have to go to faster-moving, smaller units to react to this violence of atomic threat." Salmon noted that the Marine Corps's efforts to adapt set off a serious dispute between air and ground Marines: "So, for a short period of time after World War II, the Marine Corps went to this system—BLTs and squadrons. Well this started off the great battle between air and ground. They wanted the air attached to the BLT."[5]

Donn Robertson, who had commanded an infantry battalion on Iwo Jima, showed that some ground officers understood Salmon's concerns. He noted, "There were so many emotions involved. I'm sure the people in supply and those in aviation felt they'd been done in; that they were being taken over by the ground element."[6]

Others didn't comprehend the importance of the conflict. In a well-written, tightly argued thirteen-page *Naval Institute Proceedings* article justifying the existence of the Marine Corps, one of the corps's leading thinkers, Lt. Col. Robert D. Heinl, mentioned marine aviation only in passing. In his conclusion, he devoted only a single line to close air support.[7] He either did not think marine aviation was important or simply took it for granted. His oversight was not missed by his aviation counterparts.

Like most family spats, all the blame did not lie on one side. Marine ground officers felt that marine aviators often treated close air support as an afterthought.

Twining remembered the conflicts between air and ground officers that took place on the Marine Corps board that was established to prepare for unification. He noted that the two aviators assigned to write the role of marine aviation, then Brig. Gen. Vernon E. Megee and Col. Clayton B. Jerome, neglected the close air support mission. Twining was angry that the version they wrote "was all from the fly-fly boys point of view. Nothing about close air support."[8]

The corps's leaders knew it was essential to heal the rift between aviation and ground for two reasons. First, based on the prewar doctrine and the limited times when air and ground worked together during World War II, the senior leaders firmly believed that air and ground forces fighting as an integrated team were vastly more effective in combat than fighting separately. One of those leaders was Lewis Walt, who would go on to wear four stars. In September 1946 he wrote an article for the *Marine Corps Gazette* that related his experience with marine air at Peleliu. By closely coordinating between the battalion commander and the squadron leader, marine air was able to drop twenty 1,000-pound bombs into a 100-meter target despite the fact that ground marines had completely surrounded it. Walt's experiences made him an enthusiastic proponent of marine close air support. However, he was a realist and understood the depth of the split between air and ground marines. He concluded:

> One of the first and most basic steps in this training should be a thorough in-doctrination of the aviators in the basic tactics of infantry units. Until an aviator understands how ground troops operate in an attack against the enemy and until he becomes familiar with the infantryman's language in describing the location and employment of front line troops, he cannot be efficient and accurate in furnishing close air support. It is just as important that infantry officers be fully instructed in the capabilities and limitations of the aircraft as supporting weapon.[9]

As the unification fights continued, other ground officers came out very strongly in support of marine aviation. Robert E. Cushman, then a lieutenant colonel but destined to become commandant, stated categorically, "Amphibious forces must have air." He continued to argue that since marines by law are required to be the nation's amphibious experts, the Marine Corps must include robust aviation forces.[10]

The second reason the corps had to repair the schism was the looming unification battle. It was essential for the corps to emphasize how it was different from the other services, and the air-ground team was a key element of that difference.

Although the split was clearly still an issue in 1947, the corps as an institution had recognized its impact on combat effectiveness and started working on a solution as early as 1945. As noted earlier, the commandant decided part of the solution was to ensure that all officers received the education they had missed during the war. Unfortunately, the existing institutions—Platoon Commanders' School and Command and Staff School—were not well suited to overcome the deficiencies in these officers' backgrounds. Therefore, in early 1945 the Marine Corps started the Marine Air-Infantry School to educate the officers who had not come through the prewar system. Students ranged in rank from second lieutenant to major. Individual classes averaged ninety students, with slightly more than half aviators and the rest ground officers. Many of the aviators had 1,000 hours in their aircraft and air-to-air kills to their credit, but they had never participated in close air support or been exposed to ground tactics. Many of their ground counterparts had commanded companies in combat but had never had an opportunity to work with marine aviation. Even those students who had been exposed to close air support only understood it from their own air or ground side. The school was designed to fill the major gaps in the knowledge of three groups: the aviation officers who had gone directly to flight school and then the fleet; the former enlisted men who had been directly commissioned as ground officers and had led platoons and companies but never been to school; and the prewar officers who had spent all their time on sea duty and thus had no understanding of either ground or air operations. Capt. James R. Ray, one of the first Air-Infantry School instructors, wrote an article for the *Marine Corps Gazette* to inform his peers about the school's mission and curriculum:

> Realizing the confusion and antagonism which inevitably result when specific combat techniques, requiring joint (air-ground) action by two or more arms, are involved without understanding basic differences, Headquarters, U.S. Marine Corps, ordered the Marine Air-Infantry School founded as part of the Marine Corps Schools at Quantico, Va.
>
> The Main Mission—The primary mission of the Marine Air-Infantry School is to further mutual understanding of related problems among aviation and infantry officers. At the Marine Air-Infantry School, such mutual understanding is furthered by providing the aviation officer with a broad outline of infantry organization, weapons and tactics through the regiment and the ground officer with a similar outline of all pertinent factors concerning the functioning of combat aviation, making ground-conscious air officers and air-conscious ground officers. . . .
>
> The school curriculum . . . aim(ed) at satisfying the two basic needs of such officers, a general military education, and a general familiarization of both sides of the close air support problem. Here the weight in hours devoted to general education is somewhat greater than that allotted to air-ground familiarization.
>
> An outline of maximum total hours for all students undergoing the 16-week schooling period includes 576 hours and is as follows: General Subjects, 160; Air Subjects, 127; Infantry Subjects, 250; and additional Air or Ground Subjects, 39.[11]

First Lt. Edward P. Stamford was a student in late 1946. He had been an enlisted aviation technician who had received a direct commission in 1942 and reported to flight school. After flight school he had joined a fighting squadron and remained in the Pacific until ordered to Air-Infantry School. He had had no previous contact with the ground elements of the corps. He recalled:

> The training at the Air-Infantry School at the time was a short and concentrated course. We did learn the problems of the infantry in the field from their point of view. We worked in the field as ground soldiers and then, toward the end of the course, we used aviators in the field to direct us while the other half of the class, which was made up mostly of aviators, worked from the air. Then we changed off and those who had flown directed on the ground and those on the ground learned to strike. It worked out very well and our eyes were opened a great deal. The doctrines seemed to be taking good shape. . . . All in all the training we did have at the Marine Air-Infantry School was good training and it did show the aviator the problems of the infantry. A lot of them growled about it but they do appreciate the position of the ground soldier and respect him for his work.[12]

Then Brig. Gen. Vernon E. Megee, an aviator and one of the key officers pushing for better air-ground understanding and coordination, noted that immediately after the war many, if not most, of the ground officers had no particular belief in the usefulness of marine air:

> The original version of USF63, christened "Tentative Manual for Landing Force Operations," first saw the light sometime late in 1934. Among other doctrines, so well proven during the recent war in the Pacific, it contained a chapter on the tactics and technique of providing air support for landings against hostile shores. The authors of that particular chapter, written in 1933–1934, drew upon the then extant experience of some fifteen years of air support, as played in the bush leagues of Haiti, Santo Domingo, and Nicaragua, and upon their imagination of what a major league game might be. This concept was later expanded and published by the Marine Corps Schools in 1939 as a textbook entitled: "The Tactical Employment of Marine Corps Aviation." This textbook became familiar only to those few officers who attended the Schools subsequent to its publication and prior to the beginning of the war. All those officers are today general or senior field officers, and as such fought the war. The wartime battalion and company commanders, I found, knew relatively little about the history and principles of close air support of troops: they had little enough time to learn the other tricks of their trade. . . . Those who had not seen Marine air units in action at Guadalcanal knew little about Marine Aviation, and cared less. The only planes they ever saw were Naval carrier planes, so, they asked: "Why Marine Corps aviators?"[13]

Because even regular officers through the rank of lieutenant colonel hadn't been exposed to air-ground concepts, marine leaders knew they had to expand the education beyond that provided by the Air-Infantry School. The Marine Corps also made air-ground education an integral part of the curriculum for the postwar Amphibious Warfare School. Both the junior course, designed for captains and majors, and the senior course, designed for lieutenant colonels and colonels, incorporated instruction on the employment of marines as members of air-ground teams. One of the early attendees at Junior School was then Maj. Norman J. Anderson. Anderson, who would retire as a major general, remembered not only the quality of the instruction but also the depth of the schism it was designed to heal:

> I was impressed with the Junior School. It was really the first formal military education I had had. It was kind of a strange thing to go through after 10 years essentially of active service, but it was a wonderful experience for me in many ways.
>
> Not the least of which, of course, was being associated for the first time with the ground side of the Marine Corps after World War II.
>
> One of the difficulties of the Junior School at the time was the cleavage between the aviation people and the ground people. It was very, very intense in that class.
>
> I don't know why it existed but it was—I think the aviation people felt they were being—I'm not talking about all of them, but some of the aviation people felt that their contribution to the war effort was being downgraded or submerged by the emphasis upon ground tactics and ground examples from World War II. The cleavage was so deep that when some of the instructors would take the podium some of the aviators would turn their backs on them, sit facing the back of the room. . . .
>
> I don't remember anyone being disciplined for either disrespect or impertinence to the instructor. ...
>
> In my opinion, [the downgrading of aviation's World War II contribution] was perceived. It was imagined. But that didn't make any difference to those who perceived it. Or imagined it. And if it did exist, if they perceived it to exist, it was in my view, in a good cause. The Junior School was a device for finally bringing the aviation and ground people together. Because essentially the Marine Corps experience after Guadalcanal until Okinawa was that it didn't matter where you got your air support, just so you had airplanes flying around. And one hand didn't know what the other was doing. Really, the aviation people largely didn't know, except what they would read in intelligence summaries, about the ground assaults on the islands.
>
> And similarly the ground people didn't know about what the aviation folks had been up to. The experience of MAG-24 in the Philippines was a good example. It was MAG-24 supporting MacArthur's troops and doing a great job, but it had nothing to do with the basic purpose of the Marine Corps. . . .
>
> [Amphibious Warfare School] was valuable because you really learned something about ground operations. A lot of us had been ROTC students,

which of course is principally at the platoon level and nothing more, so it gave us a chance to find out how some of these decisions were made in tactical operations at battalion and regimental sized units.[14]

The syllabus at the Amphibious Warfare School senior course also began to reflect the requirement to reintegrate the air and ground elements of the corps. In 1946 the course had only 22.5 hours on aviation matters, with only 3 hours devoted to close air support. By the 1949–1950 academic year, aviation instruction had increased over 500 percent to 114 hours, with 8 hours dedicated purely to close air support.

Not all education was formal. Much was accomplished informally, as evidenced by very lively articles in the *Marine Corps Gazette*. The *Gazette* is one of two official magazines of the Marine Corps Association, an association dedicated to the professional development of marines. The *Gazette* provided a forum for professional discussion—and often disagreement with official policy. As early as August 1946 the *Gazette* published an article titled "Stop Fighting the Japs," which was highly critical of the tactical problems and their solutions being used in the schools. The author was adamant that the corps must get beyond its experience fighting the Japanese. Studying those battles was inadequate preparation for the next war. Instead he proposed a policy of forcing the students to think about a wide range of enemies, how those enemies would fight, and what marines had to do to counter them. He wrote:

In order to promote this policy, the following specific recommendations are offered, to be applied wherever practicable in all phases of tactical training to include our tactical schools, field maneuvers, and troop training:

1. Include an appreciable number of tactical problems (not necessarily the majority) in which the student is obliged to attack an enemy who has at least temporary superiority in aviation, artillery, tanks or other supporting weapons—or in several of them.

2. Devote considerable study to the possibility of night operations to include night attacks and especially to include night reconnaissance patrolling by front line units.

3. Give the student more training in camouflage, anti-chemical defense measures, and other aspects of war which were of minor importance in the Pacific war but which may be of major importance in the war of the future. Include tactical exercises in which he will be required to utilize this knowledge.

4. Eliminate, wherever possible, those place names, terms, and characteristics of the enemy which suggest that the student is fighting Japanese troops.

5. Provide the enemy with similar organization, with respect to personnel and materiel, to our own.[15]

Clearly the *Gazette* succeeded in providing a feedback mechanism for marines to comment on what the schools were teaching. It also provided a forum to debate the issues of the day. The issues from 1945 to 1950 discuss a full range of tactical, operational, and educational matters. From the letters to the editor and rebuttal articles, it is clear the journal was having an impact on the operating forces in updating the knowledge of those officers not fortunate enough to have attended one of the corps's formal schools.

Thus, through a program of formal and informal education, the corps's leadership set out to correct the education deficiencies of the wartime corps. As part of this effort, it focused on healing the rift between its air and ground elements as an issue of primary importance. By 1950, despite some continued reservations among both ground and air officers, the effort had largely succeeded. The marines of 1950 were clearly convinced of the value of an air-ground team and were determined to make the corps the world's premier air-ground combat team.

4

Doctrine

In conjunction with filling in the gaps in the education of marine officers, the corps had to fill gaps in its doctrine. The very nature of the war the corps had fought in the Pacific meant it had not experienced a number of forms of combat that would be an integral part of any war with the Soviet Union. In particular, at the end of World War II, the commandant identified the corps's deficiency in three areas: air-ground coordination, fire support coordination, and antitank defense.[1] In parallel with the efforts to educate officers so they would understand the problems they would face in a European campaign, the corps also had to develop the doctrine to be used as guidance in the training of the Fleet Marine Force. In addition, the commandant felt that the corps had to evaluate the tactical impact of atomic weapons and, if necessary, develop doctrine appropriate to an atomic battlefield. As noted in Chapter 1, Lt. Gen. Roy S. Geiger had represented the commandant at the Bikini atoll atomic bomb trials in July 1946. At the conclusion of the test, Geiger wrote to Vandegrift, "It is trusted that Marine Corps Headquarters will consider this a very serious and urgent matter and will use its most competent officers in finding a solution to develop the technique of conducting amphibious operations in the Atomic Age."[2]

Although Vandegrift quickly assigned a team to consider the problem, he was not an alarmist about the impact on the corps's future:

> I refused to share the atomic hysteria familiar to some ranking officers. The atomic bomb was not yet adapted for tactical employment, nor would this happen soon. Accordingly, I did not feel obliged to made [*sic*] a sudden, sharp change in our organizational profile.
>
> I did feel obliged to study the problem in all its complexity. For if we believed the basic mission of the Marine Corps would remain unchanged in an atomic age, we knew that the conditions surrounding this mission would

change and change radically. The problem, in my mind, divided itself into three major considerations: how to reorganize the FMF to render its units less vulnerable to atomic warfare and at the same time retain the final assault concentration essential to success; how to decrease our reaction time or, conversely, attain and maintain a preparedness by which a large unit could mount out in hours; how to put atomic weapons of the future to our own best use.

These and other problems I gave to O. P. Smith and Bill Twining at Marine Corps Schools for analysis by special study groups—a procedure almost identical to that of the twenties when we went to work on basic amphibious doctrine. Practically nothing was deemed too fanciful for consideration. We toyed with large troop-carrying airplanes as the assault vehicles of the future, and with troop-carrying submarines, and with helicopters then in their infancy.[3]

In seeking answers to the problems he so clearly defined, Vandegrift made the refinement of amphibious doctrine a priority at Quantico. The Advance Base Team, which had led the development of amphibious doctrine in the 1930s, was formally reestablished for the specific purpose of capturing the extensive amphibious warfare experience the corps had developed during the Pacific campaign and adapting it to the changing battlefield. Brig. Gen. Oliver P. Smith, commanding general of Marine Corps Schools and Marine Barracks Quantico, assigned the Advance Base Team to work on the issues highlighted by the commandant.

AIR-GROUND DOCTRINE

One of the key deficiencies identified by the Advance Base Team was the lack of a clear doctrine for the employment of close air support. Although the Marine Corps had been aggressively developing the doctrine, tactics, techniques, and procedures to fight as an air-ground team before World War II, it had lost ground in this arena during the war owing not to lack of interest so much as to lack of opportunity. The geography of the Central Pacific campaign had prevented the marine air-ground team from working together for most of the war. The corps had entered World War II firmly committed to the concept of an air-ground team. In its first big battle at Guadalcanal, the 1st Marine Division objective was to capture the airfield to allow for the immediate arrival of marine air. Within five days of the landing, the first marine air squadrons arrived and commenced operating from Henderson Field. Nicknamed the Cactus Air Force (after Guadalcanal's code name of Cactus), the air arm grew to include marine, army, and navy aircraft. The marine and army aircraft arrived as they became available, whereas the navy aircraft sought refuge on Guadalcanal when their carrier, the *Enterprise,* was damaged. During the campaign the Cactus Air Force expended the vast majority of its sorties in protecting the ground forces from Japanese air attack and interdicting Japanese reinforcements coming by sea. Despite the fact that the marine front lines were literally one minute's flying time from the airfield, marine aircraft rarely provided close air support. In an odd twist, the majority of close air support was provided by the few U.S. Army P-400s on the island. These aircraft lacked the operational ceiling to fight the Japanese Zeros but could contribute to ground attack missions.[4] Finally, the Cactus Air Force lacked both the procedures and the radios to conduct effective close air support, so often the pilots simply drove on the ground from the airfield to the front line to look at their target and talk to the infantry commander before they flew a mission. The pressing needs of the campaign prevented the refinement of effective procedures for marine airground integration.

After Guadalcanal, the geography of the Central Pacific made it almost impossible for marine land-based aviation to provide support to marine ground forces. In these island campaigns, by the time airfields were established ashore the marine assault divisions were withdrawing and turning the islands over to U.S. Army forces for occupation. As the navy/marine team island-hopped across the Central Pacific, there were some brief opportunities for marine aviators to support their brothers on the ground:

> Although there had been some jury-rigged, prearranged air strikes on Guadalcanal (some even involving depth charges as bombs), effective close air support never developed, nor did subsequent air support ventures in the undistinguished New Georgia campaign provide much encouragement.
>
> When the 3rd Marine Division was going into commission, however, the division air officer, Lieutenant Colonel John T. L. D. Gabbert, set about a serious study of ways to make close air support effective. Using himself as a guinea pig (crouching without shelter in an open field while different weight bombs were detonated statically at measured distances), Gabbert arrived empirically at the now classic "yard-a-pound" factor for close air support; that is you can safely drop a 100-pound bomb 100 yards from friendly troops in the open. Moreover, he organized division air-liaison parties headed by Marine dive bomber pilots borrowed from the 1st Wing. These people, with suitable field radios (the best Gabbert could get, anyway) were to live with the supported troops and control Marine air from the front lines. . . . Finally, when the thing was worked out, he convoked an air support school attended by every infantry operations officer in the division.[5]

The new organization and training paid off handsomely. Marine air provided close, accurate, and timely support for the division during the Bougainville campaign. Yet despite the enthusiasm of marine ground commanders for aviation tied directly to close air support, "it is also recorded that Marine air commanders in the Solomons expressed doubt as to the efficacy of close air support missions in jungle warfare, and there appears to have been little enthusiasm among the pilots for this type of mission."[6]

During subsequent campaigns, marine air rarely had the opportunity to demonstrate its proficiency. On Peleliu, marine air did not land on the island until 12 October 1944—and the marine division had left by 15 October. However, in those three days, marine aircraft demonstrated exceptional precision in bombing just yards ahead of the advancing ground marines. In fact, one of the primary targets, the Umurbrogal pocket, was less than a mile from the end of the runway. At Iwo Jima, the only marine air in the battle was embarked on the USS *Essex,* a fleet carrier. Unfortunately, the fleet carriers spent only three days supporting the campaign before departing to raid Japan, and the marines embarked were limited to a single day of close air support before they returned to flying combat air patrol to protect the carriers.[7] In their place, navy aviators flying from escort carriers provided the close air support for the rest of the campaign.

During the battle of Okinawa (April–June 1945), Maj. Gen. Francis P. Mulcahy of the Marine Corps commanded the 10th Tactical Air Force, which was responsible both for the air defense of Okinawa and for close air support for the ground forces. Because of the nature of the threat, senior marine leadership on Okinawa had to focus almost exclusively on the air defense mission. Although marine aircraft conducted almost 40 percent of the close air support missions on Okinawa, this mission was handled largely by the air groups themselves. Mulcahy, as 10th Tactical Air Force commander, was focused on air defense to defeat the kamikaze attacks launched by the Japanese. Clearly this was a valid decision. During the campaign, kamikaze pilots sank 36 ships and damaged 368 more, killing 4,907 sailors. Despite the best efforts of fleet- and land-based air forces, the United States lost more sailors than either soldiers or marines on Okinawa. Since the marine F4U Corsair was superior to both the army P-47 Thunderbolt and the navy F6F Hellcat in speed and rate of climb,[8] Mulcahy assigned his Corsair squadrons to air defense and the Thunderbolt squadrons primarily to close air support. In the interest of protecting the fleet from the growing kamikaze threat, the Marine Corps even had ten Corsair squadrons flying from navy fleet carriers. Thus, even in marine air's biggest close air support effort of World War II, the senior marine leadership was not intimately involved in developing the concepts and doctrines necessary to create a true air-ground team.

In a separate effort initiated in early 1944, the Marine Corps argued for the creation of marine carrier air groups to ensure support for marine amphibious landings. Based on identified deficiencies in the support navy air had provided at Tarawa in November 1943, the Marine Corps requested that the navy dedicate a limited number of escort carriers (CVEs) to marine air groups. The navy did not provide the carriers until the fall of 1944; despite the delays, it eventually dedicated sixteen of the newest CVEs to the project. For its part, the Marine Corps dedicated sixteen Corsair squadrons and sixteen torpedo bomber squadrons to the carrier air group effort.[9] By April 1945 the first two CVEs with their embarked marine air groups were ready to test the concept. Unfortunately, Rear Adm. C. T. Durgin, who commanded all CVEs at Okinawa, kept two CVEs, the *Block Island*

and *Gilbert Islands,* away from Okinawa for seventy-four of the eighty-two days of the campaign. Despite the agreement between Gen. Vandegrift and Admirals King and Nimitz that had led to these "Marine carriers," Durgin wrote, "this command sees at the present writing no reason for such assignments and has no intention of allowing it to occur."[10]

Even when fully executed, the experiment with CVEs allowed only thirty-two squadrons aboard ship. Lacking sea bases, four marine air groups were assigned to support army forces operating in the Philippines. Because of the size of the islands and the corresponding length of the campaign, marine air groups were based on Luzon with the 6th Army. Established ashore fourteen days after the landing, the 168 aging marine Douglas Dauntless dive bombers worked closely with the army divisions. This association with the U.S. Army led to the development of an entirely different set of procedures and control organizations for the close air support mission from those used by the navy in the Central Pacific campaign. Using the liaison party concept developed on Bougainville, the dive-bomber groups provided continuous, immediate support to the 1st Cavalry Division in its drive to Manila. The 1st Cavalry Division commander, Maj. Gen. Verne D. Mudge, was an enthusiastic supporter of closely integrated air support:

> I can say without reservation that the Marine dive-bomber outfits are among the most flexible I have seen in this war. They will try anything, and from my experience with them, I have found that anything they try usually pans out. The dive bombers of the 1st Marine Air Wing have kept the enemy on the run. They have kept him underground and enabled troops to move with greater speed. I cannot say enough in praise of these dive bomber pilots and their gunners.[11]

The marines' reputation spread, and soon they were flying strikes for every army division in the campaign. When Luzon was secure, marine air was tasked not only to support the subsequent liberation of the southern Philippine Islands but to command the air assets dedicated to that campaign. Unfortunately, at the end of the campaign the Dauntless dive bombers were declared obsolete and the last two squadrons were decommissioned—taking their close air support expertise with them.

Because of this split between army and navy theaters, marine aviation came out of the Pacific with two different methods for controlling close air support. The first was developed during the island-hopping campaign across the Central Pacific. Since the navy commanded this campaign, marine air control was based on the navy model. It employed sea-based landing force air support control units to control the close air support aircraft. Unfortunately, the navy system suffered from key weaknesses—overcentralization, lack of flexibility, and unwillingness to turn control of air assets over to ground commanders.[12]

The second system, the Philippine model, was developed by Marine Air Groups (MAGs) 24 and 32 and later used by MAGs 12 and 14 during that campaign.[13] It was based on the modifications the marine aviators made to the army–air force system to make close air support more responsive to the ground commander:

> Separated from the U. S. Navy oversight, McCutcheon and Marine aviators in the Philippines were free to set-up a unique Marine system. They made direct communications between front line ALPs [air liaison parties] and support aircraft standard and placed competent aviators in the FAC [forward air controller] positions, a policy that was not otherwise practiced or advocated in the Marine Corps during World War II. They facilitated this by making another radio set available for direct control of air strikes, the Support Air Direction Emergency Net (SADE).[14]

Lt. Col. Keith B. McCutcheon, MAG 24's operations officer in the Philippines, was instrumental in refining and publicizing the Philippine method. The primary appeals of this method were its flexibility and the fact that it made the air responsive to the ground commander by turning terminal control of the aircraft over to the forward air controller working with that commander, or to a tactical air controller (a pilot) orbiting over his head. At the time both the navy and the official army air forces systems were set up to use air only as a last resort when artillery, mortars, naval gunfire, or direct-fire weapons could not engage the target. In contrast, the marine-developed Philippine method was designed specifically so the ground commander could use aviation as easily as artillery. It returned the corps to its prewar concept, stated in the *Small Wars Manual*, of air support as flying artillery.[15] Yet McCutcheon was also adamant that aviation units should remain under the command of aviation commanders. Like most pilots of his era, he was convinced that ground commanders understood neither the full potential of aviation nor how to take care of squadrons assigned to their commands.

Thus, depending on where they fought during World War II, marine aviators were introduced to two completely different air control systems. Each system used its own command structures, communications nets, and standard operating procedures. McCutcheon summarized the two systems marine aviators had used by 1945. In the army system, before it was modified by the Marines in the Philippines,

> the fundamental unit was the Support Air Party (SAP). The SAP usually consisted of two officers and 20 enlisted men; it was attached by an air force from a Tactical Air Communication (TAC) Squadron to divisions and higher echelons for the purpose of coordinating air strike requests and for the purpose of directing air strikes. . . . Requests for strikes originated with battalion or regiment and passed through the chain of command to the division. The division SAP received the request and coordinated with the two and three sections for approval before sending it on to corps and army. Corps or army (whichever was the highest command present) would then pass the request to

the highest air force headquarters present. The A-3 assigned the mission to a subordinate air unit for briefing and conduct. This system was of course time consuming and the chances of getting an urgent request through for action in ten or 15 minutes were slim. . . .

There is much to say in support of this centralization of control in the Division SAPs. Many officers, including Marines, firmly believe that a battalion or a regiment is too small a unit to handle air power and that the division should be the smallest unit to request the use of it.[16]

As McCutcheon noted, the lowest-level commander who had aviators directly advising him was the division commander. (He was writing about the official army system, not the informal modifications marine aviators and army ground combat forces had developed in the Philippines.) In contrast, the navy system, developed in the drive across the Central Pacific,

requires higher intervening echelons to act on a request [only] in a negative manner and does not call for any definite positive approval. As a result, of this, there have been occasions when the ASCU [air support control unit] was confronted with more requests for air strikes than there were strike planes available. Had the divisions acted on every request and assigned priorities, this condition may have been partially alleviated.

In order to correlate the two systems into a workable one that will be applicable to all branches, a joint committee was appointed by the War and Navy Departments to draw up a doctrine for the employment of air support. It has been completed and covers all stages of an operation from the purely amphibious to the land-mass stage. At the present time, it is pending the approval of the various services.[17]

The navy system was based on air liaison parties being present down to the battalion level and did not require the higher headquarters to review and approve each strike. Instead, the request was made directly from the battalion to the air control unit. As long as the air control unit did not object, the mission was immediately assigned to any available aircraft and executed. Clearly the navy system was much more responsive to the ground commander, but, as McCutcheon stated, the sheer number of requests could overwhelm the air control unit.

Unfortunately, by 1950 the services were still unable to agree on the recommendations of the joint committee and could not agree on a single system. The navy approach remained different than the army–air force approach. Between 1946 and 1950, the navy-marine team, on its own initiative, developed an approach that combined both systems. Because marines had been closely involved in the development of both systems, it was natural that the best features of both were incorporated into the eventual navy-marine system. After World War II both doctrines were written about, and the resulting analyses were circulated and discussed corpswide. Both methods had marine proponents, but the modifications marines had made to the army system in the Philippines were clearly better suited to the corps's emerging air-ground concepts and were soon adopted. In fact, the Advance Base Team at Quantico incorporated the system into the USF-63, Amphibious Instructions to Landing Forces.[18]

Between 1946 and 1948, the navy and the Marine Corps greatly expanded the specific doctrine on the use of close air support. This expansion is most clearly reflected in the listing of specific communications nets, control agencies, and procedures in the 1948 version of *PHIB 12 Amphibious Operations: Air Operations*. The 1946 version made only vague references to these critical aspects of effective air-ground integration.[19]

By 1948 the corps had developed the doctrine, organizations, and procedures to provide immediate close air support. It had established tactical air control squadrons specifically to communicate between front-line air liaison parties/forward air controllers and the aircraft arriving in the combat area. When a ground unit needed air, the forward air controller (FAC) talked directly to the direct air support center (DASC). The Marine Corps system assumed that "silence is consent." Unless higher headquarters specifically intervened, the DASC would immediately assign aircraft to the FAC, and the FAC would control the mission. If requests exceeded the number of available aircraft, the DASC would assign them according to priorities established by the overall commander. By operating in this manner, the DASC eliminated the time-consuming step of having the command approve each individual mission. When the DASC had aircraft on station, the time from request to the FAC talking to the pilots was literally less than five minutes.

In the army–air force system, an immediate air request required active approval at each level from battalion to regiment to division. Each level approved the request and repeated it to the next higher level until it reached the division. Division would then pass the request to the Joint Operations Center (JOC). The JOC was a joint center at the numbered army/numbered air force level that assigned aircraft to missions. Preplanned missions also required army corps-level approval before they could be passed to the army–air force JOC.

This cumbersome system was further hampered by organizational deficiencies. Given the lower priority of close air support in the army–air force, army regiments had only one tactical air control party. The marines had one per battalion. (In Korea the brigade initially had only two rifle companies per battalion, whereas the army had six companies per regiment spread over a much wider front.)

Even more important, the army and air force rarely trained to conduct close air support. The army units that deployed early to Korea did so without any forward air control teams. And in practice the air force more frequently passed control of aircraft to its own airborne FACs in Mosquito aircraft than to ground FACs. Although this was a more comfortable arrangement for the air force, the FACs in these light observation aircraft did not work directly for the ground commander and often lacked up-to-date knowledge of the tactical situation. This created a tendency to attack targets much farther from friendly lines in order to prevent friendly-fire casualties.

Perhaps the most important difference was simply one of priority. For marine air close air support was the number one priority. For the air force it was fourth at best—well behind "strategic" bombing, air superiority, and air interdiction.

HELICOPTERS AND VERTICAL ENVELOPMENT

The second major area of innovation in amphibious doctrine was the use of helicopters. Although Vandegrift did not think the atomic bomb had revolutionized warfare at the point where troops were in close contact with the enemy, he did direct Quantico to develop ways to reduce the vulnerability of amphibious shipping through dispersion. In a 19 December 1946 letter to the commandant of Marine Corps Schools at Quantico, Vandegrift directed

> that an immediate study of the employment of helicopters in an amphibious operation be conducted and that the following be submitted:
> a. A tentative doctrine for helicopter employment.
> b. The military requirements for a helicopter specifically designed for ship-to-shore movement of troops and cargo.[20]

The letter also directed Quantico to study the employment of transport seaplanes in amphibious operations. A special board was created to conduct the study, but it encountered a major hurdle in the lack of information on the effects of atomic weapons. The only information the board could obtain was the Smyth Report, an unclassified academic study published by Princeton University. The Pentagon refused to release the classified reports on the results of the bombings in Japan or those of the subsequent tests at Bikini atoll to the marines.[21]

Despite that handicap, on 16 December 1946 the special board submitted an advance report to the commandant recommending two parallel programs to develop a transport helicopter and a transport seaplane.[22] Although the commandant quickly approved the findings, all requests for aircraft required the approval of the chief of naval operations (CNO) because the navy actually purchased aircraft for the marines. The CNO approved the purchase of helicopters already in production for a developmental squadron, but not the purchase of seaplanes. On 1 December 1947 the Marine Corps officially commissioned Marine Helicopter Squadron 1 (HMX 1) under the command of Lt. Col. Edward C. Dyer. Despite its name, HMX 1 was not the corps's first attempt at employing helicopters. Fifteen years earlier the marines had not only tested them but tried them in combat. "In the early 1930s the Marine Corps evaluated the Pitcairn OP-1 autogyro to determine its potential military value. Field tested in Nicaragua during 1932, the four-bladed, stubby winged aircraft was found suitable only for liaison purposes and medical evacuation of the lightly wounded. Considered by those in Nicaragua as unsafe to fly when carrying loads in excess of 200 pounds, the OP-1 soon disappeared from active Marine Corps inventory."[23] Interestingly, it was then Lt. Col. Roy Geiger who recommended that the program be terminated until the technological limitations could be overcome.

Determined to explore the possibilities presented by new technology, the Marine Corps initiated an aggressive tactical testing and development program at Quantico. Under the direction of Brig. Gen. Oliver P. Smith, HMX 1 teamed with Marine Corps Schools at Quantico to develop concepts, tactics, and procedures for using helicopters in amphibious assault. Despite the fact that the available helicopters lacked the lift capacity to provide a practical platform for amphibious assault (the HO3S could lift only the pilot and three other marines), by March 1947 Marine Corps Schools had published *PHIB-31 Amphibious Operations— Employment of Helicopters (Tentative)* as a mimeographed instructional guide for the schools.

HMX 1 did not receive its first helicopters until February 1948. Nonetheless, in March Dyer agreed to participate in the Marine Corps Schools' annual Operation Packard amphibious exercise. Col. Victor H. Krulak, deputy director of Marine Corps Schools, was running the exercise and felt the squadron could be used to simulate what a helicopter force equipped with the still-under-development transport helicopters could do. It was a bold step because the exercise would stress an untested command relationship as well as new procedures for everyone involved. As the final exercise for the Marine Corps Schools' senior class, Operation Packard was a corps-level amphibious command post exercise, with students playing the roles of the corps staff, two division staffs, and four regimental staffs. One of those student staffs would act as Regimental Landing Team 9 (RLT9) and conduct operations while embarked on USS *Palau*. The student staff developed the tactical plan and the load plans for the helicopters as if they would be used to land the entire regiment. On 23 May 1948 HMX 1, operating five HO3S helicopters from USS *Palau*, conducted thirty-five actual flights that landed sixty-six Marines and their equipment several miles inland from Onslow Beach, Camp Lejeune, North Carolina.[24] These flights simulated the landing of RLT-9. For this early experiment, the command arrangements were similar to those used for naval task force aircraft supporting the landing. HMX 1 was under the command of the commander of the *Palau*. Thus, the landing force and its helicopters did not have a common commander.[25] By November the corps had released a refined *PHIB-31* as its official doctrine for the use of helicopters in amphibious operations and codified the command relationships for amphibious operations.

Based on the results of this and subsequent Packard exercises, 1st Lt. Roy L. Anderson, an HMX 1 pilot, enthusiastically promoted the helicopter in the *Marine Corps Gazette:*

Field tests have shown that a platoon can be landed, assembled, and the aircraft clear of the landing area in less than thirty seconds. This is impressive for the troops are flying at 80 mph just above the tree tops, and in less than a minute, are landed and assembled ready to thwart an attack, seize a tactical locality or observation point, or perform any of numerous missions. Operations such as these can be conducted from ship or shore bases as the tactical situation demands.[26]

Although the corps was rapidly proving the concepts and developing the doctrine, not all marines were enthusiastic about the advent of helicopters. Vernon E. Megee, then serving with the aviation branch at Headquarters Marine Corps, recalled,

. . . being so short of money, there were those of us in Marine aviation that felt the Marine Corps was going overboard on the helicopter program at the expense of fixed wing aircraft. In other words, I was one of those. We maintained that for helicopters to live in a combat environment, they had to have adequate fixed wing support and if you cut down your fixed wing support and specialize on helicopters, the first thing you know Marine aviation would be nothing more than an aerial truck organization and you wouldn't have any combat potential. And, of course, the Quantico boys were all for helicopters. They gave no thought to anything else.[27]

Dyer, the commanding officer of HMX 1, had a much blunter assessment of other marine aviators' resistance to the helicopter. He noted that the navy paid for marine aircraft and set the budget by the total number of craft. So every helicopter purchased for the Marine Corps meant one less fixed-wing aircraft.[28]

Despite these doubts and postwar financial constraints, by early 1950 HMX 1 had completed two years of testing, both of its helicopters and of the new operational concepts for employment. In a June 1950 *Marine Corps Gazette* article, Capt. Robert A. Strieby, former project officer for HMX 1, extolled the virtues and capabilities of helicopters. He noted that the corps was sufficiently confident in the helicopter to be planning the integration of helicopters with fixed-wing light observation aircraft in all observation squadrons. The helicopters would be tasked with aerial reconnaissance and observation, aerial adjustment of artillery and naval gunfire, aerial wire laying, aerial resupply and evacuation, aerial photography, and aerial traffic control of ground vehicles.[29] Strieby's article proved to be a highly accurate prediction of the actual combat use of the helicopters by the brigade in the Pusan Perimeter.

FIRE SUPPORT COORDINATION

The Marine Corps gained extensive experience in controlling and coordinating artillery fire support during World War II. On Iwo Jima and Okinawa, the Marine Amphibious Corps commanded up to eighteen artillery battalions. Yet here too marine leaders were not happy with the status quo. The Marine Corps had never developed a modern fire support coordination center to plan and coordinate air, artillery, mortars, and naval gunfire. It was not until the Iwo Jima and Okinawa campaigns that the first division-level centers were even established and tested[30]—and because they were division-level initiatives, they all operated differently. Like the two separate air support systems that evolved in World War II, multiple fire support coordination systems developed in various divisions. As noted earlier, the commandant was aware of this problem and tasked Quantico with devising a solution. In October 1946 the team at Quantico published a concept for a fire support coordination center in the *Marine Corps Gazette:*

As a result of the past war many doctrines concerning certain phases of amphibious warfare have resulted. Many have been universally accepted and tested in combat with varying degrees of success. Others were born of compromise based on individual experiences and experiment. It is because of such conflicting doctrines and individual differences that the *Gazette* feels that the accompanying article, the result of careful study in the Marine Corps Schools and combat development, represents the most up-to-date significant approach to a problem which should prove of considerable professional interest to its readers.

In the conduct of the amphibious attack the problem of insuring effective delivery of supporting fires is complicated by several factors which are not encountered in normal land operations, or which are present only in a limited degree. These factors may be summarized as follows:

a. Although air and naval gunfire are the principal supporting weapons in the early stages of the landing attack neither of those arms is under command of the Landing Force Commander, and the provision of those fires is dependent upon request and liaison alone.

b. The part played by field artillery, as the landing attack progresses, is subject to continual change progressing from complete incapacity at the beginning of the assault to a position as the dominant supporting arm when the necessary artillery material is in place ashore.

c. Control of the air and naval gunfire arms involves techniques which are dissimilar to each other and to the techniques related to control of artillery.

d. The concurrent employment of the three arms in support of the landing attack involves a succession of prompt decisions in order to resolve conflicts which arise in the distribution and delivery of fires.

The task of employing the supporting arms in a manner best calculated to overcome the complexities outlined above is a command responsibility which devolves upon commanders at all levels. In the discharge of this responsibility each commander may assign such duties to subordinates as he desires but, as in all other functions of command, the responsibility itself remains with the commander. To advise and assist him and his executive staff in the coordinate employment of supporting arms, special staff officers are provided at division and higher levels. Liaison officers provide similar advice and assistance to regimental and battalion commanders and their executive staffs. In order to insure the most effective employment of these special advisors in the coordination of the supporting arms, it is essential that there be some formalized agency within each headquarters. In the division and higher echelons this agency is termed the Fire Support Coordination Center (FSCC).[31]

In less than a year the marines at Quantico had developed a system that allowed a commander to coordinate artillery, air, mortars, and naval gunfire. Although the commander was responsible for fire support coordination, his artillery liaison officer was now formally tasked with managing the internal organization and equipment of the fire support coordination center (FSCC) as well as the plans it produced. At the same time, Fleet Marine Force Pacific developed and published SOP 3-10, which outlined the methods and concepts necessary for fire support coordination.[32]

In April 1947 Capt. Thomas N. Greene wrote an article indicating that all was not well with fire support. Even with the direction of the FSCC, he said air and naval gunfire were being limited by doctrine that forbade them to attack targets that could be engaged by artillery. He also noted a shortage of forward observers and liaison officers. Due to continuing manpower cuts, these critical billets had not been added to the T/Os. This meant that although the Marine Corps had a doctrine for an FSCC, it did not have an organization to execute that doctrine.[33]

Over the next couple of years the Marine Corps moved to fix this deficiency. With the advent of the K-Series T/Os on 1 October 1949, FSCC personnel were officially added to the wartime but not to the peacetime T/Os. Of course this meant the FSCCs would not be manned during peacetime, so there would be no way to train those staffing them until the divisions were placed on a wartime footing. Nor did the new wartime T/Os provide a corresponding table of equipment, so in wartime status the divisions would have to redistribute existing communications and transportation to provide for the FSCC. The T/Os also did not provide for any personnel below the division level. In effect, the Marine Corps had developed the concepts and doctrine for fully functioning FSCCs down to battalion level but had not provided personnel or equipment to operate them.

Thus, by June 1950, though there was still significant discussion concerning exactly what the relationships among the supporting arms would be and how the arms would be controlled, the concepts were in place and familiar to many marines. However, extraordinary budget and manpower cuts kept the corps from implementing those concepts before the Korean War broke out. The Marine Corps acknowledged as much in its 1949 Battalion Landing Team Manual, where it tasked the operations officer with fire support coordination with the assistance of "the liaison officers of artillery, naval gunfire, and air, and the commanding officers of attached or supporting tank, antitank, and assault gun units as agents to achieve coordination."[34]

Although unsuccessful in implementing a formal system for fire support coordination, the corps succeeded in implementing a new system for the delivery of artillery fire. Working closely with army artillery, the corps came up with a new approach called the target grid method. Developed in October 1948 by the U.S. Army Artillery School at Fort Sill, Oklahoma, the system moved the task of calculating the firing data from the forward observer to the artillery battery fire direction center. This simplified the forward observer's job to the point that large numbers of infantrymen could be trained as forward observers. Maj. James A. Pound III wrote enthusiastically about the system in the October 1949 *Gazette*. However, he closed on a less than optimistic note:

> This same system of observing is planned for infantry heavy weapons as well as all types of artillery. Already the Artillery School gunnery department is working on a combined range deflection fan and coordinate square that can be oriented to a compass direction and thereby eliminate the target grid sheet which currently is responsible for some of the system's inherent disadvantages. However, it is not anticipated that the new piece of fire direction equipment will be ready for general use for several years.[35]

Fortunately, over the winter of 1949–1950, 1st Battalion, 11th Marines, had implemented and trained with the new system.[36] The battalion was ready to employ the new system by June 1950.

ANTITANK CONCEPTS

The final area of major concern to the commandant was the lack of antitank doctrine, training, and equipment. He recognized that despite a wealth of combat experience in the Pacific, the corps possessed little knowledge about or capability to fight tanks. He wrote, "That we are singularly lacking in experience in the antitank field and have relatively little knowledge of it is a factual condition. While this has not constituted a weakness in the past, if it continues, it may constitute a grave fault in the future."[37]

During this period the U.S. military assumed that the next war would be with the Soviet Union. The army and Marine Corps studied the Soviet offensive campaigns against the Germans and fully understood how effectively the Soviets had used tank forces. In response the army was making both its armored and infantry divisions "heavier" in anticipation of fighting in Europe. The corps, in order to maintain its amphibious nature, could not follow suit. Rather than facing the Soviet armored divisions with masses of tanks, an amphibious force, particularly one landed by helicopter, had to find a different way to defeat tanks. Based on careful analysis of the Russian and German antitank doctrines of World War II,

Lt. Col. Arthur J. Stuart, a marine tanker, wrote that the way to stop tanks was to "achieve the coordination of the antitank roles of all arms. Thus the antitank roles of tanks, infantry, aviation, artillery, and the passive antitank functions of engineers must be carefully coordinated into one integrated defensive system."[38]

From 1947 onward the 1st Marine Division, working with 1st Marine Air Wing, regularly integrated these concepts into air-ground exercises. During Operation Demon II in October 1948, they would practice just such coordination of all arms against tank attacks. This exercise was billed as

> the biggest peacetime maneuver ever held on the West Coast. The cast included 60 Navy ships, nearly 300 Navy and Marine aircraft, and 30,000 men. It was important enough to attract a considerable gallery of observers, including 500 students of the Army's high-level Command and Staff College who were flown from Fort Leavenworth to the coast in Marine transports. Ground troops were furnished by MajGen Graves B. Erskine's 1st Marine Division, and, in the air, the Marine Corps was represented by MAGs 12 and 33 from Maj Gen Louis E. Woods' 1st Wing.[39]

Operation Demon II included coordinating the employment of infantry weapons—recoilless rifles and bazookas using massed fire—with aviation and artillery to destroy enemy armored attacks.

STATUS OF DOCTRINE BY 1950

Marine Corps doctrine writers had worked hard from 1946 to 1950 to address the key areas the commandant had identified as deficient—air-ground coordination, fire support coordination, and antitank defense.

The tactics, techniques, and procedures necessary to provide highly effective close air support had been worked out. However, the air-ground doctrine in 1950 still did not call for marine air to be under a marine commander during the amphibious phases of an operation. Because the aircraft would be based aboard carriers, the aviation element remained under control of the navy task force commander. Even when phased ashore, the aviation elements would continue to work through a separate chain of command under the theater air commander, as they had done on Okinawa. In fact, unless the Marine Corps committed a corps-level headquarters in a multidivision landing, there was no doctrinal organization designed to command a marine air-ground team. This may seem a very odd oversight, given the fact that the entire active-duty Marine Corps could not muster a full division and all the corps troops were in cadre status. However, it accurately reflected the focus of the U.S. armed forces in 1950. All assumed the next war would be with the Soviet Union and thus would require massive mobilization before major offensive actions could be attempted.

Although doctrine for a truly unified air-ground command still had to be developed, the progress made by 1950 ensured that if marine air and ground commanders communicated clearly with each other, marine air could provide highly effective close air support. Vital to this outcome were the educational steps taken during the same period. Since there was not a single air-ground command, it was absolutely essential that the air and ground commanders share a common understanding of both the potential and the difficulties of air-ground coordination. Fortunately, the educational system's location at Quantico ensured that it was closely linked to the doctrine development system, as was the case.

Fire support coordination and antitank doctrine were also well developed by 1950, and the corresponding organizations had been developed. However, as the next chapter shows, drastic personnel cuts prevented the Marine Corps from manning and equipping the organizations prescribed by the doctrine. Once again, close cooperation between the educational and doctrinal elements at Quantico ensured that the schools forced their students to employ the concepts in command-post exercises even if they would not have the appropriate personnel when they joined the peacetime FMF.

5

Post–World War II Organization

Just as the culture of the U.S. Marine Corps drove its educational approach during the late 1940s, so did doctrine drive the corps's organization and training. The doctrinal concepts developed at Quantico, constrained by the corps's limited budget and end strengths, guided the marines who wrote the Tables of Organization for the operating forces. This chapter explores how marines of that era tried to establish unit organizations that would support important doctrinal concepts while staying within strict and declining budgetary and manpower limits. In particular, it will examine how those limitations forced the marines to create two sets of organizations. The first, the wartime T/Os, included all the personnel and equipment needed to execute the corps's doctrinal concepts in time of war. The second, peacetime T/Os represented the authors' best efforts to provide a balanced combined arms force while dealing with the real-world budgetary constraints imposed by the Truman administration.

By studying the corps's experiments with its organizational structures between World War II and Korea, we can understand how it tried to balance the needs of the known battlefields of the past with the emerging needs of a potential atomic battlefield. At the same time, the corps had to meet demands for reductions in end strength that became more stringent each year.

General Vandegrift captured the importance the corps's senior leaders placed on maintaining a combat-effective organization. Testifying before the Senate Naval Affairs Committee in July 1946, Vandegrift stated, "The heart of the Marine Corps is in its Fleet Marine Force, an organic component of the U. S. Fleet, consisting of the amphibious assault divisions which spearheaded our Navy's victorious westward march across the Central Pacific, and the Marine Air Arm whose primary task is the provision of close air support for the Marines who storm the beaches."[1]

The corps would spend the next four years fighting to preserve enough of the

FMF to remain combat-effective as an air-ground team. Its leaders were willing to experiment to see if new organizations could better meet the needs of the modern battlefield and the demands of a continually shrinking budget. This willingness to examine combat-tested organizations in light of new conditions revealed an institutional intellectual honesty. But, even while demonstrating a willingness to explore new concepts, the corps's leaders required proof that the new organizations were in fact better than the old.

The Marine Corps ended World War II with thoroughly tested and highly effective ground organizations. They were the result of continual evaluation in combat and an aggressive wartime program for testing new ideas. From the fire team to the amphibious corps headquarters, the marines had built flexible organizations that demonstrated the ability to organize for specific tasks at every level. Marine leaders from the squad level up were trained to think and act using combined arms simply because it was the only way to defeat the incredibly tough Japanese defenses. Every divisional organization had been developed and then thoroughly tested in combat and found effective.

On the aviation side, the corps had grown to 120 squadrons that included an impressive array of command, control, and radar squadrons. In fact, the Marine Corps's command and control system was so highly developed that a marine, employing a marine organization, commanded the 10th Tactical Air Force responsible for air defenses during the critical Okinawa campaign, including the crucial air defense against repeated massive kamikaze attacks. Unfortunately, marine aviation's logistics and maintenance organizations were not as well designed. Each squadron had its own self-sustaining maintenance and logistics sections, with very large shipping requirements for movement across the Pacific. The perpetual shortage of shipping meant that because marine aviation logistics elements were difficult to transport, the squadrons were often left behind during the advance across the Pacific. It was not until the end of the war that marine air solved this problem by consolidating many maintenance and supply functions at the air group level.

By the end of the war, marines had developed effective ground and air units. However, as noted earlier, the nature of the war in the Pacific meant that the marines very rarely fought as a true air-ground task force. Thus, despite almost four years of war, marines had had little opportunity to refine the organizations, procedures, and attitudes necessary to create highly effective air-ground organizations.

POST–WORLD WAR II GROUND ORGANIZATION

The marine ground organizations provided a superb force for the final, brutal island battles of Iwo Jima and Okinawa. The challenges of demobilization while maintaining readiness and forward deployed forces were enormous. Yet despite having repeatedly modified its organization, training, and equipment to absorb the combat lessons of World War II, the corps suddenly found itself confronting the entirely new and uncertain specter of an atomic battlefield. Like their counterparts in the other services, corps leaders decided that the atomic bomb required them to rethink their doctrine, organization, and equipment. As noted earlier, the commandant, although not an alarmist, directed a study group to determine how the corps should respond to the advent of atomic weapons.

In response, the corps examined future tactical operations with an emphasis on amphibious operations. It concluded that its World War II organizations were vulnerable to atomic attack. In an effort to reduce the vulnerability of the division to atomic weapons, the Marine Corps did away with its World War II divisional organization of three infantry regiments; an artillery regiment; and separate battalions for tanks, engineers, reconnaissance, signals, medical, and motor transport elements. This organization was felt to provide too large a target for an atomic weapon. In its place the corps activated the J-Series T/Os. Instituted on 1 October 1947, the J-Series addressed two critical issues facing the corps. The first was the atomic battlefield, and the second was the drastic reduction in end strength. Under the J-Series T/Os, the marine division was reduced to only 10,076 marines and 466 sailors—down dramatically from more than 22,000 men in the 1945 marine division. Further, the much-reduced J-Series division had only six infantry battalions that worked directly for division headquarters, only six artillery batteries, and a 4.5-inch rocket battery that worked directly for the artillery regimental headquarters. The J-Series eliminated the infantry regimental headquarters and the artillery battalion headquarters. The division's separate battalions were each reduced from a headquarters and service company and three line companies to a much-reduced headquarters and service company and only two line companies. The J-Series division included a tank battalion with two companies, an amphibian tractor battalion with one amphibian truck company and two amphibian tractor companies, and an engineer battalion with only two companies. Its reconnaissance battalion, signal battalion, and military police battalion were each reduced to a single company and placed in the division's headquarters and service battalion. Finally, the division had a shore party regiment to handle all other support functions.[2]

The concept called for the division to operate with its forces organized into six battalion landing teams. These BLTs would contain all the units needed to operate as independent elements widely dispersed over the battlefield. Thus, they would not present a major concentration that could be destroyed by a single atomic weapon. To preserve the infantry regimental lineage, each infantry battalion was given the lineal designation of an infantry regiment. Further, since the infantry battalions were to operate as battalion landing teams working directly for the division, each battalion was commanded by a full colonel.[3]

Despite the fact that the J-Series T/Os severely reduced the strength of the division, they actually increased the personnel assigned to providing fire support coordination. This decision reflected the lessons marines had learned about combined arms warfare during World War II and codified in their doctrine. At the division level the J-Series created new special staff sections for both air and naval gunfire.[4] At the infantry battalion level they added a full-time air officer plus communicators to support the tactical air control party, the naval gunfire spot team, and the naval gunfire liaison team.[5] These additional personnel, along with the training, techniques, and procedures the corps was developing, would dramatically increase the battalion commander's ability to use and coordinate all supporting fires. In keeping with evolving marine air-ground doctrine, the new organization provided the personnel and equipment to establish a direct path from the battalion to the aviation control system. The combination of doctrine, organization, and training institutionalized the best of the air-ground procedures tried during World War II.

Even as the divisions were reorganizing in accordance with the J-Series T/Os, the Marine Corps also considered forming brigades. The proposed brigade organization looked like an even further reduced division. It was to consist of only seven battalions—a headquarters and service battalion that included a company each of engineers, amphibian trucks, amphibian tractors and tanks; a medical battalion; a shore party battalion; an artillery battalion; and three infantry battalions.[6] The brigade organization would be used when deploying ground combat forces that were smaller than a division.

It is important to note that, unlike modern marine brigades, the postwar brigade did not have an aviation element. Today a marine expeditionary brigade is an air-ground team usually built around a regimental combat team, a marine air group, and a brigade logistics element. It is essential that today's readers understand that the brigades formed before 1950 were strictly ground organizations. Between 1946 and 1950 the Marine Corps formed brigades in both Fleet Marine Force Atlantic (FMFLant) and Fleet Marine Force Pacific (FMFPac). Neither brigade had any aviation elements. The East Coast brigade was a temporary formation to provide a force in readiness until the 2nd Marine Division returned from the Pacific. Formed in January 1946 at Quantico, it was absorbed into the 2nd Division when the division arrived at Camp Lejeune, North Carolina, later that year.[7]

During the spring of 1947 FMFPac was ordered to form the 1st Provisional Marine Brigade on Guam from units being withdrawn from China. The brigade, activated on 1 June, had two infantry battalions; a service battalion; and a headquarters battalion with a tank platoon, hospital company, engineer company, truck company service, and supply company. Interestingly, the order forming the brigade specified that:

> (a.) The Force Headquarters Company and the two Infantry Battalions listed above include artillery personnel. No artillery organization will be activated until further notice. It is desired that the artillery personnel be utilized

as the nucleus of a provisional artillery organization for training and emergency employment. Artillery training of personnel, other than the artillery specialists, will be in addition to normal appropriate training for the individuals or units concerned.

(b.) The planned provisional artillery organization will consist of a tactical headquarters and two six-gun 105mm howitzer batteries.[8]

Commanded by Brig. Gen. Edward A. Craig, the brigade reflected both the challenges facing the corps and the determination of its leaders to ensure combat-readiness despite those challenges. By giving up the artillery, the corps was clearly sacrificing needed capability to save personnel. And, typical of the frugality of Headquarters Marine Corps, the brigade was dumped on Guam with no facilities of any kind but was still required to be a combat-ready force. The Marine Corps could not fund construction of facilities due to budget constraints. Despite the requirement to build his own camp, Craig insisted on a robust combat training program for the brigade.[9]

The brigade did not enjoy the luxury of two infantry battalions for long. When the Marine Corps adopted the J-Series T/Os on 1 October 1947, the brigade lost one of those battalions. Two years later the entire brigade was deactivated on 30 September 1949. Upon deactivation, its units packed up for transportation back to Camp Pendleton, California, where they were reorganized under K-Series T/Os and absorbed by the 1st Marine Division.[10] After the brigade's departure from Guam, the corps no longer had any ground units in the Pacific.

These Atlantic and Pacific brigades, both strictly ground organizations, proved to be the models adopted by the division marines when ordered to form a brigade for Korea in July 1950. Craig specifically noted that he used the Guam brigade as a model when he built the 1st Provisional Marine Brigade. Although the Marine Corps was working hard on air-ground doctrine, it did not organize its operating forces accordingly.

From 1947 to 1949 the corps maintained a total of eleven infantry battalions in two understrength divisions and the small brigade on Guam. Faced with the manpower cuts planned for fiscal years 1950 and 1951, the corps decided it had to further reduce the FMF. In 1948 the commandant directed a new study on the organization of the FMF. This report, released in December 1948, reevaluated the threats the nation faced and determined that the corps needed to return to the more robust and combat-effective triangular division and to incorporate lessons learned in logistics and aviation organization.[11] The authors felt that the J-Series T/Os did not provide an effective organization for employing the corps's limited combat power.

Thus, in October 1949 the Marine Corps once again reorganized the division by activating the K-Series T/Os. The K-Series was based on the World War II amphibious corps organization, but with major increases in antiarmor capabilities.

The marines wanted the combat-tested divisional organization back but were acutely aware that it lacked the armor and antiarmor assets required to fight the Soviet Union. The Marine Corps lacked sufficient resources to staff such an organization. Therefore, it again published both wartime and peacetime T/Os from the amphibious corps down.[12] The division wartime T/O called for three infantry regiments of three battalions each, an artillery regiment of three 105mm howitzer battalions and one 4.2-inch rocket battalion, and a tank regiment of three battalions. In addition, the division would have the following separate battalions—engineer, reconnaissance, medical, motor transport, amphibious tractor, ordnance, weapons, signal, service, and shore party. Each of the separate battalions would have a headquarters and support company and three line companies. (Line companies executed the actual duties of each battalion, whereas the headquarters and support company provide the line companies' administration, maintenance, heavy equipment and weapons, and signal support.)[13]

Essentially, the infantry regiments and artillery regiment returned to the well-tested World War II organizations. The big change was the addition of a tank regiment in response to the commandant's directive to improve antitank defense in the divisions. In addition to adding a tank regiment to the division, each infantry regiment gained an integral tank platoon assigned to the regimental antitank company. This company included the tank platoon and a platoon of 75mm recoilless rifles. The wartime T/Os reflected the corps's concepts and doctrine for future combat. Having tested the J-Series T/Os, marine leaders came to the conclusion the J-Series organization provided little advantage in an atomic conflict and major disadvantages in a conventional war. Thus, despite the cost and effort, they made the decision to return the division to the combat-tested triangular organization and increase its proposed wartime strength back to 22,000.

In October 1949 the corps lacked the personnel to man the wartime T/Os, so its two divisions reorganized based on the peacetime K-Series T/Os. These peacetime T/Os did not include the tank regiment or the tank platoons in each regiment. In their place, each division received a single tank battalion with only two companies. In addition, the corps took the 75mm recoilless rifle platoons away from the infantry regiments and consolidated them, along with 4.2-inch mortars, in a divisional weapons company.

The peacetime K-Series allowed for only one of the three wartime infantry regiments. It had a headquarters and three infantry battalions. But reducing the divisions to a single infantry regiment was not enough. To save personnel, each of the three infantry battalions would be cut to only two rifle companies of two rifle platoons each instead of the normal complement of three rifle companies with three rifle platoons each. The battalion headquarters and weapons companies as well as the rifle companies' weapons platoons would also be manned at peacetime levels. In particular, the battalion weapons company was severely reduced. The machine-gun platoon was eliminated, and the antitank assault platoon and 81mm mortar platoon each had only two sections instead of three.[14] The peacetime T/Os provided an infantry battalion with 27 officers and 543 enlisted marines, as opposed to the wartime T/Os, which called for 41 officers and 1,040 enlisted marines.[15] In practice, the battalions were manned at less than 50 percent of wartime strength. To save additional personnel, the artillery regiment was limited to one 105mm howitzer battalion. Each of the separate battalions was also allowed only one letter company and a small headquarters and service company. Even as the 1st and 2nd Marine Divisions were reorganized under the K-Series T/Os, the brigade on Guam was deactivated and its units returned to Camp Pendleton.

A key driver of these changes was the requirement to reach the strength of six infantry battalions planned by Secretary Johnson for fiscal year 1951. The K-Series T/Os did so while leaving the paper organizations in place to expand to a full-strength wartime division. Despite all the shortages, within a year the wisdom of building this organization would be tested and found correct.

With the FMF-wide reorganization on 1 October 1949, all infantry regiments, except for the 5th and 6th Marines, were deactivated. With a projected strength of only six infantry battalions, the Marine Corps chose to consolidate each division's existing six J-Series infantry battalions into three understrength K-Series infantry battalions and reduce each division to a single infantry regiment. The 6th Marine Regiment, 2nd Marine Division, immediately formed its three K-Series battalions from the six J-Series battalions already assigned to Camp Lejeune. However, the 5th Marine Regiment, 1st Marine Division, at Camp Pendleton could form only the 1st and 2nd battalions of the 5th Marines. The regiment would have to await the disbanding of the Guam brigade before organizing the 3rd battalion. The units of the Guam brigade did not return to the United States until the end of February 1950. When the infantry battalion arrived from Guam, it still had to reorganize under the K-Series T/O. In keeping with normal practice, a generous leave policy was instituted because the battalion had been overseas since World War II.[16] Thus, the battalion was not fully reorganized and manned at peacetime levels until April 1950 — just in time to join the rest of the corps in the summer turnover process.

After the reorganization under the K-Series T/Os on 1 October 1949, the 5th Marine Regiment had only two infantry battalions with a total of only eight rifle platoons instead of its wartime strength of three infantry battalions with twenty-seven rifle platoons. Even when the third battalion joined the regiment in March 1950, the regiment still had only twelve rifle platoons. Thus, the effective infantry strength of the 1st Marine Division over the winter of 1949–1950 was eight understrength rifle platoons instead of the eighty-one that were its wartime strength. With the addition of the third battalion, it grew to only twelve rifle platoons.

The same personnel cuts affected the separate battalions (tank, amphibious tractor, engineer, signals, etc.). The divisional artillery, 11th Marines, was a shadow of its wartime strength. Its wartime T/O called for three 105mm howitzer battalions and a 4.2-inch rocket battalion. The peacetime T/O called for only one

105mm howitzer battalion: 1st Battalion, 11th Marines. Even that battalion was badly understrength. Under the K-Series T/Os, "the light field artillery battalion of 329 men (instead of about 700) was organized into two firing batteries of four 105mm howitzers each—eight howitzers instead of eighteen."[17]

However, with the arrival of the units from Guam, the 1st Battalion absorbed the artillery battery that had been assigned to the brigade. Thus, the battalion finally had three firing batteries of four guns each. The artillery battalions of the Marine Corps, like its infantry battalions, had peacetime T/Os and Tables of Equipment only two-thirds the size of their wartime allocations. Under the peacetime T/O, the division had only twelve howitzers rather than the fifty-four called for in the wartime T/O. All corps-level artillery units had been deactivated.

Despite the repeated reorganizations at the battalion level and above, the corps did not modify the rifle squad after World War II. The squad had been completely changed over the course of the war, and it had been refined and tested in a series of extremely tough campaigns under a wide variety of conditions. Until 1943 the marine squad had a T/O strength of twelve men, including a sergeant squad leader and a corporal assistant. Ten members of the squad were armed with M1 rifles and two with Browning automatic rifles (BARs).[18] This organization was essentially unchanged from World War I. Unfortunately, it meant that the squad leader—the junior unit leader in the Marine Corps—had a greater number of men reporting directly to him than the company commander. It also deprived the squad leader of the triangular organization that was the rule from platoon to division. The triangular organization allowed each leader to employ three separate elements, each with its own leader, to achieve his mission. In contrast, the best the squad leader could do was divide his squad in two, with him and his assistant squad leader, a corporal, each leading half. This gave the squad leader control over a minimum of six other marines—his assistant squad leader and the four other men in his half squad. This number proved to be too large, particularly in the thick jungle terrain of the Solomon Islands.

In spring of 1943 Company L, 24th Marines, under Capt. Houston Stiff began to experiment with a new squad organization. Based on his experience with the marine raiders at Guadalcanal, Stiff organized his squads into three fire groups of three men each. Each group was led by a corporal and was built around a BAR. This organization meant the squad leader had to supervise only his three team leaders, not the entire squad. It also provided more leaders at lower levels, a 50 percent increase in automatic weapons in the squad, and the flexibility of having three units maneuver under the direction of the squad leader. The organization was adopted first by the battalion, then by the regiment, and was employed in 1944 in the Marshall Islands. As a result of that combat experience, the rifle squad was increased to thirteen men with three four-man fire teams and a squad leader. The Marine Corps adopted this organization and used it for its final campaigns in World War II. In fact, the squad has remained essentially unchanged to this day.

Under the varying conditions of these campaigns, combat revealed some added advantages of the group or fire team system. Through the cane fields and over the wooded ridges of Saipan, the use of one team as scouts preceding the squad in the advance functioned effectively. Frequent rotation of teams on this assignment was practiced. Individual groups also proved ideal for patrols.

On Tinian, replacements joined units on the front lines. In this situation, which became routine, the group system was valuable, for the new men were assigned to fire teams, putting untried men with one or two veterans. Since many infantry units also had new officers on this landing, the influx of green troops under combat conditions might have been disastrous. But each veteran was able to guide and control one or two of the replacements with little trouble.

On Saipan and Tinian, the ease with which fire teams could carry out the principles of tank-infantry coordination became apparent. The teams provided long-range and short-range support for armor over varying terrain.

On these two islands, and even more on Iwo Jima, the fire teams simplified the problem of supply under fire. One man from a team could slip back for rations and water, thus keeping dispersion at the maximum, even at the squad level.

Finally, on the nightly defensive set-up, the four man fire team broke down easily into two-man positions. With a group leader responsible for every two holes, there was effective control all along the line during every phase of the defense, from digging in until moving out in the attack. And with officer and NCO casualties heavy, the fire team leaders furnished a steady supply of tested leaders as the attack moved on.[19]

Thus, by the end of World War II the squad structure had changed completely. There were also some changes in the weapons platoons of the rifle companies. However, at the battalion level and above, the corps stayed with the triangular organization that had served it well since 1942.

In the period between 1946 and 1949, the corps had come full circle on its ground organization. It had realized that atomic weapons were not a likely threat on the tactical battlefield and had found the J-Series T/Os to be wanting. Having shown a willingness to experiment in order to meet new threats, the corps also showed the wisdom to return to the combat-tested ground organizations that had been developed by the end of World War II. This decision highlights a key cultural trait of the corps during this period. It could honestly evaluate decisions made even at the highest levels and admit that some were wrong. The decision to return to the time- and combat-tested organization was critical for the marines of the brigade. It insured that those who fought at Pusan did so in an effective, if dramatically understrength, combined arms organization.

AIR ORGANIZATION

As noted earlier, marine air was reduced from 4 wings with 120 squadrons in August 1945 to 2 wings with only 12 squadrons by June 1950; it was faced with reduction to 6 squadrons during fiscal year 1951 (July 1950–June 1951). By June 1950 the 1st Marine Air Wing (MAW) stationed in California consisted of the wing headquarters and two flying groups—MAG 12 and MAG 33. The 2nd MAW on the East Coast was similarly reduced. The only other noteworthy air organization was HMX 1. This squadron remained based in Quantico and was focused on developing the concepts and the aircraft necessary for the Marine Corps to exploit the helicopter's unique capabilities.

As noted in Chapter 4, the corps had worked hard to establish its own doctrine for close air support. Despite huge force reductions, it focused on developing the organizations that could execute the new doctrine. In parallel with the doctrinal developments at Quantico, the Marine Corps established a Marine Air Control Group (MACG) in each MAW. The function of the MACG was to provide the necessary controlling agencies to execute air support for the marine air-ground team. The MACGs were assigned to the air wings specifically to keep the aircraft under the command of aviators. Despite substantial progress in healing the air-ground rift, most aviators still did not believe that ground marines understood the needs of aviation units well enough to concede the command of air units to ground marines. However, by June 1950 the aviators were adamant that marine air existed to provide support to marine ground forces. The MACGs were specifically designed to provide the critical link between the ground commanders in the division and the aircraft supporting them.

With the MACG as the overarching control organization for close air support, the Marine Corps expanded on the lessons of World War II to provide terminal air control down to the infantry battalion level. The K-Series T/Os provided a Tactical Air Control Party (TACP) that consisted of a marine pilot and a team of enlisted communicators for each infantry battalion. The infantry regiments and divisions had similar TACPs. The pilot at the battalion level acted as both an air liaison officer (ALO) and a forward air controller. As the ALO he advised the battalion commander on all matters concerning aviation support to the battalion and worked with the operations officer in planning and executing that support. As the FAC the pilot went forward to a position where he could see the target and provide terminal direction and control for the attacking aircraft.

For immediate close air support, the battalion ALO/FAC initiated a strike by making his request directly to the Marine Tactical Air Control Squadron (MTACS) which was part of the MACG. The regimental and divisional TACPs listened to the communications nets using the "silence is consent" system. Under this system, as long as the higher headquarters did not intervene to cancel the request, it could be acted on immediately by the aviation control element. Upon receiving the request, the MTACS determined what aircraft were available and assigned them, using the priorities established by the senior ground commander in accordance with the overall requirements for all potential air missions. If aircraft were available, the MTACS ordered them to fly to a point near the battalion ALO, check in on his communications net, and execute the mission under his control. An alternative system was to pass the aircraft to a pilot orbiting over the battle space functioning as a tactical air controller (TAC). This pilot, who was in communication with the requesting unit, would provide terminal control for the air strike. This marine system combined the best aspects of both army and navy systems from World War II. By planning at the senior level, air assets could be assigned according to the priorities set by the overall commander. These priorities were then used to allocate aircraft to the requesting unit. Under the "silence is consent" system the requests traveled directly from the unit in contact to the air control unit assigning flights and from there to the strike aircraft. This system allowed for much greater responsiveness than the much more centrally controlled army–air force system. The new wing organizations had been specifically designed to make the new system work smoothly.

During late 1948 and early 1949, in a series of amphibious exercises with both marine and army units, marine aviators assigned as battalion ALOs came to the conclusion that each battalion needed a minimum of two teams to run close air support effectively. The ALO and his team would stay at the battalion headquarters to plan and prioritize air. The forward air control party would move forward with the assault companies to actually control the strikes. Unfortunately, given the austerity of the time, the Marine Corps could not afford the additional personnel or radios to provide for both an ALO and a FAC party. As a result, the single officer, using a single set of radios, had to continue to fulfill both jobs.[20]

An interesting oversight in the development of air-ground coordination was the absence of air-to-air radios in any of the corps's light observation aircraft. In 1946 the aerial observer school stated categorically that aerial observers were trained only for the control of artillery and naval gunfire.[21] Although other opportunities for FACs to provide terminal control for aircraft were enthusiastically developed, between World War II and the Korean War the corps did not purchase the necessary air-to-air radios for the aerial observer to control strike aircraft. Instead the aerial observer reported the target to the ALO at division level, and that officer initiated the air strike. This system obviously created significant delays in engaging targets detected by aerial observers.

With this minor exception, the combination of well-developed doctrine and the evolution of the MACG in the wing and the TACP in the division meant the Marine Corps was better organized to provide close air support in 1950 than it had been in August 1945. Air-ground doctrine had been codified. Air control organizations had been built, and, most importantly, detailed procedures had been worked out and practiced between air and ground units in the operating forces.

To deal with the other major organizational deficiency marine aviation suffered during World War II, the wing experimented with different ways to provide logistical support for its flying squadrons. Over the course of World War II the corps had made significant changes to ensure that the flying squadrons were light enough to be deployed along with the ground combat elements. Although the corps did not institute formal changes to the wing logistics organization, after the war Gen. Field Harris conducted an experiment with the 2nd MAW at Cherry Point, North Carolina. He attempted to consolidate all wing supplies, advanced maintenance, transportation, and other logistics support into a single large logistics and maintenance group. Even with a handpicked commander, the group could not fulfill all the required functions, and the experiment was abandoned.[22]

Harris was trying to solve a problem that had dogged marine aviation from the beginning of World War II. It had to straddle two environments—land and sea. Land-based operations required the squadron to bring full support capability with it—fuel, maintenance, ammunition, messing, billeting, etc. Yet when aviation units went to sea, all of that equipment and most of the personnel were no longer necessary because the aircraft carriers had mess facilities, fuel systems, ammunition storage, and transportation. Harris's experiment was one attempt to deal with the issue. Although it failed, the proper organization for the MAW was discussed officially in forums such as the Marine Corps board and unofficially in the *Marine Corps Gazette*.[23]

These discussions did not lead to the major T/Os changes that plagued the ground side of the corps. With the exception of the changes necessary to coordinate close air support, the air wing remained organized very much as it had been at the end of World War II. One solid recommendation did come from the "Marine Corps Board Report on the Organization of the Fleet Marine Force in War and Peace," dated 1 December 1948. The report recommended the addition of light helicopters to overcome the shortage of observation aircraft in a marine division. It stated that each division should have one observation squadron of light fixed-wing aircraft and one of light helicopters. The recommendation was accepted by Headquarters Marine Corps, but again the corps lacked the resources to actually assign a helicopter squadron to each division. Instead HMX 1, as one of many missions and concepts it was exploring, continued to experiment with using helicopters in an observation role to support the division.[24] The training HMX 1 pilots received while conducting these experiments would prove very useful in Korea.

Despite being specifically formed to study the corps's wartime organization, the 1948 "Marine Corps Board Report on the Organization of the Fleet Marine Force in War and Peace" did not have much to say about how the air-ground team would be integrated in combat. In fact, buried deep in the force troops section was a recommendation to do away with the requirement that aviation and ground units exchange personnel. The report thought the requirement for aviators to spend time with ground staffs and vice versa was unnecessary; the informal approach would be sufficient. However, it did recommend that aviators be permanently assigned to infantry regimental and battalion staffs because those organizations would conduct most of the close air support missions.[25] In an interesting oversight, the issue of who would command the aviation elements was not even mentioned. Perhaps the issue was still too contentious to enable the establishment of an official position. The board did, however, recommend a future study to determine how the new jet aircraft could be used for close air support.

The board also made note of the complexity caused by marine air's close association with the U.S. Navy. The report noted that the 1947 National Security Act stated that marine aviation existed primarily to support the FMF and that there was no distinction between aviation and other FMF elements. The report went on to say,

> In actual practice, however, it is manifest that the complexity of its status derives from the fact that within the fleet it is subordinate, with their respective spheres, to two [U.S. Navy] type commands, Fleet Marine Force and Fleet Air. This status is further complicated by the fact that Fleet Marine Force aviation in technical matters is subject to control of the Bureau of Aeronautics, while in certain administrative matters it is subject to control of Headquarters, Marine Corps. Furthermore, in the support of Fleet Marine Force landing operations, Fleet Marine Force aviation serves for the greater part or all of the operation in the carrier task force and does not normally come under landing force control until shore based squadrons are in operation on the beach and the amphibious task force has departed.[26]

Although marine aviation did not suffer from the frequent reorganizations that plagued ground forces, it continued to struggle with the fundamental reality of operating in two very different environments and within two different service administrative systems. Aviation organizations had to be designed to operate both on ship and ashore. This not only made the physical organization and equipping of the squadrons a series of compromises but also prevented the development of clear-cut command and control structures for the air-ground team. In fact, even at the corps's schools and during its major exercises, the only air-ground command and control organization tried was that of an amphibious corps-level headquarters. Obviously this would leave a gap in the command and control structures if marine units smaller than an amphibious corps were committed.

SUMMARY OF ORGANIZATION

In the late 1940s the Marine Corps struggled with a number of imperatives that affected the organization of its combat forces. The threat of atomic weapons and massive personnel cuts were primary among them. As a result, the ground forces endured a great deal of organizational turbulence as the corps experimented and tested new organization and manning levels. Fortunately, by late 1949 the corps had decided to return to the combat-tested divisional organization. Although the peacetime organizations were desperately understrength, they provided a source for the rapid deployment of the brigade and the framework for the rest of the 1st Marine Division to form around. The K-Series division proved to be a large, flexible division that could quickly be task-organized for a specific mission. In particular, the K-Series provided personnel and equipment to coordinate the air-ground team's actions into a single battle. On the air side of the house, the organizations matured as the air-ground team concept was restored and marines experimented with how to best ensure fast, effective air support to the division. Although far understrength, the wing organization of 1950 proved to have all the necessary organizations to provide the aircraft, command and control, and vital links to the ground forces of the brigade.

Although apparently mundane activities, developing, equipping, and manning the FMF organizations proved to be critical to the brigade's success. Shifting from the experimental J-Series to an improved version of the triangular division organization ensured that the corps had an organization, however understrength and underequipped, that could effectively employ the air-ground elements as well as sustain heavy casualties and keep fighting effectively. For a variety of reasons, the corps understandably failed to make the final step of integrating air and ground forces under a single command. Fortunately, the education that brought the air-ground team back together was supported by an effective training program so that, despite working for different chains of command, the air and ground marines could fight as a truly integrated team.

It is time to examine how that training prepared the newly reorganized forces for the challenge of the Pusan Perimeter.

6
Training

The state of training for marines is another of the "facts" that, according to lore and some writers, made the marines so effective in Korea. Joseph Goulden, in his book *Korea: The Untold Story of the War,* states,

> The Marines had several inherent advantages over the army. They had been in combat training in the United States; they arrived in cohesive units in which officers and men had served together for months (not hours, as was the case with many jerry-built army "companies"); they insisted on controlling their own air support, in coordinated actions based upon years of experience. Further, given the corps' stress on arduous physical training for every man, regardless of his assignment, the Marines arrived in Korea in far better condition than their army counterparts.[1]

To evaluate this claim, we need to look at the training conducted by the marines over the winter of 1949–1950 and the performance of the brigade in Korea.

GROUND TRAINING

As discussed above, the Marine Corps had shifted the divisions to the K-Series Tables of Organization on 1 October 1949. With the reorganization, the four infantry battalions at Camp Pendleton were combined into two infantry battalions and redesignated 1st and 2nd Battalions, 5th Marines. They were assigned to the newly reorganized 5th Marine Regiment under the command of Col. Victor "Brute" Krulak. As a key participant in the unification fights, Colonel Krulak was acutely aware that the corps had to live up to its motto as the nation's "force in readiness." Therefore, from the day he took over the regiment he executed a tough, thorough training regimen that kept the regiment in the field for the maximum possible amount of time.[2]

Kenneth Houghton, who would command the brigade reconnaissance element in Korea, recalled, "I was a company commander under Brute Krulak for the entire time he had it, and I was in the field for five months. My wife was about to divorce me. We would get home occasionally. He trained. He kept us in the field . . . supporting arms, live fire, night attacks."[3] Since Krulak only commanded the regiment for nine months, this regimen represented an aggressive training program.

Ike Fenton, who would become executive officer of Company B, 1st Battalion, remembered, "During the month of December, the Division had a four-day field exercise in the Horno Ridge area in Camp Pendleton. This field exercise was in mountainous terrain. The idea behind the field exercise was to move rapidly along highways, by-pass resistance on the high ground, and later come in and mop up. Close air support and artillery were utilized and gave us very good training on proper usage of these two arms."[4]

Robert Clement, a mortar section leader with Company B, 1st Battalion, and an old-timer who had enlisted in 1936, had high praise for the training regimen: "Our training under MGen Graves B. Erskine as Division Commander and Colonel Victor H. Krulak as Regimental Commander was long and relentless. Those officers who could not cut the mustard were soon transferred to such highly sought out positions as Special Services Officer or worse."[5]

Krulak's program was not a surprise. He had a well-deserved reputation for training hard. It was one of the reasons Major General Erskine picked him to lead the newly formed 5th Marines when the T/Os changed on 1 October 1949. Erskine himself had a reputation as a hard-driving commander who demanded first-class training from all his organizations. He had repeatedly stated that despite the shortages of personnel and funds, the 1st Marine Division would be as combat-ready as humanly possible. Richard T. Spooner, an NCO with World War II combat experience, remembered that the austerity of the time did not interrupt training. His company spent Monday to Friday in the field eating C and K rations left over from World War II because they were already paid for. There was no money for blanks but always enough live ammunition for rifle qualification. Spooner noted that the marines suspected that, to save even more money, the company staff selected weekend-duty personnel from those still around the barracks by the time of the evening meal on Friday. As a result, Spooner and many of his friends ate that meal off post to avoid being placed on duty—and the mess hall saved money.[6]

With the reorganization under the K-Series T/Os, Erskine knew the 5th Marine Regiment would be the only infantry regiment under his command—in fact, the only infantry maneuver unit in the division. He had his pick of colonels and selected Krulak. Erskine knew Krulak not only by reputation but also by personal observation: He had watched Krulak's performance as the commanding officer of the 1st Combat Service Group at Camp Pendleton in 1949. With the reorganization of the regiment completed, Erskine initiated a series of major training exercises during the fall and winter of 1949–1950:

- October 1949: In a simulation of the use of large seaplanes, a marine air group lifted a reinforced battalion to San Nicolas Island.
- November 1949: The 5th Marines conducted a regimental exercise supported by marine air.
- December 1949: The 1st Marine Division and 1st Marine Air Wing conducted a seven-day simulated amphibious exercise involving all principal subordinate headquarters.
- January–February 1950: 1st Marine Division elements participated in Operation Micowex 50, which stressed the use of simulated transport submarines and helicopters in an amphibious operation.
- February 1950: Marine air lifted a reinforced battalion to San Nicolas Island using the JRM-2 as a transport seaplane for the first time.
- March 1950: The 5th Marines conducted a regimental field exercise with supporting marine air.[7]

Erskine used this series of exercises to ensure that his battalion and higher-level headquarters were trained. However, Headquarters Marine Corps was deeply concerned with the status of individual and small-unit training. In his fiscal year 1950 training directive to the commanding generals of FMFLant, FMFPac, and Marine Corps Schools, General Cates specifically noted,

> The Inspector General's reports, as well as reports of individual observers attending training exercises, set forth the fact that many junior officers and non-commissioned officers do not measure up to the high standards of leadership required by the Marine Corps. . . . *Junior officers and noncommissioned officers must be required to accept and satisfactorily discharge the responsibilities incident to their rank and positions. It is particularly desired that a maximum effort be made in the training of noncommissioned officers of staff grade.* (Emphasis in the original.)[8]

It was clear that Krulak's aggressive training program for the regiment was needed. The battalions of the newly formed 5th Marines were in bad shape. Lt. Col. Frederick P. Henderson assumed command of the 2nd Battalion on 1 October 1949. His battalion had been formed on that day from the infantry elements of two of the disestablished J-Series battalions. Henderson noted that when he took command,

> the two J-table battalions I was to merge into 2/5 [2nd Battalion, 5th Marines] were out in tent camp in San Onofre; . . . I sent out the word I was going to hold morning troops inspection on every company. . . . Well it was one of the great shocks of my life. . . . I was appalled—I couldn't believe it. Here

was a Marine rifle company standing in the ranks; all of a sudden I'd walk up to a guy, here was a Marine standing in a rifle company with no rifle!

I'd say, "Son, where is your rifle?"

He'd reply, "I don't have any."

I'd say, "How long haven't you had any?" And you know, some of those guys hadn't had a rifle in a month. In a rifle squad in a rifle company! We had guys who had rifles but didn't have bayonets.[9]

Shortages of equipment were not the battalion's only problems in October 1949: "When I took over, there was [sic] about 1500 men in 2/5. We had over a month, maybe two months, in which it was supposed to go to about 700 or 800, which was our authorized strength, something like that. So it meant half the people were going to leave."[10]

Besides the personnel turbulence, the battalion needed basic equipment. Henderson noted that he had "to get property shipped out where there was surplus from the two battalions, but also to make sure the companies that were left were going to have everything they needed. We were going to have mortars, machine guns, trucks, kitchen gear, everything we should have."[11]

Once he had initiated solutions to the personnel and equipment issues, Henderson took his marines to the field to evaluate the state of their training:

We made up a simple advance guard problem type thing. You know, a battalion on the march with an advance guard. I put this outfit on the road [laughs], oh, it was the sorriest looking outfit! It looked like Coxie's Army. You know a levee en masse, stragglers, nobody knew what the hell they were doing. The radios didn't work, the point out there tried to radio back to the advance guard, and that didn't work; and I was standing along the road up there in a jeep, watching them come by, straggling. Nobody was communicating with anybody.

When they ran into opposition then I had some guys out firing some blanks; it was the biggest melee. Not only didn't they have their equipment, they weren't trained to fight! . . .

I told Brute that I was going . . . to start training at the squad level, platoon; and not any nice long schedule, but I was going to cram it down them so that by the time we moved back into barracks (another month or six weeks), they would be half way decent and a credit to the Marine Corps. After that I'm going to make 2/5 into a real expeditionary outfit. And that was Brute's idea also; and that is what we did. . . .

You will recall we listed all of the training exercises and maneuvers and that that had been done by the 5th Marines and with all of their associated units—the 11th, the Engineers, etc.—there were battalion exercises that I ran, regimental exercises that Brute scheduled and ran regularly, getting the whole outfit out, a big division field exercise, and we had CPXs [command post exercises] galore. I'd say that between September and June 2/5 went from about 25 percent combat effective to damn close to 100. It was just by drive and work and insistence on making it into a true force-in-readiness. Every man and every unit is going to have its gear, and they are going to be well trained; and anybody who can't cut the mustard we'll get rid of.[12]

Even allowing for a new commander's traditionally skeptical view of the combat-effectiveness of his command and the inevitable massive disruptions caused by wholesale reorganization, Henderson's narration is an indictment of the condition of at least his infantry battalion in October 1949.

The timing of the shift from the J-Series to the K-Series T/Os was fortunate. Under the J-Series T/Os, the commander was a full colonel, not necessarily an infantryman by profession, and he worked for a divisional headquarters, which was supervising the training of five other infantry battalions, ten organic separate battalions, four battalions of corps troops that would belong to FMFPac when a war started, and the fixed-wing observation squadron. Also under the J-Series T/Os, the battalions would all fight as BLTs directly under the division headquarters. Each BLT commander would have an infantry battalion, an artillery battery, a tank platoon, an engineer platoon, and a reconnaissance platoon assigned. Thus, the battalion commanders and staffs spent a good deal of time learning how to control the wide variety of supporting elements that would be assigned in combat. The K-Series T/Os reestablished the regimental headquarters. This allowed the battalion commanders to focus on training their infantry companies under the command of an infantry headquarters. Rather than working to keep all elements of the BLT trained, the battalion commanders could focus on training two rifle companies, a weapons company, and a headquarters and service company. This setup greatly facilitated Henderson's and Krulak's training programs. All companies remained badly understrength, but the commanders knew they were training the nucleus of the wartime battalions. Also, for reasons lost to record-keeping, the colonels commanding the J-Series battalions tended to be very senior colonels and therefore much older than the lieutenant colonels who took over the new battalions. As numerous other works have noted, older officers often lack the physical stamina to drive hard training in infantry organizations.

The 1st Battalion, 5th Marines, maintained a training schedule similar to the 2nd Battalion's. Both had to reach the levels of training required to participate in the regimental combined arms training Krulak instituted over the winter of 1949–1950.

In addition to participating in the 5th Marines' regiment-level exercises, the division's one artillery battalion conducted its own intensive training over the winter. Although ammunition limitations restricted the amount of live fire that could be conducted, the battalion worked hard at its gunnery skills. In keeping with marine doctrine and culture, 1st Battalion, 11th Marines insisted that its batteries, including headquarters and service battery, be well trained in defending their positions and guns against ground attack. This was a fundamental ethos of marine artillerymen. Col. Francis F. Parry, an artilleryman who commanded a battery in World War II; led the 3rd Battalion, 11th Marines in Korea; and fought again in Vietnam, stated,

> As far as being able to defend itself, the artillery has always considered, to my knowledge that it can defend itself. Of course, we have many more close-in weapons systems that we didn't have in World War II, and we have more M-1s and we have bazookas and types of weapons we didn't have in World War II. . . . We also split the unwieldy headquarters and service battery into two batteries—headquarters and service. This change is of great advantage to the light artillery battalion commander in that he is able to insert his headquarters element in a small area adjacent to the three firing batteries, whereas the large number of trucks in the service company can be put in a position . . . as far as half a mile away.[13]

Parry was confident that his marines could defend his batteries because "every Marine is trained basically as an infantry-man and it is only after he has become trained as such that he is permitted to specialize in something like artillery."[14]

Training for the separate battalions was also emphasized. However, they faced even greater challenges than the infantry and artillery units. As division-level support units, the separate battalions were manned at roughly one-third strength—or a single letter company with a small headquarters and service company. Thus, the separate battalions had a somewhat smaller percentage of personnel than even the infantry battalions. Further, due to the expense of training heavy weapons units, the budget limitations had more impact on these forces. According to 1st Lt. Tom Gibson, executive officer of a 4.2-inch mortar company and a World War II airborne trooper, "Peacetime austerity allowed us 24 rounds per year. That meant each gun could fire 3 rounds per year. We had enough training and comm [communications] gear to allow us 2 FO [forward observer] teams. Our FDC was trained by the 11th Marines in the states. With so little firing experience the whole company was not well trained."[15]

The tank battalion also struggled with budget and equipment limitation, not the least of which was operating out-of-date equipment. Although the new T/O called for the tank battalion to be equipped with the M26 Pershing tank, the 1st Tank Battalion at Camp Pendleton still had World War II–vintage M4 Sherman tanks. Since the Department of Defense expected the next war to be against the Soviet Union, it was only natural that the 2nd Tank Battalion at Camp Lejeune received the M26 first, while the 1st Tank Battalion continued to operate the older M4s. And of course the Sherman parts were already paid for, so it was cheaper to keep the 1st Tank Battalion training on Shermans. Fortunately, according to Sgt. Donald Gagnon, "most of the company had been together and trained as a unit for the better part of a year."[16]

A final factor limited the training of all forces, but particularly those that relied heavily on vehicles. The years of diminished budget meant the lack of funds for maintenance severely reduced the corps's ability to train. It simply could not pay for the parts to provide more than a minimal number of vehicle hours for training. On 13 May 1948 the commandant sent a letter to the quartermaster of the Marine Corps on the replenishment of vehicular operating level stocks. In it he stated,

- The actual use of operational vehicles in the fleet had been reduced to 25 percent of the initial allowance.
- These restrictions were drastic and violated the principle of maintaining a fully trained and ready Fleet Marine Force.
- The shortage of maintenance money meant 50 percent of the Table of Allowance vehicles in all units were deadlined.
- Fuel allowance had been reduced to 1.5 gallons per vehicle per day, with only twenty-two training days authorized per month. The personal signature of a commanding general was required to authorize any exception.
- Despite the fact that 3,314 vehicles at Barstow (war stocks) required repair and that reserves of ten of nineteen critical combat end items were exhausted, there would be no additional money for repair of the war stock vehicles.[17]

In short, fourteen months before the start of the Korean War, the Marine Corps's equipment was in desperate shape. There was no money to maintain the vehicles in the operating forces, so repairing the huge number of vehicles in war stocks was out of the question.

The popular narratives discussed at the beginning of this chapter are clearly correct in saying that the 5th Marines under Krulak trained very hard over the winter of 1949–1950. However, they fail to note the special circumstance under which the units trained: They were severely understrength and constrained by budget and equipment shortages. During the training from October 1949 to March 1950, the 5th Marine Regiment consisted of only the 1st and 2nd Battalions. As noted, each battalion had only two rifle companies of two rifle platoons each, and a very small weapons platoon per company. The machine-gun platoon of the weapons company had been completely eliminated.[18] The battalion weapons company and headquarters and service company were also severely reduced. Thus, each battalion had only four rifle platoons rather than the nine called for and so was training at well under half strength even when it could get 100 percent of its personnel into the field—a rare occurrence with peacetime housekeeping duties. For its part, the regiment, which had only two battalions until late February 1950, was training at less than one-third of its normal strength. This situation was both a problem and a benefit. It was a problem because when the time came to mobilize, it guaranteed a large influx of new people who had had never trained with the organizations. It was a benefit because the small units meant the leaders could focus on intensive training for fewer people. However, even this benefit would be severely undercut when, upon mobilization, the battalions had to leave behind any marines with less than eight months left on their enlistment contracts. Some units left half their core of trained marines behind. This combined with the fact that they were understrength meant most units had to absorb 50 percent new personnel in the week during embarkation—men who had never seen much less trained with their units.

Unfortunately, throughout the period commanders were assured that they would be brought to wartime strength before being committed to combat. Therefore, the battalion commanders trained as if they had three rifle companies and full-strength weapons companies. Lt. Col. George R. Newton, commanding officer of 1st Battalion, 5th Marines, remembered, "We realized that we should have our third rifle company during our training and we always trained with the idea of having a third rifle company. We used it as a maneuver element by placing this phantom element on the ground in positions as the tactical situation demanded."[19]

As a result, the battalion commanders had not trained to fight their battalions with only two rifle companies rather than the three called for in the K-Series infantry battalion wartime organization. Thus, they had not worked through the problems and possible solutions for fighting units with only two maneuver elements.

Even with the addition of the 3rd Battalion in early 1950, the 5th Marines still remained at less than 50 percent strength. As noted, the 3rd Battalion had not yet reorganized under the K-Series T/Os and had to do so upon its arrival in California.[20] The battalion's efforts to reorganize were complicated by the fact that a large number of the marines in the battalion had been with it during much of its overseas tour and were due for immediate rotation. The exception was in the rifle companies. First Lt. Robert D. "Dewey" Bohn remembered that when the companies had been formed on Guam in 1948, they had been made up of a few staff NCOs and officers, but all the troops had been fresh from boot camp. Thus, the rifle companies had an entire year to train together in Guam before joining the 5th Marines, and, as they had no NCOs, were free to appoint the best men to the corporal and sergeant positions in the companies.[21] However, even the rifle companies experienced major personnel turbulence when, upon reorganization under the K-Series T/Os, the third rifle company of the battalion was cadred (left on the corps rolls, but with no personnel) and its personnel transferred. Further, the fact that the rifle companies had had very few NCOs when they were formed in Guam meant they had virtually no combat veterans among the newly appointed NCOs.

The headquarters and weapons companies were not as fortunate as the line companies. According to Lt. Col. Robert D. Taplett, the 3rd Battalion commander, reenlistment rates were low due to poor pay and bad housing after the war. This situation added to the personnel turbulence as many marines returned to civilian life rather than reenlisting. Taplett also noted that, as the last battalion to join the regiment, the 3rd Battalion members felt like outsiders in Krulak's very tight regiment. They had missed the intensive training of the late fall and winter and thus had not bonded with the unit. Taplett remembered that his battalion "even designed their own flag depicting a lone wolf baying at a full moon."[22]

The one major exercise the regiment conducted after the 3rd Battalion joined was Demon III. Demon III was not a 5th Marines training exercise but rather an amphibious demonstration designed to showcase the corps's ability to conduct an amphibious landing. In the words of the FMF report, Demon III was "a painstakingly prepared amphibious demonstration for the students of the Command and General Staff College, Fort Leavenworth."[23] Although the actual landing was tightly scripted and, like all such exercises, rehearsed to a timetable, the 5th Marines still made effective use of the opportunity. The landing "was followed by a field exercise featuring an approach march of 15 miles."[24]

In FMFPac's analysis of the preparation for the Korean conflict, the authors wrote,

> It is particularly noteworthy that in mid-May, 1950, the ground element of the Brigade, the 5th Marines (Reinforced), and the air elements, MAG 33 (Reinf), had both participated in a three (3) day amphibious-land combined field exercise, over mountainous terrain and culminating in a live firing phase. A salient feature of the exercise was the stress it placed on close air support in order that it might demonstrate to the ground forces the impressive capabilities of close air support and provide for intensive close air support training to the air elements involved.[25]

Even at this late date, marine leaders considered demonstrating the effectiveness of close air support to the ground element to be a critical training objective. The corps was clearly continuing its efforts to overcome the residual effects of the air-ground split of World War II.

One young marine, fresh from boot camp, was very impressed with the Demon III exercise. James Sanders of the 3rd Battalion, 5th Marines, wrote, "One major field exercise took place. Hot! Near 100 degrees in May 1950. After long marches through the hills and fire breaks—we finally assaulted the major objective, a great steep hill. Marine Corsairs streaked in firing 20mm just yards in front of the rifle companies in the assault. Upon gaining the hill, the Corsairs then directed their attack on the far side with rockets and napalm."[26]

Equally impressed was then Maj. Norman J. Anderson, who was MAG 33 group tactical officer for the exercise. He noted, "The exercise was a perfect rehearsal for the job MAG-33 was required to do at Inchon and Seoul in September."[27] Obviously, it also prepared the squadrons well for the missions they had to execute during the Pusan Perimeter fight.

Unfortunately, Demon III was the only time during 1950 that the 5th Marines was able to train in the field with all three battalions. As noted in the 1st Provisional Marine Brigade special action report, less than half of the men who embarked with the battalions had participated in even this exercise.[28] In late June 1950 the regiment reported an average of 1,800 men on its rolls against T/Os calling for 3,900.[29] And of course this was before the orders to transfer those marines with insufficient time left in their enlistments to deploy.

Although Krulak focused on hard, effective training, the realities of peacetime intruded. The division was still required to provide manpower for a number of major projects in the spring and early summer of 1950. In particular, the period after Demon III was loaded with administrative requirements that made large-unit training impossible. Even small-unit training was greatly diminished. During June 1950, the division had to provide personnel to fight fires in the forests surrounding Camp Pendleton; provide patrols to find and detain illegal immigrants; help Marine Corps base prepare for the annual Camp Pendleton rodeo; prepare for a full-division combat review; conduct change-of-command parades for 5th Marines, 1st and 2nd Battalions; and daily provide a company of marines for the filming of *Halls of Montezuma*.

The additional tasks culminated at the beginning of July 1950. The Camp Pendleton rodeo, scheduled for the weekend of the 4th of July, was the Marine Corps's major public relations event on the West Coast. In the late 1940s it was attended by major Hollywood stars and tens of thousands of civilians. Handling the parking, sanitation, concessions, transportation, and other details was a major effort on the part of all units stationed at Camp Pendleton. As part of the rodeo weekend, the division had also scheduled a combat review for 3 July. The combat review was essentially a division parade with all rolling stock and combat equipment initially on display and then paraded past the crowd. Any marine who has been involved with either a major public relations event or a division parade knows the tremendous impact such an event has on training. Two such events in the first week of July would have virtually eliminated training time for division units throughout the month of June.

The only positive outcome of the support requirements came from the *Halls of Montezuma*. According to Capt. Joseph Fegan, commanding officer of Company H, 3rd Battalion, when his company shipped to Korea

> the web gear, the 782 gear, was in great shape in as much as I had had the opportunity to swap what we brought back from Guam with what the Twentieth Century Fox brought down for the filming of that movie. That is, of course, not the prescribed method, but the surplus they brought to film the movie was better than what we had in our inventory at the company level. So I merely swapped it and returned item for item of older gear since the movies were going to junk it anyway.[30]

SUMMARY OF GROUND TRAINING

The 1st Marine Division elements that would form the brigade had trained hard as individuals and units in the year before the Korean War. Unfortunately, these elements were only a nucleus of what would become' the 5th Marines (Reinforced) in July 1950. As noted, only eight rifle platoons of the eighteen the regiment would employ in Korea trained together over the winter. Four more from the 3rd Battalion joined the regiment for one exercise in May 1950. Those four platoons had been tied up in redeploying from Guam to California and then reorganizing from November to the end of March. They joined the regiment for a single exercise at the beginning of May. Of particular importance is the fact that up to 50 percent of each of these platoons would be replaced after the brigade was activated because individuals with less than eight months left on their Marine Corps contracts were not allowed to deploy.

Immediately upon completing the May exercise, the entire division went into a period of minimal training and maximum base and ceremonial support activity. As Allan Millett noted in his definitive history of the Marine Corps, *Semper Fidelis,* during the period between 1946 and 1950 "the Corps' supporting establishment was so small and its tasks for maintaining Corps bases so extensive that many FMF troops spent more time housekeeping than training."[31] And of course the final six rifle platoons that would fight in Pusan did not even exist until after the brigade was activated.

In short, while the ground elements, particularly the 5th Marines, trained hard over the winter of 1949–1950, these trained riflemen would total only the equivalent of four rifle platoons out of the eighteen that would fight. The numbers of marines of other military occupation specialties would make up similar proportions of their ground units. The men to make up the difference would join from posts and stations all over the West Coast. These new men would lack the current training and combat fitness of the marines who had trained over the winter.

Given the actual personnel strengths of the brigade units during the year before the war, it is surprising that the official Marine Corps fiftieth anniversary account, *The Fire Brigade,* contends that the brigade was composed primarily of marines who had trained very hard over the winter of 1949–1950.[32] In a July 2000 *Leatherneck* article, Allan Bevilacqua went further when he stated, "Save for those Marines hastily joined from the posts and stations up and down the West Coast, 5th Marines had been together at Camp Pendleton, for a year or more. . . . It may be that the Marine Corps never sent a better trained regiment to war."[33] Both authors paint a vivid but inaccurate portrait that has become the accepted view of the regiment as it headed to Korea.

AVIATION TRAINING

By 1945 marine aviation was organized so that entire squadrons could be easily reassigned from one air group to another. It was assumed that in a crisis the squadrons that were most ready would be deployed, regardless of the parent air group. Therefore, in order to understand the level of training of the aviation units sent to

Korea, it is essential to examine both marine air group and squadron training. The 1st MAW (Forward) deployed to Korea with MAG 33, Marine Fighter Squadrons (VMFs) 214 and 323, Marine All Weather Fighter Squadron (VMF[N]) 513, and Marine Observation Squadron (VMO) 6 as its flying squadrons. Its command and control squadrons were Marine Ground Control Intercept Squadron (MGCIS) 1 and MTAC 2. Finally, its supporting squadrons were those integral to MAG 33—Headquarters Squadron 33 and Service Squadron 33.

Despite the massive reductions after World War II, the remaining marine air groups and fighter squadrons did not undergo the repeated reorganizations faced by their ground counterparts. Although marine air was cut as deeply as marine ground forces, the cuts were made by eliminating whole squadrons and groups rather than reducing the T/O for each. Still, the requirement to go from 120 squadrons to 12 resulted in significant personnel turbulence immediately after the war, and of course the personnel shortage in the Marine Corps meant that no squadrons were manned at authorized strengths. Men were shifted around so that those with the most time overseas and the most time in service could be released from active duty first. Even those units remaining on active service suffered massive personnel turnover. For instance, VMF 323 arrived in San Diego on 28 February 1946 with 21 officers and 110 enlisted men. By 6 March 19 officers and 94 enlisted men had been transferred. Although the squadron quickly returned to full strength by absorbing the marines from three decommissioned squadrons, it obviously lacked the proficiency of the trained, cohesive unit it had been a month earlier.[34] All squadrons that remained on active duty went through similar turbulence at the end of the war. Still, because the squadrons were not faced with repeated reorganization, once the initial postwar turbulence ended, they could get on with training. Oddly enough, despite the budget crunch elsewhere, there was plenty of aviation fuel available. A marine pilot remembered, "We had plenty of fuel money. . . . You couldn't make a long distance call because you didn't have money for that. If you wanted to talk to somebody in Alameda, you couldn't telephone them, because it would cost a dollar or two, but you could take a Corsair and fly to Alameda and fly back."[35]

As for the ground elements of the brigade, the key training period for the aviation units was the winter of 1949–1950. MAG 33 participated in Operation Miki during November 1949. This was a navy-marine exercise in which MAG 33's role was defending Hawaii from an enemy fleet. Throughout this exercise all marine air was based aboard fleet carriers, which provided not only refresher flight training for the pilots but also experience for all members of MAG 33 in the challenges of commanding, flying, and maintaining aircraft while at sea.

Upon returning from Hawaii, MAG 33 headquarters began planning for the Demon III exercise to be conducted in May 1950. Like the 5th Marines, MAG 33 planned to expand the exercise well beyond the amphibious demonstration. It could have supported those operations from its home station at El Toro, California, but instead the MAG deployed to Camp Pendleton to conduct sustained operations in support of 1st Marine Division as well as to participate in Demon III. During Demon III the "Wing Headquarters, Marine Aircraft Control Group 2 and Marine Aircraft Group 33 embarked in Demon III shipping, landed all ground elements and supplies over the Aliso Canyon beaches and established an advance air field at the Camp Pendleton airstrip. . . . The period in the field was devoted to intense training in close air support and defense."[36] Upon conclusion of Demon III, the MAG remained in the field to support the 5th Marines in its extended field training exercise. Naturally, Headquarters Squadron 33 and Service Squadron 33 participated as part of MAG 33.

VMF 323, the only MAG 33 flying squadron that would deploy to Korea, also had an intensive winter training period. The squadron started that year with well-trained pilots. From 1946 through 1949, VMF 323 participated in both navy and marine exercises while maintaining an average of thirty flight hours per month per pilot. In 1948 it participated in Operation Micowex in Kodiak, Alaska, by providing mock close air support to the division maneuver units. In November 1949 VMF 323 deployed with MAG 33 to participate in Operation Miki in Hawaii. Unfortunately, Operation Miki included very little close air support. The exercise was designed to simulate the early phases of an invasion exercise for the navy. The marine squadron flew for the defending fleet, primarily sorties to interdict the invasion fleet. On the plus side, VMF 323 Corsairs conducted all operations from a fleet carrier, so all squadron pilots updated their carrier qualifications.[37] However, this would be the last time the squadron was aboard a carrier before it deployed to Korea.

During Demon III in May 1950, VMF 323 again deployed with MAG 33, this time to Camp Pendleton to conduct operations from an austere airfield with a dirt strip and no buildings. After participating in the amphibious demonstration, VMF 323 provided support for the subsequent 5th Marines exercise. Both exercises emphasized close air support to the 5th Marines, so they were an ideal preparation for Korea. In summary, during the two years before Korea, VMF 323 participated in exercises ranging from carrier operations in the arctic and in the tropics to flying from remote dirt airfields in southern California.[38]

Throughout this period, VMF 214 and VMF(N) 513 were assigned to MAG 12 and remained so until the brigade was formed on 7 July. At that point both squadrons transferred to MAG 33 to deploy with the brigade. Col. Edward C. Dyer, commanding officer of MAG 12, recalled that over the winter of 1949–1950, his air group "had a number of small tactical problems—providing air support for battalions today and a regiment tomorrow in monthly exercises at Camp Pendleton. . . . [During those exercises] they were all over me like a tent. Things like being 30 seconds, 10 seconds, 15 seconds late was cause for a great uproar."[39]

VMF 214 in particular maintained an intensive training schedule between the summer of 1949 and the summer of 1950. Maj. Howard "Rudy" York took command of the squadron in July 1949. A former ground officer, York was determined that his squadron would become proficient at close air support. Over the summer of 1949,

> utilizing the desert ranges near El Centro, California, York, in a Corsair him-self, played the part of a FAC, to instruct his pilots, also airborne, in the rudi-ments of close air support communications, and the essential skill of target identification. He related how he exercised the pilots: "I would designate a target, it might be clump of tumbleweeds, or anything that was distinguish-able on the terrain down on that desert area and set a scene for them, like 'we're dug in along this dry stream bed and so forth, and we're receiving fire from that pile of tumbleweeds over there,' and I'd give them so many number of yards to the north. When you're orbiting like that a clock position is not too good—is it my clock or their clock? So I'd say 'north of.' And they would find the target and attack it, with miniature bombs or rockets. Then I would pick another obvious target, it might be an old truck stuck in the sand or whatever, just to give them practice at discovering the target I'm trying to describe in infantry terms, and then to go ahead and set up their pattern and attack it. And I did that with many flights, where I was the airborne forward air controller so to speak, and all these guys, I'm sure I ran the whole squad-ron through at one time or another, to familiarize them with the speech of FACs and how they would go about directing a flight at targets."[40]

In his aggressive training program, York tackled the toughest part of close air support for a pilot: correctly identifying the target. His experienced pilots could put ordnance on any target they could see. The key was getting them to identify the target from information the marine on the ground might relay to them.

In October 1949 VMF 214 went aboard the USS *Essex,* a fleet carrier, and participated in exercises off the California and Hawaii coasts, including Opera-tion Miki. Upon its return to California the squadron maintained a steady pace of training throughout the winter—often filling the close air support missions as-signed to MAG 12. In March 1950 York drove his squadron to set a record for the most flight hours in a month by a single-seat squadron—and they accomplished it. Selected for a prestigious navy "E" for excellence, the squadron was back aboard ship by June. It sailed on the USS *Badoeng Strait* (CVE 116) to participate in the navy Reserve Officers' Training Corps midshipmen's summer cruise to Hawaii.

For its part, VMO 6 returned from overseas on 22 January 1947. It was based at Camp Pendleton but assigned to Marine Air West Coast and given the mission of spraying the insecticide DDT to control mosquitoes on the base. On 16 July VMO 6 was reassigned to the 1st Marine Division. However, the division, which was returning to the United States for the first time since 1942, was not ready to conduct any field exercises. VMO 6 spent the summer conducting its own tactical training while continuing the spraying assignment. On 1 October the division was reorganized under the J-Series T/Os, which did not include a VMO squadron. On that date VMO 6 was transferred to the 1st Marine Air Wing. However since the mission of the squadron was providing eyes for the division, it continued to fly in support of division exercises in the fall of 1947 as well as throughout 1948 and 1949. The primary duties of VMO 6 remained artillery spotting, aerial photography, camouflage study, and administrative flights to move personnel for the division. During 1948 VMO 6 participated with the 1st Marine Division in Operation Micowex and executed its planned mission of providing aerial artillery spotters. However, because the VMO's observation aircraft had no air-to-air radios, the VMO observers were unable to control air strikes. Instead, when the observer saw a target appropriate for air, he passed it to the division FSCC, which then passed the mission to the tactical aircraft for self-directed strikes.[41] During 1949, despite the fact that official doctrine still did not allow for VMO 6 observers to control close air support missions, the squadron experimented with controlling simulated air strikes. Although the experiments were successful, the Marine Corps could not afford to add air-to-air radios to the squadron's aircraft, so the squadron could not further test the concept. During the first half of 1950, budgetary and parts shortages restricted the squadron's flying. Despite the fact that the shortages meant none of the eight OY aircraft were reliable, the squadron still had to conduct the DDT spraying operations.[42]

The last flying squadron that would send aircraft to the brigade was HMX 1. Still stationed in Quantico, it continued a demanding training, demonstration, and experimentation schedule. By 30 June 1949 the squadron had grown to twenty-two officers and sixty-nine enlisted men, with one HTL-1, nine HRP-1s and four HOS3 helicopters. The squadron continued internal training through the summer and fall but was forced to ground its HRP-1 helicopters for long periods due to mechanical problems. Thus, during February 1950 only the squadron's four HOS3s deployed to Puerto Rico to participate in FMFLant's Fleet Exercise. In May a mix of HRP-1s and HO3Ss participated in Operation Packard III, once again refining amphibious assault procedures. Also in May the squadron participated in a demonstration for President Truman as well as conducting a squadron flyover with thirteen aircraft for a change-of-command parade. On 30 June 1950 the squadron was near both its T/O and Table of Equipment strengths with six HRP-1s, seven HO3Ss, two HTL-1s, and 109 personnel.[43] Further, its pilots and support personnel were well trained and experienced in deployments.

MGCIS 1 fulfilled its function of controlling aircraft in a tactical environment by providing ground control intercept during the various wing air exercises in southern California and Hawaii. MTACS 2 participated in all division-wing training events by providing the interface between air and ground elements during the repeated exercises over the winter of 1949–1950.

The FACs and ALOs who were assigned to the 1st Provisional Marine Brigade had received formal training at Tactical Training Unit Pacific in San Diego. The course was designed to teach a marine pilot the tactics, techniques, procedures, and communications systems necessary to control close air support for marine ground units. Upon graduating from the tactical training units, the pilots were assigned to a 1st Marine Division unit or the Air Naval Gunfire Liaison Company, where they continued to practice their skills.[44] Of course these personnel and their enlisted communicators participated in all unit exercises so that they were comfortable working with the ground commanders. Over the winter of 1949–1950, the ALOs and FACs in the 5th Marines had the opportunity to work closely with the infantry battalion commanders in repeated live-fire and simulated close air support exercises. Unfortunately, the summer rotation meant that the well-trained teams were broken up, and, like most of the brigade, the new team members would have to get to know each other on the ships en route to Korea.

SUMMARY OF AVIATION TRAINING

The squadrons were blessed with sufficient fuel to conduct full training programs during the winter; it was even more helpful that all the VMF and VMF(N) aviators were experienced fighter pilots. Even when a pilot checked back into a squadron after a nonflying tour, he retained the knowledge and experience to apply to his reacquired flying skills. The single most important factor in the training conducted by the aviation elements that year was the changed mental attitude of marine aviators. Led by men now familiar with ground operations and highly valued by their ground counterparts as essential elements of the marine air-ground team, the aviators had proven they were uniquely qualified to provide responsive, accurate close air support to their comrades on the ground.

USS *Badoeng Strait* (CVE-116) leaving San Diego Harbor loaded with marine fighter squadrons for Korea. The requirement to carry four squadrons on a CVE meant only a single helicopter could fly during the three-week transit to Japan. (National Archives Photo 80-G-416920)

Even as they were joining new marines and packing up, the logistics elements of the brigade had to carry out critical duties. Here marines of MAG-33 load ammunition aboard USS *Aishain* (AKA-55) at Naval Air Station, San Diego, California, on 9 July 1950. (National Archives Photo 80-G-416897)

This photo of marines conducting physical training during the transit shows how little space was available on the crowded troopships. The physical conditioning of the marines obviously declined during the three weeks in transit. (National Archives Photo 127-GR-32-221-A1216)

This photo shows an HO3S-1 using an external winch to lift a marine. Brigadier General Edward Craig operated such a winch when his helicopter rescued 1Lt Doyle Coyle minutes after Coyle was shot down. (National Archives Photo 127-GK-4-13I-A130015)

The terrible roads and constant movement challenged the brigade's logistics elements. Here marines complete a field repair of one of the troublesome but essential water trailers. (National Photo Archives 127-GK-27-234A-A2254)

The Corps's strenuous efforts to overcome the World War II schism between air and ground marines to regain proficiency as an air-ground team paid major dividends in Korea. Note both how low the attacking Corsair is and how close to the ground marines. (National Archives Photo 127-GR-32-217-A130949)

Whenever the brigade was out of the line, the marines trained to integrate replacements into the line companies. Here a marine rifle squad practices an assault. (National Archives Photo 127-GK-21-181-A1967)

This 75mm recoilless rifle is like the one used by Corp Ted Heckleman and his antitank section to stop the T-34s leading the North Korean counterattack on 18 August 1950. (National Archives Photo 127-GK-21-173-1462; photo by Sgt. W. W. Frank)

The open and steep terrain allowed marine heavy weapons to provide direct fire support literally over the heads of the advancing rifle platoons. Here a 75mm recoilless rifle prepares to fire in support of the attack on Obong-ni Ridge. (National Archives Photo 127-GK-21-1461; photo by Sgt. W. W. Frank)

Apparently taken from one of the hilltops on Obong-ni Ridge, this photo reveals the dominating terrain the North Koreans held. (National Archives Photo 127-GR-21-143-A1401)

7

Leadership

Examining the leadership of Fleet Marine Force units from late 1945 to 1950 is extremely difficult. Marine Corps personnel policies during this period required a frequent turnover of commanders to ensure that as many officers as possible had at least some experience in leading combat organizations. The intent was to ensure that there would be a sufficient number of officers to support the planned wartime mobilization. Tours in the operating forces were therefore quite short. During this period the 5th Marine Regiment alone had ten commanding officers.[1] As a result, there are simply too many marines involved to study even the leadership of the 1st Marine Division and 1st Marine Air Wing from 1946 to 1950.

This chapter examines the leadership of the 1st Provisional Marine Brigade when it was formed on 7 July 1950 as a representative cross-section. This specific unit and time are appropriate for three reasons. First, these officers initially led the brigade into combat. Because it was the corps's first major fight since 1945, these leaders most accurately reflect the impact of the culture, education, doctrine, organization, and training of the late 1940s. By focusing on the leadership of the 1st Provisional Marine Brigade at the time of its mobilization, the chapter can take a closer look at the backgrounds and experiences of the leaders who were faced with the sudden challenge of taking understrength peacetime organizations to war on extremely short notice. Although this chapter does not constitute a complete survey of marine tactical leadership during this critical period, these leaders are typical.

Second, the Marine Corps clearly did not anticipate a conflict in 1950. Thus, the leaders were typical of those assigned under peacetime personnel policies. The mobilization was too sudden for any significant changes in leadership. In fact, the manpower system was hard-pressed to even fill critical billets such as infantry battalion executive officers.

Finally, it is these leaders who are the source of the belief that all the officers of the brigade had been "blooded" in the fierce battles of World War II.

Perhaps the most firmly ingrained myth about the brigade concerns the combat experience of its leaders. Even the official Marine Corps history written in 1954 overstated their experience: "A glance at the NCO's, the platoon leaders and company commanders of the Brigade could only have brought a gleam of pride to the Commandant's battle wise eye. With few exceptions, they were veterans of World War II."[2] Over the years the statement that the leaders were all veterans of World War II was inflated to indicate that they were veterans of ground combat in World War II—a very different background than just being a veteran—even a combat veteran. Many marine officers spent the war aboard ship. Others spent their time in supporting organizations that never saw ground combat.

In his book *The Korean War,* Donald Knox expressed the view most commonly held about the brigade leaders: "What the brigade lacked in numbers, however, it made up for in experience. Most of its officers and two out of three NCOs were veterans of the tough island fighting of the Second World War; company commanders and platoon leaders and squad leaders had been blooded at places like Peleliu, Guam, Bougainville, Iwo Jima and Okinawa."[3]

Andrew Geer, author of *The New Breed,* supported Knox's beliefs when he wrote, "Ninety per cent of the officers of the new brigade had been in combat; sixty-five per cent of the senior NCO's had been in action against an enemy, but of the corporals and Pfc.'s [privates first class], only ten per cent have ever been under enemy fire."[4]

Allan Bevilacqua, an author writing for *Leatherneck* magazine's commemoration of the fiftieth anniversary of the Korean War, made the strongest claims concerning both training and combat experience when he wrote, "Beyond that they had the added advantage of being led by officers and staff noncommissioned officers who were almost entirely veterans of the war against Japan—men who had fought battles as ferocious as anything on record in any war."[5]

Although this is one of the most firmly established beliefs about the brigade, it is largely false. Some of the key leaders had relevant combat experience, but the majority did not.

Starting at the top, Brigadier General Craig had extensive combat experience, including command of a regiment that saw combat at Guadalcanal, Bougainville, and Guam. He won the Navy Cross in World War II and went on to command a brigade (ground units only) during peacetime on Guam. While in command of the brigade in Guam, Craig demanded an aggressive, hard training routine from his marines. Maurice Jacques, a young infantryman in Craig's Guam brigade, remembered that the NCOs demanded that troops know how to fire, clean, and maintain every weapon in the company; that the commanders marched the troops everywhere because the brigade did not have the money to run vehicles; and that tactical training included patrolling, attack of fortified positions, and defense. In particular he remembered the NCOs who were Pacific War veterans and were very intense about the training.[6] Clearly Craig more than fulfilled the description of a combat-experienced leader. Craig was also keenly aware of the power of the air-ground team. As a second lieutenant in Santo Domingo, he had been required to take terrain orientation flights in the backseat of a Curtiss before taking command of the 70th Company. Craig noted that the experience made him "air minded. My interest in aviation and its capabilities never left me from then on."[7]

The brigade chief of staff, Col. Edward W. Snedecker, also had extensive ground combat experience during World War II but did not join the brigade until 7 July 1950. He had been stationed in Hawaii and arrived in San Francisco by ship on 5 July. When he called Pendleton, he was ordered to report immediately for duty as chief of staff. Driving hard from San Francisco, Snedecker left his family to settle themselves and reported to the brigade.

Lt. Col. Raymond L. Murray, commanding officer of the 5th Marines, had earned a highly regarded record in World War II that included service on Guadalcanal, Tarawa, and Saipan. He won a Navy Cross, two Silver Stars, and a Purple Heart. However, despite months in command of an infantry battalion, his combat experience was fairly brief. His battalion arrived on Guadalcanal only after the Japanese had abandoned the remnants of their units on the island. Murray's battalion conducted small patrols to eliminate the Japanese stragglers but had no significant fights. Similarly, his battalion landed very late on Tarawa—after the primary target had been secured. Its mission was to wade to the offshore islands and eliminate any remaining Japanese. Once again the fighting was essentially at platoon level as his battalion swept forward. It was not until Saipan that his battalion landed in the assault waves. On Saipan Murray was wounded on the first morning. He continued to command his battalion until he was evacuated but was off the island before nightfall. Thus, although Murray had extensive experience in battalion command and had a corpswide reputation as a highly effective leader, he had little experience commanding a battalion in combat. Murray was widely known to have been frustrated because he had not been in the thick of things. In fact, he was the model for "High Pockets" Huxley, the battalion commander in Leon Uris's novel *Battle Cry* about marines in World War II.[8]

The 5th Marines' executive officer, Lt. Col. Lawrence C. Hays Jr., had extensive combat experience in World War II, including command of an infantry battalion in the key battles of Tarawa, Saipan, and Tinian.[9]

It is below the regimental level that the lack of ground combat experience manifested itself. The battalion commanders and their executive officers not only lacked ground combat experience but had very little experience in the ground forces even in peacetime. When they took command, none of the three infantry battalion commanders had even two years in the infantry during their entire careers, and none had ground combat experience. Lt. Col. George R. Newton, 1st Battalion, had served briefly with an infantry company in China and then been assigned to the embassy guard in Peking. He was captured by the Japanese when the guard surrendered on 8 December 1941 and held as a prisoner of war until 22

September 1945. Although he showed remarkable courage and strength in simply surviving the ordeal, the experience did not equate to ground combat experience. Between his release and taking command of 1st Battalion, Newton served on an officer selection board, attended a six-month school at Quantico, served as provost marshall at San Diego, and had periods as executive officer or commanding officer of three marine barracks. He then served as executive officer of the 1st Combat Support Group, FMFPac, before assuming duties as executive officer of the 1st Battalion in January 1950 and finally taking command of the battalion on 18 June—one week before the war broke out.[10] In the five years between World War II and Korea, Newton held eight different jobs. Between his capture in 1941 and the activation of the brigade he had a total of less than six months in an infantry battalion.

Lt. Col. Harold Roise, 2nd Battalion, served as a platoon and company commander in the infantry before World War II but spent his war years aboard the USS *Maryland* and USS *Alabama* until mid-1945. He then served in a regimental and division logistics section for the 6th Marine Division on Okinawa. From 1947 until late 1949 Roise was the 1st Marine Division athletic officer responsible for the training, equipping, and performance of a variety of division sports teams. Interestingly, Roise's two-year stint as an athletics officer seems to be the longest time any of the officers of the brigade held a single job between World War II and the Korean War. Roise took over as executive officer of the 2nd Battalion in late 1949.[11] Although the battalion had a tough training schedule, the battalion commander, Lt. Col. Frederick Henderson, assigned Roise all the administrative duties so the commanding officer could be in the field with his companies.[12] Lieutenant Colonel Roise took command of the battalion on 15 June, ten days before the war started.

The third battalion commander, Lt. Col. Robert D. Taplett, had won ten battle stars in World War II, but all for service on the USS *Salt Lake City,* a cruiser. He rose from second lieutenant to major while aboard the ship and never served a day ashore in combat during World War II. After the war he commanded four different marine barracks from 1946 to 1948. From early 1949 to early 1950, Taplett was assistant G-3 and then commanding officer, Headquarters and Service Battalion, 1st Marine Division. He took over as executive officer of the 3rd Battalion, 5th Marines on 2 April after the battalion arrived from Guam. He moved up to commanding officer on 30 April 1950.[13] This was Taplett's first time in an infantry unit. In fact, Taplett had so little time in the infantry that his military occupation specialty was still listed as 0301 basic infantry officer when the brigade shipped to Korea.[14] This was truly remarkable. The normal standard for being designated an 0302 infantry officer was six months' service in an infantry battalion. Taplett would lead his battalion into combat in Korea with a career total of four months in the infantry. Thus, despite the assertions that the brigade's leaders were almost all veterans of the bloody island campaigns of World War II, it certainly was not true for the infantry battalion commanders. In fact, when each of the infantry battalion commanders was assigned to command, the corps knew he had little or no experience either in the infantry or in combat.

The artillery battalion commander, Lt. Col. Ransom Wood, did have World War II experience relevant to his billet in Korea. After being commissioned in 1938, Wood initially served on sea duty. From 1940 to April 1944 he served with various air defense battalions, including command of the 8th Defense Battalion. However, he did not serve in an artillery battalion until he was a major, as battalion executive officer with the 5th 155mm Howitzer Battalion, a general support battalion. It was an intensive year during which the battalion participated in the battles of Saipan and Leyte.[15] Wood was not assigned to command the 1st Battalion, 11th Marines until 8 July 1950, after the brigade was activated.[16]

When we look at another key billet, the infantry battalion executive officers, we find a similar lack of World War II ground combat experience. Maj. Merlin R. Olson, executive officer of the 1st Battalion, 5th Marines, spent most of World War II aboard the USS *Pensacola*. His only experience in a ground combat campaign was as a staff officer on Okinawa.[17] The executive officer of the 2nd Battalion, 5th Marines, Maj. John W. Stevens II, spent a year in an infantry regiment immediately after his commissioning in 1939. He then served at a marine barracks before going to flight school in early 1942. Upon being designated a naval aviator, he initially flew on the East Coast of the United States until January 1945. He then served with the air staff of FMFPac. From 1946 until July 1950 he served at Marine Corps Schools Quantico. He reported to the battalion as it was embarking for Pusan.[18] The 3rd Battalion's executive officer, Maj. John J. Canney, flew fighters during World War II and rose to command Marine Fighter Squadron 351. He remained on flight status until his postwar squadron was deactivated in November 1949. He then served in various staff billets until reporting for duty as executive officer as the battalion embarked for Korea.[19]

The 3rd Battalion, 5th Marines was probably typical of the infantry battalions. Neither of the rifle company commanders had infantry combat experience in World War II. First Lt. Robert D. Bohn, commanding officer of Company G, had served aboard the USS *Monterey* during the war. From 1946 to early 1949 he served on barracks and recruiting duty. In February 1949 he reported to the 1st Marine Brigade on Guam, where in a period of only eleven months he served as a company executive officer, company commander, battalion S-2, and S-3. Returning to the United States with the battalion in early 1950, he was assigned as commanding officer of Company G in April 1950.[20] Capt. Joseph C. Fegan Jr., commanding officer of Company H, was an artillery officer in World War II. He participated in several campaigns, including on Iwo Jima as a battery commander. From 1946 to 1948 he attended advanced artillery and naval gunfire courses and served as an instructor. He did not succeed in his efforts to transfer to the infantry until 1948, when he reported to the brigade in Guam for service as assistant S-3 officer. Late in 1949 he assumed command of Company H and kept it when the battalion returned to the United States and joined the 5th Marines.[21]

Although records on company-level officers are sketchy, apparently about 50 percent of the company commanders had combat experience; the percentage was much lower among the platoon leaders and company executive officers. Of sixty-three officers in the ground combat companies, eight had definitely been in ground combat and seven had definitely not been in ground combat during World War II. An additional twenty-two had been in the service during World War II, but it is impossible to determine whether they served in combat; the final twenty-three officers came into the service after World War II. Even if one assumes that all twenty-two who served during World War II served in combat, the ground combat element had at most 50 percent combat veterans among its company-grade officers. If one assumes the twenty-two divided up roughly like the fifteen with definitive records, then combat veterans made up only 33 percent of the company-grade officers.[22]

In addition to the lack of ground combat experience in World War II, the officers of the regiment had been moved constantly between 1946 and 1950. Due to the rapid demobilization, many units were deactivated, which resulted in constant reassignment. The 90 percent reduction in the number of infantry battalions ensured a constant movement of personnel. Official records of key officers indicate that they changed jobs on average every six months. Thus, they never really learned any job.

Records for staff noncommissioned officers (SNCOs) and NCOs are insufficient to determine what percentage actually had ground combat experience or were even in the Marine Corps during World War II. Sgt. Donald Gagnon of the 1st Tank Battalion remembered, "We had more than our share of World War II combat experienced tankers, our Company Commander, XO, 1st Sgt, Company Gunnery Sgt and three tank maintenance staff."[23] It is interesting to note that Sergeant Gagnon felt that having 7 out of 181 men with combat experience meant the tank company had more than its fair share. None of these combat-experienced marines served at the platoon level or below.

Another indicator of the relative lack of combat-experienced NCOs is this entry in the brigade G-1 Journal with the date/time group of 131733Z Jul 50:

CG 1STPROVMARBDE AUTH PROM W/IN OCC FIELDS TO RANK CPL AND SGT TO FILL T/O BILLET. DISREGARDING TIG AND PASSING SCORE.[24]

The message authorizes the brigade commander to promote any marine within his occupational specialty to corporal or sergeant. At this time a corporal was an E-3 and a sergeant an E-4 equivalent since the Marine Corps did not have the rank of lance corporal. The message gave the commander permission to waive all time in grade and test score requirements. Although it does not tell us the percentage of NCOs with combat experience, it indicates that, even with the influx of personnel from all over the West Coast, the brigade was critically short of corporals and sergeants and did not have sufficient qualified personnel to promote. It would be very unusual for a marine who had served in World War II to be ineligible for promotion to corporal. To deal with the shortage, the corps took the unusual step of authorizing the promotion of personnel not qualified under peacetime standards to ensure that it had sufficient NCOs.

Even the junior marines moved constantly between posts and stations. Part of the turbulence was due to the rapid drawdown, and part was the result of Marine Corps policy to rotate as many personnel through the few FMF units to provide some experience to as many marines as possible. Even with these measures, samples of individual accounts indicate that as many as 50 percent of the junior enlisted marines had never served in the FMF before being sent to Pendleton to embark with the brigade. Effectively, they had no combat training after boot camp—and boot camp provided very limited combat training.

Perhaps typical of the young marines' training and sudden assignment to the brigade was the story of Corp. Richard A. Olson. He reported to boot camp in 1948 and upon graduation was assigned to Marine Barracks, Naval Ammunition Depot, Hawthorne, Nevada. Of his training at Hawthorne, he wrote, "During my time at Hawthorne, I served as a sentry in tower watches in the ammunition area, then as a sentry on the main gate, and then as a patrol driver providing security and enforcement of traffic laws in the Naval Housing area of the base. In April of 1950 I was promoted to Corporal and stood Corporal of the Guard watches in the three guard houses of the base."

Olson's mobilization for Korea was sudden:

> I was the Corporal of the Guard at Guard House #3 located in the ammunition area. The phone rang and I was informed that a Jeep was on the way to pick me up as I was being transferred. . . . There was no time for leave or even contact with my folks. When I hung up the phone in the guard house the Jeep was already pulling up in front. I was hustled back to the barracks and about 25 of us were processed for transfer and on a bus to Camp Pendleton that very night. We took a bus to Las Vegas where we were transferred to a Greyhound bus for LA and Camp Pendleton. We were split up and placed into various units of the 5th Marine Regiment. I was placed in "Able" Company.[25]

Despite no infantry training at all, Olson was assigned a leadership position: "Before leaving the ship, I had been assigned to 2nd fire team, 2nd squad, 1st platoon, A Company, 1st Battalion, 5th Regiment, 1st Marine Brigade, Reinforced. I was the fire team leader."[26]

Even marines with significantly more time in service often had no time in the combat forces of the Marine Corps. Sgt. Gene Dixon enlisted in late 1946 and attended boot camp at San Diego and the field telephone operators' course at Camp Pendleton. In August 1947 he transferred to Camp Lejeune, North Carolina, where he served two years with the base telephone organization as a telephone exchange operator and line repairman. In August 1949 he reported to Marine Corps Institute, Washington, D.C., for duty as an instructor and member of the drill team. In

December 1949 he reenlisted for duty at MacAlester Ammunition Depot, Oklahoma, and served six months as a gate guard. In late June 1950 he reported to Shore Party Battalion, Camp Pendleton, but was transferred to 1st Battalion, 5th Marines when the brigade mobilized. In Dixon's own words:

> With the new transfer to the Brigade, things were quite in a turmoil in my case. I knew no one in the unit to which I was assigned. I had not trained with them, and therefore I felt like an outsider in the unit. In order to be a cohesive unit, Marines must train and bond together. I did not have that opportunity. Instead, I had to do the best I could and hopefully do my job the best I could. I was a Sergeant and communicator, but prior to this time most of my duties had been with non-Combat units. I had a lot to learn in such a short time. My previous service had been limited to boot camp, Field Telephone School, and Marine Corps base at Camp Lejeune, NC. From there I was Instructor in the MCI's Air Pilot's Course, and security at McAlester, OK. Suddenly, with the outbreak of war in Korea, I was well on my way to overseas duty under combat conditions.[27]

Staff Sgt. Clarence Hagan Vittitoe did have combat experience. He was on his third enlistment when the brigade mobilized. He had joined the corps in September 1942 and shipped to the Pacific with the 1st Barrage Balloon Squadron in 1943. After almost two years protecting the harbor at Noumea, New Caledonia, he was transferred to Hawaii for base guard duty. Then he was sent to Company L, 2nd Battalion, 8th Marines as a replacement. He served as a BAR man with the company through the cleanup phase of Saipan and the invasion of Tinian. After the war he served in China, then in a series of barracks and guard posts before joining the 5th Marines in 1949.[28]

Despite the corps's best efforts to provide training for those marines not in the FMF, the fact remained that the normal day-to-day duties consumed so much of their time that little was left for training. Corp. Maurice Jacques, who would leave the corps as a sergeant major, remembered his time at Marine Barracks Pearl Harbor under the command of Col. Lewis B. "Chesty" Puller. Even Puller, a legend in the corps as a demanding officer who focused on combat training, could not find the time for barracks marines to maintain either combat proficiency or high levels of physical fitness. Jacques remembered that the best Puller could do was ensure his marines were well trained on the machine guns they would use in defense of Oahu.[29]

Jacques's experiences were typical of those marines assigned to bases and barracks around the Marine Corps. Maj. James A. Pounds captured the frustration felt by officers at barracks as they attempted to keep their marines ready for combat amid the daily press of barracks duty. He wrote an article for the December 1948 issue of the *Marine Corps Gazette* in which he detailed the problems that he confronted trying to keep non-FMF marines ready for combat:

The most trying problem of present day guard detachment commanders is maintaining their command in a state of training and physical condition so that it could function in the field as an efficient infantry company upon 48 hours notice. It is easy enough to consider that all Marines have received basic infantry training in boot camp and let the training program slide along on that theory, but it is no secret that our current boot camp graduates certainly are not polished infantrymen. . . . It was difficult to realize that a large percent of the command had never served in a Fleet Marine Force unit, had only a hazy idea at best how even a squad operated.[30]

The major went on to describe the extraordinary measures his post took to maintain even minimal combat-readiness among his marines, who had a full-time job guarding the naval station. He lacked range facilities, transportation, and ammunition with which his men could train, and he made it clear that despite his best efforts, the marines were minimally prepared to take their place in a rifle company. Unfortunately, when the brigade formed, many marines would come from barracks with officers not as driven as Puller or Pounds. These men would often have not only to fill in as riflemen but to assume roles as squad and team leaders despite never having served in an infantry company.

When we examine the training of the ground and support units, we find that most of the men in the units had not trained together and were not physically fit because they had joined their units from posts and stations all over the West Coast during the week of embarkation. They were confined in very crowded ships for the three-week transit of the Pacific Ocean. Although all personnel worked to maintain or gain some kind of fitness, the crowding limited physical training to about thirty to forty-five minutes per day. The lack of fitness would be painfully obvious in the first days of combat in Korea.

Within the brigade's aviation element, the combat experience was significantly higher. The aviators had two major advantages. First, the only people who fought in the squadrons were the pilots. As part of the downsizing from 120 squadrons at the end of World War II to the 12 squadrons still active in June 1950, the corps had emphasized retention of combat-experienced aviators. According to then Col. Edward C. Dyer, the commanding officer of MAG 12 from 1949 to 1950, "all the pilots were ex World War II guys; most of them had been doing nothing but flying fighters since they came into the Marine Corps, let's say in 1942. So these guys had been eight years doing nothing but flying fighters and they were good. They were real pros. They were the first pilots that went to Korea."[31]

Second, the Marine Corps had simply stopped training aviators at the end of World War II because it had so many surplus pilots. Those who were flying in 1945 kept flying. There were simply no new pilots who had to be introduced to the FMF. However, despite the extensive combat experience, the one area in which most of the pilots were lacking was flying close air support missions in combat. The Corsair squadrons in World War II had focused heavily on the air defense mission and rarely had the opportunity to fly in support of ground marines.

Still, the turnover in the aviation commands was as high as that in the ground commands. Brig. Gen. Thomas J. Cushman, who had been an aviator since 1918, took command of the 1st MAW (Forward) when it was established on 7 July. He had been the assistant wing commander. Col. A. C. Koonce retained command of MAG 33 for the deployment but would be relieved by Lt. Col. R. C. West in Japan on 20 August.[32] Maj. J. E. "Hunter" Reinburg arrived at El Toro the first week of July. He was returning from a tour of night flying with the Royal Air Force in England. Reinburg took command of Marine Night Fighter Squadron 513 on 7 July. He had so little time with the squadron before embarkation, that he said, "On the way over there, I got to know the pilots and enlisted men."[33] Lt. Col. Walter Lischeid took command of Marine Fighter Squadron 214 on 7 July after it returned to California from Hawaii. Because he took over while the squadron was embarking, he had no time to obtain his carrier landing qualifications. Maj. Arnold A. Lund took command of Marine Fighter Squadron 323 on 7 July also. And Maj. Vincent J. Gottschalk had assumed command of Marine Observation Squadron 6 on 3 July. Thus, every flying squadron was led by a commanding officer who took over during the week 1st MAW (Forward) was activated. They would have less than one month in command—and no time in the air—before leading their squadrons into combat. As the next chapter will show, one week of that time was spent in embarking, three weeks were spent aboard ship with no flight time, and then only one to three days were spent in flying training before entering combat.

SUMMARY OF COMBAT EXPERIENCE OF BRIGADE LEADERSHIP

The belief that the majority of the brigade's ground combat leaders had extensive combat experience "on the bloody beaches and in the jungles of the Pacific" is clearly an exaggeration. Although all key ground leaders at battalion level and above had served in World War II, less than 50 percent actually had significant ground combat experience. Of the company-level officers, probably only 33 percent or so had combat experience. The aviation element was in fact led by combat veterans of World War II, but even the squadron commanders admitted they had participated in few if any close air support missions. During World War II the Corsair community had been focused on air defense and air attacks on Japanese bases for the vast majority of the time.

Yet by the year 2000, the fiftieth anniversary of the war, the myths had solidified. In the official Marine Corps publication *Fire Brigade: U.S. Marines in the Pusan Perimeter,* released for the anniversary, the author stated that "90 percent

Table 7.1
Dates Key Commanders Assumed Command of Their Units in 1950

1st Marine Brigade (Provisional)	Brig. Gen. Edward A. Craig	7 July
1st Marine Air Wing (Forward)	Brig. Gen. Thomas J. Cushman	7 July
5th Marines	Lt. Col. Raymond L. Murray	20 June
1st Battalion, 5th Marines	Lt. Col. George R. Newton	18 June
2nd Battalion, 5th Marines	Lt. Col. Harold Roise	15 June
3rd Battalion, 5th Marines	Lt. Col. Robert D. Taplett	30 April
1st Battalion, 11th Marines	Lt. Col. Ransom Wood	8 July
Marine Air Group 33	Col. A. C. Koonce	Summer 1949
Marine Fighter Squadron 214	Lt. Col. Walter Lischeid	8 July
Marine Fighter Squadron 323	Maj. Arnold A. Lund	7 July
Marine All Weather Fighter Squadron 513	Maj. J. E. "Hunter" Reinburg	7 July
Marine Observation Squadron 6	Maj. Vincent J. Gottschalk	3 July

of the brigade's officers had seen combat before on the bloody beaches and in the jungles of the Pacific. This was also true for two-thirds of the staff noncommissioned officers."[34]

By 2000 the corps's myths had become accepted. The brigade had been a cohesive, well-trained organization led by combat veterans, almost all of them "blooded" on the beaches or in the jungles of the Pacific. Further, these men maintained high standards of physical fitness and so were ready for the stress of fighting in the heat of a Korean summer. These later accounts never mention the fact that over 50 percent of the organization joined during the week of embarkation. Nor do they mention that every battalion commander and executive officer was new to the battalion and lacked ground combat experience during World War II—or even much time in infantry organizations.

Table 7.1 shows the dates the key commanders took command of their units. The vast majority of the commanders had less than a month in command before entering combat with their units. For all but one of the commanders (Taplett), Korea would be the first time they would be with their units in the field.

Despite all the challenges listed in Chapter 6 and this chapter, when the mobilization orders were issued in July 1950, the marines responded. It is time to turn to how they managed to form, assemble, equip, and embark the brigade in less than ten days.

8

Mobilizing and Embarking
the Brigade

The 1st Provisional Marine Brigade, FMF (Reinforced) was activated on 7 July 1950 as a combined air-ground team for combat duty in the Far East. Practically all of the combat units of the Fleet Marine Force stationed on the west coast were included in this organization. No table of organization and no recent experience were available upon which to organize this Brigade, certain essential combat equipment was still in supply depots, and organizations were below authorized peacetime allowances. Despite these difficulties, ground and air elements were brought to full peace time strength plus a third platoon for each rifle company. Loading commenced on 9 July and the Brigade sailed from San Diego and Long Beach on the 14th of July.[1]

This paragraph, the introduction to the brigade's after-action report, does not begin to capture the intensive, time-compressed effort required to form and embark a brigade from the sadly depleted Fleet Marine Force of July 1950. As noted in Chapter 1, almost five years of progressively steeper cuts in manpower and funding had reduced the Marine Corps to a shadow of its World War II strength. By June 1950 the entire Marine Corps had only 74,279 men. Only 15,000 of those were in the marine operating forces in the Pacific theater.[2] Of those, 7,825 were in the 1st Marine Division and 3,722 in the 1st Marine Aircraft Wing.[3] The roughly 4,000 other marines assigned to FMFPac were scattered in posts and stations across the command.

When word first reached the marines of the Korean invasion, most felt they would not be called to fight. The corps continued business as usual. There was so little concern that the Marine Corps continued its normal summer personnel transfers. As noted earlier, in 1950 marines received little or no combat training until they reached the FMF. This meant that with the FMF getting smaller and smaller, it was very difficult to maintain a trained base of personnel to support the envisioned rapid wartime expansion for conflict with the Soviets. In response the Marine Corps instituted a policy of short tours in the operating forces. Although this caused significant turbulence in those units, it ensured that the largest possible number of marines received the advanced combat training that was essential if they were to be leaders in a wartime corps. Thus, by late June 1950 the normal summer rotation of personnel was well under way, and no one thought it necessary to stop the routine. As noted in Chapter 7, most of the key commanders had recently been transferred, and in some cases their replacements had not yet arrived. In even more cases a hasty change of command would take place after the brigade was activated but before it embarked. At the top, ill health had required Lt. Gen. Thomas Watson, commanding general of FMFPac, to depart his post without a face-to-face relief. The situation in early June 1950 was so relaxed that his replacement, Lt. Gen. Lemuel C. Shepherd, had taken command by dispatch and been given permission to take a month's leave to travel across the United States by car before flying to his new post in Hawaii. According to Shepherd,

> I was in Colorado Springs when the Korean War erupted. I read about it in the morning paper, and said to myself, "Well, that's MacArthur's bailiwick, I won't worry about that one." I mean, the war was in Korea and we didn't have any Marines there so I continued on my trip up to Yellowstone, with my family. When I got to Cody the war was getting hot and I thought, I'd better notify Admiral Radford that I would come if he wants me to. . . . [A day later] I opened up the telegram. It was from Admiral Radford but the wording was rather ambiguous. It said "Prefer that you come by air rather than by transport and take the rest of your leave some other time."[4]

Despite the lack of urgency in the message, General Shepherd decided to terminate his leave and proceed by air to Hawaii. When he arrived two days later, on 2 July, he was handed a dispatch directing him to send an air-ground brigade to Korea. Shepherd noted, "We had no plan for the emergency confronting us and only a small staff with whom I had never worked."[5]

Thus, a new commander working with a staff that had significant turnover due to summer transfers had to develop a plan to deploy a brigade within days. Complicating the problem was the fact that no such brigade existed, nor did the depleted FMF have sufficient formed units to produce a brigade. For a smoothly functioning staff, this would have been a challenge. In July 1950 not only had Shepherd never worked with the staff, the staff itself had never worked together. Many members, including the key players in the operations section (known as the G-3), were in transition. Krulak and Henderson, two new members of the FMFPac G-3, had given up command of the 5th Marines and 2nd Battalion, 5th Marines, respectively, during mid-June and arrived in Hawaii on 29 June, four days after the war had started. Although due for transfer, Col. Alpha Bowser, the FMFPac G-3, had not yet received his orders. He was in the awkward position of knowing that the incoming commanding general, Shepherd, had specifically asked for Krulak as his G-3, but Headquarters Marine Corps had forgotten to transfer Bowser. Thus, even when there was limited continuity in the staff, the working relationships were still unsettled by the summer transfers.

Facing its biggest crisis since World War II, FMFPac was starting from scratch with both its staff and its plan. Further complicating the planning was the strained relationship between the FMFPac staff and the Pacific Fleet staff. Shepherd, Krulak, and Henderson all noted the tension between the two staffs.[6] Still, even while Shepherd was making his way to Hawaii, the two staffs had to work together to make critical decisions without Shepherd's input. The most critical was to commit the Marine Corps to providing forces on short notice. Krulak remembered that he arrived in Hawaii and joined the G-3 section on the same day that the staff received a message from the commander in chief of the Pacific Fleet asking, "'How soon can you sail for Korea: (a) a BLT (b) a RLT [regimental landing team]?' Krulak recalled he went back to his office and wrote the reply, '(a) 48 hours, (b) five days.' Since it had only taken ten minutes to type the message, when he took it to Col. G. A. Williams, FMFPac chief of staff, who was acting in place of Shepherd, Krulak was asked, 'How do you know we can do this?' Krulak, still acutely aware of the recent efforts to do away with the Marine Corps, replied, 'I don't. I don't know if we can afford to say anything else.' Krulak noted that the answer came back quickly to the effect, 'We opt for b and let's see you do it.'"[7]

The FMFPac staff immediately generated a formal warning order to the 1st Marine Division and 1st Marine Aircraft Wing in California. At the same time the FMFPac staff began planning with the Pacific Fleet staff to arrange amphibious shipping for the brigade. Although the division and wing did not receive the official warning order until 5 July, they started planning on 2 July based on informal warning orders from Headquarters Marine Corps. Although it may seem odd that Headquarters Marine Corps would bypass FMFPac on such an important warning order, on 2 July Shepherd was just arriving in Hawaii. Thus, there was no general officer in Hawaii. The warning orders were passed from general officer to general officer over the telephone.

Given the fact that the Marine Corps was adamant that marines must fight as an air-ground team, it was a bit schizophrenic about forming the brigade. The commanding general of FMFPac's July message to the commanding general of the 1st Marine Division designated the Regimental Combat Team–Marine Air Group task force as 1st Provisional Marine Brigade FMF (Reinforced).[8] The commandant of the Marine Corps approved this designation the same day. Yet in all subsequent orders, starting with the activation of command letter written by the acting commanding general, 1st Marine Division Brig. Gen. Craig (because of the rush, Craig wrote his own activation letter), only the ground elements were referred to as the 1st Provisional Marine Brigade.[9] The air elements were initially referred to as Marine Air Group 33 (Reinforced). Later their title was changed to Forward Echelon, 1st Marine Air Wing (1st MAW [Forward]). Regardless of the name, air assets remained under the command of Brig. Gen. Thomas J. Cushman rather than that of Brig. Gen. Edward A. Craig. Upon arrival in Japan the 1st MAW (Forward) would be placed under the operational control of the commander of Naval Forces Far East, although administrative control remained with 1st MAW and the commander of Air Forces, Pacific Fleet. Thus, despite the corps's insistence on fighting as an air-ground team, it did not organize its forces as an air-ground brigade. Rather, the air and ground elements remained essentially separate organizations, with the air element supporting the ground. This arrangement seemed to grow from two considerations: the absence of any doctrinal air-ground command below amphibious corps level and the fact that the planners assumed the brigade would conduct an amphibious landing and that the air elements would therefore fly from carriers and work for the fleet commander. The Marine Corps had not written any doctrine for a single commander for both air and ground forces below corps level. Even the amphibious corps of World War II had not included aviation assets as integral elements of the corps, and the Packard exercises at Amphibious Warfare School always dealt with corps-level amphibious landings. Since there was no formal command and control relationship between the marine air and ground elements, the air-ground culture that had been reinvigorated since 1945 would prove to be absolutely essential to the success of the brigade.

Even Craig made it clear that although the marines in Korea fought as an air-ground team, he did not think of the air wing as part of his brigade. "We organized the 1st Marine Brigade from practically what was then the 1st Marine Division, consisting of a little over 8000 men. The Brigade mounted out together with the air wing consisted of about 7000 and some. . . . Being in command of the base and the division at the time, I had my choice of taking anybody I wanted. Naturally, I took the best I could find."[10]

SHEPHERD GOES TO JAPAN

With the mobilization of the brigade underway, Adm. Arthur D. Radford, commander in chief of the Pacific Fleet, called Shepherd and instructed him to go to Japan to discuss the situation with MacArthur. Shepherd recalled, "It was a day or two later that Radford said to me, 'Tommy Sprague's coming in today. I think you both had better go out to Korea and see General MacArthur and find out what this thing's about. We're getting a lot of dispatches here which are rather confused. I want somebody to tell me what the situation is out there.'"[11]

Shepherd departed from Hawaii on 7 July and arrived in Japan on the morning of Sunday, 9 July. He received a briefing from Adm. Turner C. Joy, commander of Naval Forces Far East, then moved on to MacArthur's Far East Command to commence planning with that staff. On 10 July he had a private meeting with MacArthur during which MacArthur expressed his desire to have the entire 1st

Marine Division in order to conduct an amphibious envelopment. Shepherd said the Marine Corps could provide the division, less one regimental combat team, by 1 September. MacArthur told him to write a message to the Joint Chiefs of Staff requesting the 1st Marine Division and MacArthur would sign it immediately. Shepherd did so.

In his war diary, Shepherd noted that the conference with MacArthur alleviated one of his primary concerns:

> During my flight from Honolulu to Tokyo, I had given considerable thought to the operational command status of the 1st Marine Brigade upon its arrival in Korea. I feared that the Brigade, which was only a reinforced regiment at reduced strength, would probably be attached or integrated into an Army Division and thus loosing [sic] its identity as a Marine organization. Furthermore, I felt certain that the Marine aircraft and helicopter squadrons would be assigned to the Far Eastern Air Force Command. My apprehension was based on attempts by the Army and Air Force to dismember the Marine Corps and reduce its rolls and missions during discussions of the recently enacted "Unification of the Services" legislature. To insure that the Marine Units in Korea would be under command of a Marine General officer of sufficient rank to protect the interests of the Corps, I had determined to suggest to General MacArthur that he request a Marine Division be sent to Korea. The First Marine Division, stationed at Camp Pendleton was under my administrative command and I felt with a first class war developing in the Far East that the Marine Corps, as the Nation's Force in Readiness, should be represented by a Marine Division supported by a Marine Air Wing. Anticipating General MacArthur's approval of my proposal I had drafted, during my flight to Tokyo, a carefully prepared dispatch to the JCS for General MacArthur's signature, which I brought with me to my conference with him on July 10th.[12]

Shepherd departed that evening after finalizing arrangements for marine squadrons to use Itami Airfield upon their arrival in Japan. From 10 July onward, other than his visit to the brigade just prior to its departure from California, Shepherd focused the efforts of the FMFPac staff on the mobilization and deployment of the 1st Marine Division and 1st Marine Air Wing in support of MacArthur's amphibious hook. His discussion with MacArthur indicated that the marine division-wing team would assemble in Japan, reabsorb the brigade, and complete preparations for the amphibious landing. Although not officially approved until 10 August,[13] MacArthur's request required Shepherd to concentrate on the much larger task of forming the division and wing, which inevitably caused tension between the brigade and FMFPac. Both staffs competed for the same critically short assets to fulfill their assigned missions. The brigade staff was obviously focused on assembling the strongest possible team for immediate deployment, and the FMFPac staff was concerned that the brigade would not leave enough of the division behind to provide the nucleus for mobilization. The FMFPac staff had rank, but the brigade staff had proximity.

THE BRIGADE FORMS

To understand these tensions, we need first to examine what happened in California while the FMFPac commander was traveling to Japan. The 7 July deployment order could not have hit the division and wing at a worse time. Both units, and the rest of the Marine Corps, were in the middle of their annual summer personnel rotation. It had long been the practice in the U.S. military for permanent change-of-station orders for career servicemen to take place during the school vacation months of June, July, and August. Thus, units across the Marine Corps were undergoing the turbulence of summer rotation. Since it was also customary for a majority of personnel to take their annual leave in conjunction with the transfer orders, it was impossible to sequence the reliefs. As a result, many billets went unfilled for a month or more as personnel departed before their replacements arrived.

Summer is also the time when most units change command. As noted, FMFPac was struggling with the turnover of key personnel, including the commander. The same was true of the units in California. All the way down to the company level, the annual change-of-command process was well under way. On the ground side of the house, Maj. Gen. Graves Erskine, division commander, was due to turn over command in August to Maj. Gen. Oliver P. Smith, who was currently the deputy commandant. At the time of mobilization Erskine was on a trip to Vietnam to decide what kind of equipment the French might need from the United States during 1951. Despite being the division commander, Erskine had been assigned to the three-month mission to evaluate the French requests for assistance in their efforts to reestablish their rule in Indochina. He had departed in May and would not return until late summer. Upon his return he was to be replaced by Smith, who was still at Headquarters Marine Corps.

As previously noted, Krulak had just given up command of the 5th Marines to Lt. Col. Raymond L. Murray. All three infantry battalions of the 5th Marines had also changed command recently, as had the 1st Battalion, 11th Marines, the only artillery battalion in the division. The only good news was that in each case the new battalion commander had served for between one and ten months as executive officer of the same battalion before taking command. This provided some continuity. As noted earlier, the bad news was that the infantry battalion commanders had extremely limited time in the infantry prior to taking command.

Although the FMFPac warning order directed the formation of an air-ground team, the division and wing actually mobilized as separate entities. This is not surprising because it was the normal system of operation. Despite the corps's enormous efforts to reintegrate marine air and ground forces after World War II, headquarters had never taken the final step of creating a peacetime air-ground command element. Although FMFPac was the common administrative headquarters, it was not an operational command. Operational orders passed down through the type commanders.

Brigadier General Craig, acting division commander, first heard about the North Korean invasion on his car radio. He commented to his wife, "'Well, this is it again and it looks like another war for the Marines.'"[14] Then, on 28 June, Craig received a call from General Smith, who was assistant commandant of the Marine Corps, instructing him to hold all leave for his marines. Craig took the additional step of ordering his staff to start planning for the movement of the division. On 2 July Smith called again and instructed Craig to "prepare plans for and prepare for mounting out a Marine Brigade including an air group."[15] As noted, these calls were general officer to general officer. Once Shepherd arrived in Hawaii, all further instructions from Headquarters Marine Corps were passed through FMFPac.

Upon receiving the 2 July warning order, Craig immediately convened a division planning conference. One of the first decisions was whether or not to continue with the combat review scheduled for the following morning. Craig decided that since all the equipment was already staged on the parade ground and senior navy and marine officers from the West Coast were attending, he would execute the parade as scheduled. However, he decided to cancel the rodeo after its first day.[16] After the conclusion of the parade, he wanted the division focused on getting the brigade to war.

On 3 July President Truman and the JCS officially approved the commitment of a marine brigade to Korea. Activated on 7 July, the brigade had to commence embarking aboard ship not later than 9 July to make a sailing date of the 14th. Clearly the brigade could not have made this schedule without commencing planning based on the warning order of 2 July. As a first step, Craig had to form a brigade staff and headquarters battalion. Although he could quickly take the men from the 1st Marine Division staff, there were no formal T/Os or Tables of Equipment for a brigade staff or its headquarters elements. In his oral history Craig noted that he had given up command of the Guam brigade in May 1949, and though that brigade was much smaller than the one he was forming for Korea, he chose to model his new staff and headquarters units after the old.[17] Even with this model, Craig and his brigade staff literally had to make it up as they went along because there was no written guide for the personnel and equipment needed for each staff section or the supporting headquarters battalion that would supply the critical communications, transportation, security, and other support for the staff. In addition to building a brigade staff and headquarters from scratch, Craig had to put together a logistics element to support the brigade's combat units. He formed the headquarters and service battalion from the separate logistics battalions that supported the division. Once again there were neither T/Os nor Tables of

Equipment for a brigade support element. The same applied to the separate combat and combat support companies the brigade would form out of the corresponding battalions that supported the division. As noted in the brigade special action report, "Indications at this state of the planning were that the Brigade would be used in an amphibious assault against the enemy."[18] The units of the brigade were built accordingly.

Because Craig was acting commander of the 1st Marine Division, he wrote his own activation of command letter, complete with the organization list. By the time the brigade sailed, Craig had claimed over 5,300 of the 7,798 marines and sailors on the 1st Marine Division's muster rolls.[19] The letter laid out the organization and strength of the brigade, as shown in Table 8.1.

In addition to providing a unit list and strength for the brigade, the activation letter also provided the organization for the brigade staff. In keeping with the times, the staff was small, consisting of only twenty-three officers and fifty enlisted marines.

Finally, the letter established the brigade Headquarters and Service Battalion to provide the support, supply, communications, and motor transport for the headquarters. Led by a major, this was a lean organization. The total for both the staff and the headquarters battalion was only 31 officers and 197 enlisted men.[20] Although the 28-member marine band looked like an odd extravagance for

Table 8.1
Organization 1st Provisional Marine Brigade, FMF (Reinforced)

	Officers	Enlisted	Total
Brigade Headquarters Provisional	25	107	132
Det, 1st Signal Battalion	16	186	202
Co A, 1st Motor Transport Battalion (Reinf)	8	107	113
Co B, 1st Medical Battalion (Reinf)	5	90	95
Co A, 1st Shore Party Battalion (Reinf)	10	170	180
Co A, 1st Engineer Battalion (Reinf)	6	200	206
Det, 1st Ordnance Battalion	4	115	119
Co A, 1st Tank Battalion	8	165	173
1st Battalion, 11th Marines (Reinf)	37	455	492
4.2" Mortar Co, 1st Weapons Battalion	4	124	128
75mm Recoilless Gun Co, 1st Weapons Battalion	4	81	85
5th Marines, 1st Marine Division	113	2,068	2181
Det, 1st Service Battalion, 1stMarDiv	9	156	165
Det, 1st Combat Service Group, FMF	4	100	104
1st Amphibious Truck Platoon, FMF	1	73	74
1st Amphibious Tractor Company, FMF	9	235	244
1st Platoon, Reconnaissance Company, 1st Marine Division	2	35	37
1st MP Traffic Platoon, MP Company, 1st Marine Division	2	35	37
	267	4,508	4,769

Source: Headquarters, 1stMarDiv Activation of Command, Enclosure (1) letter, dated 6 July 1950. Slight errors in totals are in the original table.

a brigade going to war, the band section's doctrinal role in combat was to provide close-in security for the brigade command post; therefore, it had a critical role.

The activation of command letter directed the division's separate battalions (signal, motor transport, medical, shore party, engineer, tank, ordnance, service, combat service, amphibian tractor, weapons, and reconnaissance) to provide task-organized, company-sized elements to the brigade. This was a major test for these units. Not only were they manned at such a low level that a company would take the vast majority of their personnel but they also had to provide reinforcements for each line company they formed in order to provide for the general support functions normally covered by the battalion headquarters and service companies.

For instance, Company A (Reinforced), 1st Engineer Battalion, 1st Provisional Marine Brigade, not only had to be organized to execute its normal combat engineer functions of mobility and countermobility, it also had to execute the support engineering functions of operating water points, engineer equipment repair points, and bridging. These functions were normally done by the Headquarters and Service (H&S) Company, 1st Engineer Battalion, but of course that company would not deploy with a brigade. Thus, while reinforcing marines arrived to fill its own combat platoons, it had to attach a support platoon formed from the marines of H&S Company. Then the newly formed company had to split into four elements for embarkation on the USS *Alshain,* USS *Henrico,* USS *Pickaway,* and USS *Gunston Hall.*[21]

The often unnoticed but critical supporting companies actually faced even greater challenges than did the major combat units. Further, these units were led by officers much junior to those leading the major combat elements. Although the major combat units were all led by lieutenant colonels or majors, these support elements were led by captains and, in some cases, even lieutenants. Another complicating factor for the support elements was the need to attach additional personnel and equipment to their organizations. Like the engineer company, each would have to provide critical support that exceeded their normal capabilities.

As if they didn't have enough problems, these young officers had to deal with the fact that some of their units had not yet converted to the K-Series T/Os. The commander of Company A, Motor Transport Battalion, noted that in the midst of embarkation he was ordered to reorganize his company to the K-Series T/Os before reporting to the brigade. He also had to absorb both a supply platoon and an auto-repair platoon from the battalion H&S Company. These platoons were also in the process of reorganizing to K-Series T/Os. Like all brigade units, the motor transport company had to accomplish these tasks while simultaneously boxing and crating its equipment and thirty days' worth of supplies for delivery to San Diego by 8 July. And of course, as in all military operations, "hurry up and wait" was an integral part of the process. As part of its preparations the company carefully loaded twenty-two trucks with supplies critical for the truck company's operation. Then, upon arrival at the pier, the company had to unload those supplies into a warehouse due to the shortage of shipping.[22]

Other key elements of the brigade not only had to form companies for embarkation but had to execute duties critical to the embarkation of the brigade. Unlike the combat units, which could focus on preparing their personnel and equipment for embarkation, these supporting elements had to execute their support functions while simultaneously preparing for embarkation. Company A (Reinforced), Ordnance Battalion, provides insight into the challenges these units faced in embarking at such short notice. First Lt. Meyer LaBellman had to form his company from elements of the Ordnance Battalion's maintenance, supply, motor transport, ammunition, and medical companies. In short, he had to form a unit from men assembled from all over the battalion as well as absorbing some of the newly joined marines pouring in from all over the West Coast. Even as the lieutenant was trying to form his company and assemble and pack its supplies, he had to meet one of the very early embarkation dates. His ordnance maintenance and ordnance supply sections had to depart for the piers on the morning of 7 July.

Complicating his job was the requirement to send one officer and sixteen men on 5 July (two days before the official formation of the brigade) to Fallbrook Naval Ammunition Depot (next to Camp Pendleton) in order to draw five units of fire for the still forming brigade. At the same time he had to provide a similar detail to load the ammunition aboard ships as the ammunition and ships arrived at Naval Air Station Coronado, California. The rest of his ammunition personnel were responsible for issuing a basic load to every unit as it embarked. Upon loading the ships and issuing ammunition to all the other units, the ammunition sections still had to prepare and embark their own personnel and equipment. Obviously they were among the last to load, going aboard on 12 and 13 July just before their ships got under way. Thus, the lieutenant and his marines had simultaneously to organize, pack, and embark while getting to know each other and providing extensive support to the brigade in multiple locations.[23]

Given Marine Corps air-ground doctrine, one of the most vital detachments was the Air Section, 1st Provisional Marine Brigade. It too was formed on the fly, and although the division air section was conceived as a planning and advising organization, the brigade's air section was clearly organized for tactical usage. The Air Naval Gunfire Liaison Company (ANGLICO), 1st Marine Division, was tasked with providing tactical air control parties for the 5th Marine Regiment and its infantry battalions. It took every ANGLICO marine trained in air control procedures to bring the regimental and battalion parties up to the one officer and six men each rated. There were insufficient men to provide for a brigade air control element, so it was formed by providing the brigade air officer with six men transferred from the 1st Signal Battalion just prior to embarkation. The sudden attachment of personnel at battalion, regimental, and brigade level "necessitated a great amount of familiarization with equipment and indoctrinational schooling during the movement to the objective."[24]

The Air Observation Section, which would control artillery fire while flying as observers in VMO 6's OY aircraft, was formed by combining the few marines in the 1st Battalion, 11th Marine's Air Observation Section with those from the 1st Marine Division Air Observation Section. According to the section after-action review, "there was no training for the air observation section except for school which was held while enroute to the objective. There were no rehearsals held for operations to be conducted in the objective area due to the time factor."[25]

The medical section of the brigade formed "along lines similar to those of a [medical section for a] reinforced regiment, with partial T/O organization in the various service elements such as the Shore Party, Service Battalion, etc."[26] Although the medical officers had a model of how many staff members and what equipment they should take, they simply lacked trained personnel. The infantry battalion's medical sections deployed at their peacetime strength of only one medical officer (50 percent of wartime) and eleven hospital corpsmen (28 percent of wartime) to care for roughly 700 Marines, over 66 percent of wartime strength. The Clearing and Collecting Company, which provides immediate, definitive care, had only two sections rather than the three called for in wartime. Even at these greatly reduced strengths, only 60 percent of the hospital corpsmen deploying had received any field training, and according to the after-action review, most of that training was inadequate. Of the fourteen total medical officers, only two came from the division. With the exception of the brigade surgeon, the others had neither experience nor training in field medicine. Since the vast majority of medical personnel had to be transferred from other units, issued field equipment and clothing, and taught how to use and wear those items, the only training accomplished was two lectures on medical operations in the field. Due to the lack of knowledge across the medical community, no instructions other than first-aid lectures were conducted during the transit. The special action report dryly noted that, due to the press of organization and embarkation, no medical planning was conducted.[27]

Although reassured that the brigade would train in Japan until it was joined by the rest of the division to conduct an amphibious assault,[28] Craig was adamant that his brigade be ready for combat when it sailed. Acutely aware of the diminished strength of his infantry and artillery units, Craig remembered, "I immediately, of course, made requests that the 3d Company be put into the battalion and the 3rd Platoon be furnished. I also requested additional guns for the artillery battalion. They were only equipped with four guns per battery. These requests, except for the addition of the 3d Platoon, to the two companies, were disapproved although I made strenuous and very forceful arguments to get what I wanted."[29]

The FMFPac staff also argued aggressively in support of Craig's request. In particular, Krulak and Henderson, fresh from the 5th Marines, were adamant that the brigade's requests must be filled by Headquarters Marine Corps. "One of the most crucial problems was: trying to get the commandant to authorize us to put the third rifle platoon in each company before the Brigade went to Korea. You know, Headquarters didn't want to do that! If you sent out two-platoon rifle companies, they wouldn't have lasted any time. That was a hell of a battle to get that done."[30]

Although FMFPac won the argument about the third platoon per rifle company, Headquarters Marine Corps did not authorize them until 8 July, leaving less than five days to find the marines and equipment and get them to the units.[31] Unfortunately, Headquarters Marine Corps simply could not find the men to fill the third rifle companies in each battalion or the additional six gun crews for the artillery battalion. The corps was already stripping the entire West Coast just to provide the men necessary to fill the peacetime T/Os plus the third platoons. The best headquarters could do was order the division to prepare "a further 1,135 men earmarked for the as yet unformed rifle companies [that] would later sail from San Diego in August with the rest of the 1st Marine Division."[32]

Taplett, commanding officer of the 3rd Battalion, 5th Marines, captured the state of readiness of his battalion as it embarked. He noted that although the battalion had trained hard since its return from Guam in late February, it had done so largely with new officers and NCOs.[33] Further diluting the core of trained marines, the battalion incorporated over 50 percent new personnel who had arrived by air, bus, and train from posts and stations all over the corps during the week before the battalion embarked. Taplett noted that his executive officer, Maj. John J. Canney, and most of the battalion staff had joined the battalion in the four days before sailing. In the few days before embarkation the battalion had to assimilate all the new personnel, issue their equipment, and conduct battle-sight zeroing for their weapons. There was no time even for fire team, squad, and platoon tactics. And of course the battalion still had to provide men every day to support the filming of *Halls of Montezuma*, fight forest fires, support base efforts for the rodeo, and prepare for the combat review.[34] The one bright note was the rifle companies of the 3rd Battalion. First Lieut. Robert D. "Dewey" Bohn, commander of Company G, felt that these two companies were better off than the rest of the battalion. He remembered, "I had only 2 platoons in the company; however, we had a full platoon of machine guns, a full section of mortars and the 2 platoons I had were right up to strength."[35]

Capt. Joseph C. Fegan Jr., commanding officer of Company H, noted that the short period of time the 3rd Battalion had been with the 5th Marines and the hectic schedule of training and support activities meant that the officers of the regiment had not had a chance to get to know each other. Although he was one of two rifle company commanders in the battalion, he noted, "there were other members of the regiment I hadn't even met at this point . . . other company commanders. For example, a couple in the 1st battalion I had not met. Our training kept us busy, and other duties."[36]

In a July 1951 *Marine Corps Gazette* article on the brigade, Lynn Montross summarized the impact the shortage of troops had on the deploying units: "The 1st Battalion . . . was fairly typical. About 300 men had been training at Camp

Pendleton when the Brigade was activated. Most of the remaining 400 troops of the battalion had thereafter joined from posts and stations on the West Coast. The latter had received no training with the battalion on field problems."[37]

Capt. Francis I. "Ike" Fenton, executive officer of Company B, 1st Battalion, 5th Marines, remembered the problems caused by the sudden arrival of so many new men:

> On approximately 9 July we received a number of men from various posts and stations on the West Coast to form the 3d Rifle Platoons. We also received enough men to give us an extra 5%. Our company utilized these extra men to form a third machine gun section.
>
> These men were shipped from the posts and stations by air, most of them arriving with just a handbag. Their seabags were to be forwarded at a later date. They didn't have dog tags and had no health records to tell us how many shots were needed. Their clothing generally consisted of khaki only, although a few had greens.
>
> They had no weapons and their 782 equipment was incomplete. We had a problem of trying to organize these men into a platoon and getting them all squared away before our departure date, set for 13 July.
>
> We didn't put all the new men together as a 3d Platoon. We took key noncommissioned officers and good privates and pfcs from the other platoons and built the 3d platoon around them. This proved very successful. We had competent men that we could rely on in that 3d Platoon, and they helped the new men along. When we actually formed this platoon on 9 July we had many housekeeping details to take care of, such as issuing weapons and 782 equipment. We didn't have time to take these men out and train them tactically as a unit or give them any field work.[38]

First Lieut. Francis W. Muetzel noted that the Marine Corps was not too picky about where it got the marines to fill up the companies before deployment. He noted, "We drained the dregs of personnel sources. I even had a General Courts Martial prisoner released to us from the prison at Mare Island. If he fouled up, he was going back to jail."[39]

Sergeant Clarence Vittitoe, Platoon Guide for 2nd Platoon, Company A, 1st Battalion, 5th Marines, has only fragmented memories of the mobilization:

> I remember very little of what was going on during this time. . . . We were receiving replacements daily. Also, some that had been TAD [temporary additional duty] were returning to the company. One such was S/Sgt Charles Martin. I had been Platoon Guide since I'd joined 2nd Platoon, but when Martin returned from TAD, he being senior to me became Platoon Guide and I became squad leader of 3rd squad.
>
> Before the war, we didn't have a 3rd squad. When the Brigade started its build-up, we had Marines come out of the woodworks. Some came from

guard units all over the western United States, and even some reserve units were called up for active duty. Some hadn't been in a line company for several years, and some had the wrong MOS [military occupational specialty]. These Marines may have had to take positions under Marines of lower rank than themselves. This didn't last long since all Marines are infantrymen first. By the time we arrived in Korea, they were in the position their rank called for and able to handle the position well.[40]

As Fenton noted, Headquarters Marine Corps authorized the brigade to fill its units past the peacetime authorized strength.[41] Theoretically, each unit was supposed to add 5 percent to its personnel number. Some units increased that number; in particular the 1st Battalion, 11th Marines, took advantage of the opportunity. Lieutenant Colonel Wood, commanding officer of the 1st Battalion, recalled, "Before we left Camp Pendleton the battalion received sufficient numbers of personnel to bring us up to about 20 per cent over the number allowed by the K Tables of Organization, Peacetime. This cushion, so to speak, was invaluable, as we learned of the enemy's tactics of infiltration, since these men were used primarily in a local security role."[42]

While Headquarters Marine Corps gave, it also took away. On 3 July 1950 the commandant of the Marine Corps ordered all sergeants and below whose enlistments were to expire before 28 February 1951 to be transferred from the brigade. (Note that this administrative directive predates the official activation of the brigade.) Although many of those marines immediately reenlisted to deploy with their units, several hundred were transferred to units remaining at Camp Pendleton.[43] The order hit the infantry and artillery battalions particularly hard. Lieutenant Colonel Newton, commanding officer of the 1st Battalion, 5th Marines, noted, "Of the personnel who had been previously trained, about 50% were cut off the sailing lists or taken away from us because they didn't have sufficient time to do in the Marine Corps before they were discharged."[44]

This single administrative order significantly weakened the brigade on the eve of its embarkation. Despite the aggressive training schedule the regiment had conducted throughout the winter of 1949–1950, after these transfers were completed, only about one-quarter to one-half of the marines in any unit had trained together. Compounding the issue, many of the new arrivals lacked any advanced field training in their military occupational skills. As noted in Chapter 7, even the best barracks provided very little advanced combat training, and many had grown soft in various billets outside the FMF. Although the Marine Corps had a theoretical dedication to physical fitness, many of the scattered marines did not participate in any regular physical training.

Despite the crush of preparation for embarkation and the personnel turmoil, unit commanders tried to provide some last-minute training. The 1st Battalion, 5th Marines, noted in its special action report that it had conducted three days of dry-net training (training on the ground to simulate climbing down the side of a ship via a cargo net) and amphibious lectures at the debarkation mock-ups prior to embarking. The emphasis on dry-net training was based on the belief that the brigade would conduct an amphibious assault as its entry into Korea. The battalion commander knew that less than half his battalion had participated in the Demon III exercise in May, so many would be unfamiliar with this critical and difficult evolution that was the starting point for any amphibious landing. The special action report noted that once embarked, the units rotated on deck to allow each unit to conduct half an hour of physical training per day. All elements gave lectures on weapons, tactics, amphibious doctrine, and debarkation drills.[45] Even more important was obtaining some training for the marines who would be equipped with weapons they had never fired before. The 5th Marines stated that "indoctrination firing for the new 3.5″ anti-tank rocket launchers was conducted."[46] However, personal accounts all indicate that the only training received on the 3.5-inch launchers consisted of shipboard lectures on the way to Korea. The 2nd Battalion, 5th Marines, stated that all personnel who had not fired the weapon with which they were armed were given an opportunity to do so, and the rocket teams fired seven rounds. Unfortunately, they had to fire the 2.36-inch launchers because the 3.5-inch ones were not available.[47] This would be the only training the crews received until they were in action in Korea. The 2nd Battalion report also noted that the battalion spent a day at the range to ensure that the newly arriving marines, who had never fired the weapon they would carry in combat, had an opportunity to battle-sight zero and then conduct familiarization fire with the weapon.[48] There was no time for qualification courses.

Of the ground combat elements, the tankers of Company A faced the greatest challenges. Although the 1st Tank Battalion had previously received five of the new M26 Pershing tanks, they were all assigned to the H&S Company. Company A, the single tank company in the battalion, still had World War II–era M4 Sherman tanks. Upon activation of the brigade, Company A was ordered to trade its M4 tanks for the new M26s. Additional tanks were brought down from Barstow Logistics Base by train to the Marine Reserve Center San Diego. Upon arrival, the crews had to make them operational. Unfortunately, the Steam Jennys that were supposed to remove the preservation grease did not work, and the company didn't have any solvents. As a result, the crewman had to spend sixteen-hour days using gasoline to clean their tanks. The crews also welded metal racks to the outside of the tanks so that the supporting infantry units could fill them with rifle and machine-gun ammunition cans. The combat veterans knew the value of the tank-infantry team and willingly dedicated some of the precious preembarkation time to this task.[49]

Since his crews had never trained together on the M26, Captain Gearl M. English, the company commander, managed to transport two of the new tanks to the range and allowed each gunner and leader to fire two main gun rounds. Unfortunately, his drivers and other crew members received minimal training in operating the new tanks.[50] They would learn to fight, drive, and maintain their tanks in combat.

In one area the Marine Corps was completely ready. Despite the budget shortages, the corps's leadership had been adamant that thirty days' worth of supplies must be maintained for immediate deployment in support of combat forces. To ensure that the supplies were present and packed on pallets for easy movement, the 1st Marine Division regularly inspected each site where its wartime supplies were stored.[51]

MOBILIZING THE 1ST MARINE AIR WING, FORWARD ECHELON

On the air side, the situation was every bit as hectic. Although the FMFPac order stated that the air group would be part of the brigade, the assets did not belong to the 1st Marine Division, so the 1st MAW wrote its own Operations Order 1-50, dated 12 July 1950. In it 1st MAW (Forward) was designated as the senior command in the organization. The 1st MAW operations order gives no indication that the MAW (Forward) was either a part of or subordinate to the brigade but simply directs MAG 33 to provide VMF, VMF(N), and VMP (photo) aircraft to support the brigade.[52]

Like the brigade, the 1st MAW (Forward) was an ad hoc organization established specifically to provide a command element for the aviation units deploying with the brigade. Its personnel and equipment had to be taken from the parent 1st MAW, and like the brigade staff, the 1st MAW (Forward) staff had no T/Os or Tables of Equipment. Like the division, the 1st MAW had been caught on the back foot by the sudden mobilization orders. As the 1st MAW historical record noted, MAG 12 and MAG 33 had just completed spring exercises, and MAG 25 (Provisional) was heavily engaged in moving aircraft and personnel for the annual reserve training program. Therefore, training and readiness were good. However, like the rest of the corps, the wing was in the midst of both summer leave and summer rotation. Many well-trained personnel had departed, and their reliefs had not yet arrived.

The wing staff immediately started planning when General Smith called General Cushman on 2 July with the warning order. However, the command structure was very different. Because FMFPac was essentially a type command (like destroyers or submarines) for Pacific Fleet, the air elements of FMFPac worked through a navy aviation command structure. As a result the wing did not plan directly with FMFPac but instead with the commander of the Air Force Pacific Fleet. The wing immediately recalled all personnel on leave; rescinded transfers; and, in anticipation of deploying the entire wing, accelerated training programs.

On 5 July, 1st Marine Aircraft Wing received official orders directing the deployment of two day-fighter squadrons, a ground control intercept squadron, and an air control squadron together with supporting, administrative and service elements. . . . To meet this directive Marine Aircraft Group–33 (Reinforced) with Hedron-33 (8 F4U-4B's and 2 F4U-5P's), Service Squadron–33, VMF-214 (24 F4U-4Bs), VMF-323 (24 F4U-4B's), VMF(N)-513 (12 F4U-5N's), MGCIS-1 and MTAC-2 were organized as the Forward Echelon, 1st Marine Aircraft Wing under the command of Brigadier General T. J. Cushman, USMC.[53]

As a first step, Cushman had to establish a wing forward staff. He drew it from the wing staff with the understanding that the staff would be reunited before the marines were committed to combat. According to the 1st MAW historical record, Cushman reported to Craig for duty on 5 July. The same day, Cushman and an advance party left El Toro by air and arrived in Japan on 19 July. It is interesting to note that Craig and Cushman did not travel together. At this point the marines were still under the impression that the brigade was traveling to Japan to train and would not be committed until it was joined by the rest of the 1st Marine Division and 1st MAW. As a result, Cushman's primary function was to plan and prepare for the arrival of 1st MAW in Japan. On 20 July operational control of the Forward Echelon, 1st MAW was assumed by the commander of Naval Forces Far East.[54] Effectively, this placed all marine air under the fleet commander.

The official wing operations order task organizing MAG 33 was not released until 12 July 1950, by which time the group had almost completed embarkation. Of particular interest, the 1st MAW Operations Order 1-50 tasked the 1st MAW (Forward) to

formulate plans for the formation of appropriate infantry organization whose mission will be to:
a. Provide internal security against sabotage, espionage and infiltration by hostile elements.
b. Provide external security against surprise attack by guerrilla forces if and when directed.[55]

The message was clear. Even within the air wing, every marine remained a rifleman, and units defended themselves.

MAG 33, although a standing organization, was caught with forces deployed for training and required heavy reinforcement prior to embarkation. Further complicating its preparation, the MAG was on holiday routine from 1 to 5 July to celebrate the nation's birthday.[56] Although Headquarters Squadron (Hedron) 33, Marine Service Squadron (SMS) 33, MGCIS 1, and MTACS 2 already existed, they were all badly understrength. MAG 33 headquarters required additional personnel in the areas of supply, communications, embarkation, transportation, and ordnance.

Personnel shortages were among the highest priorities. In the seven days between activation on 7 July and sailing on 14 July, MAG 33 absorbed 250 new arrivals at the group headquarters. Complicating the preparation for embarkation, elements of MAG 33 were still "in the midst of redeploying from the maneuvers at Camp Pendleton during May 1950. There was also a large turn-over of personnel being transferred and joined from other stations and quite a number of personnel were on leave over the fourth of July holidays. These had to be recalled and in some cases it took five or six days for them to return to their organization."[57]

In addition to bringing the MAG headquarters elements back from Camp Pendleton, MAG 33 had to recall VMF 214, which was at sea on a carrier training deployment:

> The squadron was enroute to Hawaii on board the escort carrier *Badoeng Strait* (CVE 116), having been awarded the privilege of hosting the annual Naval Academy midshipmen's cruise, when it received word of the North Korean invasion of South Korea. It was not long before the squadron's commanding officer, Major Robert P. Keller, was summoned to Headquarters Fleet Marine Force, Pacific, at Camp Smith. After flying off the carrier, Keller met with Colonel Victor H. Krulak, Lieutenant General Lemuel C. Shepherd, Jr.'s chief of staff [*sic*]. With a tone of dead seriousness only Krulak could project, he asked Keller: "Major, are you ready to go to war?" Keller, reflecting on the training and experience level of the squadron, assured him that the Black Sheep were ready. With no time to enjoy Hawaii, the midshipmen were offloaded and the carrier made a beeline back to California in anticipation of mobilization orders.[58]

Upon arrival in California, Lt. Col. Walter E. Lischeid took command of the squadron, and Major Keller became the squadron's executive officer.

Since VMF 214 was the only MAG 33 squadron ready to go to war, the group had to transfer its other squadrons to MAG 12 and join new squadrons from MAG 12 and MACG 2. On 7 July the commanding general of air FMFPac dispatch ordered the transfer of MAG 33's VMF 312 and VMF(N) 542 to MAG 12. Under the same authority, MAG 33 joined VMF 323 and VMF(N) 513 to its command from MAG 12. At the same time, MAG 33 had to absorb MTACS 2 and MGCIS 1 from MACG 2.[59] On 12 July the commanding general of FMFPac dispatch assigned MAG 33 administration control of VMO 6 but gave operational control to the commanding general of the 1st Provisional Marine Brigade. Included in administrative control of VMO 6 was the requirement to receive the HMX 1 detachment arriving from Quantico and transport the six helicopters the detachment had borrowed from West Coast navy organizations.[60] And of course, in the midst of the scramble to reorganize and embark, every flying squadron conducted a change of command.

Another complicating factor in the transfer of VMF 323 was that the squadron was in the process of returning to El Toro after several months deployed to Camp

Pendleton. It was literally scattered over hundreds of miles of southern California. The marines had to consolidate their people and equipment at El Toro, clean the gear, and prepare both gear and people for embarkation.[61] To add one final major complication, VMF 323 was in the process of being decommissioned in order to meet the projected strength of six squadrons in fiscal year 1951. Equipment was being crated for shipment to depots, and many personnel had already been transferred.[62] Although the personnel turbulence was difficult to overcome, the fact that a significant portion of the squadron's parts and maintenance equipment had already been crated for shipment made it easier for VMF 323 to embark.

The massive transfer of squadrons caused as much confusion in the MAW as they did on the ground side of the house. MAG 33 noted that "during the period 7 July 1950 to 13 July 1950 over two hundred and fifty (250) personnel were joined and assigned. . . . Most personnel reported to the Group without orders or service records. . . . This practice presented a problem in that it allowed the section no advance notice with which to plan the processing and assigning of personnel."[63]

Of course all of these transfers had to be conducted simultaneously with planning and executing an embarkation by a severely understrength MAG staff in the throes of summer turnover. The personnel section had only three marines—a technical sergeant, a private first class, and a private. It would not be reinforced until 29 August, when the MAG, by then in Japan, would receive 104 officers and 495 enlisted men to bring it up to wartime strength.

To make the sailing deadline, embarkation had to commence on 8 July. On that day the group supply officer started sending supplies to the staging area in Long Beach. Unfortunately, MAG 33 had no supplies on hand for either the F4U-5N night fighters or the F4U-5P aerial photo aircraft of VMF(N) 513 and Hedron 33. The group supply officer immediately requested that MAG 12 release the supplies in its possession. MAG 12 did so after packing and loading them on pallets for embarkation.[64]

In keeping with standard operating procedures, all supplies were packed on pallets and marked. Unfortunately, upon arrival at Long Beach, the shortage of shipping required the pallets to be broken down into individual boxes, which were not marked. Although this allowed more supplies to be loaded, it would create a nightmare when the group unloaded in Japan. Group marines would have to open every single box to determine what was in it and what unit it belonged to.[65]

FMFPac Operation Plan 1-50 had designated ten amphibious ships for the brigade, all the shipping that was available on such short notice.[66] It was not enough. Transport shipping was in such short supply that all ships were loaded administratively rather than according to combat loading plans. That meant cargo was loaded to maximize the ship's load without any consideration for when it might be needed. Combat loading very carefully organizes material so that it will be available when needed ashore. Although obviously essential for any amphibious landing, combat loading significantly reduces how much can be loaded in each ship. Since the brigade had been assured it would offload in Japan for training, the planners opted for administrative loading. Although this allowed a great deal more equipment to be carried, it precluded any normal operations or training while under way. The deck load of the USS *Badoeng Strait* illustrates how tightly loaded the ships were. Between its hangar deck and main deck, the *Strait* carried fifty-six F4U-4Bs, two F4U-5Ps, twelve F4U-5(N)s, six HO3S-1s, and eight OY-2s.[67] To understand the challenges the MAG faced in maintaining its aircraft during transit, refer to the photo of the ship under way in the photo section. Note that only the one HO3S had space to fly. It would fly daily administrative runs for the task group—and as such be the only aircraft to fly the entire transit.

As if these problems were not serious enough, the supply officer also produced a list of critical shortages that were filled on a rush basis from marine and navy supply depots all over the country. Critical parts and equipment were being flown to Marine Corps Air Station El Toro up to and including 14 July, when the ships sailed.[68]

In addition to supply shortages, the MAG ordnance section discovered that Naval Magazine, Port Chicago, California, was unprepared to provide ordnance for embarkation. As a last resort, the 1st MAW emptied the magazines at El Toro to provide at least some ammunition. Unfortunately, the MAW had only 352 tons of 500-pound general-purpose bombs, 20mm cannon ammunition, 5-inch rockets, a few 3.25-inch smoke rockets, and a small amount of napalm. The normal mount-out requirements for the mix of aircraft assigned to the MAG called for 1,960 tons.[69]

Every section of the group headquarters faced challenges like those of the supply section. The communications section was manned and equipped at only 40 percent of its peacetime T/O and Table of Equipment.[70] As a final hurdle, the group motor transportation section did not have sufficient trained and licensed drivers to move the supplies and equipment from the bases to the ports of embarkation. As a result, untrained drivers were used—literally learning on the job by driving heavy trucks in highway traffic. Given the huge number of vehicles needing repair at the Barstow depot, some of the vehicles trucked in from war stocks were not operational—six Jeeps did not have clutches. Upon arrival in Japan, fully 20 percent of the rolling stock had to be towed off the ships. Yet despite the challenges, the group was embarked and ready to sail on 14 July—although due to the shipping shortage, fully 30 percent of its 318 pieces of motor transport equipment were left on the pier to be shipped later.[71]

The squadrons faced similar challenges, but with much smaller and less experienced staffs. VMO 6 probably faced the greatest challenges. On 7 July, on his third day in command, Major Gottschalk was ordered to embark his squadron. But in reality, Gottschalk would have only forty-eight hours to form a composite squadron that would be the first to employ helicopters in combat operations. Gottschalk had to combine a detachment of eight fixed-wing pilots, thirty-three enlisted marines, and four OY-2 light observation aircraft from his own squadron with a detachment from HMX 1. The HMX 1 detachment of seven helicopter pilots and thirty enlisted marines did not arrive in California until 12 July.[72] Headquarters Marine Corps had decided to execute its plan to incorporate light observation headquarters into the VMO squadrons. Unfortunately, rather than the careful integration it had planned, the helicopters were integrated with an existing VMO in a matter of days. In fact, the Marine Corps did not even have the ability to ship helicopters from Virginia. Instead VMO 6 "borrowed" six HO3S helicopters from navy commands on the West Coast—two each from Inyokern and Point Magu naval airbases and two from the overhaul and repair facility in San Diego.[73] Due to a remarkable effort, the marines from HMX 1 and the helicopters managed to marry up with VMO 6 as the squadron was embarking. As if the integration of the squadron were not sufficiently complicated, Gottschalk knew his OY-2 aircraft were in bad shape. To ensure that he had the required four operational OY-2s he scavenged all eight of his assigned aircraft. The HMX 1 detachment took a similar approach with the borrowed navy helicopters. They scavenged the six they borrowed to embark four operational birds.

SHEPHERD RETURNS FROM JAPAN

As the brigade was loading onto ships, Shepherd completed his trip to Japan. After a stop in Honolulu to brief Admiral Radford, Shepherd flew to California to confer with General Craig. In his war diary Shepherd noted that he and Craig had a long talk during which they "discussed several personal matters which were not satisfactory about his [Shepherd's] actions and frequent unnecessary requests, especially his having cleaned out the Division in forming the Brigade."[74]

Craig, having almost completed the incredible task of forming and embarking a brigade in less than a week, was understandably "a little disappointed when CGFMFPac made a trip from Honolulu to Camp Pendleton. I received a little dressing down because I had requested additional shipping than that authorized by FMFPac. I required this shipping to take my authorized compliment [sic] of vehicles with the Brigade. I was told I had put the Marine Corps in a difficult position by requesting additional transportation after they had already told the Navy what they needed."[75]

In addition, Shepherd criticized Craig for taking Col. Edward W. Snedecker as his chief of staff and Lt. Col. Joe Stewart as his G-3. Shepherd felt that both officers were essential for mobilizing the 1st Marine Division. Smith, the new division commander, was not due to arrive until early August. Although Shepherd relented regarding Snedecker, he struck Stewart from the sailing list and refused Craig's request to reconsider the order. Fortunately for Craig, General Cates, commandant of the Marine Corps, had decided to fly out to see the brigade off. Using quiet diplomacy, Craig managed to have Cates reverse Shepherd's decision and instruct Shepherd to let Stewart go with Craig. Even as Cates, Craig, and Shepherd conferred, the brigade was completing its embarkation.

Despite Shepherd's displeasure with Craig's decisions concerning the division's personnel and equipment, the brigade sailed as Craig had built it. The two landing ship docks (LSDs) got under way on 12 July, only ten days after the first warning order had been received at FMFPac and four full days after the activation order. On 14 July Craig drove to San Diego to see the rest of the ships off. He gathered the troops on the pier for one last talk before their departure. Early in his talk he set the tone for the brigade when he said, "It has been necessary for troops now fighting in Korea to pull back at times, but I am stating now that no unit in this Brigade will retreat except on orders from an authority higher than the 1st Marine Brigade. You will never receive an order to retreat from me."[76]

David Douglas Duncan, a reporter and photographer for *Life* magazine, observed Craig as he spoke to the assembled marines on the pier that morning. Duncan, himself a former marine, noted that the marines were

> dead-panned . . . expressionless. Then Craig, with his Brigade Surgeon standing at his side, told his men that as long as there were any Marines alive in Korea who could still fire a rifle, or toss a grenade, no other Marines would be left behind upon the battlefield, either wounded or dead. Over four thousand men shouted in unison as his Leathernecks gleefully slugged each other in the ribs, grinned happily and wanted to know when the hell they were going aboard ship.[77]

The marines filed aboard the ships, and the task group got under way.

As soon as the ships cleared the pier, Craig and a small planning staff departed by air for Hawaii to coordinate with the FMFPac staff. He would continue on to Japan to make arrangements for the arrival and unloading of the brigade. Craig and his advance party spent 16 July conferring with FMFPac staff members. During the meetings Craig repeatedly emphasized several key points. First, he was adamant that he needed the third rifle company for each battalion. Second, he needed a replacement draft to replace battle casualties. He also stated his need for additional motor transport and artillery. He pointed out that his artillery batteries had only four guns each instead of the wartime allowance of six. As a result, the 1st Battalion, 11th Marines, had only twelve guns instead of the normal eighteen, and he had no general support artillery. Craig was clearly concerned about fighting with peacetime-strength infantry and artillery organizations.[78] Given the hasty formation of the brigade, all hands felt it essential that they be prepared to take advantage of all available training time once the brigade landed in Japan. During the conference in Hawaii Craig was told that he would "probably go to Japan, and there we would sit until such time as the rest of the division came out; and for that reason they were not too concerned about the additional rifle companies."

In a direct reference to the recent unification fights, he replied that we "are Marines and we might have to go into Korea at any time, and the future of the Marine Corps might well rest on what the Marines did there in view of the very critical situation of the Marine Corps at that time."[79]

Despite Craig's arguments, the corps was simply unable to mobilize and ship the additional rifle companies or artillerymen or even to institute the replacement draft in time for the brigade's initial commitment in Korea. And of course the shipping was simply not available to immediately transport the motor vehicles the brigade had left on the pier in California. After completing the visit with FMFPac, Craig and his team also paid a brief visit to the navy's Pacific Fleet staff to coordinate with it. Then, with the planning in Hawaii completed, the advance party departed for Japan.

It arrived on 19 July. Craig reported his presence to Adm. Turner Joy, commander of Naval Forces Far East, and then immediately proceeded to general headquarters, Far East Command, where he was joined by Cushman and conferred with General Douglas MacArthur. This conference was critical for the success of the brigade. Craig was concerned that the air force would demand that marine air fight under air force command.

Craig remembered,

MacArthur greeted me most cordially and asked me to sit down. He lit his pipe and talked at length on the situation in Korea. He expressed his pleasure at having Marines under his command again and said that he had the greatest admiration for the Corps after having had the 1st Marine Division and an air wing under his command in WWII. He then went into a long discussion as to how he was going to employ the Marines after the remainder of the 1st Marine Division arrived in Japan. He spoke of Inchon and of how he was going to land us there and cut the North Koreans off by advancing to Seoul and then North. That he would cut their lines of communication and cause the Pusan Perimeter to collapse thus allowing the 8th Army to advance and complete the defeat of the enemy. We then talked of the organization of the Brigade and I mentioned that we were a trained air-ground team, and that though we were few in numbers that we carried a big punch if we were used together as a team and not split up. I said that I hoped that we would not be split up nor that our air support be taken away. General MacArthur then stated that he would keep us together as a team and that the Air Corps [sic] would not be allowed to take over our air support except in an emergency. . . . The General then told me that the Brigade would probably be kept in Japan until the remainder of the Division arrived and for me to make arrangements with his staff for billeting areas.[80]

Craig's staff commenced planning with the army's general headquarters staff on the morning of 20 July. However, that same morning Craig had a meeting scheduled with Gen. George E. Stratemeyer, commanding general of the Far East

Air Force. Because Craig had a personal commitment from MacArthur, he felt confident when he met Stratemeyer and found that Stratemeyer had already issued an order stating that the brigade would retain operational control over marine air. Craig had achieved his goal—if committed, the brigade would fight as an air-ground team. MacArthur had also placed the brigade under Admiral Joy so that it could focus on training for the amphibious envelopment MacArthur was planning. Thus, immediately after his meeting with General Stratemeyer, Craig reported to Joy for a planning conference. At this conference Joy surprised Craig by asking him to detach his reconnaissance platoon for assignment to the navy's commando units to operate from submarines. Craig objected strongly and suggested that Joy ask for one of the platoons still at Camp Pendleton. Joy agreed.

By the end of the day marine and army planners had agreed that the planned training locations for the brigade were inadequate to support the entire division and too far removed from the planned 1st MAW airfields. The staffs agreed that the marines would travel to Itami Airfield, Osaka, to examine bases in the Kyoto-Osaka-Kobe area and develop a plan for the arrival of both the brigade and the division/wing team. Craig and his planners arrived at Osaka on 21 July and fanned out to reconnoiter billeting and training areas. By late on 23 July the reconnaissance was completed and the advance party returned to Tokyo to gain approval for its billeting plans. Craig received approval on 24 July and boarded an airplane early on 25 July to return to Itami and establish his headquarters to continue preparations for the arrival and training of the brigade and division. Halfway there he received orders to return immediately to Tokyo.

With the crisis worsening in Korea, Craig was issued oral orders by the G-3 of general headquarters Far East that the brigade would proceed directly to Korea. There it would report to the commanding general of the 8th Army for duty but remain prepared to withdraw from the Pusan Perimeter to participate in amphibious operations. Craig himself was directed to leave for Korea the next day with his staff to coordinate the employment of the brigade with the 8th Army. Craig and his staff arrived in Taegu, Korea, at noon on 26 July and reported to Lt. Gen. Walton "Bulldog" Walker, commander of the 8th Army. Craig noted, "He was very cordial but told me that he did not know exactly where the Marines would be used at that time; that the situation was changing so rapidly that they might be used anywhere on the perimeter but that probably I would be used on the left flank."[81]

Due to the navy's strict adherence to radio silence, Craig did not know and could not tell the 8th Army when the ships carrying the brigade would arrive at Pusan. Craig and his staff spent the next four days in Taegu working with the various staff sections to gather all the information they could. During this period Walker lent Craig his personal plane and pilot so Craig could make repeated aerial reconnaissance flights over the entire Pusan Perimeter. The pilot, who flew frequently with Walker, was very helpful in pointing out key terrain and the positions of friendly troops.

On 28 July, still uncertain about his mission or the arrival date of the brigade,

Craig moved his staff to Pusan to conduct reconnaissance and preparation for the arrival of the brigade. On reaching Pusan, Craig immediately wrote an order to the brigade detailing what the units should do upon landing and providing key information he felt they needed. He dispatched the message through the 8th Army message center. Craig then established a temporary command post and continued planning and coordinating for the arrival of the brigade.

THE BRIGADE SAILS

The commander of Amphibious Forces, Pacific, designated the naval force Task Group (TG) 53.7. Under the command of Capt. Louis D. Sharp Jr., U.S. Navy, TG 53.7 sailed from San Diego at 9 A.M. on 14 July, less than one week after the official activation of the brigade. All embarked assumed that the brigade would sail to Japan to offload; train; and, after being joined by the rest of the division and wing, reembark to invade Korea. The marines were acutely aware that the ships were administratively rather than combat loaded and therefore would have to be reloaded before the brigade could conduct an amphibious assault.

In addition to the uncertainty of when and how they would enter combat, the embarked marines had to deal with various crises. The two LSDs departed ahead of the main force on 12 July. On 13 July, one day out of San Diego, the well deck of the USS *Fort Marion* (LSD-22) flooded to a depth of 4 to 5 feet, damaging 14 tanks; 300 rounds of high-velocity armor-piercing 90mm gun ammunition; and 5,000 rounds of .30-caliber machine-gun ammunition. The ship's damage-control team stopped the flooding and pumped the well deck dry. Then, on orders from the brigade, the damaged ammunition was jettisoned over the side and the ship ordered to return to San Diego for new tanks. After conferring with his marines, Captain English reported that he could repair the tanks. And, despite the fact that very few of the marines had worked on the M26 before, the tank crews and maintenance teams of Company A managed the task—resorting to such field-expedient fixes as drying the electronic components in the ship's ovens. By the time they arrived in Korea, all but one tank were ready for combat.[82]

No sooner had the *Fort Marion* been pumped dry than, on 15 July, the USS *Henrico* (APA-45) reported a boiler casualty and requested permission to return to port for repairs. After an examination by the ship's crew, the commander of Amphibious Forces Pacific notified the commander of the Pacific Fleet that it would take "six to seven working days on 24 hour basis including holidays to make repairs HENRICO."[83] Based on the estimated time of repair, the 5th Marines staff transferred at sea from the *Henrico* to the USS *Pickaway* (APA-222).[84] The *Henrico* steamed independently to San Francisco for repairs and arrived on 16 July. The repair teams were waiting for it when it arrived at the dock. Captain Fenton noted that the battalion took advantage of the ability to go ashore in the port to train:

When we arrived at San Francisco on 16 July, security was emphasized. There was, of course, no liberty, and it was ordered that no one make any telephone calls. We emphasized fire team formations and hand and arm signals. New men were given the opportunity to familiarize themselves with company weapons. They were given lectures on the machine gun and 60mm mortars. We were very concerned about trying to keep the men in condition and emphasized calisthenics and body conditioning.[85]

Despite an initial estimate of a week to complete repairs, the shipyard completed repairs in two days, and the *Henrico* sailed on 18 July with orders to catch up to TG 53.7.

As the *Henrico* sailed toward San Francisco, the rest of the brigade settled down for the long ocean transit. Due to radio silence, the only news the marines received concerning the fighting in Korea was via commercial radio broadcasts the ships monitored. Naturally this news source faded as the ships pulled away from the United States. The incomplete information led to a great deal of speculation and even bets as to whether the North Koreans would seize all of Korea before the brigade arrived.

The extremely crowded ships provided little room for training. The brigade was instructed to conduct officer and NCO schools daily but space limited the training to squad or at most platoon level. Fenton noted,

It was an impossibility to get the whole company together at one location. Consequently, we used passageways, boat decks, holds, any space we could find to lecture to the men and give them the little information we had as to what was happening in Korea. We lectured on the characteristics of the T-34 tank and told the men about the kind of land mines we might expect. A lot of time was spent on blackboard tactics for the fire team, platoon, and company. We had the 3.5 rocket launcher but no one present had ever fired one. So we used the handbook and obtained as much information as possible. . . . We also emphasized first-aid, hygiene, water discipline and no eating of native foods. . . . We were looking forward to a few days in Japan where we could let the new men fire their weapons, something they hadn't had the opportunity to do while in Pendleton. We were also hoping to get in one or two days of platoon tactics in the hills of Japan.[86]

The view of training from belowdecks was even less encouraging. In the words of Sgt. Gene Dixon of Communications Platoon, H&S Company, 1st Battalion, 5th Marines:

As I recall, it took about 14 to 15 days to sail to Korea. Our only entertainment was perhaps a movie or two. During the trip, I was in the Communication center, handling messages to and from unit commanders on the ship and to other ships. There was no further training, although we did get some lectures on what to expect when we got to Korea. The ship had no stopovers once we left California. It was a straight shot to Pusan, South Korea, where we landed on August 2, 1950.[87]

Sgt. Clarence Vittitoe recalled,

There wasn't much to do on the trip over. We saw a few movies on the fantail. We did calisthenics when we could find space topside—most anything rather than lay around all day. We had no duties, but Lieutenant Johnston and Gunny Lawson held several lectures on various subjects. I think it was more to have something to do than to impart something of use. No one knew much about Korea, and I believe most of the lectures given were guess work. They were about climate, terrain and the varmints we might run across. We knew almost nothing about the North Korean Army.[88]

Corp. Richard A. Olson remembered the transit more graphically:

The ship was like a cattle car. A number of my buddies from guard company in Hawthorne were aboard. Spencer, Koslowski, and I hung together for the ride over, even after I was switched from the third platoon to the first platoon. There were 150 men bunked in a space probably no larger than 40x40 feet. There were metal-framed canvass [sic] bunks from floor to ceiling. I weighed only 150 pounds and was very slim, but when I lay in my sack, my nose and feet were within inches of the bunk above me. Conditions were gross down there. Good hygiene wasn't practical and the place just stunk. There was nowhere to go on the ship where we could be alone. In order to eat we had to stand in line for hours. I had no duty on the ship. I just rode it all the way across the Pacific.[89]

These first chapters have shown that the organizational myths that have grown up around the 1st Provisional Marine Brigade are largely untrue. These myths—that the brigade was led by combat-experienced officers who had trained the units hard as teams over the winter—have become part of the corps's story. Like the rest of the corps's history, the stories about the brigade honor the men who fought and, by their example, add to the combat-effectiveness and cohesion that are hallmarks of the corps. Yet these myths mean that today's marines underestimate the incredible accomplishments of the brigade. We have seen that the brigade was not the fully trained, combat-experienced, physically fit organization of myth but rather men struggling with all the shortages of peacetime who were suddenly thrown together in a hastily formed organization and shipped off to war. The next three chapters will show how, despite these enormous handicaps, the brigade established an exceptional combat record that should take its place among the greatest of the corps's victories.

9

The Sachon Offensive

As Task Group 53.7 sailed across the Pacific, the brigade marines still believed they would land in Japan to train and wait for the arrival of the rest of the division, although there was some speculation about other possibilities, including whether the brigade could arrive before U.S. forces were driven off the peninsula. This belief was strongly reinforced on 24 July when the commander of TG 53.7 received orders to proceed to Kobe, Japan, and debark the brigade with all its supplies and equipment. On the same date the brigade staff traveling with the task group received Operation Plan 2-50 from the commanding general of the 1st Provisional Marine Brigade, directing them to occupy staging billets upon debarkation in Kobe. Upon arrival, the brigade was to "debark and occupy staging billets in accordance with detailed instructions to be issued and that arrangement should be made for a conference aboard the U.S.S. GEORGE CLYMER (APA-27) of all unit commanders upon arrival. Bulk supplies and vehicles over ten tons would remain in the dock area to facilitate later embarkation. All units were to maintain readiness for re-embarkation on 48 hours notice."[1]

Thus, on 24 July the marines were looking forward to an intensive training program in Japan to prepare their units for combat. The next evening the brigade received the first official indicator that it would not train in Japan:

On 25 July Brigade administrative headquarters received dispatch 250702Z directing that ships with air elements embarked proceed to Kobe and debark air personnel, supplies and equipment. The VMF squadrons and VMO squadrons were to be prepared to reembark aboard carriers for close air support operations. CTG 53.7 with remainder of shipping was directed to proceed to Pusan, Korea and debark ground elements non-tactically at Pusan Korea. The Commanding General, 1st Provisional Marine Brigade directed Brigade administrative headquarters to cancel his Operation Plan 2-50 and to execute provision of Brigade Operations Plan 1-50, and upon landing Pusan, Brigade to be prepared for land operations. Non-essential amphibious personnel and equipment were ordered to Kobe, Japan. As a result of this directive, The Commanding Officer, 1st Amphibian Tractor Company with Amphibian Truck Company attached was ordered to debark from the U.S.S. GUNSTON HALL (LSD-5) at Kobe, Japan, and to report upon arrival to the Deputy Commander, 1st Provisional Marine Brigade, Kobe, Japan.[2]

TG 53.7 split. Despite the promise of time to train in Japan, the ships with the brigade's ground forces aboard (USS *Fort Marion, Gunston Hall, George Clymer, Henrico, Alshain, Whiteside,* and *Pickaway*) were ordered to sail directly to Pusan. The ships carrying the air group (USS *Badoeng Strait, Anderson,* and *Achenar*) were ordered to steam to Kobe, Japan, to offload the 1st MAW (Forward).

As USS *Badoeng Strait* approached Japan, the marine fighter squadron commanders wanted to fly their aircraft off the carrier on 30 July while the ship was still at sea. They knew the ground marines would need their support very soon, and the squadrons needed every hour of training they could get. Unfortunately, the ship's captain decided this maneuver was unsafe. Over the strong objections of at least one squadron commander,[3] the *Badoeng Strait* proceeded into Kobe Harbor on 31 July without having launched its aircraft. The marines were ordered to crane their F4U Corsairs onto the pier and then tow them sixteen miles to the airfield. After craning several planes off, the marines were suddenly ordered to put them back aboard. Someone further up the chain of command had realized that the narrow roads and low-hanging power lines made towing the aircraft impossible. The OY aircraft of VMO 6 were left on the pier, VMO 6's helicopters were flown to a nearby parking lot, and the Corsairs were reloaded in the order in which they were expected to launch. The *Badoeng Strait* returned to sea and launched the day fighters of VMF 214 and VMF 323 late on 31 July. Unfortunately, the indecision had cost the day fighter squadrons two full training days.

The night fighters of VMF(N) 513 were not launched until 1 and 2 August, with a group of six aircraft leaving each day. As soon as the last of those aircraft were launched, the *Badoeng Strait* returned to dock to complete the unloading required to deliver the remaining marines to the ships and bases from which they would operate.[4]

The captain's reluctance to fly the aircraft off the ship is not as odd as it first seems. VMF(N) 513 aircraft were first in line to be launched. The squadron had not trained on carriers for months, and its pilots had not flown at all for over three weeks. Nor, owing to the exceptionally tight deck loading, had any of the Corsairs been flown during the transit of the Pacific. The lack of shipping had left no choice. It was pack the aircraft on, or don't go to the war. The only aircraft that had flown during the transit was a single helicopter from VMO 6, which had made daily guard mail and passenger flights between ships of the amphibious group. During the unloading and reloading scramble in port on 31 July, the aircraft were rearranged on the deck so that VMF 214, which had trained aboard carriers in June, was in position to launch first. As each aircraft left the deck, the next had that much more room to take off. The marines of VMF 323 had not trained aboard carriers since the previous November but successfully launched all their aircraft next.

Acutely aware of the possible problems, the marines had worked hard throughout the transit to keep the aircraft flyable. Despite the incredibly crowded conditions on deck, they inspected each aircraft every day. Every other day, they started each aircraft. The squadron commanders were confident they could fly safely off the ship, and they were right. Every Corsair launched successfully and headed for the Itami Airfield near Kobe. The advance party had made arrangements with the U.S. Air Force for the 1st MAW (Forward) elements to operate from Itami Air Force Base.

With the fighter aircraft clear, the *Badoeng Strait* again went pierside to continue unloading. Although VMO 6 was assigned to the 1st MAW (Forward), upon arrival in Japan it was transferred to the brigade and remained with the brigade throughout the Pusan campaign. The VMO 6 squadron worked all night on 2 August to unload its equipment and supplies into a warehouse on the pier. The squadron's aircraft had been craned over the side but were not towed to the airfield. Instead, early on the morning of 2 August, ten officers and six enlisted marines of the advance party departed for Korea. To the amazement of the Japanese citizens, VMO 6 deployed the advance party by taking off from the streets of Itami after the mechanics had given the aircraft a quick check and fueled them.[5] Four helicopters and four OY planes made the short hop to Pusan.[6]

Lt. Harold Davis later told the story this way: "It was a kick to see thousands of Japs lining the streets to watch us. . . . We all made it okay but Vince. He tore off a part of his wing on a telephone pole. He couldn't land on the street so he flew to Itami for a new wing. The planes we were flying were horrible junk and crossing Tsushima Straits to Chinhae was hairy, but we made it."[7]

Of course the helicopters had been borrowed from the navy. Although they had been inspected prior to embarkation, the first chance the pilots of VMO 6 had to fly their borrowed helicopters any distance was when they took off from Kobe and flew to Korea.

The rest of VMO 6 spent 2 August loading personnel and equipment on a landing ship tank (LST), departed late that evening, and arrived in Pusan on the morning of 3 August. That morning the squadron commenced operations under brigade command. Despite the fact that the squadron had been formed only two days before sailing, no additional training was possible for the pilots or ground crews. They would learn in combat.

General unloading of the *Anderson* and *Achenar* had begun in Kobe on 31 July. On the evening of 2 August *Badoeng Strait* also commenced general unloading. MGCIS 1 and the air defense section of MTACS 2 unloaded in Kobe and moved to Itami to begin operations. On 4 August the Close Air Support Section,

MTACS 2, offloaded from the *Anderson* directly to LST Q-019 and departed to join the brigade headquarters in Korea. Due to the extensive confusion in the Pusan Perimeter, the section had to scrounge its own transportation and then move twice in two days, but it was operational and ready to support the brigade from Chinhae Airfield by 7 August. In the midst of the chaos of unloading while deploying some elements and training others, MAG 33 headquarters and support elements managed to establish themselves at Itami Air Force Base, Japan. From there they provided support to the far-flung elements of the group.

VMF 214 and VMF 323 were urgently needed in Korea, so the squadrons were allowed minimum training time before embarking on the escort carriers: "VMF-214 was able to operate approximately one day in the Itami area and VMF-323 was allowed three days prior to their flying aboard. Both squadrons concentrated on field carrier landing practice since most of the pilots had not flown for a period of three weeks to a month. Their operations were hampered by a lack of tools and ground handling equipment still in the process of being offloaded."[8]

The reason the squadrons lacked tools and ground handling equipment was that the squadron's maintenance sections were loading aboard the USS *Sicily* and USS *Badoeng Strait*. As soon as the ships arrived in Kobe, VMF 214's ground support staff unloaded their equipment and personnel from the *Badoeng Strait* and reloaded it aboard the *Sicily*. Since the squadrons had loaded their equipment administratively to maximize the space on the *Badoeng Strait*, VMF 323's ground personnel had to rearrange their gear on the ship in order to support flight operations.

On 3 August VMF 214 flew its twenty-four Corsairs to rendezvous with the USS *Sicily* at sea. In the late afternoon of the same day VMF 214 flew an eight-plane strike from the *Sicily* against Chinju with incendiary bombs and sixty-four high-velocity aerial rockets.[9] On 5 August VMF 323's twenty-four aircraft flew aboard the *Badoeng Strait*. Despite no carrier training since November 1949, VMF 323 experienced only one landing mishap. The pilot was fine, but the aircraft had to be jettisoned over the side. Clearing the fouled flight deck quickly, the squadron immediately launched an eight-plane close air support strike and then flew twenty-two more missions that first day of operations.[10]

Once stationed aboard the carriers, the squadrons were no longer under the command of MAG 33. In keeping with the usual command arrangements, the squadrons passed to navy command. If the two carriers were operating together, the marine squadrons worked for the senior marine afloat, who reported to the admiral. If the ships were operating separately, the squadron reported to the commanding officer of the ship. In their first week at sea the squadrons were operating under what Capt. John S. Thach, commanding officer of the *Badoeng Strait* and inventor of the famed Thach Weave fighter tactic in World War II, called "the best orders ever." The situation was desperate, and the air force could not provide any control for navy and marine aircraft, so it simply let them plan and fly their own missions under the "spirit of coordinated control." Over the next few days the squadrons averaged over twenty sorties each per day, focused on "targets at the Perimeter's southwest corner. They bombed bridges near Chinju and Uiryong to impede vehicular traffic and attacked villages that had been taken by the enemy. Their rockets, bombs, napalm tanks and cannons left large fires burning in several such villages that day."[11]

Back in Japan with MAG 33, Maj. Hunter Reinburg, the new commanding officer of VMF(N) 513, struggled to get into the fight. Reinburg felt the senior marine leadership simply did not understand the capabilities of his squadron. He recalled a conversation with Brig. Gen. Thomas Cushman, commanding general of the 1st MAW (Forward):

> "Hunter, I don't know what to do with your outfit, so we'll just sit here and wait to see what happens."
>
> And I said, "Well, let's try some night strikes over Korea."
>
> And he said, "Oh, no, no, night flying is very unsafe. We don't want that."[12]

Frustrated by the inactivity, Reinburg went to Itazuke Airfield to meet with the U.S. Air Force general responsible for night operations over Korea. The air force elements tasked with night operations over Korea had very little night flying training and no radar in their aircraft. They welcomed both the marines' night flying experience and their F4U-5N radar-equipped Corsairs. After the initial meeting, the air force general sent a message to MacArthur's headquarters requesting that VMF(N) 513 be assigned to his operational control. The request was approved and sent to Cushman at Itami. Cushman concurred, and VMF(N) 513 immediately moved to Itazuke, where it joined the fight under the operational control of the 49th Bomber Group, 5th Air Force.

The first night, 8 August, Reinburg established the pattern for his squadron's operations over Korea: "We went out for four hours every night. All night long, I had four planes out. . . . At night, you can't work in formation, you run together. You have to turn your lights out. So, I gave everybody a sector. . . . It just paid off beautifully. . . . Just the passiveness of your presence there, hearing the engine drilling up there pins them down."[13]

Although not flying in support of the marine ground elements with which they had trained, the marine night fighters were in the fight quickly and making a difference.

With its flying squadrons scattered to the winds, MAG 33 still faced enormous problems trying to sort out the ammunition and parts that had been dumped on the pier. The shortage of shipping had forced the embarkation team to break up the pallets that had been marked by squadron and section and load the unmarked individual boxes into the ships. Obviously the boxes were further scrambled during the hurried unloading and trucking to Itami. And, not surprisingly, critical elements were mislabeled. VMF(N) 513 noted significant problems with the ordnance; in particular, the 20mm aircraft guns did not come equipped with any of the necessary F4U-5N installation parts. . . . The ammunition pans were found to be mislabeled as to right or left in some cases and also numbered wrong. When the supply of MK-8 links was replenished with MK-7 links there was a noticeable increase in gun malfunctions due to link breakages. . . . The quick connect splices [on the rockets] had come apart. . . . Some of the rocket nose plugs could not be removed.[14]

Finally the squadron discovered that firing the four new 20mm cannons (recent replacements for six .50-caliber machine guns) consistently knocked the radar out of operation. Before they ceased using the cannons, several pilots had to use dead-reckoning navigation to get back to base.

The MAG's logistics section would spend weeks sorting through the disorder—all the while supporting squadrons at sea and at multiple locations in Japan and Korea. Despite being scattered over two countries and two carriers, by 4 August marine air was ready to support forces on the ground in their first action.[15]

THE BRIGADE ARRIVES AT PUSAN

As noted earlier, the ships carrying the ground elements had separated from those carrying the aviation elements off the coast of Japan. Late on the afternoon of 2 August marines lined the rails as those ships entered the port of Pusan, Republic of Korea. Sweating in the hot, humid air, they were amused to see a small Korean band attempting "The Marines' Hymn." Little did they know that although they had just arrived, they were hours behind schedule.

Craig and his advance party were on the pier. Looking up at his marines, the general was surprised to see that they were not ready to disembark.[16] He soon found that his orders for immediate debarkation and action, sent through the 8th Army, had never arrived. He quickly convened a conference aboard the USS *George Clymer* to issue Operations Plan 3-50. Commanders were ordered to disembark their troops; draw ammunition, weapons, and rations; and be ready to move out by 6 A.M. on 3 August.[17] The last transport did not even tie up until 9:10 P.M.[18] on 2 August. The commanders immediately returned to their units and started to disembark at a frenetic pace. The marines and sailors had no idea where they were going. A few hours before they had been waving to the Korean band greeting them. Now they were unloading as rapidly as possible with orders to move out tactically. The fact that the ships were not combat loaded meant the marines had to scramble to get to ammunition and critical equipment. Second Lieutenant Tom Gibson of the 4.2-inch Mortar Company captured the feeling well:

> The word was spread aboard ship. "Before you go down the gangplank, load and lock!" Now that's an incredible order to receive. We marched down the gangplank, loaded and locked.
>
> In Pusan, there was tension and excitement that was palpable. It was like

being in a college town on homecoming Saturday. There was also another emotion you could sense, almost feel—fear. The people were scared to death. The North Koreans were very close. In the distance, you could hear artillery.

The kids were terrific. We had a number of seventeen-year-olds in the company. They didn't walk off the dock, they swaggered off. Their attitude said, "Don't worry about it. The Marines are here!"[19]

The real challenge lay in getting the heavy equipment off the ships in time to move out with the brigade in the morning. Maj. William L. Batchelor's shore party company worked through the night to insure the howitzers and trucks as well as the critical engineering equipment for the 1st Battalion, 11th Marines, were craned over the side to the waiting units.[20]

Even as the unloading began, the brigade commander did not yet have orders from the 8th Army on where to position his brigade. Not until 11 P.M. did "Eighth Army verbally designate Chang-won as the immediate destination of the Brigade."[21] Chang-won is just north of the city of Masan and positioned the brigade well for operations on the southwest flank of the Pusan Perimeter.

Despite the late notification, Craig was prepared to designate a specific assembly area and defensive positions to his commanders. Before the arrival of the brigade's main body he had conducted a thorough helicopter reconnaissance of potential mission areas across the perimeter. Then, guessing where his force would most likely be employed, Craig had conducted ground reconnaissance by Jeep of the area between Pusan and Chindong-ni. His staff had also been very active, so they were prepared to provide routes for the vehicles of less than 2.5 tons and rail transport for vehicles over 2.5 tons. Despite the failure to deliver the original message, the marines were on the move by 6 A.M. Capt. Joe Fegan Jr. noted,

> Upon landing in Pusan, it was startling to see the mood of the people who were already there. I'm talking, particularly, of some of the Army people and the press we met, how almost . . . I guess the word is "defeated" they appeared. They were so downcast. What impressed us was seeing the movement. . . . We were going against the tide. Everyone that we saw seemed to be going in the opposite direction.[22]

Fegan had encountered the despair that characterizes all armies in retreat. The men who have broken have to justify their flight and thus tell everyone they meet how bad the situation "up front" is. And of course those who are still fighting are not present in the rear to contradict the despair.

As the brigade moved out,

> Craig took off early on 3 August in one of its helicopters and put in a remarkable day that demonstrated the amazing versatility and usefulness of the new aircraft. He stopped to give instructions to the lead battalion on the march; he

then selected a site for his forward command post (CP); and then he flew to Masan to confer with Lieutenant General Walker and Major General William B. Kean, USA, commander of the 25th Infantry Division, to which the Brigade would be attached. Finally on his return trip, Craig landed three more times to meet his unit commanders.[23]

Although he had never worked with helicopters before, Craig clearly understood and exploited the new capability they offered:

I found that by putting commanders in a helicopter, within a few minutes they could reconnoiter the area their unit was to move into or operate in and be back to their command. And it was invaluable due to the lack of good maps that we had at the time. Many of the maps were old Japanese maps, and some of them had villages with different names than were on the 8th Army map. Whereas our fire control map was the old Japanese map to start with, and other units were issued the 8th Army map. So by getting up in the air you could really find out where you were.[24]

Uncertain what the brigade was facing, Craig ordered it to move out in tactical formation. The brigade reconnaissance platoon led, followed by the 1st Battalion, 5th Marines, and then the rest of the brigade. Upon arrival, the 1st Battalion immediately took defensive positions. As each battalion arrived, it too assumed a tactical defensive position. The artillery was sited and headquarters established as if the brigade commander expected immediate contact. The 3rd Battalion, 5th Marines, which traveled by train, was the last battalion to arrive. Lieutenant Colonel Taplett noted that it was a long, miserable trip. The train frequently broke down in tunnels, so the marines spent long periods choking on the smoke and sweating in the heat as they waited for repairs. Taplett recalled that even the night temperatures were over 100 degrees, and his battalion suffered its first heat casualties while still in reserve. He immediately instructed his leaders to look to water discipline (restricting consumption) in the battalion.[25]

Despite the fact that the brigade was well behind the lines, Craig was adamant about remaining tactical. "It was the first chance the brigade had to operate as a unit under combat conditions. . . . The only training we had while we were there were the nights in this position. . . . We carried out tank training and a certain amount of artillery training. We also carried out reconnaissance to our flanks with our reconnaissance company."[26]

This day set the tone for the brigade. A brigade unit would never assume that anyone else was responsible for its security. This policy, which included not only combat units but also all headquarters and supporting elements, was based on the precept that every marine is a rifleman first. The policy paid off. No brigade unit was ever overrun. Craig also established the policy that whenever a unit was out of action, it would conduct combat training.

Marine doctrine provided additional sound guidance. It called for commanders to establish themselves well forward. Craig found that "the closer I could get to the front, the better control I had due to congestion on the roads and lack of good communication. I also found that the matter of security was generally solved by being close to the front lines where the combat units were."[27] This simple tactical expedient greatly mitigated two of the problems that plagued many U.S. Army units throughout the Korean campaign—communications with subordinates and protection of critical artillery and supporting units against North Korean infiltration. Command and support were protected by the line units simply because they were moved as close to the front as possible.

As the combat elements of the brigade moved out, the 1st Combat Support Group (with 4 officers and 100 enlisted marines) was left behind in Pusan to unload the brigade's supplies and organize and warehouse them. The 8th Army ordered that all common items be placed in the Pusan Base Command supply dumps for issue to all allied forces. Army units that had been in combat for a month were desperately short of some of the items the marines brought, and the supply system rightly filled their requests. Though it would mean later shortages for the marines, the 8th Army situation was so desperate that it was literally surviving a day at a time. Only marine-peculiar supply items remained under marine control.

The combat elements of the brigade spent two days (4 and 5 August) in the vicinity of Chang-won. These two days were invaluable for several reasons. First, they gave the units an interval to conduct training and patrolling with their new personnel. As part of this training, the brigade began to integrate VMO 6 into its daily operations. One of the ground patrols resulted in the first helicopter combat medical evacuation and resupply in Korea. A 5th Marines patrol was sent to drive North Korean elements off the high ground overlooking a bivouac area. By the time the patrol reached the ridgeline, one marine was overcome by the heat, and all needed water. VMO 6 launched a helicopter to deliver water and evacuate the heat casualty. This tactic proved so useful that the brigade quickly established a standard operating procedure of keeping two of its helicopters at the brigade command post during all daylight hours. The helicopters were available for leaders' reconnaissance, immediate resupply, evacuation of casualties, and liaison visits. When not busy with those tasks, "the helicopters would move in and post outposts on surrounding hills, enabling security to be posted around the CP area in ten minutes, and eliminate the normal hour and a half climb. Unless the helicopters were busy elsewhere, these outposts were fed hot meals three times a day."[28]

Second, this period ensured that the brigade was tied to its air support. On 5 August the brigade completed assembling the air-ground team when MTACS 2, having completed its move to Chinhae, established communications with the fighter squadrons aboard the carriers. This critical communication and coordinating link between the marine air and ground forces was in place and in use before the first contact with the enemy. A greater challenge was establishing communications between MTACS 2 and the 1st MAW (Forward) in Kobe. "Since the only communications channel available was over loaded with high priority messages, it often necessitated a four to six hour delay in getting communications. This was finally solved by using a frequency which was unassigned and unauthorized."[29]

Finally, the two-day interval was also essential to let individual marines get over the jitters characteristic of men in combat for the first time. Of course, in keeping with marine doctrine, it was not just combat arms units in the perimeter: every unit and headquarters provided its own defense. PFC Fred F. Davidson related what the first night ashore looked like from his point of view:

> I raised my carbine and squeezed the trigger. The muzzle flash blinded me. For the next few seconds, I saw lights and stars. Andy shouted, "Hey, you almost hit me!" Oh, God, I didn't know I was aiming in that direction. It was so dark I couldn't see my front sight. I said to myself, "You better take it easy, ol' buddy, before you kill some Marine." Over to my rear someone else pulled off a round. Next it was someone to my front. Then the firing pinballed from place to place all over the hill and back down toward the railroad track. . . . Finally . . . all firing ceased. . . . The rest of the night I lay awake, scared, my finger on the trigger.[30]

The next morning the officers and SNCOs of the brigade conducted some serious small unit counseling. The firing was greatly reduced the second night in position.

On 6 August elements of the North Korean People's Army 6th Division were only eight miles west of Masan and less than forty miles from Pusan.[31] Loss of the port of Pusan would mean defeat of the U.S. forces. Lt. Gen. Walton H. "Bulldog" Walker, commanding general of the 8th Army, had to stop the North Korean advance or lose the war. To do so, he formed Task Force Kean, using two regiments from Kean's 25th Infantry Division, the newly arrived U.S. Army Regimental Combat Team (RCT) 5, and the marine brigade. The brigade was tasked with moving eight miles to Masan and staging behind RCT 5. RCT 5 would then move out, attacking west to seize Chinju. When RCT 5 cleared a key intersection in the vicinity of Chindong-ni, the 5th Marines would move south to Kosong, then west to seize Sachon. As a first step, the 5th Marines would relieve the army's 27th Infantry Regiment west of Chindong-ni on the night of 6 August.

As the marines moved into place, artillery doctrine superseded the brigade's command and control arrangement. Lieutenant Colonel Wood noted that "the Brigade was under the operational control of the 25th Division during its first operation; consequently, my artillery battalion was under the operational control of the division artillery commander."[32] Thus, although the brigade was theoretically fighting as an integrated air-ground team, in reality most of the aviation and all of the artillery was under the operational control of commanders outside the brigade.

Taplett's battalion, reinforced by the artillery of Wood's battalion, an engineer platoon, and a 75mm recoilless rifle platoon, led the brigade's move. In keeping

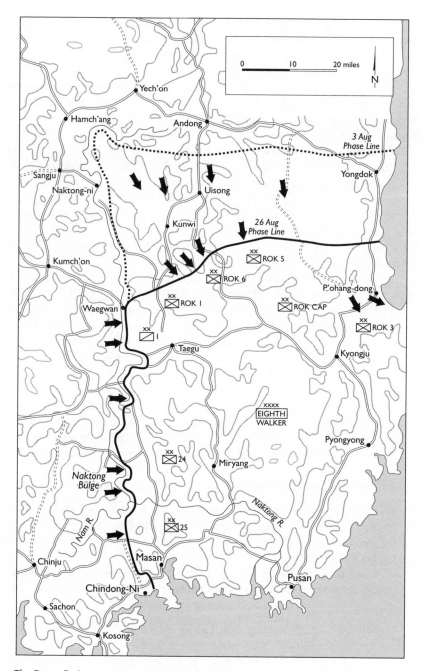

The Pusan Perimeter, 1 August–1 September 1950.

with doctrine for a relief in place, his force was under the command of Lt. Col. John H. Michaelis, commanding officer of the 27th Infantry. Taplett arrived at the 27th Infantry's command post about noon but was unable to find the regimental commander. He moved forward to the command post of the 2nd Battalion, 27th Infantry, and again could not find the commander. During his initial discussion with the army battalion staff, they recommended that the marines occupy the army command post in the schoolhouse. Taplett replied, "My men are going to fight in the mountains and ridges and that is where our command post staff people will be . . . high on the reverse slope of the hill. Besides, as I look around your command post, I'm sure the enemy artillery has this village well zeroed in."[33] He rapidly moved out of the village and placed 1st Lieutenant Bohn's Company G in position west of a small airfield and Captain Fegan's Company H facing north toward Hill 255, with one platoon covering the south side of the main supply route. Taplett established his command post on the reverse slope of a ridgeline just behind Company G, his most forward company. It was a good decision. Later that night the North Koreans shelled the schoolhouse.

About midnight Michaelis contacted Taplett. The 25th Division wanted the marines to send a reinforced rifle platoon to relieve Company F, RCT 5, on Hill 342. This odd intervention, with a division giving orders to a platoon, indicates the importance that the division placed on Hill 342. It had been the scene of fierce fighting and had already changed hands twice. Company F needed relief badly. The marines were astonished at the order to send a single platoon to relieve a company, but Taplett, after objecting strongly, obeyed. Second Lt. John J. "Blackie" Cahill's platoon, Company G's reserve, got the job. It moved out and met Pvt. Ivan W. Russell, the guide sent by Company F, RCT 5. On the pitch-black night, the guide took a wrong turn, and the platoon had to backtrack. Then the platoon came under fire from the 2nd Battalion, 27th Infantry. As a result, it had only reached the foot of Hill 342 by 5 A.M. Cahill decided to wait for first light to start the climb.

At first light Cahill's platoon struggled up the steep, slippery slope:

> Stumbling, gasping for breath, soaked with perspiration, every Marine reached the point at which he barely managed to drag himself up the steep incline. There were choked curses as men gained a few feet, only to slip and fall back even farther.
>
> Water discipline collapsed as canteens were quickly emptied. Marines began to drop along the slope, some unconscious, others doubled over and retching.[34]

Contending with the intense heat and hit by automatic weapons fire about halfway up, the platoon didn't get to the crest of the hill until 8 A.M. Only thirty-seven of the original fifty-two men made it. Among the casualties were Cahill's platoon sergeant and platoon guide.[35] Cahill found Capt. Stanley Howarth and informed him that Company F was relieved. Howarth indicated that his soldiers

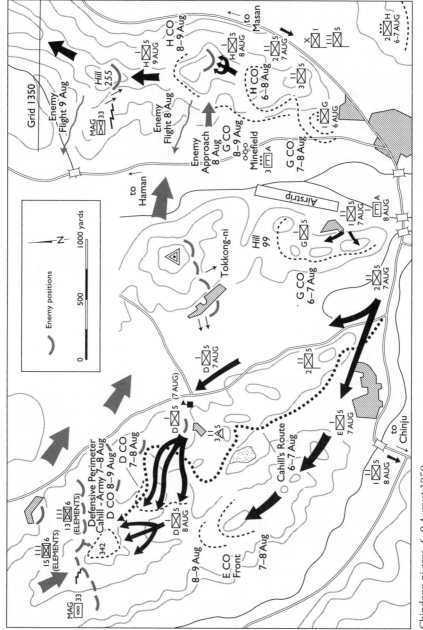

Chindong-ni area, 6–9 August 1950.

had pulled in tight for the night and had been unable to return to their daytime positions. Just then the increased activity on the hill drew heavy fire from the North Koreans, killing nine Americans, including Howarth.[36] Howarth's executive officer, Lt. Frank B. Brooks, took over the company. Cahill called for artillery fire and requested aerial resupply of water and ammunition. Eight of Cahill's marines were suffering from heat exhaustion. Each man had only one canteen and had quickly drained it as temperatures rose to 112 degrees Fahrenheit.[37] An air force R4D transport responded to Cahill's request but missed the perimeter with its airdrop. VMO 6 stepped in to fill the gap. By flying its OY-2s very low and slowly, it managed to deliver the ammunition and water within the perimeter. Unfortunately, every five-gallon can burst upon impact, so each man received only a few sips of water. Then, according to Cahill, "the water ran out. Some people went down with canteens and came back with rice-paddy water. As a result, we all ended up with worms. Hell, in that oven we were so thirsty we'd have drunk anything."[38] This would not be the last time a water shortage reduced marine combat-effectiveness. Despite the heat and the North Korean fire, Cahill's marines and the remnants of Company F clung to the hilltop.

Adding to the confusion, the NKPA 6th Division attack commenced at dawn but did not reach the crest until about 8 A.M. as Cahill's men struggled to the crest of Hill 342. The 6th Division was an elite unit formed in 1949 by redesignating the 166th Chinese Communist Forces Division. Composed of North Koreans who had fought with the communists in China, the 166th had returned to Korea as a well-trained, well-equipped, and combat-experienced unit.[39] The division not only hit Hill 342 hard but also moved around the U.S. frontline positions to seize Hill 255, which lay north of and dominated the main supply route. From here the North Koreans could clearly observe the schoolhouse designated as the dismount point for the 5th Marines.

As a result, the 5th Marines faced a fight from two directions while attempting a relief in place to be followed by a forward passage of lines. Any of these maneuvers would have been difficult for a green unit. Yet this was the situation that greeted the main body of the brigade as it moved up early on the morning of 7 August. PFC Doug Koch captured the fear, the confusion, and the steadying effect of the combat-experienced NCOs:

When we drove through Masan, it was dark and very eerie. I was twenty years old. Except for the officers and staff NCOs, most of us were kids — eighteen-, nineteen-, and twenty-year olds. No doubt we were gung ho. We thought we were pretty tough too. Underneath, though, we were pretty scared. Anyone who says he wasn't is lying. West of Masan, in the distance, I could hear artillery. Then, not more than 100 yards away, an enemy shell exploded! Right then and there we kids were ready to bail out of the truck and hit the ditch. Old Gunny Reeves stood up and growled, "Shit, set your ass down. By God, when you see me get nervous and excited, that's the time to really get nervous and excited." We sat back down. The gunnery sergeant had settled us kids right down.[40]

As the 2nd Battalion, 5th Marines, and 1st Battalion, 11th Marines, moved into position, they came under indirect fire. Despite the North Korean fire, the 1st Battalion quickly established its own firing positions. Unfortunately, the North Korean fire was both accurate and heavy, knocking out the number 3 gun in Battery B.[41] The 1st Battalion commenced counterbattery fire, which silenced the Korean guns, but the North Korean artillerymen had shown that they were well trained and effective—a lesson they would demonstrate repeatedly throughout the Pusan campaign.

The rugged Korean terrain demanded exceptional flexibility from the artillery. Lieutenant Colonel Wood noted,

> The Korean terrain certainly is not the best for artillery position areas. Mountains and rice paddies see to that. Ground which often looked favorable was found later to be inaccessible due to lack of solid ground approaches, principally because of ubiquitous rice paddies. . . . As the 5th Marines moved against NKPA troops, 1/11 was forced to displace often. Because of the terrain, the 105s had to be placed much closer to the infantry lines than is normally recommended. When 2,000–3,000 yards would have normally been the distance between the artillery and frontline infantry positions, often in the Pusan perimeter the distances were 500–1,500 yards.[42]

Wood said he placed his artillery "well knowing the risks involved of being within enemy mortar range most of the time, because we did not want the distance to be too great between us and the infantry, and thus give the North Koreans an opportunity to pass wide around the infantry flank and surround our position areas." Despite the proximity to the infantry, the artillery still had to deal with a number of infiltrators. The marine ethos that artillerymen had to protect their guns from ground assault was reinforced during the artillery battalion's first week in combat. "Due to the fluidity of the situation, the position, the smattering of enemy troops, and the fact that an enemy officer was killed within fifty (50) feet of the CP, local security was a doubly important element. All machine gun positions were doubled and the perimeter reinforced by every available man."[43]

With observed artillery fire falling on the command post and the enemy attacking from two directions, Lieutenant Colonel Murray, commanding officer of the 5th Marines, pitched in to sort out the situation. He sent Lieutenant Colonel Roise's 2nd Battalion to take Hill 255 to protect the supply road. Unfortunately, even as the battalion started to move out, Murray received orders from TF Kean to immediately relieve the 2nd Battalion, RCT 5, on Hill 342. TF Kean knew about the attack on Hill 342 but did not seem to know the Koreans were also on Hill 255. Murray changed his battalion's orders and sent it to relieve the 2nd Battalion, RCT 5. He then tasked Taplett's 3rd Battalion with clearing Hill 255.

Meanwhile, atop Hill 342, "Cahill and his remaining NCOs crawled around the perimeter to insert Marines in positions among those of the Army troops. This psychology was sound, for each infantryman, eyeing his Army or Marine neighbor, prided himself on setting a high standard of military conduct. From that time on, every man discharged his responsibility in a most exemplary manner."[44]

As the 2nd Battalion, 5th Marines, moved out to relieve the 2nd Battalion, RCT 5, TF Kean ordered the 1st Battalion, RCT 5, to attack to the west. For a still unknown reason, the battalion turned south at the first road intersection instead of continuing west. As a result, it was attacking along the axis assigned to the marines while no one was attacking along the axis assigned to the army.

With TF Kean attempting to control the action from twenty miles away and with two regiments mixed together and under attack, the task force was in chaos. Craig described the confusion that greeted him upon arrival at the front:

My first combat action in Korea was one of the most confusing in which I have participated. . . . I arrived at the front in my helicopter and Communist artillery and mortars dropped a concentration all around me. Colonel Joe Stewart my G-3 and I took off at a run and gained cover behind a low stone wall running out from the village but found that we were in the middle of an odorous pile of Korean fertilizer. We finally gained the road and with the artillery still falling climbed the steep hill to the place picked out for our CP. There we conferred with LtCol Bob Taplett who had already arrived with his 3rd Bn, 5th Marines. The 5th RCT, U.S. Army was holding the line in front of us and as we had no communications with them Stewart and I drove down there in a jeep and talked with the CO. We found him well protected in a deep hole and noticed that he was visibly concerned over the situation his outfit was in. He said he could not let his men get out and string wire to our CP. It was then that Stewart and I commandeered one of his wire jeeps and heading for our CP laid the wire ourselves—probably the first time a general officer has had to do such a thing. As the brigade arrived in the area for the jump off, they were whittled down by a number of separate engagements taking place all around us and as a result the drive made little progress for the first two days. To complicate and confuse a very critical situation the following series of events was taking place in the vicinity of Chindong-ni as my Brigade moved toward the line of departure: Sporadic mortar and artillery fire was falling on the area, the 5th RCT, US Army, which was to clear a road of enemy troops in order that the brigade could cross the line of departure was unable to accomplish its mission and I had to send a rifle battalion from the 5th Marines to assist them; An enemy attack on the ridge directly behind and above my Brigade CP developed and was only beaten off after two companies of the 3rd Bn, 5th Marines had been committed and fought all day and part of the night; the 24th RCT, U.S. Army, which was marching from the rear to take over defense of the Chindong-ni area at H-hour, was held up by enemy action just outside the town and did not arrive till August 9th; Shortly after H-Hour I received orders from General Kean the Task Force Commander to assume control of all troops in the Chindong-ni area until further orders and to assure clearance of the contested road fork. (This meant command of the equivalent of a division, reinforced.) The MSR from Masan to Chindong-ni was cut by enemy action at various times during August 8th. The 2nd Bn, 5th Marines, had to assist U.S. Army troops in holding Yaban-san, a hill mass on the brigade right flank which was under heavy attack by the enemy; The 1st Bn, 5th Marines was to relieve an Army battalion holding part of the line of departure, but on arrival after an all night march found the line abandoned; Marine casualties by the time the line of departure was crossed amounted to 30 killed and 132 wounded, plus numerous heat casualties.[45]

In short, immediately upon arriving in combat, Craig found one army battalion attacking in the wrong direction, one mixed army-marine company clinging to Hill 342, and one understrength marine company trying to reopen the road by retaking Hill 255. The main road, a dirt track one lane wide, was clogged—under fire and jammed with vehicles and personnel. The 27th Infantry was trying to execute its orders to move back; the marine brigade, the 24th Infantry, and RCT 5's support vehicles and artillery were trying to move forward. Craig's artillery, the 1st Battalion, 11th Marines, found itself with "one battery laid on an azimuth generally South, one battery on an azimuth generally West, and the third battery laid North."[46] And as soon as Craig arrived, General Kean, seeking to sort out the mess, gave Craig operational control of all troops in the Chindong-ni area, including the army's 24th Infantry and RCT 5.[47]

In an act typical of his leadership style, Craig moved to the critical point. He approved of Murray's initial dispositions and issued orders for renewing the attack the next morning. Craig tasked Col. Godwin Ordway, commanding officer of RCT 5, with moving his unit west on the correct road by the next morning, 8 August. Murray was to have the 3rd Battalion, 5th Marines, open the main supply route by clearing the enemy off Hill 255; the 2nd Battalion, 5th Marines, was to continue its relief of the 2nd Battalion, RCT 5, on Hill 342; and Lieutenant Colonel Newton's 1st Battalion, 5th Marines, was to commence an attack on the southern route as soon as RCT 5 was clear of the intersection.

Roise ordered his Company D (under Capt. John R. Finn) to relieve Cahill on Hill 342 while Company E (under 1st Lt. William E. Sweeney) took the western spur of the same ridge. This deployment would allow the 2nd Battalion to dominate the ridge and adjoining valleys. Finn's marines, worn from almost twenty-four hours without sleep, started the climb in the late afternoon. The heat, humidity, lack of water, enemy fire, and viciously steep slopes took their toll. After losing twelve men to heat exhaustion, losing one to a broken leg, and having five wounded in action, Finn stopped less than 1,000 meters from the top and dug in for the night. He sent a runner to advise Cahill and Brooks that his company would relieve them early on the morning of 8 August. They replied, advising him to move under cover of darkness, but Finn chose not to. VMO 6 attempted to drop water cans to Company D, but once again almost all of them broke. That night each marine and soldier on Hill 342 received only a few sips of water.

During this period marine Corsairs had continued the fight with a vengeance. VMF 214 averaged twenty-four close air support sorties per day from 7 to 9 August. They stopped only when the USS *Sicily* sailed to Japan for replenishment. Upon the *Sicily*'s return on 12 August, VMF 214 upped its average to thirty close air support sorties per day for the rest of August.[48] VMF 323, which had flown from the USS *Badoeng Strait* only on 5 August and had not had the advantage of a carrier training tour before deployment, started somewhat more slowly. It averaged only fourteen close air support sorties a day from 7 to 9 August. But when the *Sicily* went off station on 10 August, VMF 323 picked up the slack, averaging forty sorties a day until the *Sicily* returned. The *Badoeng Strait* then returned to Japan for two days for replenishing. Upon its return, VMF 323 averaged twenty-five close air support sorties a day while also providing combat air patrol for both carriers.[49] "Relieving each other on station, flights from one or both squadrons were on tap above the front lines to strike within a matter of minutes."[50] In fact, the two squadrons generated more sorties than the brigade could employ. The excess was passed to air force controllers for use throughout the perimeter. The F4U Corsairs were superb close air support aircraft. They had a long loiter time and large ordnance loads. In addition to four wing-mounted 20mm cannons, the Corsairs normally carried high-velocity aerial rockets, bombs, and napalm. Understanding napalm's powerful physical and psychological effect, the squadrons attempted to ensure that it constituted at least 50 percent of an aircraft's bombing load.[51]

In addition to the high sortie rates, the squadrons rapidly adapted. Within two days they had shifted from a standard four-plane division to five planes. Four would load ordnance while the fifth loaded primarily smoke rockets and acted as a TAC. This greatly reduced the load for the FACs on the ground. Now they only had to get the TAC's eyes on target; then he would control the individual aircraft or sections in the attack. This system was not only safer for the ground FAC but also more effective because aircraft-to-aircraft communication was more reliable than ground-to-air. VMO 6's OY-2 light observation aircraft and crews became another part of the close air support team. The OY-2 was the ideal platform for the mission because it could fly low and slowly enough to see the enemy despite the North Koreans' excellent camouflage discipline. When the terrain prevented a ground FAC from seeing the enemy, he talked to the observer in the OY-2, who would give him targeting information. The FAC could then relay the observer's instructions to the TAC to commence the air attack. Although awkward, this system was necessary for two reasons. First, the observers and FACs had the same maps as the ground commanders, but those maps were not available to the TACs.

Second, the OY-2 radios could not communicate with those in the Corsairs.[52] Yet the marine team worked out the procedures to optimize the role each member played in providing close, nearly continuous air support for the brigade.

Unfortunately, VMF(N) 513 was still under air force command. The air force did not think close air support after dark was possible. In keeping with its pre-war doctrine, the air force tasked the night fighters with attacking fixed targets, conducting night interdiction missions, or running armed reconnaissance over specified routes. Although they were not allowed to fly close air support missions, the VMF(N) 513 pilots became very proficient at knocking out North Korean artillery by bombing the muzzle flashes. The enemy forces soon learned to cease firing whenever they heard an airplane overhead. In response, the 8th Army controllers requested that marine aircraft remain overhead even when their ordnance was expended.[53]

During the first thirty days of operations, VMF(N) 513 managed to conduct only eighteen close air support missions, and then only by checking in with U.S. Army L-19 observation aircraft for immediate support missions.[54] It would not be until 4 September that VMF(N) 513 would fly its first night close air support mission for the brigade. It then provided eight sorties on 4 September and four on 6 September.[55] These proved to be the squadron's last sorties in support of the brigade, as the brigade then came out of action.

Dawn of 8 August found TF Kean attacking in four directions while three full regiments and supporting elements clogged the single-lane dirt supply road. Adding to the confusion, as the U.S. forces moved out at dawn, the North Koreans made a final attempt to overrun Hill 342. Cahill and Brooks's combined force of marines and soldiers held their ground as Company D, 2nd Battalion, 5th Marines, hearing the fight, immediately attacked to relieve them. The attack was successful, but at a high price. According to then 2nd Lt. Ralph E. Sullivan,

> The following morning the 1st and 2d Platoon Leaders were KIA [killed in action] and the 3d Platoon Leader had the back of his head shot off. The Company Commander was hit between the horns, and in his left shoulder by HMG [heavy machine-gun] fire. (In this case a shot in the head was the equivalent of a flesh wound.) The Company XO [executive officer] had gone down from heat exhaustion and did not recover until well after the sun went down. The MG [machine gun] Officer had been left behind to guide up the Army company that was to relieve us.
>
> All but two of the Staff NCOs were down, and one of those two had been painfully hit in the hand. Many if not most of the Sergeants and Corporals were dead or wounded. That's what happens in combat.
>
> So you could observe that D Company went from strong leadership to no leadership in a matter of a few minutes. Those officers and NCOs who had been responsible for D Company at 0800 that morning by 0815 had not been decimated, they'd been eliminated.[56]

With four officers in Company D killed or wounded and the executive officer down with heat exhaustion, M.Gy.Sgt. Harold Reeves took over the company and fought it until the executive officer recovered and took command in the evening. Reeves was assisted by 2nd Lt. Douglas Wirth, an artillery forward observer from the 1st Battalion, 11th Marines. As Reeves rallied the company, Wirth took charge of all available artillery and air assets to bring devastating fire down on the attacking North Koreans.

Finally relieved by Company D, Cahill and Brooks brought their commands off the hill. In its two days on the hill Cahill's platoon had lost 6 killed in action and 12 wounded in action out of the 52 he had led up the hill. Brooks had only 8 survivors of almost 120 who had gone up with him four days earlier.[57] Hill 342 had been an intense introduction to the NKPA for both regiments.

As the 2nd Battalion, 5th Marines, cleared Hill 342, the 3rd Battalion moved to drive the enemy off Hill 255. Thinking it was held by a minor force, Fegan, Company H, sent the 1st Platoon alone into the attack. It was driven back. As the platoon reorganized, Fegan ordered the 3rd Platoon to pass through and continue the attack. The platoon leader refused and was relieved. Fegan then took command of the platoon personally and led it in the attack. The platoon drove through the hilltop below 255 but had to blast the Koreans out of their fighting holes one at a time. Daylight ran out before it could move on to Hill 255 proper. The company dug in at the base of 255, registered its supporting arms, and prepared to continue its attack in the morning. Once again the heat had taken an enormous toll. Murray remembered that at one point he had "at least a third of my regiment lying at the side of the road with heat exhaustion."[58]

With the heat causing large numbers of casualties, rapid resupply of water became critical. To provide faster resupply, Company A, 1st Engineer Battalion, established water purification points as far forward as 200 yards from the front line—often moving ahead of the main body to have water points "in operation and filling canteens as the Main Body reached that point."[59] Getting water forward to the line companies would be a continual problem, so the marines sought expedient solutions. Sgt. Paul Santiago of H&S 1st Battalion, 5th Marines, remembered,

> Someone thought to take the top or bottom of a can of dry C-rations, bend it, then jam it into a wet crevice in the rocky side of a hill. The water seeping down the side would then flow over the bent metal, a FAUCET! We could then place a canteen cup under it to capture a couple of ounces of water per man. The water was as clean and cool as I remember it. It worked almost every time the column stopped.[60]

With the rear areas being secured, RCT 5 was free to attack to the west but once again was unable to clear the intersection. The 1st Battalion, 5th Marines, received orders to move out at 8 A.M. and follow the 2nd Battalion, RCT 5, until it cleared the intersection. At that point, the 1st Battalion would turn south to commence the marine attack on Sachon. Unfortunately, when the battalion arrived at the intersection, RCT 5 still blocked it. No sooner had RCT 5 started west than it ran into a roadblock and was stopped. The 1st Battalion was ordered to move back about a mile and wait. It was advised not to try to go around RCT 5 because the only path was a 1,200-meter-long rice paddy covered by "heavy machine-guns and small-arms fire and defended by many troops."[61] Then, at 9 P.M., the battalion was ordered to jump off at 11 P.M. to relieve the 1st Battalion, RCT 5, which was still astride the intersection. The marines were understandably apprehensive about this mission. "Earlier in the evening, a couple of Army men came staggering into the Battalion CP and said: 'My God! That rice paddy is murder to cross.'"[62]

The marines waited in the dark for their army guide. When the guide failed to appear, the battalion found local Koreans willing to guide it. Just as it moved out, an army company from the 1st Battalion, RCT 5, withdrew past them. The battalion had withdrawn before being relieved by the marines. As a result, the 1st Battalion, 5th Marines, faced the prospect of crossing 1,200 meters of contested ground to move into positions that might be occupied by North Koreans. Newton made the decision to move out. The battalion crossed in single file without contact and moved into position about 4 A.M. At 4:30 A.M. on 9 August, Murray ordered it to seize the high ground before it (Hill 308). Exhausted from two nights without sleep, almost out of water, and badly dehydrated, the battalion moved out at 6 A.M. After moving constantly to seize ever higher terrain, Company B was ordered to return to the road at 1 P.M. Murray had intelligence that there were no enemy ahead, and he wanted to seize as much ground as possible before the North Koreans recovered and moved into the void. Only two officers and thirty men from Company B made it back to the road. The rest were heat casualties, many out cold. All needed water and rest to continue. Once again the "chiggy bears," contracted Korean civilians, came through. Tough and acclimated, the Koreans delivered water to the marines on the hill and carried the fifteen worst casualties down to the battalion aid station.

With his rifle companies effectively out of action, Newton used his headquarters and weapons companies to continue the advance. As they moved out, Newton discovered that his Japanese map did not match the actual terrain. It showed only one road, whereas the ground showed two. He took the road his map indicated. About 300 meters on, the battalion ran into mines that had apparently fallen off an army truck. While waiting for the engineers to clear them, Newton was joined by Murray, who had a better map that showed both roads. Murray ordered Newton to reverse direction and take the southern road. Then, in another display of the flexibility that helicopters could provide, Murray took to the air to confirm that he had made the right decision. As Newton was reversing his personnel and vehicles, Craig showed up—mad as hell about the delay. Throughout the campaign, senior marine officers characteristically went well forward to identify and solve problems, even if it meant going all the way to the front. After having advanced

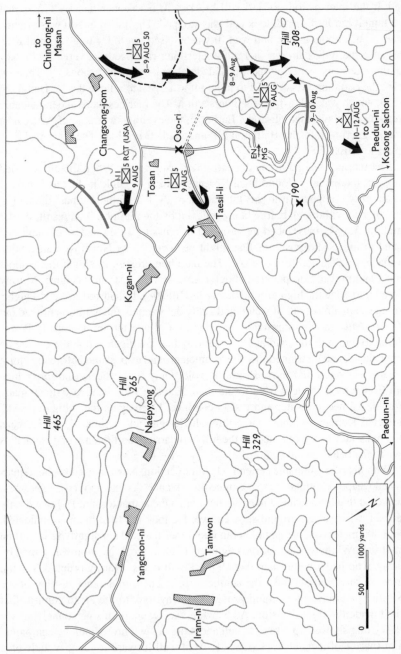

Sachon offensive, 8–10 August 1950.

less than two miles south on the correct road, the 1st Battalion, 5th Marines, was ordered to dig in for the night.

At 5 P.M. Kean decided the situation was properly sorted. RCT 5 was moving in the right direction and away from the brigade, so he took control of army forces in the area back from Craig. About the same time, the 2nd Battalion, 5th Marines, was relieved in the vicinity of Hill 342 and trucked forward to catch up with the 1st Battalion.

During this first day of forward movement, the brigade's air element introduced another innovation—the squirrel-cage advance. Under this system the ground FAC placed himself very near the point element of the ground force. Two F4Us flew "a squirrel cage around the point ready to pounce on the first machine gun that opened fire. Two more fighter aircraft would be under control of the F.A.C. and standing nearby to reinforce the fires of the circling aircraft. . . . The (airborne) forward air controller would be an OY-2 aircraft also circling the point and its flanks."[63]

While the 1st and 2nd Battalions moved out to seize Sachon, the 3rd Battalion, 5th Marines, spent 9 August clearing the enemy off Hill 255 to remove the threat to the supply road. Taplett started his attack with well-planned heavy artillery fire. He followed the artillery preparation with Corsairs delivering napalm, rockets, and cannon fire. When his riflemen climbed the last few meters to the crest, they found almost no opposition. Later that day, the 3rd Battalion linked up with the 2nd Battalion, 24th Infantry, which had been attacking from the other end of the long ridge leading to Hill 255. The last fight of the melee around Chindong-ni was over. It had cost the 3rd Battalion, 5th Marines, sixteen killed and thirty-six wounded in action. Company H suffered most heavily, losing 25 percent of its strength.[64] The 3rd Battalion also suffered thirty-three heat casualties.[65] But, having defeated the NKPA 6th Division's offensive and driven it back, the marines could now focus on attacking in a single direction. Taplett turned the area over to the 24th Infantry and started his battalion up the road to catch up with the rest of the 5th Marines.

That night Murray ordered the 2nd Battalion to pass through the 1st Battalion and continue the attack. The 2nd Battalion moved out at 1:15 A.M. on 10 August. This day set the pattern for the rest of the attack to Sachon. The restricted terrain forced the regiment to move in a column of battalions, leapfrogging a fresh battalion through when the lead battalion was exhausted. The 2nd Battalion moved quickly until about 5 A.M., when a bridge collapsed under the lead tank. The second tank threw a track trying to bypass the first, and the whole column had to wait while engineers and local labor built a bypass. Even with the delay, the battalion cleared Paedun-ni by 8 A.M. Murray, aggressive as always, decided to shuttle his battalions forward to Kosong by truck. Unfortunately, the clogged supply road prevented the trucks from moving forward quickly. Once again, as Murray and his battalion commander were trying to sort out the problems, Craig showed up to see what the delay was. Finally sorted out, a small convoy of ten

Jeeps and five trucks, with most of Capt. Andrew Zimmer's Company D aboard and led by the brigade reconnaissance platoon (under Capt. Kenneth Houghton), got rolling west.

At 3 P.M. this lead element entered Taedabok Pass and was engaged by machine guns and antitank guns. Houghton extracted his marines from the ambush and pulled back to meet Company D. Zimmer maneuvered his two platoons against the enemy positions. Having lost eleven men and expended all his 60mm mortar ammunition in driving back the NKPA forces, he elected to wait for the battalion to catch up before continuing. At 4:30 P.M. the battalion closed up and the lead tanks, joined by marine air, finished off the enemy roadblock.

By this time Taplett's battalion had arrived by truck. Murray ordered it to pass through the 2nd Battalion and continue the attack. Taplett gave the task to Bohn's Company G, and it moved out by 5 P.M. Climbing the 300-meter-high hill to the right of the road, Bohn's marines drove off the enemy. They continued to advance, only to be held up by two machine guns on a hill across the road. Taplett sent Company H up the ridge to the left of the road to clean out the machine guns. It did so just before dark. At about the same time the regiment received orders from the brigade to dig in for the night. Company G was assigned to kick off the attack the next morning, 11 August, at 6 A.M.

As the infantry battalions leapfrogged rapidly forward, the 1st Battalion, 11th Marines, struggled to stay in position to provide artillery support. The single road combined with the extremely restrictive terrain presented major challenges to the artillerymen:

> The Korean terrain is anything but ideal for artillery position areas. This battalion experienced considerable difficulty in locating areas containing sufficient gun position space, motor park space, etc. with any enfilade or defilade protection. Temporary roads often had to be cut by our dozers and the guns were dug in as well as the FDC, CP, and Aid Station. Dry river beds or semisolid bean patches invariably constituted the chosen position. For security reasons, villages were avoided.[66]

Just before daybreak on the 11th, the Koreans attacked. Apparently drawn to the sound of Company G's radio, they hit the command post with grenades and machine-gun and rifle fire but were quickly driven off. With the enemy routed, Bohn, who was having his wounds tended, realized he was late crossing the line of departure for the day's attack. As he hurried to get his company reorganized and moving, he saw Murray coming up to give him hell for being late. Murray was adamant that his units cross the line of departure on time. Fortunately, Taplett had also arrived and intervened. Despite the Korean attack, Bohn had his company moving by 8:30. Bohn recalled, "I felt that I was the most powerful man in the Marine Corps that day. . . . I had everything in support—tanks, artillery—air constantly overhead and I had a FAC . . . with me. We had the main body on the

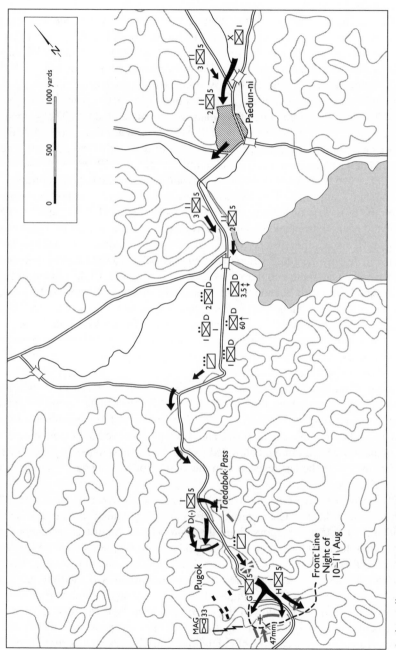

Sachon offensive, 10 August 1950.

road and had flank patrols on the high ground. People on the flanks were running to keep up so I relieved them frequently."[67]

The marines moved so fast that they surprised a NKPA machine-gun team and wiped it out before it could respond. To further speed the movement of the battalion, Taplett used Corsairs to cover his flanks "just like we did, last April, during the amphibious landing exercise at Camp Pendleton."[68] The column reached Kosong before 10 A.M. Company G moved through the town and commenced an attack on Hill 88 to the southwest. Using air and artillery, Company G engaged what it believed to be hundreds of Koreans as it assaulted the hill. The Koreans fled, and the marines had the hill by 1:30 P.M. Once again Craig arrived at the head of the column. His helicopter had landed to the rear of the advance, and Craig had met M.Sgt. Robert L. Collier, a military police (MP) NCO who served as his driver and bodyguard. They drove forward to the 3rd Battalion's command post and then went forward on foot to observe a flank platoon supporting an attack on the hills west of Kosong. When the attack concluded, Craig moved to a schoolyard near the front and was fired at by an antitank gun in a house just down the street. He and Collier observed as a marine squad employed a 3.5-inch rocket launcher to destroy the gun.[69] Craig then returned to the 3rd Battalion's command post, where he and Taplett conferred while under sniper fire. Craig wanted to get moving quickly toward Sachon. Taplett recalled Company G from the hill and, while it was coming back down, ordered Fegan's Company H to take the lead and move out. Once again Taplett used marine air to cover his flanks. He later said, "I always figured it [marine air] was my best weapon in Korea, particularly because we weren't responsible for lugging its armament resupply through the rice paddies and primitive treacherous roads."[70]

While Company H was assembling, a Jeep ambulance raced in to pick up some Company G casualties. On its way out, the driver turned the wrong way and passed through Company H, headed toward Sachon. His unfortunate mistake triggered an NKPA antitank-gun ambush. The Koreans destroyed the Jeep but didn't hit Company H. Fegan immediately led two tanks forward to destroy the North Korean guns. With the last resistance in the vicinity of Kosong destroyed, he led his company west.

By uncovering Kosong, the brigade gained access to a side road that led south to a small harbor. Characteristic of its superb planning, the brigade staff had identified potential harbors along the route. On 11 August Detachment 1st Service Battalion had loaded fuel, rations, and general supplies aboard an LST to establish a floating dump of Class I (food), II (clothing, individual equipment), and Class III (fuel). As a result, the LST was ready to enter the harbor as soon as the marines seized it. On 12 August the LST commenced unloading at Tangdong-ni.[71] This expedient allowed the marines to keep their frontline units supplied despite the single narrow, congested road. This was possible only because the supply marines were capable of defending themselves as well as running each supply point. The training invested in every marine being a rifleman continued to pay off handsomely. The brigade special action report highlighted this approach: "Army policy generally places Supply Points 6–12 miles to the rear. We do not have transportation to accomplish this length of haul. Our supply points were up close, from 3–5 miles from front lines. We concentrated service and supply elements and provided all around security by Shore Party."[72] Although no combat units were dedicated to protect them, no marine rear units—command posts, artillery pieces, or supply points—were ever overrun by the numerous North Korean infiltrators.

Further exploiting its naval advantage, the brigade outfitted a second LST as a floating aid station to allow for rapid evacuation of lightly wounded personnel. With the badly wounded flown by helicopter directly to the field hospitals and lightly wounded trucked or flown to the nearby LST, the brigade was relieved of the problem of moving its casualties.

About 2 P.M., as the 3rd Battalion, 5th Marines, continued moving, the 1st Battalion, 11th Marines, fired a base-point registration on a road intersection west of Kosong. By chance it hit the heavily camouflaged 83rd Motorcycle Regiment. Thinking it was observed and about to be subjected to heavy artillery fire, the regiment broke cover and sped down the road toward Sachon. For the 83rd, the disaster was just starting. Maj. Arnold Lund, VMF 323, was overhead as TAC for a division of Corsairs. He had a perfect target—almost 100 vehicles in a column on a narrow road. He sent his Corsairs after them. When the first division of aircraft had expended its ordnance, a second came on station and continued the attack. As the marine Corsairs pulled off target, U.S. Air Force F-51s arrived to join the attack. The combined attack left forty vehicles burning. Although getting hammered, the North Koreans fought back. They damaged two Corsairs badly enough to force them to land. The first, piloted by 2nd Lt. Doyle Cole, ditched in the bay. Fortunately for Cole, at this time Craig was returning to his headquarters by helicopter and diverted the aircraft to pick up the pilot almost immediately after Cole had climbed into his life raft. As Cole was pulled into the helicopter by "an elderly sergeant," he slapped him on the shoulder and said, "Thanks for the lift, buddy."[73] He then realized that the winch operator was General Craig. Unfortunately, the second pilot, Capt. Vivian Moses, who had survived a shoot-down the day before, was killed.

Referred to as the "Kosong turkey shoot," this event highlights how closely marine air was integrated with the ground forces. The marines were fighting a truly three-dimensional battle. Craig noted, "During the advance on Sachon, we used the helicopters to the limit—for reconnaissance of our flanks and to the front. In addition to that, we had our O-1 [sic] planes, which had reconnaissance personnel in them"[74] This combined with the squadron's flying squirrel cage meant marine ground forces effectively moved in a bubble covered by marine air.

The marines of the 3rd Battalion were particularly appreciative of the turkey shoot. Not only did it destroy a major enemy force on their route but, as the first infantry battalion on the scene, they had the opportunity to liberate twelve

Russian Jeeps (which had U.S. lend-lease engines and transmissions) and four motorcycles with sidecars.[75] These were added to the battalion's motor pool on the fly.

Company H continued past the wreckage of the 83rd Motorcycle Regiment, maintaining a rapid pace until about 6 P.M., when a machine gun engaged the point. Although three marines were wounded, the company quickly destroyed the gun position. Taplett ordered the battalion into night defensive positions to ensure that it was set before dark. The brigade had done well. Its lead elements were less than a day's march from Sachon. But the North Koreans still had fight in them:

> At first light, 1/5 passed through 3/5 to continue the attack. Reinforced by a platoon of M26 tanks, 1/5 was led by a jeep-mounted reconnaissance detachment. The reconnaissance element would stay about a mile ahead of the battalion while observation and helicopter aircraft closely patrolled the battalion's flanks and Corsairs circled overhead. Crossing the line of departure at 0630, the battalion moved so rapidly that by 1300 it entered the Changallon[76] Valley, less than four miles from Sachon. The valley was a natural cul-de-sac, with high ground to the front and both flanks. The reconnaissance element saw two enemy taking cover in the village and opened fire. Once again, the marines had detected a well-laid North Korean ambush.
>
> The enemy had cunningly picked their terrain for this ambush. The low ground to either side of the road was flooded rice paddies with the high ground 300–500 yards to each flank. Our tanks and vehicles were restricted to the road and there was no cover or concealment for the foot troops. The enemy had made full use of camouflage and had well-concealed positions from which they could place interlocking bands of fire on the road.[77]

The North Koreans poured fire in from the front and both flanks but once again engaged only the point of the column. In response, Capt. John Tobin sent his 1st Platoon with two tanks to reinforce Houghton. He ordered his 2nd Platoon to close up and sent word to his executive officer to request an air strike on the high ground to the right of the road and then to have the 3rd Platoon assault it. Tobin himself moved forward to coordinate with Houghton in neutralizing the threat from the left. At the first burst of enemy fire, everyone had scrambled into the flooded rice paddies for cover. Unfortunately, the water was two feet deep and immediately took a toll on the company's radios. Soon all platoon radios were out of commission, and the company command group had only two that worked. Compounding the problem, the company had to fight back initially with only its own weapons and the tanks. The artillery was moving into position, and the regimental mortars were facing that perpetual problem of Korea: finding enough flat, dry ground to set up.

Still, by the time the 3rd Platoon was ready to move out, all supporting arms were firing. Supporting Tobin's actions, Newton ordered Capt. John R. Stevens's Company A to use two squads to clear the high ground to the left of the road

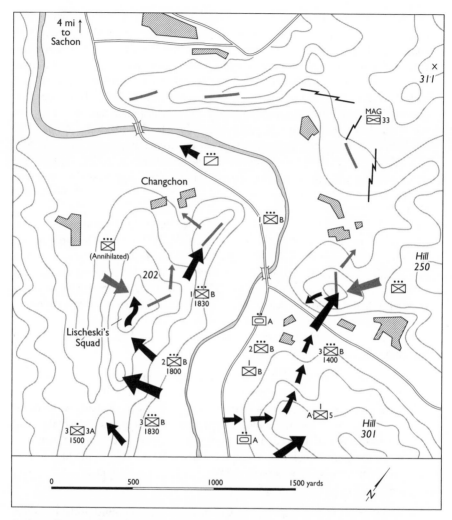

Sachon offensive, Changallon Valley Ambush, August 1950.

and to check the high ground south of where the 3rd Platoon, Company B, was assaulting.

Everything was working. Marine air was on target within five to seven minutes of being requested.[78] The air strike silenced the Korean machine guns. The 3rd Platoon assaulted immediately behind the air strike. Then, as the 3rd Platoon cleared the crest, about 100 North Koreans emerged from the reverse slope and hit it hard. The sharp surprise, the ferocity of the attack, and the fact that the platoon had not begun to organize its defense meant that it was driven halfway back down the hill by the Koreans' initial rush.

Newton immediately ordered a twenty-minute artillery and mortar preparation on the hill, to be followed by an air strike. He then ordered Company A to pass through the 3rd Platoon, Company B, and take the hill. By 5 P.M. Company A had destroyed the enemy on the fingers leading from Hills 301 and 250 on the right side of the road. However, the battalion column was still taking heavy fire from Hill 202 to the left of the road. Newton ordered Company B to clear that ground. Tobin rapidly coordinated artillery and mortar preparation and then sent the 1st and 2nd Platoons across the rice paddy. The 3rd Platoon, Company B, reoriented itself to make up the left flank of the company's attack. By 6:30 P.M. Company B had cleared the objectives. As the 2nd Platoon moved over the crest of its objective, it saw an enemy platoon withdrawing. Sgt. Frank J. Lischeski maneuvered his squad quickly into an ambush position and killed all thirty-nine Koreans.[79]

The battalion was then ordered to dig in for the night. Unfortunately, Company B had to cover two-thirds of a mile of ground with three understrength rifle platoons. The company registered night fires, established platoon positions, and put listening posts in the major gap, but there was a gap between the 1st and 2nd Platoons. Though it was as well prepared as possible, the company still had only two radios that worked and was also short of communications wire. It wasn't until midnight that the company finished consolidating its position—digging in, moving casualties back across the rice paddies, running wire lines, and redistributing ammunition. The marines were exhausted. They

> had covered a distance of about 29 miles, not counting all the hills we had gone up and down. The tenseness of the fire fight we had been in all afternoon sapped the men of a lot of their energy. We hadn't had any water or rations since noon and we couldn't expect any that night, as the battalion did not have any natives to carry supplies to us. . . . To be certain we would be ready for them if they did attack, we ordered 50 per cent of the men to stay awake at all times. That was a mistake. . . . The men were just too tired to try and stay awake half the night.[80]

At about 5 A.M. the 2nd Platoon, Company B, reported noise to its front and requested illumination. The company tried to alert its other platoons and the battalion, but they did not respond. Company B fired a 60mm illumination round and discovered a large enemy force making for the gap between the 1st and 2nd Platoons. As those platoons opened fire, a runner arrived from the 3rd Platoon reporting that its position had been overrun and the platoon had fallen back 100 yards. Tobin sent the runner back with orders to the 3rd Platoon to hold what it had. He would put supporting arms fire on its old position. First Lt. Fenton, the company executive officer, raised Company A on the radio. It relayed Company B's requests for fire support to the battalion. Within minutes artillery and mortars were pouring fire onto the old 3rd Platoon position. Fenton continually adjusted

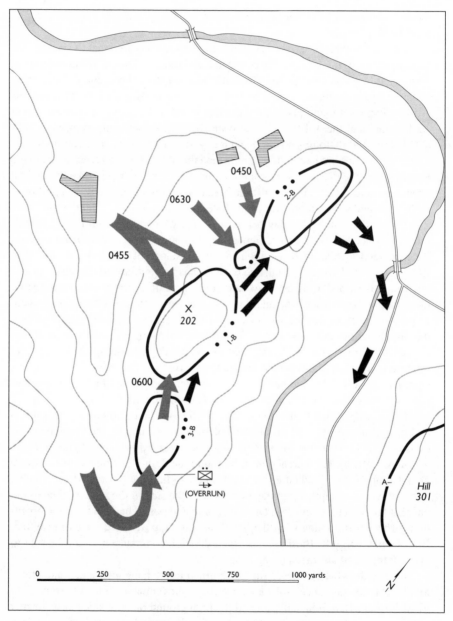

0450

2-B

0630

0455

×
202

1-B

0600

3-B

⊠
↳
(OVERRUN)

A–

Hill
301

0   250   500   750   1000 yards

N

Enemy counterattack, Changallon Valley, night of 12–13 August 1950.

the fall of the rounds closer until they were falling within 100 yards of the platoon's new position.

Just as that threat was dealt with, the 2nd Platoon reported that the enemy had succeeded in driving into the gap between it and the 1st Platoon. Tobin ordered all platoons to withdraw to the 2nd Platoon's position, hold there, and counterattack at dawn. Again the marines showed a mastery of supporting arms by adjusting the artillery impacts to land just behind the rear guard as headquarters, weapons, the 1st Platoon, and the 3rd Platoon fell back. By 6 A.M. the company was consolidated at the 2nd Platoon's position and ready to counterattack. The continuing artillery and mortar fire had greatly diminished the fire they were receiving from the Koreans, and the marines were confident that they could quickly take the ground back. Just before they jumped off, the battalion ordered Company B to pull back to the road and get on trucks for immediate movement back to Chindong-ni.

Events that started the day before had finally caught up with the 1st Battalion. About noon on 12 August, General Craig had received orders from General Kean to send a reinforced battalion to the assistance of the 24th Infantry. The RCT 5 attack had bogged down, and the Koreans had outflanked the regiment and overrun at least one army artillery battalion. The 24th Infantry could not restore the situation. Kean tasked the marines with recovering the guns. Craig once again displayed the flexibility of the air-ground team. He took his helicopter to find the 3rd Battalion and issue orders for the new mission. En route he found two elements of his trucks. He landed and instructed them to dump their loads and proceed to a pickup point for the 3rd Battalion. He then found the 3rd Battalion's command post, briefed the battalion commander, and offered him the helicopter to conduct his leader's reconnaissance and coordinate with the 25th Division.

Craig simply told Taplett to meet the 25th Division liaison officer at a specified bridge and resolve the problem. Taplett, accompanied by the brigade operations officer, Lt. Col. Joe Stewart, flew to the specified bridge but couldn't find the liaison officer. He searched until he found the 25th Division Reconnaissance Tank Company and hitched a ride south to try to find the liaison officer. Unable to find anyone, he tapped into the wire lines by the side of the road until he found one that let him talk to the 25th Division command post. The 25th Division operations officer had no idea what the battalion was supposed to do. He did say that Brig. Gen. George B. Barth, the assistant division commander, would be sent to take command of all forces in the area.

Free to do what he chose, Taplett returned to the helicopter and conducted a low-level reconnaissance of the area. He found the remnants of the overrun 555th Field Artillery Battalion and searched the high ground on both sides of its former positions, now known as Bloody Gulch, for the enemy. He had been told the Koreans were present in strength. Unable to find any sign of them, he flew back to show his battalion the route to the dismount point. He then flew ahead, landed, and found the commanding officer of the 555th Field Artillery Battalion. The commander guessed the enemy "was in the ridges and hills, immediately northwest

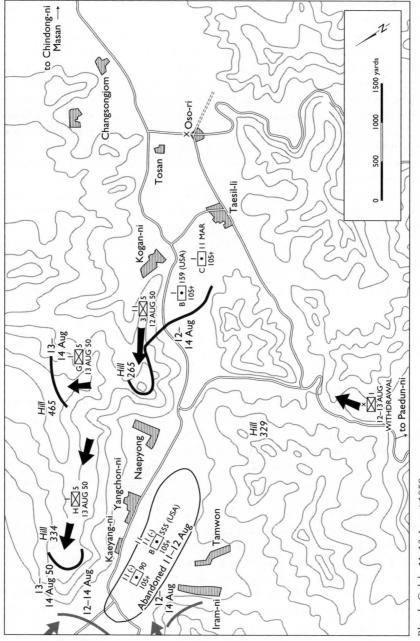

Bloody Gulch, 11–13 August 1950.

and possibly southwest"[81] of the high ground that was his position. With no guidance from 25th Division, Taplett decided to send Company H to clear the high ground. Taplett met Company H as the troops were dismounting from the trucks and issued his orders; the company moved out. As was Taplett's norm, he fired a fifteen-minute artillery preparation and then sent Corsairs to make napalm runs on the ridge. Taplett had also coordinated with Lt. Col. John H. Daly of the 555th Field Artillery Battalion to provide fire from the 155mm battery that had not been overrun. Company H took the objective with no casualties but found signs that a large Korean force had departed hastily. About 7 P.M. General Barth showed up and asked Taplett when he would attack. Taplett must have enjoyed informing him that the 3rd Battalion had already attacked and taken the objective. The battalion dug in for the night and prepared to continue the attack the next morning to recover the lost artillery pieces.

As the 3rd Battalion moved to restore the situation around the 555th, Craig continued forward to his lead elements. He was in a tough position. He had only two understrength infantry battalions supported by eight howitzers and still had to seize Sachon. Right then one of his forward battalions was engaged in a tough fight, and his reserve was rapidly moving over twenty miles in the wrong direction. He stayed with the lead element until the day's fight was over and units were digging in. Then he was again summoned to the 25th Division headquarters. Arriving at 6:30 P.M., he was told that the Koreans had broken the line on the Naktong River and was ordered to withdraw his brigade to its original assembly area. He returned to his command post at Kosong and issued the orders by 7:45 P.M. Clearly the exceptional speed of marine actions was possible only because of Craig's use of his helicopter and excellent staff work.

The brigade settled in for the night, with one battalion preparing to attack near Chindong-ni and two battalions twenty-nine miles down the road toward Sachon with orders to break contact and conduct a tactical withdrawal at first light. Both missions had to be accomplished while in contact with the aggressive, highly professional but now badly shattered NKPA 6th Division.

These were the events that led to the sudden orders for Company B to pull back at dawn on 13 August. Tobin objected violently. He knew he could quickly clear the enemy from the 3rd Platoon's old position. The bodies of nine of his marines were there. It was an article of faith that marines never left anyone behind. They knew all nine were dead, but that didn't change the basic ethos of bringing them back. Newton replied that Company B had to withdraw now. There was a crisis in the rear. The marines did not know it at the time, but the North Koreans had moved behind the U.S. Army units to their right rear. Army commanders were very concerned that the marines were miles ahead with an exposed flank and might be cut off by the continuing attacks against the army forces well behind the marine advance.

To extract his company, Tobin ordered Fenton, his executive officer, to use the 3rd Platoon and the mortar section to evacuate the wounded and dead while the 1st and 2nd Platoons fought as rear guards. Fenton captured the difficulty of withdrawal in contact:

> Getting the wounded off that hill and moving through those rice paddies was a pitiful sight. Everyone who could walk had to carry the more seriously wounded and dead back. Seeing a wounded Marine, badly hit but walking, trying to carry another wounded man who couldn't walk was like watching the blind leading the blind across New York's 5th Avenue during the rush hour. All told we had suffered 19 wounded and 20 killed during the morning's fight. Few words were spoken. The men didn't have to talk to express their sentiments—you could read the bitterness in their faces and eyes. They had gone 29 miles in four days and were only three and a half miles from Sachon, the Brigade's objective. Twenty-nine miles had been paid for with much blood, sweat, and tears. Now they were turning around and handing it back to a badly beaten enemy on a silver platter. As far as they were concerned, it was a hell of a war.[82]

The brigade used every asset to quickly move back to its original assembly areas at Miryang, east of Chindong-ni. Company B passed through Company A's position and mounted trucks for the move back. To make room for the company, all the supplies had to be removed. The marines had to watch as food, clothing, PX supplies, and personal equipment were crushed or burned to keep them from the Koreans. It particularly hurt to see the food that would have been their first hot meal since arriving in Korea destroyed. As Company B drove away, Company A broke contact and marched to Tang-dong-ni, the small port south of Kosong. There the support units had reloaded the LST and were prepared to embark along with Company A for transportation rearward. The flexibility of the navy/marine team not only allowed them to move supplies well forward but also allowed them to recover most of the supplies rather than destroying them.[83]

A tank platoon reinforced by a combat engineer platoon served as the rear guard for the rest of the brigade on its march back to Chindong-ni. The engineers destroyed bridges and culverts, cratered the road, and laid antitank mines as they withdrew. They also destroyed all the equipment the North Koreans had abandoned during their retreat—43 motorcycles, 24 trucks, 8 antitank rifles, and 10 tons of ammunition.[84] VMO 6 and the fighter squadrons maintained their constant presence overhead, and the 6th Division did not try to interfere with the withdrawal.

Although the 1st and 2nd Battalions, 5th Marines, were pulling back from Kosong on the morning of 13 August the 3rd Battalion kicked off its attack along the ridgeline as planned. By 10 A.M. it had cleared the ridge against minimal resistance. The marines again found many signs of recent activity and concluded that the enemy had pulled out ahead of the marine attack. According to one prisoner interrogation report, an NKPA major stated, "Panic sweeps my men when they see the Marines with the yellow leggings coming at them."[85] The prisoner was referring to the fact that the marines still had low quarter shoes and therefore had to wear yellowish canvas leggings in the field. The brigade had earned the marines yet another nickname—"yellow legs."

With the regiment withdrawing, Murray came back to check on the 3rd Battalion. When he arrived, he and Taplett discussed options for continuing the attack to relieve RCT 5. The commanding general, 25th Division, canceled those plans and ordered Taplett's battalion to remain in place on the ridge. On 14 August the 2nd Battalion, RCT 5, came forward to relieve the 3rd Battalion but refused to come all the way forward. It dug in over a mile behind the 3rd Battalion's position. Unable to convince the 2nd Battalion to move up, Taplett informed the 5th Marines of 2nd Battalion's refusal and then got his battalion moving to join the rest of the brigade. It arrived at Miryang near midnight.

While the combat organizations fought a tough, tenacious enemy in the form of the NKPA 6th Division, the logistics and support personnel fought the Korean terrain. In particular, the roads took a toll. After the brigade's first road march from Pusan to Chung-wan, the Motor Transport Company had to repair 97 vehicles and replace 146 tires damaged by the terrible roads. This would set the pattern for the brigade's entire time in the perimeter. In a single day's motor march on 15 August, the communications platoon noted that a 6x6 broke an axle, one trailer lost a wheel, and one radio vehicle burned out a motor. The jarring was so bad that every radio in a communications vehicle was rendered inoperative. The platoon commander recommended that all further movements for communication vehicles be done by rail. His recommendation was adopted.[86] The Motor Transport Company also recorded extensive damage. Given the intense heat, there was particular concern that of 38 water trailers, 6 had to be abandoned on the side of the road, too broken to tow, and 19 others were damaged beyond repair.[87] Despite the extensive damage caused by the incredibly tough terrain, the support units never let the combat organizations down.

THE BEAN PATCH

Arriving by train and truck, the brigade reassembled its ground elements and established a bivouac in a bean field next to a fast flowing river. The troops immediately nicknamed the site "the Bean Patch." The marines took their first baths and received their first hot meals since arriving in Korea two weeks earlier. As always, the marines were alert to acquire more equipment. On the first day in the Bean Patch, 2nd Lieutenant Muetzel's platoon had the opportunity to use a field shower unit. As they finished up and returned to their gear, he asked the NCO he'd left to guard his platoon's gear who owned the gear next to theirs. The NCO noted it belonged to the army unit using the shower. Muetzel recalled, "With that I selected an M1919AG light machine gun, threw it on the back of the truck, mounted up, and ordered the truck to move out. The gun proved to have some minor deficiencies, but who was I to question a gift."[88]

The brigade spent all day on 15 August at Miryang, cleaning gear and rebuilding the rifle companies. Since no marine replacements had arrived in Korea, the brigade filled its badly depleted rifle companies with men from the rear—staff positions, logistics elements, and even the combat support elements such as artillery and tanks. Corp. Carl E. Lawendowski, a school-trained draftsman, found himself suddenly moved from the 1st Battalion's S-3 shop to assistant BAR man in the 3rd Platoon, Company B. The ethos that every marine is a rifleman was to be tested in the weeks ahead.

During its first week of combat, the brigade had lost a total of 66 killed, 240 wounded, and 9 missing in action (those the 1st Battalion had been ordered to leave behind). Official estimates placed enemy losses against the brigade at 1,900 killed and wounded.[89] The NKPA 6th Division and 83rd Motorcycle Regiment, which had not had a major setback before meeting the marines, had been driven back twenty-six miles in four days and, according to army reports, rendered combat-ineffective. The brigade had come together as a first-rate combined arms team ready to face the even more severe test awaiting it. Even as the marines rested and reorganized at Miryang, the situation at the Naktong continued to deteriorate.

10

The First Battle of the Naktong Bulge

From 4 to 14 August, as the brigade attacked toward Sachon, the 8th U.S. Army was desperately fighting to hold the perimeter as a whole, and particularly the Naktong Bulge. Having committed its fresh reserves against the NKPA 6th Division, the most critical threat to the perimeter, the 8th Army had only the exhausted 24th U.S. Infantry Division to try to hold the Naktong River bulge. As early as 3 August NKPA 4th Division patrols had crossed the Naktong north of Ch'angnyong. Once established on the east bank, the division strove to break through 8th Army lines. To hold off the 4th Division's attacks, the 8th Army had committed the badly battered 24th Infantry Division (19th, 21st, and 34th Infantry Regiments), then reinforced it with parts of the 27th Infantry Regiment, the newly arrived 9th Infantry Regiment, and all available artillery. For eleven days the army regiments held, answering each North Korean attack with a counterattack. Despite heroic efforts on the part of many of the army units, they had been unable to drive the 4th Division back across the river. The Korean penetration threatened to cut the bulk of the 8th Army off from the port of Pusan.

Lieutenant General Walker had brilliantly juggled his small reserves to deal with one crisis after another. Under intense pressure, the perimeter still held. But the penetration by the 4th Division genuinely threatened to destroy it. On 15 August Lieutenant General Walker told Brig. Gen. John H. Church, commander of the 24th Infantry Division (Church had taken over the division after William F. Dean was captured), "I am going to give you the Marine Brigade. I want this situation cleaned up—and quick."[1]

The situation was desperate, and many believed it was only a matter of time before U.S. forces were driven from the peninsula. A British military observer who watched the marines move up noted in a dispatch to Tokyo, "I realize my expression of hope is unsound but these Marines have a swagger confidence and hardness that must have been in Stonewall Jackson's army of the Shenandoah.

They remind me of the Coldstreams at Dunkerque. Upon this thin line of reasoning, I cling to the hope of victory."[2]

Church immediately convened a conference to outline his plan to his commanders. The attack would commence at 8 A.M. on 17 August with the marine brigade as the main effort, supported by the 9th Infantry Regiment on its immediate right and the 19th Infantry north of the 9th.

Upon returning from Church's conference, Craig called his commanders together for a quick planning session. The MAG had been alerted, and the deputy group commander, Lt. Col. Norman Anderson, flew ashore to join the orders group.[3] The brigade worked quickly, and the 5th Marines received the order by 10:30 A.M. on 16 August. Lieutenant Colonel Murray, commanding officer of the 5th Marines, went forward to conduct a personal reconnaissance and coordinate with the 9th Infantry while the brigade elements moved from the bivouac at Miryang to assembly in areas behind the 24th Division front lines. Although Craig had expressed full confidence in the 9th Infantry, Murray's closer coordination determined that it had suffered heavy casualties in its defense of the bulge. Further, the ground was such that a simultaneous attack by the 5th Marines and the 9th Infantry would have both regiments crossing the low ground at the same time. Murray recommended that the 9th Infantry support the 5th Marines by fire while the marines took Obong-ni Ridge. Then the marines could return the favor as the 9th Infantry took Finger Ridge. Brig. Gen. Church approved this change to the plan.

With external support established, Murray ordered the battalions forward by truck. With a promise of 144 trucks from the 8th Army, he felt he could get his battalions in position with plenty of time to allow the leaders to conduct reconnaissance and integrate supporting arms into the attack. Unfortunately, the brigade was once again haunted by the shortage of motor transport. Although the 8th Army had promised 144 trucks, only 43 showed up—and they were three hours late.[4] Ever conscious of the power of supporting arms, Murray assigned priority of movement to the 1st Battalion, 11th Marines, to ensure that his artillery was in place to support the attack. However, because of bad roads and a series of delays (such as the requirement to repair 87 tires),[5] the battalion did not establish firing positions until 10 P.M. According to its special action report, the battalion immediately fired registration fires. This is an essential step to ensure that the first volleys of fire are on target—particularly when operating with poor-quality maps.

With the trucks dedicated to artillery, the infantry battalions began moving on foot. The movement covered more than fifteen miles and continued throughout the night of the 16th. The men in the assault battalion, the 2nd Battalion, 5th Marines, marched until 1:30 A.M. to reach the assembly areas and prepare for a 8 A.M. attack. The 3rd Battalion was also late arriving and could not find the 34th Infantry to conduct the ordered relief. Part of the confusion came from the fact that the army and marine units called two different hill masses Cloverleaf Hill, although the hills were several hundred meters apart. For its part, the 34th Infantry moved out without relief but could not get into position in time to participate in the attack.

Having failed to find the 34th Infantry, the 5th Marines simply picked a point and prepared to attack. The marines of Company A, 1st Tank Battalion, required engineer support to build a number of bypasses simply to get their tanks from the assembly area to the line of departure. The company could not even move out until 3 A.M. and did not arrive until 7:25—just minutes before the preparation fires were supposed to commence. The tank company's third platoon immediately moved into position but had little time to coordinate with the 2nd Battalion. The plan was already unraveling, and it wasn't even H-hour. Last in the order of march, the 1st Battalion did not arrive until after daylight on the 17th.

Several events reveal how the hurried execution of this attack resulted in major failures in staff planning and unit execution. The 2nd Battalion's special action report noted that "no intelligence information was received by this battalion prior to the action on Obongni Ridge other than that the enemy was present."[6] It further noted that the planned artillery preparation was not fired. And, despite the fact that the deputy air group commander's attendance at the orders group meant the squadrons had map overlays, only a single air strike hit the objective before the battalion moved out.

Obviously the report reflects only one battalion's perception of the battle. In fact, the 1st Battalion, 11th Marines, fired an extensive preparation. Perhaps as a result of the poor maps or the confusion concerning the fact that the army and marines had named two different hills "Cloverleaf," or just the normal fog and friction of war, the 2nd Battalion didn't even know the preparation fires had been executed. Thus, it entered the attack not knowing if it could count on supporting arms. Command relations were also a bit confused. U.S. Army doctrine called for all artillery to be assigned to the division level. Thus, the marine artillery battalion was now assigned to the 24th Division artillery and no longer worked directly for the brigade. Since marine artillerymen were trained by the army at their artillery schools, the technical aspects of the assignment created no problems. But the shift in command required the marine artillery staff and commander to establish communications and coordination with the 24th Division artillery commander. As a result, they did not have their usual liaison elements with the brigade headquarters. The brigade could not quickly determine the cause of the apparent lack of support for the 2nd Battalion's attack. On the positive side, the 24th Division artillery commander, Brig. Gen. Henry J. D. Meyer, assigned two army artillery battalions, one light and one medium, to reinforce the fires of the 1st Battalion, 11th Marines, since the 5th Marines were the division's main effort.[7]

As for the single air strike, the VMF 323 unit diary notes a ten-plane strike as preparation for the attack, and VMF 214 launched seven more aircraft. However, the flights arrived late, so only about half the aircraft were able to strike before the assault started. Worse, the squadrons were almost out of their favorite ordnance: They had only four napalm tanks between them. Further reducing the impact of the air strike, one napalm canister missed the target and one failed to ignite.[8] For the first time the brigade was not functioning well as a team. The combination of confusion over the ground, inadequate planning with the army, the late arrival of units, and just plain fatigue seems to have accumulated to the point where the normal crisp coordination of all elements of the brigade failed. Another major factor in the failure of the preparatory fires was the fact that the North Koreans had prepared a reverse-slope defense, whereas artillery and air fires were delivered against the forward slope and crest of the ridge. Finally, in the absence of any information on the enemy, Murray ordered a single-battalion attack. This force was clearly insufficient.

In contrast to the brigade's hasty preparation, the enemy it faced had prepared their positions well. The NKPA 4th Division had been given the honorary title of "Seoul Division" for its part in seizing the South Korean capital. Holding the area the brigade would attack was the division's 18th Regiment, supported by a battalion of the 16th Regiment of the same division. Over 1,000 North Korean soldiers with at least thirty-six machine guns and supporting 82mm and 120mm mortars[9] opposed the attack of two understrength marine rifle companies. The commander of the 18th Regiment, Colonel Chang Ky-dok, a Soviet-trained combat veteran of the Chinese Communist Army, had motivated his soldiers by telling them their well-prepared positions were impregnable. They would be the first Koreans to defeat the U.S. Marines—and he would take instant action against anyone who tried to withdraw. He intended his regiment to defeat the marines or die in place. Chang's exhortations were not just hot air. He had carefully prepared positions on the reverse slope of the ridge. From these positions his soldiers could engage the marines while well protected from both direct and indirect fire. Additional reverse-slope-fortified bunkers gave them a place to retreat to during air attacks but were close enough that they could man their fighting positions before the ground marines could close in.[10]

Despite the delays in movement, the 2nd Battalion attacked on schedule at 8 A.M. Company D (under Capt. Andrew Zimmer) was on the right, closest to the village of Tugok, and was to attack the north end of Obong-ni Ridge. Its front line would run from the road to "Red Slash Hill," a hill showing a distinct red line of erosion. Company E (under 1st Lt. William Sweeney) was to move against the ridgeline directly through Obong-ni village. Each company put two platoons in the attack and kept one in reserve. The total strength of the two companies was only 339 men.[11] The marines were outnumbered by the defenders by almost three to one. (Two accounts claim the four assault platoons had only 130 men between them.)[12] The inadequate forces the 5th Marines committed to a frontal assault on a numerically superior enemy were a major mistake, which the line companies would pay for. It is yet another indicator of the rushed nature of this attack.

The companies moved quickly across the low ground, but when they reached the base of Obong-ni Ridge, they received heavy fire from two directions—the village of Tugok in the 9th Infantry's zone and the reverse-slope defenses on the

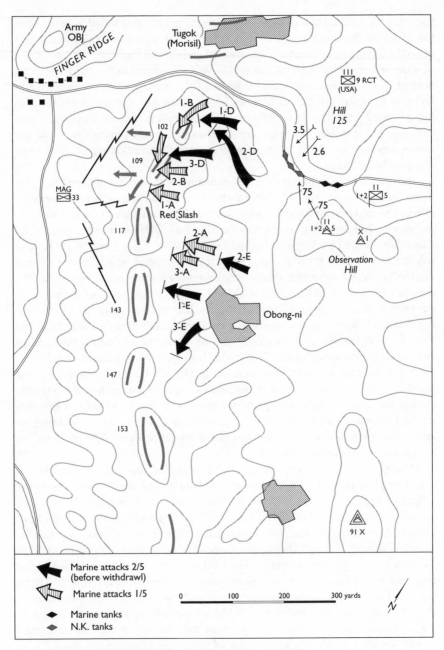

First Naktong counteroffensive—Obong-ni River, 17 August 1950.

ridge itself. The reverse-slope defenses allowed the North Koreans to put flanking fires into the assaulting marines without being subject to direct fire except from those marines they were shooting at. Hit hard from two directions, the companies slowed but continued to drive forward. Scrambling upward against heavy fire and waves of hand grenades, the marines moved "always upwards by fire and maneuver, roll under a bush or other ground cover . . . quickly catch a few breaths, then get up and charge upwards a few more precious yards."[13]

Company D's 3rd Platoon (under 2nd Lt. Michael Shinka) managed to reach the top of Hill 109 but could not hold. Enemy fire from the higher hills to the south and Tugok village to the north was so intense that Shinka had to order his platoon off the hill. When he pulled back, he had only fifteen effective men left of the thirty who had commenced the assault. Captain Zimmer, seeing Shinka's platoon driven back but S.Sgt. Albert Crowson's 1st Platoon continuing to move, sent his 2nd Platoon (under Tech.Sgt. Sidney S. Dickerson) to reinforce the 1st Platoon. Even with the 2nd Platoon's support, the attack stalled. The 3rd Platoon was pinned down in a small cut in the hill and could pull back no further. The 1st and 2nd Platoons clung to their position on the side of the hill, continuing to take heavy fire from Tugok. Zimmer identified the source of the fire in Tugok and requested artillery fire, but his request was denied by the battalion because the target was in the 9th Infantry's zone. Each of three requests was denied, and the 2nd Battalion was unable to coordinate with the 9th Infantry to attack the target.

Frustrated at his inability to provide indirect fire, Zimmer coordinated the fire of the 75mm recoilless-rifle platoon and the tank platoon against Tugok. The tanks moved so far forward that they received a total of twenty-three hits from antitank rifle fire, but none penetrated the armor. Paul DiNito, a loader with 1st Tanks noted that the marines were still learning about the M26:

> We discovered once in combat with the M-26's that we had to keep the hatches open on top of the turret because the automatic breach came back by itself and opened up, letting all the fire and gases out into the turret. The opened turret did not stop the heat from burning our faces or the fumes from burning our eyes, but it let the gases out just a little faster and gave us some air to breathe.[14]

Meanwhile, the tanks and recoilless rifles accounted for numerous NKPA antitank and machine guns. While the direct-fire weapons worked to support his marines, Zimmer called in an air strike on Hill 109. Shinka assaulted immediately on the heels of the strike and seized the top but had only nine men. In his own words,

> Fire from Hill 143 was gaining in intensity, and they had observation over our position. Fire was also coming from the hill to our front [Hill 207]. I reported the situation to Captain Zimmer. A short time later phosphorous shells were exploding in Hill 143. This slowed the fire but it never did stop.

My resupply of ammo did not arrive. Running short of ammo and taking casualties, with the shallow enemy slit trenches for cover, I decided to fall back until some of the fire on my left flank could be silenced. I gave the word to withdraw and take all wounded and weapons. About three-quarters of the way down, I had the men set up where cover was available. I had six men who were able to fight.

I decided to go forward to find out if we left any of our wounded. As I crawled along our former position [on the crest of Hill 109], I came across a wounded Marine between two dead. (This was a man named Hric.) As I grabbed him under the arms and pulled him toward a foxhole, a bullet shattered my chin. Blood ran into my throat and I couldn't breathe. I tossed a grenade at a gook crawling up the slope, didn't wait for it to explode, turned and reached under the marine's arms and dragged him as far as the military crest.

Another bullet hit my right arm, and the force spun me around. I rolled down the hill for a considerable distance before I could stop myself.

I walked into my line and had a battle dressing tied to my face and arm. I learned that the ammo was up and that relief was contemplated; and then I walked back to 2/5's aid station where they placed me on a jeep and took me to regimental aid.[15]

To the south of Company D, Sweeney's Company E moved across the rice paddies from its assembly area on Observation Hill toward Obong-ni village. Just before the lead platoons reached the village, heavy fire poured into the marines from Obong-ni Ridge. Second Lt. Nicholas Arkadis's 1st Platoon managed to fight through the village, but not 2nd Lt. Charles Christiansen's 2nd Platoon. Unable to contact the artillery or find his 4.2-inch mortar forward observer, Sweeney committed 2nd Lt. Roger Eddy's 3rd Platoon into the fight. Eddy took his platoon south of the village and attacked up a small spur. His attack took some of the pressure off the other platoons, but heavy fire from even farther south pinned his men down. Sweeney committed his last reserve: 1st Lt. Paul Uffleman, the company executive officer, led the marines of the headquarters and company mortar section to engage the enemy at the south edge of the company position. Sweeney himself moved to the center of the action at the base of the objective.

Using highly effective 81mm mortar fire, the 1st Platoon started up the hill again. Unfortunately, the marines were hit by a friendly barrage of white phosphorous just as they crested the hill. Still, the platoon managed to hang on near the top until 11:30 A.M. Then it was ordered to fall back because an air strike was coming in. Six Corsairs made repeated passes, delivering bombs, rockets, and 20mm cannon fire. Yet as soon as the Corsairs pulled off target, the Koreans swarmed out of their bunkers and delivered a withering fire into Company E's left flank. The attack was stopped cold. Companies D and E were clinging to the front slopes of Obong-ni but were unable to continue.

Years later General Craig still remembered the confidence the North Koreans showed: "They were the damndest bunch of people I ever saw. With a full-scale air attack on that ridge, I've seen many of these North Koreans jump out of the foxholes and just wave at us and then perhaps get shot down. But they were very cocky and were sure they were going to win, because they had been pushing the American troops back ever since the war started."[16]

It was noon, and the exhausted companies could not continue. The battalion had had 23 killed and 119 wounded in just four hours.[17] It was also dealing with a small number of North Korean infiltrators who had worked their way into the battalion rear to snipe. With no third rifle company, the battalion had no reserve to commit. Marine supporting arms kept working the ridge and the enemy rear, but Colonel Chang's fortifications had paid off. His men could hunker down during the artillery and air attacks and come out to deal with the infantry.

In retrospect, it is easy to see that a cross-corridor attack on a fortified position with a numerically superior force following inadequate preparation was doomed to fail. With no clear picture of the enemy situation or even a good idea of where the Koreans might be, the regiment employed the quickest and most direct method—a single-battalion frontal attack. Clearly the rushed preparations, unknown situation, and delays in getting units into place had disrupted what had been a very smoothly functioning team. For the first time in Korea, the brigade had suffered a serious setback.

With the attack stalled, higher headquarters acted to get it moving. Craig, upon finding that Murray had agreed to the 9th Infantry supporting by fire but not attacking, tried to get supporting arms firing into the 9th Infantry's zone. Murray, unable to get in touch with Col. John G. Hill, commander of the 9th Infantry Regiment, contacted General Church in an attempt to get the 9th Infantry to attack to neutralize the heavy fire coming from Tugok. Church told Murray that the 9th Infantry would attack after preparatory fires. This is one of the few times the coordination between brigade headquarters and the 5th Marines broke down— and at the worst possible time. The 2nd Battalion's attack was stopped cold.

Understanding that the 2nd Battalion could not continue the attack, at 12:45 Murray ordered the 1st Battalion to attack through the 2nd and seize Obong-ni Ridge. This time air, artillery, and mortars were in place and registered. Joined by Company A, 1st Tank Battalion's tanks, supporting arms raked the ridge and the positions they now understood were dug in on the reverse slope. As supporting arms hammered the objective, Murray visited Church and confirmed that the 9th Infantry would attack to eliminate the fire from Tugok.

In keeping with doctrine, the 1st Battalion commander, Newton, and his staff joined the 2nd Battalion commander, Roise, and his staff in the 2nd Battalion's command post. The two commanders and staffs had a good view of the battlefield in order to coordinate the passage of lines. Company B, Captain Tobin, moved forward to the right of Observation Hill to relieve Company D. Company A, Captain Stevens, moved directly over Observation Hill and down across the rice paddies to reach Company E. By 4 P.M. both companies had relieved the battered 2nd Battalion units and commenced their attacks on objective 1.

Company B attacked with the 1st Platoon on the right, 2nd on the left, and 3rd in reserve. All company machine guns were in general support from Observation Hill, where they could mass fires in front of the assault platoons. The 1st platoon initially made good progress up the draw to the north of Hill 102. Then, about 100 yards short of the top, it was pinned down by fire from Hill 109. By shifting farther right and attacking Hill 102 from the north, the platoon found a covered approach and seized Hill 102 just after 5 P.M. While holding Hill 102, the 1st Platoon continued to receive fire from Tugok, as the 9th Infantry had not yet cleared it.

As the 1st Platoon, Company B, held on to Hill 102, the 2nd Platoon fought its way up the draw between Hills 102 and 109 to seize Hill 109. Tobin was seriously wounded in the final assault. The company executive officer, 1st Lieutenant Fenton, took over and called his 3rd Platoon, mortars, and machine guns forward. With their arrival, Company B consolidated in a company perimeter straddling Hills 102 and 109. Fenton later remembered,

> John Tobin was on my left, the radio operator on my right. An enemy machine gun opened up and stitched John six or seven times. It also hit the radio operator. I wasn't scratched. . . . All of a sudden it dawned on me that he had the only map in the Company that showed our objective. Immediately, I knew I had to get the map before John bled all over it. I also hoped the gooks hadn't shot any holes in it. It shows you how you think in combat: here was a good friend of mine badly wounded and I thought about a map.[18]

Fenton immediately retrieved the map, cleaned the blood off it, and then had Tobin evacuated.[19]

As Company B took and held its hills, the 1st Platoon, Company A, fought its way to the top of Hill 117. When it crested that hill, it was immediately pinned down by heavy fire from Hill 143—the next peak south. Company A's 2nd Platoon was fighting its way up the draw between Hills 117 and 143. Due to numerous casualties, including platoon leader 2nd Lt. Thomas E. Johnston, the platoon could not seize 143. With two platoons pinned down, Captain Stevens committed the 3d Platoon of Company A to pass through his 2nd Platoon and seize Hill 143. Heavy fire from higher peaks to the south pinned the platoon in the draw between 117 and 143. At the same time, the fire drove the 1st Platoon back to the front slope of Hill 117. Despite the heavy and constant use of supporting arms, Company A could not seize the top of either 117 or 143. Every time the supporting fires lifted, North Koreans rushed more troops forward to occupy the trenches on the hills. As dark fell the company tied in with Company B on its right, dug in on the front slopes of Hill 117, and registered night fires.

As the rifle companies of the 1st Battalion, 5th Marines, dug in, four North Korean tanks attacked down the road between the 9th Infantry and the 1st

Battalion. Company B immediately reported the attack to the battalion. Newton instructed Company B to let the tanks pass through, and the battalion would deal with them in the rear. The 1st Battalion deployed the 3.5-inch rocket section of its antitank platoon at the base of Hill 125. The 75mm antitank gun company already had its 1st Platoon set up on Observation Hill to support the day's attack. That platoon simply shifted its focus to the road. The 2nd platoon, which was moving up to reinforce the 1st Battalion for the next day's attack, moved into a ravine below and to the rear of the 1st Platoon. Nearby were three M26 tanks of the 3rd Platoon, Company A, 1st Tank Battalion, which had been supporting the infantry attacks all day. At 6 P.M. they had withdrawn about 1,000 yards to refuel and rearm. They were still rearming when they received the report of enemy tanks. They immediately moved forward to the gap between Hill 125 and Observation Hill. The North Koreans didn't know it, but they were about to encounter a defense in depth that would subject them to fire from three directions by tank-killing weapons.

The 3.5-inch rocket teams engaged first at the point-blank range required by their weapons. They hit the lead tank and disabled the second. The 75mm antitank guns then joined in from a range of 350 yards. The lead M26 hurried forward from the rearming point, drove around the corner, and found the lead T34 only 100 yards away. The M26 immediately opened fire, and the first two Korean tanks were quickly killed. A third tank came up the road about ten minutes later and was destroyed. A fourth tank saw the destruction of the others and attempted to retreat but was caught by marine air and destroyed. Marine air also routed the infantry forces that were accompanying the tanks. Despite their quick demise, the T34s proved to be very tough targets. Corp. Ted Heckelman, Weapons Company, 1st Battalion, 5th Marines, captured the intensity and confusion of the fight against the tanks:

Major Russell, our Company Commander, came running up the hill . . . pointed to the road and the jeeps and pinpointed on the map the area where we were expected to be to encounter the enemy tanks. . . . As we proceeded to round the curve, I stopped the caravan. The first enemy tank was penetrating the pass, the position where we were to be. We turned around and I immediately directed the guys to go up on the side of the hill, positioning them in a skirmish line. . . . Our instructions to all were to let the first tank round the curve and then Cpl. Thomas was to hit the bogey wheel and knock the track off the tank causing it to become immobile. Then Cpl. Bowles was to concentrate on aiming for the gas tank and blow it up. I believed the second tank would then proceed to the curve and try to move the first tank out of the way. It was at that point, when the second tank made contact with the first tank, that Cpl. Bowles was to knock the bogey wheel out and Cpl. Carrow was to aim for the gas tank and destroy it. When the third tank came to the bend and made contact with the second tank, Cpl. Carrow was to aim for the

gas tank and destroy it as well. All of us would then work out an instanta-
neous plan of attack should there be a slip up or slight deviation.

The first tank went around the bend as planned and Cpl. Thomas did his
job. Because that tank was now exposed to our main line of resistance and
our troops, our own tanks fired armor piercing shells that went straight
through the front of the tank and out the back, exploding in the rice paddy
several yards away. It must have been a horrifying experience because we
could hear the activity of the Koreans inside the tank trying to start the engine and make things happen. As the escape hatch on the turret opened, out
came the tank commander. I think everybody in the section cut loose with
their carbines, rifles and pistols.

It was at this point that Cpl. Thomas Fava stood up from his fox hole and
fired a white phosphorous round into the turret. Now we were not in the position that we were supposed to be in, and had no way to communicate with
our troops as to our actual position. When Cpl. Fava stood up, our troops
behind us thought he was a North Korean and opened up with a machine gun
that riddled Cpl. Fava from his head to his waist, or he was shot down by our
Air Force planes strafing the area. Either way, it was friendly fire that took
his life.

We had no corpsman—we were out of position—no means of communication—and three more tanks coming at us. After checking Cpl. Fava, we
could see that there was nothing we could do to save him. All we could do
was to offer a prayer to the Almighty. I tried to comfort Cpl. Fava as best I
could. It was the most agonizing death that I have ever witnessed in my life.
When all was over I returned to my original position to watch the progress of
the second tank that was now coming around the curve in the road. But I shall
never forget his calling out for "Mama, mama." I have heard that for years.

I advised Cpl. Bowles to hold his fire until that second tank made contact
with the first. As the tank made the contact and proceeded to back up, he was
to aim for the gas tank rather than the bogey wheel. It was at this point that I
noticed that Cpl. Bowles's rocket launcher was not loaded properly and had
he fired, in all probability, would have wiped us all off the map. I yelled to
Cpl. Bowles not to fire and I immediately scrambled from my position down
to Cpl. Bowles, grabbed the rocket launcher from his grip and returned to my
position up the hill where Sgt. Bernard properly loaded the rocket and gave
me the OK to fire. I aimed where I thought the gas tank was and when the
spot was sighted in, pulled the trigger and Eureka—pay dirt! I had hit the
tank in the gas tank and it immediately exploded like a roman candle—a
sight that I can still see to this day but cannot explain to others. It was a good
thing that I made that direct hit because as I fired the rocket, the turret with its
cannon was turning to our position on the side of the hill and one round was
all that he would need to wipe us all out.

It was apparent the enemy troops that were some 1500 yards in front of our position had observed our positioning and communicated this to their incoming tank. We waited for what felt like hours after the explosion for the third tank to make its appearance. Although it seemed like hours, I'm sure it was almost momentarily—the third tank made its appearance and plowed into the second tank, trying to push it off the road or cliff. As contact was made, Sgt. Bernard yelled to Cpl. Carrow to aim for the gas tank. Cpl. Carrow fired his rocket after Sgt. Bernard and myself decided where we thought the most vulnerable spot would be—just in front of the back bogey wheel and a little to the top of the track. Cpl. Carrow's aim was true and accurate and he hit the gas tank dead center. Another roman candle appeared in the night sky. Now it was a case of waiting for the fourth tank and/or the enemy troops—whichever came first.

We did not dare move because we did not know the password for the night. We did not know where our friendly troops were and we did not know exactly where we were. So we decided the best thing to do was to lay low and hope that the Almighty was on our side and would look after us.

As luck would have it, the Air Force came in, saw three tanks immobilized on the open road and began to strafe them. As they strafed the tanks, we took the brunt of their devastating fire power. I do not know to this day how or why we were not hit and wiped out but we would survive. After about an hour or what seemed to be an hour, no other tank or infantry arrived. But we were taking some sniper shots from the enemy troops that were approximately 1500 yards in our frontal area. Nobody moved—nobody panicked—but we were one scared anti-tank section that wishes [*sic*] we were somewhere else. As it developed, Lt. Brown made the decision that we would grab our equipment, start singing the Marine Corps Hymn—make as much racket as we could and head back toward our line. We made it through the listening post.[20]

With the tank threat destroyed before 8:30 P.M., the battalion settled into its night defensive positions. Since the day's heavy casualties had left the rifle companies unable to defend the ground they had seized, Newton sent forward men from his H&S Company to extend the left flank of the position. As they moved forward, the 1st Battalion implemented a detailed fire plan that included registering fires for company 60mm mortars, battalion 81mm mortars, regimental 4.2-inch mortars, and artillery. Once registered, the mortars and artillery maintained harassing fire all night. This intelligent but routine use of supporting arms allowed the battalion to survive.

At 2:30 A.M. on the 18th, the North Koreans counterattacked from Hill 143. They moved downhill and flowed around both sides of Hill 117. The attack broke through the lines of Company A's 1st and 2nd Platoons and isolated the 3rd Platoon on the left flank. Those Korean units that had moved north of 117 continued downhill to hit Company B on 109. In forty-five minutes of intense fighting,

Company B managed to eject the North Koreans from their lines and reestablish an intact company defense, but not before they had penetrated all the way to the company command post:

> Upon receipt of the news that the enemy had broken through, I immediately ordered my 2d platoon to pull back toward the company and form company perimeter defense with my other platoons. The enemy took full advantage of their break through, and a great number of them managed to overrun my 2d platoon. Some of them pushed into my Company CP, where it was actually a case of hand-to-hand fighting. About then the Battalion Commander notified me that it was of utmost important that I hold at all costs. A Company had three breakthroughs on their company front, and if B Company was pushed off the ridge, we'd have to do it all over again in the morning. The situation was confused. It was very dark, there was considerable firing going on, and it was impossible to see the enemy except at very close hand. Several of my noncommissioned officers displayed outstanding gallantry by personally re-forming members of the company and leading them in a counterattack against the enemy. We closed out the enemy from our perimeter.[21]

Although Company B ejected the enemy, the North Koreans still held the high ground above Company A and were in position to throw or roll grenades down into the company's positions. The intensity of the enemy's attack is captured in the narrative of the 1st Battalion's special action report:

> The enemy method of attack was to have one squad rise up and throw grenades and then advance a short distance, firing to their front and flanks with automatic weapons. They would then hit the deck and another squad would repeat the same movement. . . . One trick of the enemy was to work in close to our machine gun positions, drawing their fire. When our machine gun position was disclosed it would be fired on by an automatic weapon set up at a greater range.[22]

After the North Koreans drove Company A off Hill 117, the intensity of their fires kept Company A from consolidating a company position or counterattacking. However, near dawn the enemy attack faltered. The intensity of the fighting was reflected in the casualties sustained by both sides. The marine rifle companies started the attack with about 190 men each. The next morning each company had only about 100 effective men. The North Koreans suffered even more severely. In a single small cut the marines counted "120 dead North Koreans with 12 cart mounted machineguns."[23] They had been caught by an artillery barrage and wiped out.

Despite the heavy casualties suffered the day before, Company A counterattacked. This time the aviation was on time and conducted repeated strikes on Hill 117 just prior to the company jumping off at 7 A.M. The scattered elements of the company came at the Koreans from multiple directions—one squad that had fallen back on Company B attacked along the ridge from Hill 109, the 1st and 2nd Platoons attacked up the draw from the hillside of 117, and the 3rd Platoon, which had been separated during the night, joined the attack up the draw. Marine air continued to provide very close support. Held up by four North Korean machine guns, Company A requested an air strike. In less than five minutes the lead Corsair placed a smoke marking rocket directly in the machine-gun position, and the second Corsair delivered a 500-pound bomb directly on the mark, knocking out all four Korean machine guns. This strike was immediately followed by strafing and a napalm run.[24]

Captain John S. Thach, commanding officer of USS *Sicily*, captured the trust that had evolved between the marines on the ground and the aviators supporting them. He graphically described one strike:

> They had to fly right down over the ridge then start shooting right away, or start shooting really before they got to the ridge, with rockets. After the first one came down, the Marines on the ridge were standing up and looking. They wanted to watch the shells! The last pilot that came down after they'd put these rockets in there called the controller again and he said: "Would you please have the people in the front row be seated. I can see the back of their heads in my gunsight and it makes me nervous!" That's how close these Corsairs were. These pilots would come back and talk to me and say: "Captain, those people on the ground think we're really better than we are and we're worried. We had a fellow today—we were doing some real close work, right over his head . . . and he [the FAC] said, "Shoot at the top of my head. I'll duck and let it go by."[25]

The 3rd Platoon followed up the air strikes by seizing the top of the hill and then attacking along the saddle to Hill 143. Temporarily pinned down, the 3rd Platoon again called for supporting arms. Marine air as well as 81mm and 4.2-inch mortars hammered the top of 143. The Koreans withdrew, and Company A consolidated its hold on both Hills 117 and 143. As it did so, the company reported that the enemy had broken. Large numbers of Koreans were fleeing, many without weapons. Newton immediately requested permission to continue the attack to ensure that the Koreans had no chance to reorganize. At 10 A.M. the 1st Battalion received orders to attack. By 12:30 it had seized Hills 147 and 153 and consolidated positions along the forward slopes of the entire Obong-ni Ridge.

During a very brief inspection of Obong-ni Ridge, 1st Lieutenant Fenton found "about 25 heavy Browning machine guns, 15 light machine guns, numerous small arms and BARs, one 3.5 inch rocket launcher with nine rounds, four anti-tank rifles with large amounts of ammunition, and numerous hand grenades. The enemy also had one SCR 300 radio on our Battalion tactical net, and five or six SCR 536 radios laying [*sic*] around in the general area."[26]

Fenton's list reveals both the tenacity of the Korean defense and the adaptability of the Korean soldier. The Browning heavy machine guns, BARs, 3.5-inch rocket launcher, and radios were all equipment captured from U.S. Army units during the drive south from Seoul. The Koreans had clearly integrated the weapons as key elements of their defense. Newton walked the terrain after his battalion captured it and noted that the North Koreans had dug more than 1,000 fighting positions on the reverse slope of the ridge.[27] The Koreans were learning how to minimize the impact of marine supporting arms.

As Fenton returned to his command post, he found Nick Shriver. Shriver, the only other surviving officer in the company, had been evacuated the night before with a head wound. Fenton remembered,

> In the morning, Nick came back with head encased in bandages. I said, "Nick what are you doing here?" He said "While I was in the aid station I got to thinking that very seldom does a 2nd Lt. ever get a chance to command a company and I thought your luck is running short, you haven't been hit yet, I figured I'd get back and I might get a company."

Fenton noted that it became a running joke between them, particularly since Fenton fought through Seoul and the Chosin Reservoir and was never hit.[28]

As the 1st Battalion cleared Obong-ni Ridge and consolidated its positions, Murray ordered the 3rd Battalion to pass around the right flank of the 1st to seize brigade objectives 2 and 3. The 3rd Battalion was prepared to move quickly. Murray had issued a warning order the night before, and Taplett had taken his company commanders forward for a personal reconnaissance. As a result they knew the ground and the plan and simply had to execute it when ordered. The 3rd Battalion moved forward from its assembly areas, passed around the right of the 1st in a column of companies, and then spread out with both rifle companies on line to attack objective 2. Once again Taplett used all supporting arms—tanks, recoilless rifles, air, artillery, 4.2-inch and 81mm mortars—to smother the enemy positions as his companies advanced through "moderate" resistance to seize the objective by 12:30. As the rifle companies fought through the few Koreans remaining on the hill, a platoon of North Koreans tried to move around the flank of Company H. Company A tanks spotted the platoon and poured 90mm tank main-gun and machine-gun fire into them. The Koreans who were not immediately killed withdrew quickly to the north. As the 3rd Battalion cleared the top of the objective, it continued to pound the retreating enemy with all available fires until the last of the Koreans withdrew from sight.

The marines of the 3rd Battalion could not see that the North Korean 4th Division had broken and the vast majority of the Koreans were desperately trying to cross the river to escape. The VMO 6 observers, overhead as always, could see this and immediately called in 105mm and 155mm artillery. The TAC marshaled section after section of Corsairs to slash at the retreating Koreans. Numerous pilot and observer reports note that the Naktong was full of floating bodies and seemed to run red with blood. The 4th Division was shattered.

At 2:40 P.M. Murray ordered the 3rd Battalion to continue the attack to seize

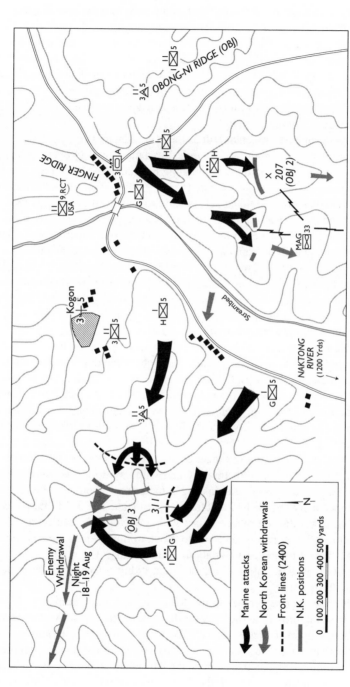

First Naktong counteroffensive—Objectives 2 and 3, 18 August 1950.

objective 3. Once again Taplett put both companies into the assault (objective 3 was huge) and led them with both indirect and direct fire. As the companies advanced, the tanks, recoilless rifles, and 81mm mortars moved forward to keep the lead companies within range. The lead companies moved up adjacent fingers leading to the top of Hill 311. The hill was so steep that the tanks could continue to fire overhead with the 90mm main gun until just before the infantry reached the crest. The North Koreans on Hill 311, isolated and deprived of machine guns, mortars, or rifles, continued to fight.

Having occupied as much of Hill 311 as it could with two companies, the 3rd Battalion dug in for the night, sent patrols down the fingers to overlook the Naktong, and continued to mop up the remaining Koreans. About 9:15 P.M. the Koreans launched a final counterattack with twenty to thirty men against Company G. Company G killed eight of the attackers and drove the rest off but lost two killed and eight wounded. This last day of the first Naktong fight was costly for the 3rd Battalion. Both Captain Fegan and 2nd Lt. Cahill—two superb combat leaders who had been in the fight from day one—were wounded and evacuated.

At 11 P.M. Company H received orders to continue the attack in the morning, 19 August. Following an intense seven-minute preparation by 81mm mortars, the company jumped off and moved through the objective without making contact. The rest of the day was spent patrolling, tying the two marine rifle companies together, and making contact with the army unit on the 3rd Battalion's right flank. The 5th Marines found 1,200 Korean dead, 34 artillery pieces, hundreds of automatic weapons, and thousands of rifles. Throughout the day marine air and artillery under the control of aerial observers and TACs continued to attack the 4th Division on the far side of the river. According to General MacArthur, "Here, the enemy 4thDiv was decisively defeated, lost its bridgehead and was thrown westward across the NAKTONG River, suffering very heavy losses in both personnel and equipment."[29]

At 1 P.M. the commanding officer of the 5th Marines received orders to pass control of the area to the 19th Infantry and withdraw to a bivouac area east of Yongsan. The 1st and 2nd Battalions began motor movement at 4 P.M., arrived at 5, and immediately established a defensive perimeter. The 3rd Battalion continued patrolling but did not make contact with any North Korean forces. At 2:50 P.M. the 3rd Battalion received orders to move to the bivouac area as soon as it had been relieved by the 2nd Battalion, 19th Infantry. The relief was not completed until 10:30 P.M., and the 3rd Battalion didn't arrive at the bivouac until 3 A.M. on 20 August.

During the intense fighting in the Naktong, VMO 6 continued to innovate. Well rehearsed in providing the eyes for the brigade, the squadron sought to provide greater support to the wounded. "Two helicopters were modified to carry stretcher patients. This was accomplished by removing the window on the right side and installing straps in the cabin on the left side to hold the stretcher securely. With this modification, each of the helicopters could evacuate one stretcher case."[30] The increased speed of evacuation certainly saved the lives of some of the marines. Even more important, it gave them the comfort of knowing rapid evacuation was available if they were hit badly.

All day on 19 and 20 August, VMF 214 and 323 ran strikes along the Naktong in front of the brigade to ensure that the North Korean forces had no opportunity to reorganize. As soon as the brigade pulled off the line on 20 August, marine air provided all its sorties to the air force controllers. From 21 August until the brigade reentered combat on 3 September, the squadrons maintained the same high operational tempo that characterized their support of the brigade. In fact, VMF 214's biggest effort came on 29 August, when it launched forty-seven sorties in support of U.S. and ROK troops in contact.[31] On that single day the Black Sheep in their Corsairs almost doubled the bomb tonnage a U.S. Air Force F-80 squadron had dropped in seventeen days of operations, an incredible testament to the disparity of the combat punch of the two types of aircraft as well as the different operational philosophies of the two services.[32]

Lacking training in true close air support, the army observers tended to use the marine strikes somewhat farther from the front than did the marines. In particular, they took advantage of the Corsairs' ability to find enemy artillery and mortars and destroy them without further guidance. Although marine air continued in the fight, the First Battle of the Naktong Bulge was over for the ground marines.

11

The Second Battle of the Naktong Bulge

Early on 20 August the marines moved to their assembly area in the vicinity of Miryang. Just after they arrived, the brigade was ordered to move back to Chang-won and counterattack to recover the ground the 25th Division had lost. The significance of attacking back over the same terrain they had taken during the Sachon offensive was not lost on the marines:

> You can imagine how they felt when they received word that they were going back to Chang-won and move up once again to Chindong-ni because the enemy had moved down that Sachon-Kosong road to Chindong-ni. All of our 29 miles had been lost. The news went over like a "lead balloon." If we were depressed before, we really felt bad this time. The question in everyone's mind was: how long will the Army hold the Naktong River area before the Gooks come across again and the Marines are called back? We had only been ashore about two weeks, but we felt that we had done more walking and attacking than any outfit in Korea.[1]

Regardless of how the marines felt about it, they executed the order smartly. Movement to the Bean Patch near Masan commenced at 7:10 P.M. and was completed by 2 P.M. on 21 August. Upon arrival the units established local security and commenced patrolling. In an interesting look at how effective the grapevine can be, the official 5th Marines special action review does not note receipt of a warning order to counterattack in the 25th Division zone until 22 August, yet the marines seemed to have known about it early on the 21st.

Fortunately, the brigade was not committed to counterattacking in the vicinity of Chindong-ni. The commanding general, 8th Army, ordered the brigade to detach its artillery battalion and assign it to the commanding general of the 25th Infantry Division, which was assigned to defeat the North Korean advance to Chindong-ni. The 25th Division artillery commander, Brig. Gen. George B. Barth, assigned the 1st Battalion, 11th Marines, to direct support to RCT 5 and reinforcing fires for the army artillery battalion supporting RCT 5. Since the 1st Battalion, 11th Marines, provided forward observers to a single infantry battalion in RCT 5, that battalion in effect had a battalion of artillery in direct support.[2] The 1st Battalion continued to fire in support of the 25th Division throughout the period the brigade was assigned to 8th Army reserve.

From the afternoon of 21 August to the morning of 1 September the rest of the brigade remained at the Bean Patch, resting, reorganizing, refitting, and training. The ground combat elements in particular needed time to absorb replacements. Casualties, particularly among junior officers, had been terrible. Five of six company commanders had been wounded, and platoon leaders had also suffered badly. Of eighteen rifle platoon leaders who had started the campaign, four had been killed and nine wounded. Fortunately, some of the wounded officers returned to duty. However, the 368 replacements and 98 who returned to duty did not make up for the 122 killed, 489 wounded, 13 missing, and 279 nonbattle casualties the brigade had suffered.[3] The regiment's strength, already well below wartime T/Os, had been reduced by another 437 men since landing in Korea.

Although the replacements were welcome, they had been traveling since the beginning of August and had essentially no physical training while in transit. Craig had specifically requested that a replacement draft be sent to Japan at the earliest possible moment, but the belief that the brigade would not fight until it was joined by the rest of the division made his request a lower priority than that of filling the division. As the brigade sailed across the Pacific, FMFPac and Headquarters Marine Corps starting working to provide the replacement draft promised to Craig. The commandant of the Marine Corps ordered a first replacement draft of 800 officers and men to be formed at Marine Barracks, Treasure Island, San Francisco, and shipped to the Far East by 1 September. However, when the orders went out to activate the 1st Marine Division, these marines were diverted to the 7th Marines. A subsequent draft of over 3,000 men was ordered to be formed at Marine Barracks, Camp Pendleton. These men were absorbed by the 1st Marine Division. It was not until 3 August—after the brigade landed in Korea—that FMFPac directed the division to send 10 officers and 290 enlisted men by air to the brigade. The men were ready by 9 August, but the U.S. Air Force's military air transport service refused to provide airlift. On 14 August the men were moved to San Francisco by rail and airlifted by the navy's commander of the Western Sea Frontier from there to Japan.[4] After more than a week of travel by train, truck, and air, the replacements arrived at the Bean Patch. Unfortunately, the replacements did not include the critical third rifle company for each infantry battalion or the two howitzer sections for each battery. At the same time that headquarters gave, it took way. Even as the replacements were being assigned to their new units, Headquarters Marine Corps notified the brigade that all seventeen-year-olds had to be transferred out of the brigade and evacuated from Korea. They could not return until they turned eighteen. Until then they would serve elsewhere in the Far East.[5]

During this period VMO 6 marines provided their ground buddies with a major boost in morale. The squadron flew in three hot meals, mail, and a beer ration of one can per man per day. On the negative side, the brigade was unable to replace its badly damaged equipment and uniforms. The marines had to patch things together as well as they could.

While most of the ground combat elements of the brigade rested and refitted, the artillery and fighter aircraft shifted to supporting U.S. Army and United Nations forces. Even though both carriers managed to make port calls at Sasebo for replenishment and repairs, VMF 214 and 323 flew 373 strike sorties from 21 August to 1 September in support of the Pusan Perimeter.

In a notable event for VMF 214, "at 1509 on 24 August, a Corsair bounced down on the deck of the *Sicily* and caught the arresting cables. Lieutenant Colonel Walter E. Lischeid, the squadron commanding officer was back at the helm of VMF-214. Lischeid had remained in Japan since the squadron's arrival in the Far East for extra carrier landing practice. Lischeid needed this extra work-up time, because he had been out of an operational squadron in his duties immediately prior to taking command of VMF-214."[6]

As noted, the 1st Battalion, 11th Marines, was immediately assigned to support the hard-pressed U.S. 25th Infantry Division:

> On 24 August, the battalion was ordered by 25th DivArty to support the defensive positions of the US Army 5th RCT, and reverted to operational control of the 25th DivArty. . . . From 24 through 31 August, one hundred and thirty (130) missions were fired, totaling two thousand, four hundred and thirteen (2,413) rounds. Until [*sic*] 2400, 31 August, to 0500, 1 September, the majority of the missions were night defensive fires and results were problematical and undetermined. The enemy counterattacked at midnight on 1 September, and the firing batteries fired continuously until 0500, 1 September, successfully breaking the attack in the sector of direct support. Counterbattery fire was extremely heavy during the same hours and the fact that there were no serious casualties can only be attributed to good cover discipline and some protection from the high land mass to the west. All security elements were doubled and remained awake and alert during the entire night. . . . At 1200, 1 September, the battalion displaced to the Masan front area.[7]

The artillery believed it was moving back to join the brigade in the rest area and prepare for the amphibious landing at Inchon. The marines knew Craig had received orders to prepare the brigade to reembark and join the 1st Marine Division for a planned landing. They just didn't know the landing would take place at Inchon. Craig sent his chief of staff, Colonel Snedecker, and a team of planners to Japan to join the division staff in planning the landing. Not only was the timeline very short but the division was not complete. Due to the massive cutbacks after

World War II, the division had been able to assemble only a single additional infantry regiment (1st Marines) and its supporting troops after sending the brigade out in early July. The 7th Marines, the division's third infantry regiment, was on its way but had been delayed because two battalions of the regiment were formed almost entirely from activated reservists and the third, a regular battalion, had to sail all the way from the Mediterranean Sea to join the regiment in Korea. In fact, the planners put together a plan knowing that the 7th Marines would not arrive at Inchon until seven days after the landing. Increasing the complexity of planning was the fact that General Walker, commanding general of the 8th Army, was adamant that he could not lose the brigade during this critical phase of the defense of Pusan. The marine and navy leaders were every bit as adamant that they had to have the brigade if the landing was to succeed.

While the planners struggled to put together a viable plan, the brigade began training its replacements while simultaneously sending its heavy equipment ahead to Pusan for embarkation. Unable to get complete sets of new dungarees, boots, or even sufficient numbers of BARs and machine guns, the marines nonetheless set about a tough, focused training program. Although it was supposed to be a well-kept secret, most members of the brigade knew they were pulling out for an amphibious landing. Only a few selected officers knew the actual objective, but the marines were happy at the prospect of fighting alongside other marines. They were eager to rejoin the 1st Marine Division.

Company commanders were notified of the top-secret location of the landing, and although they could not tell the troops where it would be, they were tasked with conducting appropriate training. The brigade constructed a crude rifle range, and every marine fired his weapon. Crews were trained for heavy weapons. Mornings were dedicated to integrating the new troops into companies, platoons, and gun crews (mortars, machine guns, recoilless rifles) and to hard physical exercise to acclimate the new marines and navy corpsmen. Afternoons were dedicated to weapons and equipment maintenance. The new men were mostly hastily mobilized reserves. William Fisher, a hospital corpsman third class and veteran of World War II, described how his reserve company, Easy Company, 13th Marine Infantry Battalion, Tucson, Arizona, had been mobilized:

> The other guys were asked how long they had been in the reserves—one year or two. They were also asked how many summer camps had they attended. I think if they had attended one summer camp and been in the reserves for two years, they were considered to be "trained." Those who hadn't gone to any summer camps were sent to boot camp. But a lot of the guys found this out and lied. They said they had been in two summer camps so that they could end up with all their buddies. You have to realize that at this point a lot of them had had no Marine Corps training. A lot of them were 16 or barely 17 years old. But they didn't want to be separated from their buddies. Another peculiar thing about this whole situation was that there was this rule, I think,

that brothers weren't supposed to be serving in the same combat zone. My brother Bob ended up in the 1st Marines in Korea, and I ended up in the 5th in Korea. There were a lot of brothers and cousins, however, who were in the same outfits. I guess they didn't screen that too well.

With no training and being young, we all started on our trip to Korea. In my case, I had no Marine Corps training. Nor did I have any field med training as a corpsman. When asked, "What did you do in the war, Dad?" my answer has always been, "I delivered babies." I didn't really know anything about field training. Corpsman schooling at Pendleton would have been nice, but I was never in combat corps school or field medical training. I certainly did need it. Even when I got to Korea, I couldn't convince anybody that I had had none. But there, of course, you were a warm body and that's all that was needed.[8]

Many of the replacements arrived without weapons. Short of weapons and equipment themselves, the seasoned marines of the brigade invoked the age-old right of scrounging to reallocate government equipment between army and marine units. Even the chaplain got involved. As Taplett inspected his motor pool, accompanied by his motor sergeant, S.Sgt. Alvie Queen, he

found the assistant Regimental Chaplain, Lieutenant (jg) Bernard Hickey, and a jeep with a trailer attached. In response to my surprised query, Alvie replied, "It is my jeep and trailer and he is the driver." Confronted, the faithful priest explained he "had acquired" an "abandoned army jeep with trailer" while we were fighting at the 1st Naktong. I knew enough not to further question him as he was a great "midnight procurer." The biggest surprise came when I asked him to remove the tarp covering the trailer. This he reluctantly did. Alvie and I laughed when we saw his "treasures." Besides his authorized chaplain kit, the trailer contained assorted pairs of shoes, green dungarees in various sizes, .30 caliber ammunition boxes, 60mm mortar rounds, boxes of hand grenades, a couple of rifles and carbines, first aid equipment and boxes of "C" rations. He sheepishly explained "the army units leave a lot of stuff lying around and I know our front line Marines are always short of this stuff." I congratulated him on "cleaning up the battlefield after the army units" and moved on.[9]

On 29 August the president of the Republic of Korea, Syngman Rhee, visited the brigade to conduct an awards ceremony. Like all ceremonies, this one created some problems for the troops:

One platoon leader, Second Lieutenant Muetzel, received two Purple Hearts (with the Silver Star to come later for his heroic actions on Obong-ni). . . . It was a strain to try to look presentable for the ceremony, as Muetzel later remarked: "My leggings had been thrown away, my trousers were out at both knees, my right boot had two bullet holes in it, and my dungaree jacket had a corporal's stripes stenciled on the sleeves. I grabbed a fast shave with cold water, hard soap, and a dull blade. Gene Davis loaned me a clean set of dungarees, Tom Gibson loaned me his second lieutenant's bars, and off I went with my troops."[10]

The break ended for the brigade on 1 September. On the night of 31 August the NKPA launched a last massive offensive against the perimeter. Selecting five major points for breakthroughs, the North Koreans threw 98,000 men at the battered U.S. and South Korean divisions holding the line. Once again General Walker was faced with shuffling his weak reserves to deal with breakthroughs. Early reports indicated that the most serious penetration was in the 2nd Infantry Division's zone. The NKPA had sent its 2nd, 9th, and 10th Divisions as well as the remnants of the 4th Division to destroy the U.S. 2nd Infantry Division and drive to Pusan. Maj. Gen. Laurence B. Keiser, commanding general of the 2nd Division, reported that the North Koreans had penetrated deeply. Given the fact that the marine brigade had just cleared the area in which the U.S. 2nd Infantry Division was operating, the 8th Army at first discounted the reports that the 9th Infantry had effectively been overrun. However, General Walker did send a warning order to the marine brigade at 8:10 A.M. to be prepared to counterattack to restore the line. By 9 A.M. he had also requested that the 5th Air Force make a maximum effort to support the 2nd Infantry Division. The 8th Army also sent light liaison aircraft forward on an hourly basis to report on the situation as well as drop water and ammunition to isolated units of the 2nd Division. By late morning the scope of the disaster became clear. The 9th and 23rd Infantry Regiments of the 2nd Division had been deeply penetrated. The infantry battalions were cut off, and some companies had been wiped out. Worse, the penetration was already eight miles deep and six miles wide in the division's zone.

At 11 A.M., with the situation now clearly critical, Walker ordered the brigade back into the fight. By 1:30 the brigade, with its artillery battalion reattached, moved out from its billeting areas near Masan to its old assembly area in the vicinity of Miryang. Although ordered forward, the brigade was not formally attached to the 2nd Division until the morning of 2 September. The brigade was an essential element of MacArthur's plan for the Inchon landing, but Walker felt he could not restore the perimeter without it, so he called MacArthur's Chief of Staff, Maj. Gen. Doyle Hickey, to confirm that he could use it. Hickey informed Walker that MacArthur had approved the use of the brigade. Thus, at 1:35 P.M. on 2 September, Walker officially attached the brigade to the 2nd Division with the understanding that as soon as the situation was resolved, the brigade would be released to prepare for Inchon. That afternoon Craig attended a planning conference at the 2nd Division headquarters. The division had collapsed. Isolated elements were fighting hard, but many others were withdrawing without being attacked. The army planners wanted to commit the brigade piecemeal as it arrived from Masan. Craig recalled,

I conferred with the commander of the 2nd Division. At that time the chief of staff of the Eighth Army was at the CP, and I remember his idea was to commit the brigade immediately despite the fact that our air control units had not arrived from Chinhae, nor had one of my battalions arrived in the area. This was the only heated discussion I had with the army while in Korea. I insisted that the attack be held up until all my troops arrived, and I had my air support properly coordinated, and they finally gave in on this.[11]

As Craig convinced the army to wait until his brigade assembled, the 2nd Battalion, 5th Marines, and the brigade and regimental command posts arrived by motor convoy. They had commenced movement at 11:30. By 6 P.M. they had covered the eighty-four miles to Miryang, had set up, and were operating. The rest of the brigade was moving by rail to Miryang. Once again there were too few trucks, so the units had to shuttle from the Miryang railhead to assembly areas near the 2nd Division headquarters. The last element of the brigade did not close until 6:30 on 2 September.[12]

While Craig and the ground elements were assembling in Korea, VMF 323 was scrambling to set up operations at Ashiya Air Force Base near Kokura, Japan. On 28 August the squadron had flown off the USS *Badoeng Strait* before the ship entered harbor for repair and replenishment. On 1 September the squadron received a warning order from the brigade to be ready to support immediate operations. Since the *Badoeng Strait* could not take the squadron back aboard until 4 September, the squadron commander improvised aircraft maintenance and support in order to conduct operations from ashore. Fortunately, the rear echelon of VMF 323, which had been left behind in California due to shipping shortages, joined MAG 33 on 31 August and immediately moved to Ashiya to support operations. On 1 September VMF 323 was joined at Ashiya Air Base by VMF 214 when the USS *Sicily* returned to Sasebo, Japan, for required repair and replenishment. The longer range to target and bad weather over Korea would significantly reduce the air support available to the brigade in the upcoming battle, but the air elements would be in the fight.[13]

As noted, Craig had prevailed at the conference and won time to assemble the brigade for a coordinated attack rather than committing it piecemeal. After the conference the 8th Army issued a warning order to the brigade. Received at 11:35 P.M. on 2 September, the order specified that "one reinforced battalion of the brigade would move beginning at daylight to the vicinity of Yongsan to cover movement of the remainder of the brigade into an assembly area that vicinity, prepared for operation in the 2d Infantry Division sector."[14] By 1:30 A.M. on 3 September the 5th Marines had issued regimental Operations Order 12-50. By 4:15 the leading battalion, the 2nd, had issued its order, briefed supporting arms and unit commanders, and moved out. According to the 2nd Battalion's special action report,

The battalion was informed that the enemy's 1st regiment of the 9th division was located in the area into which we had been ordered. No information as to strength and actual location was available. The battalion was further informed that an armored Brigade was in support but there was no information as to possible strength. The only information concerning enemy mortars and artillery was that there was a good deal of it.[15]

Despite the lack of information, the regiment felt the situation was well developed enough and the terrain wide enough to allow a two-up (two battalions abreast) attack. This would be the first time the regiment had committed two battalions to the attack at the same time. The regiment ordered the 2nd Battalion to lead the column, occupy the line of departure, and wait for the 1st Battalion to come up on its left before commencing the attack. By 4:45 A.M. the 2nd Battalion had arrived at the assembly area and moved out in tactical column to occupy the line of departure. Unfortunately, as it moved up, the North Korean 9th Division attacked again, driving the U.S. Army 9th Infantry Regiment 1,000 yards to the rear of the line of departure. Thus, the 2nd Battalion's first action was to move Company A, 1st Tank Battalion, forward to support the 9th Infantry soldiers as they fell back and passed through marine lines. Roise used the time to mass supporting arms on his new objective so that he had full support of tanks, recoilless rifles, mortars, artillery, and air as the 2nd Battalion attacked at 7:15 A.M. The 2nd attacked to restore the line of departure as the 1st Battalion moved up on its left. Moving through the line of departure, the 2nd Battalion continued across the rice paddies toward its assigned objective, Hill 117.

In an act typical of his leadership style, Craig was well forward to observe. In fact, he was just behind the tanks that were supporting the 2nd Battalion. When the tank platoon leader, 2nd Lt. Robert Winters, standing in the hatch firing the .50-caliber machine gun, was hit, it was Craig and his aide, Lt. Jack Buck, who pulled Winters out of the tank and dragged him to cover.

Company E, supported by direct fire from tanks, moved south of Yongsan to seize three small ridges and support the attack of Company D on the main objective. Company D first had to move through Yongsan and then through Myong-ni to get into position to attack Hill 117 from its flank. Once in position, Company D moved out, supported by direct fire weapons from Company E; the 2nd Battalion; and Company A, 1st Tanks as well as mortars, artillery, and air strikes. Company D got a foothold on the north edge of the Hill 117 complex before the enemy responded with massed artillery and mortars while feeding infantry reinforcements in from the back side of the hill. Stopped and with no support on either his right or left, the commanding officer of the 2nd Battalion ordered Company D to dig in and hold its gains until friendly units could move up. Combat reports indicated that two to three battalions of the NKPA's 9th Division held Hill 117 and Hill 91 to the south. The North Koreans positioned crew-served weapons on the

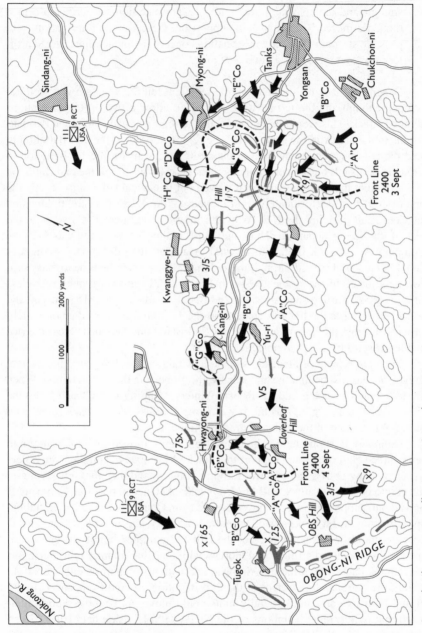

Second Naktong counteroffensive, 3–5 September 1950.

reverse slope to enfilade the advancing marine units. Until the 1st Battalion could move up, Roise felt he could not advance, so he ordered his battalion to dig in for the night. During the day's intense fighting the battalion had lost eighteen dead and seventy-seven wounded.[16] As the battalion dug in, Roise ordered one platoon from Company E to move north of Company D and fill the gap between Company D and the 9th Infantry to the north. With this final disposition, the battalion was set for the night.

Moving up behind the 2nd Battalion, the 1st was not able to cross its line of departure until 8:50 A.M. Company A moved out on the battalion left and Company B on the right. They were subjected to long-range small-arms fire as they crossed the line of departure. Newton, the 1st Battalion's commanding officer, moved forward to an observation post near the line of departure and ordered 81mm and 4.2-inch mortar fires placed on the battalion objective to protect the companies as they crossed the intervening rice paddies. Halfway across Company B was pinned down by heavy machine-gun fire. Newton requested an air strike. With its usual speed and accuracy, marine air destroyed the position in minutes. But now Company A was held up by increasing fire from the high ground before it and to the left. Once again the battalion turned to air support. The Corsairs struck quickly but could not completely silence the fire. Newton directed Company B to shift right to make contact with the 2nd Battalion and Company A to shift right to maintain contact with Company B.

Despite the continued heavy small-arms fire, the two companies were tied in and ready to attack by 9:50. Unfortunately, they still had to cross 800 yards of rice paddy. Newton directed 81mm mortars to fire onto the reverse slope of Hill 91, where the enfilading fire was originating. At the same time he had the 75mm recoilless rifle platoon fire high explosive and white phosphorous rounds into the small village in front of Company A. As these fires began to take effect, a new North Korean heavy machine-gun position opened up from the front slopes of the 1st Battalion's objective. Newton turned to his 4.2-inch mortar and artillery observers for immediate suppression of these guns and quickly silenced them. As the artillery and mortar fire lifted at 10:55, Company B reported that it was at the base of the objective and ready to assault. Ten minutes later Company A reported that it was also in position to assault. The two companies kicked off the attack together as the battalion continued to work the objective with supporting arms. Company B moved quickly and seized its portion of the objective by 11:15, but Company A was unable to seize its portion until 12:05. As both companies began to consolidate their positions on Hill 91, North Korean forces opened up from the next high ground before them. The battalion responded with an air strike. When the strike hit, Company B reported that it could see the enemy running away to the west. The battalion immediately placed artillery fire on the fleeing enemy and achieved "excellent results."

Not content to let the artillery finish the retreating North Koreans, marine riflemen joined in. They quickly demonstrated that accurate rifle fire at ranges of

400 to 500 yards was possible. Determined not to let the enemy regroup and dig in, marine riflemen and artillery continued to work over groups of fleeing North Koreans. As the North Koreans fled out of sight of the ground marines, the TAC and aerial observers took over, employing a technique the marines had developed to coordinate the effects of air and artillery: "During those periods when large groups of enemy were retreating before our forces, it became a practice to drive him to shelter with aerial strafing and rockets. When a large group concentrated in one shelter, that is, a village or road culvert, artillery would be called in to flush them out and the aircraft would then hit him again as he ran."[17]

At the same time the battalion resupplied the companies with ammunition and water while evacuating the wounded. By 1:50 P.M. both companies were ready to resume the attack. The brigade reconnaissance platoon moved up on the battalion left to screen that flank while the battalion arranged an air strike followed by a five-minute artillery preparation on objective 2. At 3:10 the companies moved out in the attack and moved quickly until 3:45, when Company A started to receive enemy mortar fire. The orbiting VMO 2 observation aircraft immediately located the enemy mortars and called in artillery to destroy them. VMO 2 had been active all day—finding and engaging enemy artillery and mortars before they could bring fire onto the advancing marine battalions. Using both air and artillery, VMO 2 destroyed sixteen gun and mortar positions through the day. With the enemy mortars destroyed, the advance continued, and by 4:30 both companies were on objective 2 and preparing night defensive positions. With the companies digging in, the 1st Battalion's command post moved forward to ensure that it was close to the front lines.

Badly spread out, with each battalion covering frontages of well over 2,000 yards, the marines were certainly vulnerable to a North Korean counterattack. Given the skill and ferocity with which the enemy had conducted such attacks in the past, the frontline companies worked hard to prepare. For the first time engineers had sufficient material to place antipersonnel mines and booby traps along the flanks. As usual, the battalions registered night fires with all indirect fire weapons. And, for the first time since arriving in Korea, VMF(N) 513 was on station to conduct night close air support. Despite the rain and poor visibility, the "Flying Nightmares" delivered six strikes in close support of the marines. The fires, obstacles, and miserable weather, combined with the severe beating the North Koreans had taken, allowed the marines to pass a relatively quiet night. The only North Korean attack was a weak, halfhearted effort that was easily driven off.

As the brigade was fighting its way west on 3 September, the planners in Tokyo set a deadline for the return of the brigade. It must be out of the line by midnight of 5 September to give it time to embark and sail to join the 1st Marine Division's assault on Inchon on 15 September. Even as MacArthur's headquarters was setting the deadline for the brigade to withdraw, the 1st Marine Division liaison officers were working with the 5th Marines staff to fill out the landing schedule and boat assignment table. This schedule showed which units down to squad and team level were in every boat in every wave of the upcoming landing. Thus, the 5th Marines were simultaneously executing a critical counterattack in the Naktong Bulge and conducting detailed planning for the assault waves of an amphibious landing at Inchon.[18] The planning was made more complicated by the selection of Inchon as a landing site. The combination of thirty-foot tides and the island of Wolmi-do guarding the port meant the 5th Marines had to plan to land one battalion to seize the island at morning tide, withdraw all shipping ahead of the falling tide, and then return on the evening tide to land the other assault battalions at Inchon. The island approaches were so restrictive that the morning assault would have to be conducted with old destroyers converted to amphibious transports—a type of shipping the 5th Marines had not worked with before.[19]

At 11 P.M. Murray ordered Taplett's 3rd Battalion to pass through the 2nd to continue the attack in the morning. At 8 A.M. on the 4th, the 3rd passed through the 2nd and, together with the 1st, moved out into the attack. Within forty minutes the 3rd Battalion had completed its pincer movement and held the top of Hill 117. The North Koreans had had enough, and the previous day's stiff resistance was rapidly turning into a rout. The 1st Battalion moved just as quickly in its zone. Within minutes it had overrun the abandoned command post of the NKPA's 9th Division, complete with tents, equipment, and two operational T34s. The battalion took prisoners as North Koreans came out of hiding to give up. As they advanced the marines saw "the bodies of many dead NKPA soldiers and piles of abandoned or destroyed equipment, souvenirs of low-flying Corsair strikes and accurate fire from the 11th Marines poured on the retreating enemy. Among the litter were captured American guns, tanks, mortars and vehicles which were returned to the 2d Division."[20]

By 3 P.M. the battalions had overrun objective 1 and were overlooking a 1,600-meter-wide series of rice paddies before the next high ground. The only vehicle route across the valley was the one road that served as the boundary between the 1st and 3rd Battalions. There was also a series of the small dikes characteristic of rice paddies that the infantry could move along. The 1st was ordered to move out and seize the high ground west of the rice paddies. About three-quarters of the way across, Company B, 1st Battalion, was suddenly subjected to heavy small-arms and machine-gun fire. Fenton, recently promoted to captain and commanding officer of Company B, moved up his tanks and called in air to neutralize the enemy fire. He noted, "The amazing part of this was that we didn't have a single casualty. Not one man wounded or killed and I would say that the fire we received was just as heavy as any fire we had received in a daylight attack."[21] With the supporting arms suppressing the fire, Company B continued the attack and rapidly seized the high ground west of the paddy. Company A then crossed and seized the southern half of the same high ground.

During one of the last strikes of the day, the brigade demonstrated how tightly the helicopters at brigade headquarters were tied to the strike aircraft coming out of Japan. At 6 P.M. a Corsair pilot reported that he had been forced to bail out:

"Before his chute opened an HO3S (helicopter) stationed at Brigade command post was airborne and was ready to pick the pilot up almost as his feet touched the ground. The fighter pilot estimated he remained on the ground three minutes before being picked up."[22]

At this point the brigade made the decision to hole up for the night. This left Company A and B almost 2,000 meters in front of the 3rd Battalion and manning a very thin line almost a mile long. The 3rd was almost as isolated. It could not make contact with the army's 9th Infantry, which was supposed to be attacking on its right. Thus, both battalions dug in with their flanks in the air and large gaps between their companies. To protect the gaps, the marines again called forward engineers to place mines, wire, and booby traps. As always, fires were adjusted, and they prepared to defend against an attack from any direction. Apparently the pounding the 9th Division had taken over the previous two days had taken the fight out of it, and there was not even a token ground attack that night. The North Koreans did open fire with a fairly heavy concentration of artillery—hitting the 1st Battalion's command post and line companies. The Flying Nightmares immediately conducted a strike that silenced the enemy artillery for the rest of the night. Once again the marines spent a miserable night in a cold, driving rain.

Craig ordered the brigade to continue the attack on the 5th. At first light the 3rd Battalion observed a North Korean attack developing against the 9th Infantry to its right. It took advantage of its high ground to pour direct and indirect fire into the attackers. The attack was destroyed before it ever started, and the marines were ready to move out. In preparation for the marine attack, the 1st Battalion demonstrated how smoothly marine and army artillery could work together as its preparatory fires were reinforced by the U.S. Army 15th Field Artillery Battalion (105mm) and the 503rd Field Artillery Battalion (155mm) to provide the heaviest artillery preparation to date.[23] As the units moved off, they knew they were just a few thousand yards from Obong-ni Ridge—in fact, the 1st Battalion's first objective was Observation Hill, which had been the line of departure for the attack on the ridge. The battalions moved forward swiftly, the companies working together smoothly. In each battalion one company would act as a base of fire while the other moved forward quickly to seize the next hilltop. Then it would provide a base of fire as its sister company moved up.

The attack moved so quickly that the 3rd Battalion was pinched out by the advances of the 1st Battalion and the 9th Infantry. It was ordered to hold up and then sideslip to the left to pass behind the 1st and become the left flank of the regiment. When it was in place, the two battalions would launch an attack on Obong-ni Ridge. As the day progressed, the rain got heavier and a fog moved in. Marine air was grounded. The North Koreans took advantage of the weather to launch a vicious counterattack against the 1st Battalion. Only 400 yards from the main enemy position on Obong-ni Ridge, the 1st was suddenly subjected to heavy mortar and artillery fire as well as raking heavy machine guns. The marines were pinned down, and the rain knocked out all the company radios. Fenton sent runners to the army unit on his right, requesting all available artillery fire. He also sent runners to battalion, both to update it and to request fire, and a final runner to the tanks to warn them that three North Korean tanks were moving up the road as part of the counterattack. Unfortunately, that runner did not arrive in time. The marine tanks were focused on supporting the marines on the ridge and were thus facing the wrong direction. The North Koreans quickly knocked out two of the tanks. They in turn were engaged and destroyed by 3.5-inch rocket-launcher teams from the battalion and Company B.

Fenton's runner to the army, upon arriving at the unit's position, requested all available fires. Just as the army officer was making the fire request, he was wounded badly and evacuated. The runner, PFC William A. Wilson, a twenty-two-year-old graduate of Ohio State University, took over and directed several artillery fire missions in front of his fellow marines. He then called the army platoon leaders up, pointed out the marine positions, advised them where to place their platoons and machine guns, and then returned to report to Fenton. Fenton later related that one of the army officers told him "Lieutenant Wilson" had done a great job.[24]

Despite the artillery support, the North Koreans assaulted Fenton's position with 300 to 400 infantry troops. They aggressively sought out and found the blind spots in Company B's extended defense. Fenton fed every man he had into the line to hold it. He was running out of ammunition and was also low on grenades when 2nd Lieutenant Muetzel arrived with two platoons from Company A. Most importantly, the marines of Company A brought five boxes of hand grenades and a radio. The marines simply opened the boxes and started heaving grenades at the Koreans, who were within 100 yards of their positions. With the working radio, Fenton adjusted the 81mm mortar fire by slowly "walking" it closer and closer to his lines until it was within 100 yards and finally broke the attack. The Koreans fled west in disarray toward the Naktong.

At 4 P.M., the deadline for withdrawal almost upon them, Murray ordered his battalion commanders to halt, dig in, and prepare for relief by army units. For security reasons, most marines had no idea why they had halted and were even more puzzled by the orders to withdraw. Fenton was informed by David Douglas Duncan, a *Life* magazine photographer, that the brigade was headed back to Pusan. Battalion commanders had been informed but would not put out the word over the radio for fear the North Koreans would intercept the messages.

That evening U.S. Army units moved up. Unfortunately, in the three days the marines had been in the attack, the battered 2nd Division had not been able to recover from its collapse. As a result, only small, poorly equipped and trained platoon-sized units were available to relieve the marine companies on the line. Single army companies took responsibility for the sectors held by marine battalions. The 8th Army simply had no more forces to relieve the brigade.

Taplett noted that instead of a battalion, he was relieved by a decimated rifle company led by a lieutenant. Taplett gave him radios, mortars, ammunition, batteries, food, and water as his battalion pulled back. The lieutenant had decided not to go as far forward as the 3rd Battalion but to set up well to the rear.[25]

As the infantry pulled back, the 1st Battalion maintained its batteries to cover the relief. Despite having been in continuous action since the first Naktong battle, the 1st Battalion fired approximately 5,000 rounds from 1 to 4 September in the second Naktong fight. The targets were generally mortar, machine-gun, and artillery positions, plus a few large troop concentrations.[26]

In his after-action comments, Wood noted that his battalion had learned six key lessons that would be very important during the Inchon-Seoul and Chosin Reservoir campaigns. They were:

1) Stay out of villages and towns if at all possible in selecting position areas for artillery.

2) Wherever possible, so site one gun from each battery that it may be used in an anti-tank role. Our 105mm high explosive anti-tank ammunition will stop a T-34 or similar tank.

3) As part of the battalion's standing operating procedure, carry local security personnel on the battalion commander's reconnaissance for position. Place local security posts on the hills commanding the valleys, especially those to the rear and the flanks. Establish your own patrols, and always have an aggressive patrol policy in operation. It's good life insurance.

4) Keep civilians, refugees, and especially children, out of the position area or camp if in a rear area. Children were used extensively, especially in the early days of the war, to enter camps for the sole purpose of leaving an armed hand grenade near some unsuspecting person.

5) Wherever possible, select and organize positions to be occupied by the battalion so that at least one battery will be able to fire in any direction.

6) Every Marine, regardless of his rank, primary MOS, or job, is essentially an infantryman when it comes to shooting the weapon with which he is armed.[27]

By midnight the brigade had been relieved and was moving back to Pusan to prepare for Inchon. The brigade had been in action for one month. It had lost a total of 903 marines and sailors: 149 killed, 14 died of wounds, 730 wounded, 1 died of disease, and 9 missing (7 confirmed killed).[28] It had restored the 8th Army lines in three separate offensives, inflicted an estimated 9,900 casualties while smashing in turn the NKPA's 83rd Motorcycle Regiment; 6th, 4th, and 9th Divisions; 16th Independent Brigade; and elements of the 16th Mechanized Brigade.[29] Yet, the marines knew they still had a tough fight ahead. With only days to absorb replacements; integrate the third rifle companies, which had finally arrived; repair or replace worn-out equipment and clothing; and embark for an amphibious landing, the brigade had no time to rest.

The brigade arrived on the piers at Pusan on 7 September. With no shelter available, the marines slept on the docks while preparing for embarkation. On the plus side, they ate hot food aboard the ships three times a day. As usual, the Marine Corps supply system did not have the gear the marines needed. Fortunately, army supply did, and the marines soon discovered they could simply enter any boxcar or warehouse and take what they needed. The soldiers did not contest their choices. Inevitably, one of the foraging parties found beer and ice. They immediately filled a jeep trailer with ice and beer and started a major party alongside the USS *Henrico*. The foragers made numerous runs to maintain the beer supply, but unfortunately soon encountered army MPs. In the ensuing flight from pursuit, the somewhat handicapped marines drove the jeep and trailer off the pier.

On a more serious note, the marines had been ordered to turn in the various items of captured North Korean and U.S. Army motor transport. As a result, they were short of necessary vehicles for the invasion. Second Lieutenant Muetzel recalled, "Consequently, vehicles were purloined from the army. The worst offense I saw was the theft of the MP company commander's jeep. After a fast coat of paint and phony numbers were slapped on, it was presented to Lieutenant Colonel George Newton, our battalion CO."[30]

Along with acquiring vehicles, the brigade absorbed 1,135 officers and men, including the sorely missed third rifle company for each battalion. For the first time the 5th Marines were near wartime strength. The units worked hard to integrate the new marines while repairing or replacing worn weapons, maintaining heavy equipment, and preparing everything for an amphibious landing.

In the six days (7–12 September) between its withdrawal from heavy combat until it had to sail, the brigade had to move almost sixty miles, absorb replacements that represented 30 percent of its infantry strength, incorporate the new rifle companies and the corresponding increases in weapons and H&S companies, complete planning, issue orders, and embark. To add yet another complication, upon arrival in Pusan the brigade was made responsible for the Korean Marine Regiment, which was to land with it at Inchon. Unfortunately, one of the Korean marine battalions did not even have weapons. Thus, in addition to the massive effort necessary to prepare the brigade to conduct an extremely difficult amphibious landing, the staff had to find the personnel and equipment to provide very basic weapons training as well as supervise the embarkation of the Korean marines and teach them how to live aboard ship.

Detailed planning started with the brigade's arrival at the piers on 7 September; embarkation had to commence on the 9th, and the convoy would sail on the 12th. In the few days available, the brigade had to refine the embarkation plan and develop the scheme of maneuver, boat assignment tables, landing plans, and fire support plans—all for a target most of the planners had never heard of until they arrived at the piers.[31]

Fortunately, the planners had access to aerial photos of the Inchon area. Two F4U-5P photo reconnaissance Corsairs and a marine photo reconnaissance detachment had sailed with the brigade in August and had been quietly working from Japan to support current brigade operations as well as planning for Inchon. Once again the brigade proved the usefulness of a task-organized air-ground team with a culture of working together. Despite the fact that they were not under a single commander, marine air always found a way to support marine ground elements.

The brigade sailed on schedule, and at 12:01 A.M. on 13 September, somewhere in the Yellow Sea, it ceased to exist. All elements returned to their parent units in the 1st Marine Division and 1st MAW.[32] Thirty hours later the 3rd Battalion, 5th Marines, supported by other elements of the brigade, spearheaded the landing at Inchon.

WHAT DID THEY ACCOMPLISH?

So what did this hastily assembled brigade of marines accomplish in its sixty-seven days of existence? According to Volume 1 of the U.S. Marine Operations in Korea, the brigade "inflicted total casualties of 9,900 killed and wounded on opposing NKPA units. Enemy losses of arms and equipment were on such a scale as to impair the effectiveness of the forces concerned." However, the cost was high: 172 marines died, and 730 were wounded—almost 14 percent of the original strength of the brigade.[33] As always, the vast majority of the casualties were concentrated in the rifle companies. According to the unit diaries, the rifle companies dropped an average of 127 marines from their rolls during their time in the Pusan Perimeter.[34] Although not all these men were casualties, the sheer number indicates the turbulence the rifle companies endured.

Entering the fight with badly understrength units and suffering heavy casualties, the brigade nonetheless succeeded in three offensive operations during a month in combat. Despite having to repeatedly shift in and out of the line and travel a distance of over 380 mile with only one-third of its organic transportation, the brigade met every challenge.

One month after activation and less than seventy-two hours after arriving in Korea, the brigade went into the attack with TF Kean. Meeting the relatively fresh NKPA 6th Division head-on, the brigade would need only two days to defeat the North Korean attack and then four more to drive the Koreans back twenty-six miles. In doing so, the brigade and its army counterparts effectively destroyed one of the freshest and best-equipped North Korean divisions. More important, they turned back the most serious threat to the port of Pusan. Showing true flexibility, the brigade sustained the main attack while dispatching a battalion twenty-six miles to the rear to restore the lines of the adjacent army unit.

Terminating their attack only on orders from the 8th Army, the marines moved quickly back to a staging area, then counterattacked in a different direction. This First Battle of the Naktong resulted in some of the hardest, closest fighting in Marine Corps history. The tactical choice to assault Obong-ni Ridge frontally with only two understrength rifle companies was clearly a poor one—perhaps driven by time constraints, lack of information about the enemy, or even simple overconfidence. Yet the combination of tenacity, effective use of combined arms, and sheer courage allowed the marines to drive a tough, experienced NKPA regiment out of well-prepared reverse-slope defenses. Exceptional small-unit skills and effective use of combined arms, particularly air, turned the initial failure to seize Obong-ni Ridge into a massive rout of the NKPA 4th Division and restored the Naktong River line. The blow was so heavy that it would take the North Koreans ten days after the marines left to reestablish a beachhead over the Naktong.

Pulled off the line to prepare for the landing at Inchon, the brigade shifted focus to preparing for embarkation. It had to plan not only for the landing but for how to disband the brigade and rejoin its elements to their parent units. The units immersed themselves in the innumerable details of amphibious planning and embarkation while simultaneously refitting and absorbing the limited replacements available. In the midst of this intense activity, with the brigade staff split between Japan and Korea and heavy equipment being embarked, the brigade was suddenly committed to the Second Battle of the Naktong. Once again the marines conducted a hasty attack. Once again they drove the North Koreans back with heavy casualties. However, there would not be a repeat of the massacre of the NKPA 4th Division. As the brigade picked up momentum, driving almost 3,000 yards on the third day of the attack, it was recalled to embark for Inchon. The embarkation process was already days late in starting, and any further delay in leaving the line might mean the landing would miss the one night per month on which tidal conditions were adequate for the landing at Inchon.

In a final burst of activity, the brigade managed to complete the plan, absorb replacements, reequip its units, provide basic training for a ROK marine regiment, and embark the entire force in just five days. As with every other challenge the brigade faced, it succeeded.

12

Why Did They Win?

In this book I set out to examine how the Marine Corps maintained a high level of combat-readiness between the end of World War II and the corps's sudden commitment to combat in Korea. I measured this effectiveness by the 1st Provisional Marine Brigade's remarkable combat record in the early days of the Korean War. Over time popular literature identified and then reinforced the belief in certain "truths" about why the brigade fought so well. In reality, because the brigade was hastily assembled and existed only from 7 July to 13 September 1950, its performance was shaped primarily not by its activities as a brigade but by how individuals and units developed in the period before the war. The Marine Corps's culture, educational system, doctrine, organization, training, and leadership between VJ Day (15 August 1945) and North Korea's invasion (25 June 1950) shaped the brigade. Thus, the real question becomes: How did these elements of "fighting power" allow the brigade to succeed despite the enormous handicaps it faced?

The popular and later even official Marine Corps literature on the Korean War came to credit the brigade's success to several key factors: leaders with extensive ground combat experience, unit cohesion based on a long period of training together, arduous physical training, and the effectiveness of the air-ground team. As this book has shown, although there is an element of truth in each factor, for the most part, other than the effectiveness of the air-ground team, these notions are not supported by the actual personnel and training records of the era.

Like most legends, the story of the brigade accumulated over time. Early official reports stuck close to the facts. One of the first, "A Report on the Activities of FMFPac from 25 June 1950 to the Amphibious Assault at Inchon" was written by Headquarters, FMFPac. Released on 6 December 1950, less than three months after the brigade was deactivated, the report covered the activities of both the brigade at Pusan and the 1st Marine Division and 1st MAW at Inchon. In discussing the success of the early-arriving marine forces in Korea, FMFPac noted:

Their subsequent success in action appears to validate the tactical doctrines and techniques of the ground combat arms and services. The homogeneity of the Marine Corps moreover insured that these doctrines were held and understood throughout the Corps, largely through the medium of instruction at the Marine Corps Schools coordinated with practical application in the Fleet Marine Force. Painstaking adherence to this practice made it possible for units to be assembled from widely diverse sources and committed to combat with confidence, although they had participated in far less than the optimum amount of training. Despite the fact that in many cases units were not able to exercise in the many coordinate details which must be perfected to insure effective combat performance, there was nevertheless a justifiable assurance that all hands knew what to do and how to do it because of a uniform Marine Corps program of instruction.[1]

The report went on to detail the extensive training conducted by the elements of the 1st Marine Division and 1st MAW over the winter of 1949–1950. Although written by the headquarters that was responsible for the prewar training of the marines, it was remarkably candid about the shortcomings of that training. It noted that many of the marines who fought with the brigade had not participated in the previous year's training because they were not in the operating forces but stationed at various posts and bases on the West Coast. The report stated that these posts and stations had only conducted annual weapons qualification and individual military training, but it made no mention of any unit training, thus indicating that they had not conducted any. However, the report contended that this failure was partially overcome by the Marine Corps policy of rotating marines through the combat forces on short tours. FMFPac seemed satisfied with its training program and but did note "that the fact Division, Wing and Headquarters, Fleet Marine Force, Pacific were undergoing their annual personnel turnover period, with a number of key command and staff positions involved, was the single factor tending to lower the combat effectiveness of the units concerned."[2] Thus, the initial report by the senior marine headquarters in the Pacific attributed the success to a combination of education, doctrine, and training. It concluded that although many of the marines in the brigade had not served together long enough to develop unit cohesion, the underlying culture of corpswide conformity in doctrine, instruction, and training had provided a different form of cohesion. This conclusion seems to defy the conventional wisdom that training together is essential for unit cohesion.

Despite its admirable frankness, the report had numerous shortcomings. Although it acknowledged the impact of turbulence, it failed to appreciate—and due to the speed of the mobilization may not have realized—that over 50 percent of the brigade was composed of men who joined it during embarkation. Although it admitted that "a number of key command and staff positions turned over," it badly understated the 100 percent turnover of commanders at battalion level and above. Further, the report ignored the physical-fitness deficiencies noted by Murray's frustrated comment that "at least a third of my regiment [was] lying at the side of the road with heat exhaustion"[3] as well as the over 80 percent losses of Company B, 1st Battalion, 5th Marines, to heat exhaustion during its first offensive action. It also did not acknowledge the brigade special action report of 11 September 1950, which recorded that "more casualties occurred from heat prostration in August than anything else."[4] Although the marines who had trained in the FMF over the winter were in good physical condition, many who joined in that hectic week before embarkation clearly were not. And of course, their condition deteriorated during the transit across the Pacific.

However, the FMFPac report captured the key organizational factor that contributed to the brigade's success: the common education, doctrine, and training throughout the corps that allowed these forces to be assembled at short notice and still fight well. This analysis was very different from the mythology that would develop over the next fifty years.

CULTURE

Although not specifically saying so, the FMFPac report credited marine culture with creating "a justifiable assurance that all hands knew what to do and how to do it." It implied that the brigade was able to overcome a lack of cohesion because the culture that required common doctrine, education, and training for all marines meant they shared a common tactical approach. Even more important, the common identity as marines created trust that was essential to effective combat units. In short, marine culture substituted for the normal methods of building unit cohesion. This is a remarkable conclusion given the importance both serving officers and historians place on time served together as an essential element of unit cohesion.

Analyzing the corps using the six elements of "fighting power," I have come to a similar conclusion: The corps's culture made up for serious deficiencies in individual and unit training and conditioning. In this case I define "culture" as the values, norms, and assumptions that guide human action. Culture enables choices to be made by predisposing people to interpret situations in a limited number of ways. For example, the individual marine's predisposition was to assume that other marines would never leave him behind. The statements of marines who fought at Pusan demonstrate that this factor had a major impact on how they responded to the stress and fear of combat.

However, I see the role of marine culture as more expansive and important than discussed in the FMFPac report. The impact of culture can be seen in almost everything the corps did between 1945 and 1950 to maintain its combat-effectiveness. Marine culture guided the actions of the institution and the individual marines because it enjoined marines both to remember and to learn. Both aspects clearly drove the other elements of fighting power during those lean times.

Remembering

The corps has long been recognized as an organization that honors and defends its traditions. As noted by Cameron, new marines "were treated more as initiates than simple inductees, and their drill instructors claimed for themselves a larger role as proselytizers and not mere teachers."[5] Although the U.S. Army made significant changes to its training methods after World War II, the Marine Corps refused to yield on the training methods it had developed to instill marine culture. In particular, the corps defended the philosophy that each recruit must first become a marine, and therefore a fighting man, before he could go on to specialized training. Robert D. Heinl, one of the leading historians of the Marine Corps and at the time a serving lieutenant colonel, believed organizational culture was central to the success of the corps. In 1950 he wrote,

> Yes—all things considered—perhaps the Marine Corps is an elite force. But why? Whatever the reasons may be it is not because the incoming recruits and potential officers of the Corps constitute any elect body of supermen. The recruit who passes through Horse Island Gate at Parris Island is just an average American boy in physique, intelligence, and background. He is no different from the youngster the Army drafts. It is what happens to him *after* he enlists, and while he is becoming a Marine at boot camp, that begins the long process of making him elite. It is the Marine Corps system, not the raw material, which counts.[6]

For individuals, the remembering aspect of marine culture came through clearly in almost every personal account of the fighting. The marines who wrote about their time in the brigade echoed Heinl's sentiments. Each spoke about the reinforcing power of the marine history inculcated into them at boot camp and repeated constantly in the FMF in the form of "war" stories from the veterans, ceremonies, and celebrations. They also recalled the "presence" of every marine who had fought before them and the intense feeling that they could not let their predecessors down. In particular, the marines going into their first fight noted two dominant feelings. First, they couldn't let their buddies down, and second, they could not let the marines of the past down. Keep in mind that a 1950 rifle platoon was led by a lieutenant and had only one staff NCO assigned. The other forty or so men were sergeants (enlisted grade 4s) or below. Thus, the vast majority who would fight at the tip of the spear in Korea had been too young for World War II. Since most of the men in the rifle platoons were not combat veterans, this determination not to fail provided important support to these men as they entered their first fight.

The corps's institutional remembering was reflected in a number of other ways. For units it lay in maintaining the combat-proven small-unit organizations developed during the harsh Pacific campaigns. Despite the postwar reality of drastically reduced strength, marine leaders refused to reduce the T/O of the rifle squad or platoon. In large organizations it is often the smallest units that are reduced in times of austerity. The obvious manpower savings of ten-man World War I squads over thirteen-man World War II squads must have made the rifle squad a tempting target. Yet the veterans of the vicious fighting in the Pacific who led the corps were convinced that the thirteen-man squad was superior in every way and maintained it against all pressure to change.

However, the corps's leaders were clearly willing to evaluate new approaches. After experimenting with the J-Series T/Os and finding them ineffective, the corps leadership was willing to admit its mistake and return to the robust, effective World War II–era divisional organization. Even though end strength cuts meant it could not man the division at even half strength, the corps recognized the value of having the organization in place for rapid mobilization. The wisdom of this decision is reflected in the rapid mobilization and deployment as well as the combat-effectiveness of the 1st Marine Division in 1950.

Another aspect of marine culture directly improved the brigade's performance against the North Koreans. The corps required officers to lead from the front—even senior officers were expected to be well up front in combat. This tendency favored the brigade and, at times, frustrated the North Korean tactics, which focused on finding a gap and going deep to destroy the U.S. headquarters and support units, such as artillery. Often the North Koreans went too deep and could not find the marine headquarters or support elements. Newton, commanding officer of the 1st Battalion, 5th Marines, noted, "The problem of defense was comparatively easy in that the battalion CP was held very close to the front lines. It was within 400 yards at night time. The members of the headquarters company were placed in the low lands and acted as a perimeter within the long avenues of approach up to the CP and to the rear."[7] The general rule was that a leader should be immediately behind the first subordinate element so that he could observe the situation and know how to employ his other elements most effectively. The brigade's leaders all the way up to General Craig followed this rule.

Pushing the command post forward was just as effective in the offense, starting with the brigade's very first fight in Korea. One of the reasons Kean, the 25th Division commander, passed control of his regiments to Craig during the first two days of the Sachon fight was because Craig was present on the scene. His command post was within a few miles of the front, whereas the 25th Division's command post was twenty miles to the rear. The poor roads and communications networks made it physically impossible for the army leaders to influence the battle from that distance. Craig was adamant that leaders had to be positioned well forward. "I found throughout my operation in Korea that the closer I could get to the front, the better control due to the congestion on the few roads and the lack of good communications."[8]

The forward presence of marine leaders allowed for rapid, informed decision-making each time the brigade faced a crisis. From the confusion at the intersection on the first day of the Sachon offensive to the passage of lines during the Naktong fights, both personal and official accounts show that the immediate presence of marine leaders—platoon, company, battalion, regimental, and brigade commanders—had an immediate impact on the fighting. Craig's instant grasp of the potential of the helicopter reinforced this trait. Repeatedly Craig either used a helicopter to personally reconnoiter the scene or provided one to his regimental and battalion commanders so they could do so. Yet, though they used the helicopters to conduct reconnaissance, marine leaders never tried to control action from the air. Instead they landed and moved forward on the ground. This allowed them to see and feel the battle as their subordinates did as well as letting them confer face to face.

In contrast, army doctrine and practice placed leaders much farther back. As noted, Kean's divisional command post was twenty miles behind the front lines. An army officer remembered that, in contrast to marine battalion commanders who were within a few hundred yards of the front line, army leaders were often out of touch with the fighting: "Our infantry lines were along the forward slope, the battalion command post was four or five miles back of us, and the trains were two miles beyond that."[9]

Another aspect of remembering was the corps's near religious devotion to the concept that every marine is a rifleman: Every man fights. Ransom Wood, the artilleryman who commanded the 1st Battalion, 11th Marines, recalled the impact this idea had on the marines in Korea:

> Finally, one lesson learned by Marines long ago was recalled. Fortunately, we hadn't forgotten it in our training in the States, and we hadn't forgotten it when the Chinese entered the picture in Korea. That lesson is that every Marine, regardless of rank, primary MOS, or job, is essentially an infantryman, when it comes to shooting the weapons with which he is armed. What with the extraordinary tasks imposed on the infantrymen, the combat support troops and the combat service support troops, there are many of them who are alive today because that lesson has not and will not be forgotten in the Marine Corps.[10]

As part of this creed, every marine was a marksman. Despite the massive firepower supporting the marine infantryman, marine leaders never let up on the fundamental concept that every marine must be able to hit his target. From dedicating two weeks of boot camp to basic marksmanship instruction to the value placed on it by marines in the operating forces, the corps reinforced this idea at every opportunity. The performance of the marines at Second Naktong when riflemen hit fleeing North Koreas at 400 to 500 yards proved it was not just a motto but a reality.

The final remembering aspect was the fundamental commitment never to leave a marine behind. From the cheers that greeted Craig's statement on the pier at San Diego to the tough fighting on the Naktong, marines were confident they would not be left behind and therefore did not have to retreat.

Learning

The learning aspects of marine culture were illustrated by numerous aggressive efforts to improve the performance of the corps's combat forces after World War II. Despite having just finished its most successful war ever and being assured of a "Marine Corps for another 500 years," the corps's leadership immediately examined key aspects of the corps's performance. The commandant himself noted the failures in air-ground cooperation, fire support coordination, and antitank tactics. And like all the services, the corps had to grapple with the possible changes wrought by atomic weapons. Vandegrift did not let the corps rest on its laurels. Instead he reinstituted the Advance Base Group at Quantico specifically to examine how the corps could become more effective in combat. This effort to learn from recent operations was vital to the success of the brigade in 1950.

One of the truly critical factors in the brigade's success was the post-1945 development of the attitudes, organizations, tactics, techniques, and procedures necessary to create a true air-ground combat team. The corps had entered World War II with a firm belief in the air-ground team. By 1941 marine aviators had been working for two decades to improve their ability to provide close air support to their ground counterparts. Yet the peculiar circumstances of the Pacific campaigns and exigencies of wartime training eroded that belief to the point that some aviation and ground officers were barely on speaking terms by 1945.

Even before the end of the war Vandegrift became concerned about both the education of his marines and the schism that had occurred between air and ground. In late 1945 he made the critical decision to dedicate a significant portion of the corps's decreasing assets to restoring educational standards and developing an effective air-ground team. Only by dedicating extensive resources in terms of education, doctrine, and training was the corps able to build an air-ground team that could successfully operate based on mutual trust despite being physically separated and in different chains of command.

Today marines take it as a matter of faith that they will deploy as part of an integrated air-ground team. Today's marine expeditionary brigade is an air-ground team under a single commander. It is built around a regimental combat team, a marine air group, and a brigade logistics element. However, it is important that today's readers understand that the brigades formed before 1950 were not based on this model. They were strictly ground organizations. By 1950, despite the focus on developing air-ground teams, the corps's aviation elements, even when phased ashore, worked through a separate chain of command unless it was an amphibious corps-level landing. There was simply no doctrine or organization for marine units below amphibious corps level to command both air and ground elements. The appointment of a single commander for an air-ground team at the brigade level had simply not happened. Even as the corps refined air-ground doctrine and training, the brigades it actually formed in FMFLant and FMFPac between 1946 and 1950 were ground-only organizations.

On 26 January 1946 the FMFLant brigade was established at Quantico. The brigade was formed by taking marines from all over Quantico. It was composed of a composite infantry battalion and supporting attachments, and like previous marine brigades, it was purely a ground organization. On 4 March the 1st Brigade moved to Camp Lejeune and was eventually absorbed into the 2nd Marine Division upon the 2nd Division's arrival from Japan in the summer of 1946.[11]

During the spring of 1947 FMFPac was ordered to form the 1st Provisional Marine Brigade on Guam from units being withdrawn from China. The brigade, activated on 1 June, had two infantry battalions; a service battalion; and a headquarters battalion with a tank platoon, hospital company, engineer company, truck company service, and supply company. Interestingly, the order forming the brigade specified no artillery batteries. Instead select brigade personnel would be given additional duty as artillerymen.[12] This brigade, also known as the 1st Provisional Marine Brigade and commanded by Brigadier General Craig, was purely a ground organization, and it did not enjoy the luxury of two infantry battalions for long. When the Marine Corps adopted the J-Series T/Os on 1 October 1947, the brigade lost one of its infantry battalions. When the corps reorganized under the K-Series T/Os on 30 September 1949, the brigade was deactivated. Upon deactivation, its units packed up for transportation back to Camp Pendleton, where they were reorganized under the K-Series T/Os and absorbed by the 1st Marine Division.[13]

These brigades, both strictly ground organizations, were the mental models the division marines adopted when ordered to form the 1st Provisional Marine Brigade for deployment to Korea in July 1950. Thus, despite the fact that the Marine Corps was working hard at air-ground doctrine, it was not organizing its operating forces to operate under a single commander. The primary reason was the corps's focus on amphibious warfare. The assumption was that marine aviation would be ship-based to support the landing and would not come ashore until the assault phase was over. The navy was adamant that aircraft operating from ships would be under naval command. Since there was nothing the corps could do to change the navy command structure, it had to accept a split command for its forces in the early phases of amphibious operations.

The awkward command structure made the corps's return to the concept and culture that marines fight as an air-ground team absolutely essential to the success of the brigade in Korea. The exceptional support MAG 33 provided to the 5th Marines proved that a deep understanding and mutual respect could overcome the problems inherent in the marine air and ground elements operating under different chains of command with no mutual superior below MacArthur himself. It also showed the importance of the theater commander recognizing the power of that team and ensuring that subordinate commanders did not interfere. Had MacArthur placed marine air under air force control, the situation would have been very different. As noted by numerous observers and summarized by Fred Allison, "Air Force neglect of tactical air had resulted in atrophied air support. Now working outside a common uniform (from the US Army), with distinctly separate missions, there existed little reason to improve a cumbersome air support system, nor maintain the necessary skills and equipment air support required."[14]

As a result of the very different ideas on the proper use of air between army–air force and navy-marine teams, the start of the Korean War saw two different systems of close air support in existence:

> The Air Force system had largely been developed in the European theater. There, the exercise of command over aircraft was not given to the frontline units; employment of aircraft was jointly coordinated at the Army level by two officers—one air, one ground. Strike planes did not orbit the battlefront, but were assigned to a particular mission as approved by the joint operations center (JOC). Upon arrival at the scene of conflict, planes would be directed and controlled by airborne, liaison-type aircraft, not by ground parties. Close air support targets were considered to be those within the immediate battle zone, as much as ten miles away.
>
> At the time of the outbreak of the Korean war, the army–air force system was not immediately ready.
>
> The Navy-Marine systems, on the other hand, had largely been developed in the Pacific war as an indivisible part of an amphibious assault. A certain number of aircraft were committed for use and control by the ground commander, who could use their services as and where he saw fit. A few planes constantly orbited the battlefield, ready to strike "close air support" targets that were within 50 to 200 yards of the immediate front lines. The pilots received guidance and information for their attacks from a trained crew directly in the front lines.
>
> At the outbreak of the Korean war, this system was ready.[15]

The U.S. Air Force simply did not have an institutional ethos that valued close air support. In fact, in establishing an air force culture separate from that of its parent service the army, air force leadership had aggressively sought a distinct mission. The air force was determined to prove air power could win wars by itself and therefore was hostile even to airmen who sought to improve close air support after World War II. Obviously, an organization focused on winning wars through strategic bombing did not expend scarce resources in training to support ground troops.

Without the commandant's focused effort to rebuild the air-ground team, the poisonous relationships in late 1945 could easily have led to a split within the Marine Corps similar to that between the army and air force. Like their Army Air Forces counterparts, marine aviators had focused on air superiority and interdiction efforts during World War II. Marine aviators came out of the war resentful of marine ground officers who did not acknowledge their contributions to the war. For their part, marine ground officers questioned the corps's heavy investment in aviation, particularly at a time of sharply decreasing budgets. Only the sustained investment in education, doctrine, training, and organizations focused on the reintegration of the corps's elements prevented such a split. Between 1945 and 1950,

> the Marine Corps induced its aviators to be more "ground-like," to seek their identity first as Marines and secondly as aviators. Thus a common uniform, integrated training and cross-training held together with esprit de corps gave Marines a common mission. Professionally executed close air support, then, became a Marine Corps specialty through common training and a common military culture. Pilots identified with the ground battle and in the CAS mission subordinated their skills and airborne weapons to the ground commander.[16]

Interviews with Corsair pilots after their combat tours in Korea reflected how completely the Marine Corps had healed the split between air and ground. Robert Keller expressed the intensity of the bonds that had developed between air and ground Marines: "When the chips are really down, and you saw what those troopers had to do, hell you almost ran your airplane in the ground to take somebody out . . . we got religion. This goes back to the difference in the organization of the armed forces. Marines are a team and the cutting edge of the sword of the team is the troops, the grunts."[17]

Lt. Col. Emmons Maloney's views were similar and highlighted how he, as a pilot, became involved in the ground battle: "The guns would freeze up sometimes, I was strafing some troops one time and my guns froze up and I was going to show them, I was going to go down and cut their heads off. I got down there and then I thought, 'What the hell am I doing?' I could go down and cut their heads off but I could auger in [crash] doing something like that."[18]

Although marine aviators were not seeking a new mission to justify their existence as a separate service, they performed the full range of aviation functions. With the exception of strategic bombing, which the air force claimed for itself, the emaciated MAWs were prepared to conduct almost all other aviation missions—air defense, surveillance, aerial photography, aerial interdiction, strike, transportation, and control of aircraft. They trained for all these missions, yet the change in culture between 1945 and 1950 was so complete that marine aviators were adamant that their most important mission was providing close air support.

Ground officers were every bit as enthusiastic about the air-ground team. Of course for ground officers the benefits of responsive, effective close air support were obvious and immense. By 1950 the intensive effort by Headquarters Marine Corps to build an effective air-ground team had succeeded.

And marine ground officers weren't the only ones enthusiastic about marine air. Gen. Mark W. Clark, strongly encouraged by Lt. Gen. Ned Almond, wrote to the army chief of staff Gen. J. Lawton Collins, "More recently, the operation of Marine Air in Korea in direct support of Army and Marine Corps units has demonstrated a great advantage which the Marine Close Air Support System has over the Army–Air Force system. The Marine System operated on command instead of a cooperative basis, thus assuring the ground commander operational control of his support air units."[19]

Almond, who as commanding general of X Corps had the 1st MAW flying in support of his corps, was a very strong proponent of marine aviation. He had seen the effectiveness of the marine air-ground team during both the Inchon-Seoul campaign and the Chosin Reservoir campaign. He argued vociferously and repeatedly for the army to have aviation similar to that of the Marine Corps. He stated, "The chief objection I had to the support that we received in Northeast Korea was the fact that the Air Force high command desired notification of tactical air support requirements 24 hours in advance. . . . We need an Air Force commitment to respond to unplanned tactical air support requests within 30–50 minutes of the initial requests."[20] Almond put his resources where his mouth was. Since the army–air force system provided only four TAC parties per division (one at division and one at each infantry regiment), Almond took ground officers and communications soldiers to create the thirteen TACPs per division that were part of the navy-marine air control system. He assembled them, trained them, insisted that the air force certify them, and then deployed them to the army divisions that were part of X Corps.

Testimony from marines and soldiers show that the commandant had clearly succeeded in fixing the schism between marine air and ground that grew out of World War II. Historian Max Hastings noted,

> From the first days of the war there was intense and often bad tempered debate between the ground commanders and senior officers of FEAF [Far East Air Force] about the quality and quantity of close air support they received. This was heightened by Army jealousy of Navy and Marine organic air support, which the soldiers considered both more dedicated, and more professional, than that of the Air Force. The argument hinged upon the weight of Air Force effort that should be given directly to the ground forces, and at whose discretion this should be allotted.[21]

The Marine Corps was less successful at fixing the second problem that General Vandegrift identified—fire support coordination. By 1950 the educational, doctrinal, and organizational requirements had been worked out in detail to provide a system for fire support coordination, but only at the division level. However, the peacetime K-Series T/Os did not provide personnel for a fire support coordination center even at that level. That organization would not be activated until the division shifted to a wartime organization. Even the wartime T/Os did not provide for FSCCs below division level. When interviewed after returning from Korea, Lt. Col. Francis F. Parry, who commanded the 3rd Battalion, 11th Marines—an artillery battalion—noted,

> The supporting arms center at (infantry) battalion level is fairly much an organization in name only. Each battalion runs it differently. I'd say in the majority of battalions, the battalion commander is supporting arms coordinator for all practical purposes; he usually decides whether he wants an air strike or artillery. . . . Usually it's a race between air and artillery to see who can bring fire down on a target first. In this respect, the air occasionally uses dubious tactics in that they get planes up in the air and the artillery has to stop shooting. Then the planes take several minutes locating the target, whereas the artillery could by that time have brought fire in.[22]

While highlighting the problems caused by the lack of an FSCC at lower levels, Parry's comments dramatically illustrate how the attitude of marine aviators had changed since the early days of the Air-Infantry School.

Despite the lack of FSCCs, the battalions clearly integrated all forms of firepower. Based on firsthand accounts, a primary reason for this integration was the terrain. Being both hilly and largely deforested, Korea provided good fields of observation. A battalion commander could often move to an observation post and through his supporting arms representatives coordinate the fires ahead of his companies. In a similar fashion, the company commander or the company executive officer could coordinate the fires for his company. A second important factor was that during the initial Sachon offensive a single company was in the lead. This virtually eliminated the need to coordinate fires with other ground forces. The lead company had only to coordinate fires with the movement of its own platoons. The FACs could work with the forward observers to ensure that air, artillery, and mortar fires did not conflict with each other. Finally, informal coordination worked well when the North Koreans broke and ran. The brigade's special action review recorded that "during those periods when large groups of enemy were retreating before our forces it became a practice to drive him to shelter with aerial strafing and rockets. When a large group concentrated in one shelter, that is, a village or road culvert, artillery would be called in to flush them out and the aircraft would hit him again as he ran."[23]

This informal fire support coordination system was not as successful when attacking with two regiments in line as part of a larger offensive such as that of the Naktong Bulge. In those situations the units had significant problems coordinating across service lines and suffered serious casualties because of their inability to do so. After-action reports acknowledged this deficiency, and after the war the corps formalized the FSCC down to the infantry battalion level.

Antiarmor defense was another deficiency identified by the commandant. Here too the educational, doctrinal, and organizational foundations were well established by 1950. Unfortunately, like the FSCCs, the antiarmor organizations added to the units were never manned. However, the education, doctrine, and training clearly worked on the two occasions when the brigade faced tanks. In each case the marines executed a doctrinal defense in depth that used all available tank-killing weapons together to destroy the North Korean armor.

An important aspect of the cultural willingness to learn was the corps's willingness to admit that a new idea didn't work. The experiment with the J-Series T/Os was a rational attempt to deal with the quantitatively different impact that atomic weapons could have on the battlefield. However, after two years of working with the new organization, the marines admitted that it did not significantly improve the corps's capability on an atomic battlefield, whereas it decreased its capability to fight a conventional war. Despite the major investments made in reorganizing the force, the corps's senior leadership was able to admit the mistake and return to the combat-proven triangular division.

POSTWAR IMPACT OF KOREA

The Korean War shaped a generation of marines. Although World War II was obviously much larger and involved many more of the corps's leaders, it is clear that Korea helped form the modern Marine Corps in two major ways. First, it changed the corps's air-ground concept from a doctrinal belief to a cornerstone of marine culture. Second, it changed the thinking of marines concerning what it meant to be a "force in readiness."

The first, and most clearly traceable to the Korean War, is the corps's intense belief in fighting as an air-ground team. The marines who fought at the Pusan Perimeter and then went on to Inchon, Seoul, and the Chosin Reservoir daily observed the timeliness and accuracy of marine air. Many of the ground officers—particularly those who fought their way out of the encirclement at Chosin—believed they owed their lives to the presence of marine aviators. Some of these officers remained with the 1st Marine Division when it reentered the fight in South Korea without the dedicated support of the 1st MAW. This happened when, upon withdrawal from North Korea, the 1st Marine Division was taken out of combat to replace casualties and equipment. It then entered the line under command of the 8th Army. During the division's rest period, the 1st MAW was placed under air force command. When the division returned to the line, the air force argued successfully for keeping the 1st MAW under its command. Thus, the MAW's sorties were assigned through the air force air support system, which made them less responsive and spread the effort across the entire ground force in Korea. Although air force officials argued that this was the most efficient use of resources, the marine ground officers, who were used to air support within minutes from the 1st MAW, were angered that air support now took hours or sometimes even days to arrive.

As noted earlier in this chapter, marine officers were not the only ones who felt that the air force's close air support was inadequate. The different emphases between the services naturally produced very different battlefield results. For ground-oriented observers, the marine system was vastly superior to that of the air force—so much so that U.S. Army officers appealed to their chain of command for better support. Col. Paul Freeman, commander of the 23rd Infantry, witnessed marine close air support when his regiment fought alongside the brigade in the Pusan Perimeter. He later wrote to Gen. Matthew B. Ridgway in Washington,

> We must have Tac Air in direct support of infantry regiments just as we have artillery; and communications must be direct and simplified. Infantry can't do the job alone. Infantry and artillery is a good team, but only by adding adequate and efficient air support can we succeed without devastating losses. . . . The Marines on our left were a sight to behold. Not only was their equipment superior or equal to ours, but they had squadrons of air in direct support. They used it like artillery. It was, "Hey, Joe, this is Smitty, knock the left of that ridge in from Item Company." They had it day and night. . . . General, we just have to have air support like that or we might as well disband the Infantry and join the Marines.[24]

Another army officer was impressed with the determination and single-minded purpose of marine pilots. He wrote in the *Combat Forces Journal,* "Our tactical air arm should spend a few months with the Marines. I don't know what causes the difference, but it is there. The Marine pilots give us the impression that they are breaking their hearts to help us out and are as much in the show as we are."[25]

Naturally the air force did not appreciate the comparisons. And its resentment was heightened when the press picked up on the controversy and articles reflecting the army officers' complaints began to appear. In response, Lt. Gen. George E. Stratemeyer, commander of the 5th Air Force, requested that Gen. Walton Walker, commander of the 8th Army, rebut one of the articles. Walker's reply was not what Stratemeyer expected:

> As for the support rendered my troops by the Fifth Air Force, I have every praise for the cooperation and assistance of Partridge and his people and have gone on record in this regard. Without the slightest intent of disparaging the support of the Air Forces, I must say that I, in common with the vast majority of officers of the Army, feel strongly that the Marine system of close air support has much to commend it. . . . I feel strongly that the Army would be well advised to emulate the Marine Corps and have its own tactical aviation.[26]

Like the marine aviators in 1945, air force personnel felt that their contributions to the war were being overlooked. The resulting long-running controversy over close air support is beyond the scope of this book. However, it is clear that the marine officers who first experienced marine close air support and then experienced the lack of aviation support from the air force became vocal and aggressive proponents of keeping marine aviation under marine command.

The exceptional support provided by marine air is clearly the result of the cultural shift that took place after World War II. The corps's efforts to rebuild the concept of an air-ground team were obviously successful. In fact, the idea of an air-ground team exceeded the doctrinal and organizational capabilities of the corps. In keeping with the concept of fighting as an air-ground team, FMFPac ordered that the 1st Provisional Marine Brigade be formed as an integrated air-ground team under a single commander. However, in July 1950 the Marine Corps simply had not worked out the command and control or interservice agreements necessary to operate as an air-ground team under a single commander. Both the original documents and the statements of members of the brigade show that the division and wing each created a separate organization. In various interviews and his own memoirs, *Incidents of Service,* Craig never referred to the 1st MAW (Forward) as part of the brigade. Nor did he treat it as such in his written orders. The brigade special action report never listed any aviation elements as being part of the brigade. Obviously, although the corps had developed the doctrine to fight as an air-ground team, the requirement was not yet a deep cultural value. However, the performance of the brigade in the Pusan Perimeter had changed the air-ground concept from mere doctrine to nearly gospel. In short, it became a cultural belief of the corps during the opening months of the Korean War.

Despite this belief, the pattern of split command was repeated when the division and wing operated as separate entities in different chains of command during the Inchon, Seoul, and Chosin campaigns. The same two factors made it work as well for the division as it did for the brigade. First, the strong belief inculcated in both marine air and ground personnel ensured that the division received extremely effective and responsive air support in these campaigns. And, just as important, MacArthur ensured that the 1st MAW remained under navy command. The navy continued to treat marine operations ashore as extensions of amphibious operations and gave priority to close air support. It was only after this relationship was severed when the 1st Marine Division returned to South Korea that the separate chain of command created any problems for the marines. When the marines came out of North Korea, command of marine air was passed to the air force. The air force command insisted that the most effective use of air was to interdict enemy supplies rather than to provide close air support. Therefore, it focused marine aviation on this mission to the detriment of the close air support mission. At the end of the war, Lt. Gen. Merrill B. Twining commented,

> The winning combination that had taken Inchon and Seoul was broken up. The surface ships, operating as a form of floating artillery bombarded Wonson and the northern ports for years with no discernable result; the carriers participated with the Air Force in operations against the enemy lines of communication—the 1st Marine Air Wing was separated from its teammate, the

1st Marine Division, thereby destroying the most effective air-ground team the world has ever seen.[27]

To marines, the lesson was painfully clear. Unless marine air was under marine command, ground marines could not count on effective close air support. This became a major point of contention between the services for decades to follow.

In addition to its aggressive, continuing efforts to protect the air-ground relationship, the corps also worked to improve its effectiveness. By the end of 1950 the Marine Corps had rewritten its requirements for tactical air observers, who flew in the light observation aircraft, to include the ability to mark targets and control air strikes.[28] Further, based on the lessons of Korea, the corps improved both the strength and communication capabilities of its battalion and regimental TACPs. It doubled the number of aviators and communicators assigned to the infantry battalion to provide each with an air liaison team and a forward air control team.[29]

In December 1951 the commandant issued his decisions on the recommendations of the Harris Board (Board to Study and Make Recommendations on Air-Ground and Aviation Matters). He decided "that a composite staff of air and ground officers [should] be formed when Fleet Marine Force air-ground task organization are employed in training and or/combat." Further, "the aviation officers [should] be integrated within each staff section and not formed into a separate aviation section."[30]

The very different viewpoints of the air force, army, and Marine Corps concerning close air support were not resolved immediately following the war. The services continued to fight over this issue for the next forty years. They seem to be in agreement on the use of aviation in the current conflicts in Iraq and Afghanistan, but the nature of those conflicts makes close air support aviation's primary mission, so there have been no other missions competing for fighter or bomber assets.

The second major impact of Korea was a deepening of the corps's dedication to its role as a force in readiness. Although "First to Fight" had been a marine slogan since the early twentieth century, the Korean experience modified its impact. Before Korea marines trained hard but believed there would be a period of mobilization to bring peacetime units to wartime strength before they fought. After Korea the concept of "First to Fight" came to include the idea that marines would fight with what they had on the day the war started. They trained accordingly and incorporated that concept into their contingency planning.

In addition to shaping the modern Marine Corps's attitude about the air-ground team and readiness, the fight at Pusan reinforced its concept that every marine must be a rifleman. The Chosin campaign made that an absolute requirement. This concept reinforced and was woven into the "first to fight with what you have ethos" and has been a hallmark of marine recruiting and public relations as well as the foundation of the corps's combat training ever since.

INSTITUTIONAL PARANOIA

The final marine characteristic reinforced by the Korean War was the corps's institutional paranoia. Unlike the corps after World War II, the post–Korean War Marine Corps did not believe its combat performance provided any protection in the budget battles inside Washington, D.C. The efforts to eliminate the corps during the late 1940s came after two very successful combat performances. In addition to the post–World War II trials, the corps's critics had tried to eliminate it after World War I. Despite its exceptional combat performance in 1918, by 1919 the corps "numbered just 1,570 officers and men and its demise seemed imminent."[31] If these two lessons weren't enough, the corps continued to fight for its existence in Washington even while fighting with great success in Korea. Brig. Gen. Ronald D. Salmon recalled that during the Korean War, the fight for marine air continued. "Remember we had 128 [squadrons] in World War II. We were fighting for 21 active squadrons in aviation. General Vandenburg of the Air Force had put in a request that he would allow us to have 12 squadrons, providing at the end of the crisis—emergency [the Korean War], they would all revert to the Air Force."[32] Thus, the Korean War and its aftermath deepened the corps's institutional paranoia. As Terry Terriff noted, "the Marine Corps sense of organization paranoia is not only firmly fixed in its organizational culture, a critical aspect of its identity, it arguably is one of the, if not the, dominant organizational cultural artifact that exerts an influence on other key organizational cultural attributes of the Corps."[33]

THE BRIGADE SET THE STANDARD

The fact that many of the myths about the brigade are not true does not in any way reduce its incredible accomplishments. If anything, the real circumstances of the formation and deployment make what those marines achieved even more epic. In less than ten days they had to

- Form a brigade, MAW (Forward), and service support headquarters without any Tables of Organization or Equipment;
- Transfer up to half of the men out of the units that did exist and had trained together;
- Bring those units up to peacetime strength by incorporating 50 percent or more new men from posts and stations all over the West Coast (in many cases this included commanding officers, executive officers, and key staff members);
- Integrate those people into units, including creating personnel and health records, drawing personal equipment and weapons, and establishing battle sight zero on the weapons;

- Reorganize the supporting units based on the K-Series T/Os while absorbing the necessary attachments from their battalion headquarters;
- Draw organizational equipment such as heavy weapons, vehicles, radios, and tents from war stocks (most of this equipment was left over from World War II, but some—for example, the M26 tanks and 3.5-inch rocket launchers—was so new that none of the marines in the brigade had yet seen it);
- Embark all the men and equipment from two ports over 100 miles apart;
- Spend three weeks in incredibly crowded amphibious shipping thinking they would unload and train prior to conducting an amphibious operation; and
- Commit every element of the brigade into combat within three days of getting off the ships.

The brigade was a hastily formed, badly understrength organization that succeeded. Although it did have a core of well-trained marines, the majority were hastily mobilized, not well conditioned for combat, and had little if any training in their combat assignments. All commanding officers were new to their units. The brigade's incredible record of only nine missing in action during the tumultuous first month of combat is a solid measure of its cohesion. What makes it even more remarkable is that the cohesion was achieved without the men having trained together as a unit or served together for any significant period. The cohesion came from the common culture based on education, doctrine, and training.

Between 1945 and 1950, the corps had both remembered the fundamental truths about men in combat and learned how to better combine the tools of modern warfare. In existence for only two months, the brigade proved the validity of the corps's post–World War II theories on air power, organization, discipline, and leadership. Even more important, the brigade once again validated the corps's cultural emphasis on esprit de corps, readiness, and even paranoia. Although often overlooked because of the momentous campaigns to follow, the brigade's performance matched that of its storied predecessors. The combat performance of the brigade's marines was so remarkable that it led to myths that clouded their true accomplishments.

Understanding the true nature of the brigade's challenges highlights the remarkable courage and cultural heritage that allowed these ordinary men to accomplish legendary feats. T. R. Fehrenbach, in his book *This Kind of War,* captured the essence of the impact marine culture had on the young men of the brigade who were thrown into battle with little preparation. He wrote, "These men walked with a certain confidence and swagger. They were only young men like those about them in Korea, but they were conscious of a standard to live up to, because they had had good training, and it had been impressed upon them that they were United States Marines."[34]

Notes

PREFACE

1. Joseph C. Goulden, *Korea: The Untold Story of the Korean War* (New York: Random House, 1982), 175.
2. Donald Knox, *The Korean War: Pusan to Chosin, an Oral History* (New York: Houghton Mifflin Harcourt, 1985), 84.
3. Andrew Geer, *The New Breed: The Story of the U.S. Marines in Korea* (Nashville, TN: Battery Press, 1989), 4.
4. Allan C. Bevilacqua, "Send in the Fire Brigade," *Leatherneck* 83, 17 (July 2000): 15.
5. John C. Chapin, *Fire Brigade: U.S. Marines in the Pusan Perimeter* (Washington, DC: History and Museums Division, Headquarters, U.S. Marine Corps, 2000), 3–4.
6. Stephen Biddle, *Military Power: Explaining Victory and Defeat in Modern Battle* (Princeton, NJ: Princeton University Press, 2004), 6.

1. FROM "A CORPS FOR THE NEXT 500 YEARS" TO A FIGHT FOR EXISTENCE

1. Trumbull Higgins, *Korea and the Fall of MacArthur: A Précis in Limited War* (New York: Oxford University Press, 1960), 8.
2. Joseph C. Goulden, *Korea: The Untold Story of the Korean War* (New York: Random House, 1982), 25.
3. Allan R. Millett, *The War for Korea, 1945–1950: A House Burning* (Lawrence, KS: University Press of Kansas, 2005), 190.
4. Ibid., 192.
5. Ibid., 215.
6. Ibid., 199.

7. Excerpts from Acheson's Speech to the National Press Club, January 12, 1950, http://web.viu.ca/davies/H323Vietnam/Acheson.htm (accessed 26 April 2009).

8. Letter from Brig. Gen. W. L. Roberts to Maj. Gen. C. L. Bolts, 8 March 1950 (National Archives and Research Administration, College Park, MD, Records Group 319, U.S. Army, stack location 631-32-09, box 121).

9. Roy E. Appleman, *South to the Naktong, North to the Yalu (June–November 1950)* (Washington, DC: U.S. Government Printing Office, 1960), 35.

10. Ibid., 38.

11. Ibid., 46.

12. Uzal W. Ent, *Fighting on the Brink: Defense of the Pusan Perimeter* (Paducah, KY: Turner Publishing Company, 1998), 32.

13. Appleman, *South to the Naktong, North to the Yalu*, 263.

14. Office of the Chief of Military History, U.S. Army, "Peace Becomes Cold War, 1945–1950," extracted from *American Military History*, www.army.mil/cmh-pg/books/amh/AMH-24.htm.

15. Ronald H. Spector, *At War at Sea: Sailors and Naval Combat in the Twentieth Century* (New York: Viking, 2001), 316.

16. Robert D. Heinl, *Soldiers of the Sea: The United States Marine Corps, 1775–1962* (Baltimore, MD: Nautical & Aviation Publishing Company of America, 1991), 510.

17. Ibid., 511–512.

18. Allan R. Millett, *Semper Fidelis: The History of the United States Marine Corps* (New York: Free Press, 1980), 447.

19. Alexander A. Vandegrift, *Once a Marine: The Memoirs of General A. A. Vandegrift, Commandant of the U.S. Marines in WW II* (New York: Marine Corps Association, 1964), 312.

20. Clifton La Bree, *The Gentle Warrior: General Oliver Prince Smith, USMC* (Kent, OH: Kent State University Press, 2001), 94.

21. Millett, *Semper Fidelis*, 453–454.

22. Heinl, *Soldiers of the Sea*, 512–513.

23. Millett, *Semper Fidelis*, 430.

24. Gen. Clifton B. Cates, USMC (Ret.), Oral History, 1973 (Bound Volumes, Marine Corps Oral History Division, Quantico, VA), 233.

25. Brig. Gen. Frederick P. Henderson, USMC (Ret.), 1976 (Bound Volumes, Marine Corps Oral History Division, Quantico, VA), 472.

26. Interview with Lt. Col. George R. Newton, 5 March 1951 (National Archives and Research Administration, College Park, MD, Records Group 127, U.S. Marine Corps, stack location 370/B/22/03, box 1, folder 6), 49.

2. MARINE CULTURE

1. John A. Lynn, *Battle: A History of Combat and Culture* (New York: Basic Books, 2003), xxv.

2. Ibid., xx.

3. Terry Terriff, "Warriors and Innovators: Military Change and Organizational Culture in the US Marine Corps," *Defence Studies* (June 2006): 215.

4. Tom Clancy with General Tony Zinni and Tony Koltz, *Battle Ready* (New York: Putnam, 2004), 141–143.

5. Korean War Educator, "Veterans' Memoirs: Joseph Alfred Crivello, Jr.," http://koreanwar-educator.org/memoirs/crivello_joe (accessed 17 July 2007).

6. Korean War Educator, "Veterans' Memoirs: Dean F. Servais," http://koreanwar-educator.org/memoirs/servais_dean (accessed 17 July 2007).

7. John W. Thomason, *Fix Bayonets! And Other Stories* (Washington, DC: MCA Heritage, 1980), p. xi.

8. Eugene B. Sledge, *With the Old Breed* (New York: Presidio Press, 1981), 315.

9. Philip Caputo, *A Rumor of War* (New York: HRW, 1977), 8.

10. *Leatherneck's* Famous Marine Quotes, www.mca-Marines.org/leatherneck/quotes.asp (accessed 7 February 2008).

11. "War: The First Team," *Time* magazine, 14 August 1950, www.time.com/time/magazine/article/0,9171,858895,00.html (accessed 22 August 2009).

12. Victor H. Krulak, *First to Fight: An Inside View of the U.S. Marine Corps* (Annapolis, MD: U.S. Naval Institute Press, 1984), 176.

13. Bruce Norton and Maurice Jacques, *Sergeant Major: The Biography of Sergeant Major Maurice J. Jacques, USMC (Ret.)* (New York: Ballantine, 1995), 21.

14. David J. Danelo, *Blood Stripes: The Grunt's View of the War in Iraq* (Mechanicsburg, PA: Stackpole Books, 2006), 13.

15. James Brady, *Why Marines Fight* (New York: Thomas Dunne Books, 2007), 42.

16. Korean Educator, "Veterans' Memoirs: Wilfred 'Will' Diaz," http://koreanwar-educator.org/memoirs/diaz_will (accessed 17 July 2007).

17. Korean Educator, "Veterans' Memoirs: Richard A. Olson," http://koreanwar-educator.org/memoirs/olson_richard (accessed 17 July 2007).

18. Gerald P. Averill, *Mustang: A Combat Marine* (Novato, CA: Presidio Press, 1987), 3.

19. Robert Speights, interview with the author, 13 February 2007.

20. Raymond E. Stevens letter to Uzal Ent (U.S. Army Military History Institute, Carlisle Barracks, PA, Uzal Ent Papers, box 17, folder 6).

21. Terry Terriff, "Innovate or Die: Organizational Culture and the Origins of Maneuver Warfare in the United States Marine Corps," *Journal of Strategic Studies* (June 2006): 477.

22. Frank Marutollo, *Organizational Behavior in the Marine Corps: Three Interpretations* (New York: Praeger Publishers, 1990), 1.

23. Clancy, Zinni, and Koltz, *Battle Ready,* 141.

24. Marutollo, *Organizational Behavior,* 70–71.

25. Allan R. Millett, *Semper Fidelis: The History of the United States Marine Corps* (New York: Free Press, 1980), 459.

26. "Statement by General Alexander A. Vandegrift, USMC, Before the Senate Naval Affairs Committee Hearings on S. 2044," *Marine Corps Gazette* (May 1946): 1A.

27. Marutollo, *Organizational Behavior,* 79.

28. Krulak, *First to Fight,* and Marutollo, *Organizational Behavior,* provide excellent accounts of these events.

29. Krulak, *First to Fight,* 51.

30. Extracts from the Marine Corps Board Report on Organization of the Fleet

Marine Force, War and Peace, 1 December 1948 (National Archives and Research Administration, College Park, MD, Records Group 127, U.S. Marine Corps, stack location 370/B/22/0, box 5, folder 5).

31. Millett, *Semper Fidelis,* 465.

32. Robert D. Heinl, *Soldiers of the Sea: The United States Marine Corps, 1775–1962* (Baltimore, MD: Nautical & Aviation Publishing Company of America, 1991), 524.

33. "James V. Forrestal, 1st Secretary of Defense, Truman Administration," www .defenselink.mil/specials/secdef_histories/bios/forrestal.htm (accessed 7 January 2008).

34. Heinl, *Soldiers of the Sea,* 525–526.

35. Ibid., 527.

36. Robert D. Heinl, "Inchon, 1950," in *Assault from the Sea: Essays on the History of Amphibious Warfare,* ed. Merrill L. Bartlett (Annapolis, MD: Naval Institute Press, 1983), 338.

37. James A. Warren, *American Spartans: The U.S. Marines: A Combat History from Iwo Jima to Iraq* (New York: Free Press, 2005), 107.

38. Jeffrey G. Barlow, *Revolt of the Admirals: The Fight for Naval Aviation, 1945–1950* (Washington DC: U.S. Government Printing Office, 1994), 188–190.

39. Ibid., 217.

40. Millett, *Semper Fidelis,* 472.

41. Robert D. Heinl, "The Marine Corps: Here to Stay," *Naval Institute Proceedings* (October 1940): 1085.

42. Statement of General A. A. Vandegrift, USMC (Ret.), delivered before the House Armed Services Committee Investigating the B-36 and Related Matters (National Archives and Research Administration, College Park, MD, Records Group 127, U.S. Marine Corps, stack location 370/B/24/04, box 6, folder 23-2), 5.

43. Statement of General Clifton B. Cates, Commandant, USMC, before the House Armed Services Committee Investigating the B-36 and Related Matters (National Archives and Research Administration, College Park, MD, Records Group 127, U.S. Marine Corps, stack location 370/B/24/04, box 6, folder 23-3), 2–8.

44. Barlow, *Revolt of the Admirals,* 273–277.

45. Heinl, *Soldiers of the Sea,* 530–531.

46. Ibid., 534.

47. Krulak, *First to Fight,* 121.

48. Warren, *American Spartans,* 107.

49. Even when the corps was heavily engaged in Korea, President Truman was adamant that it would remain small. In response to a request made during the Korean War by Congressman Gordon McDonough that the commandant be appointed a member of the JCS, Truman wrote, "For your information, the Marine Corps is the Navy's Police Force and as long as I am president that is what they will remain. They have a propaganda machine almost equal to Stalin's." The ensuing uproar from former marines and friends of marines resulted in one of Truman's few public apologies, delivered to the national meeting of the Marine Corps League. Still, it was not until 1952 that Congress passed Public Law 416 fixing the corps's strength at three division-wing teams and legislating that the commandant would be present whenever the JCS discussed matters of concern to the Marine Corps. Millett, *Semper Fidelis,* 507.

50. Krulak, *First to Fight,* 15.

51. Terriff, "Innovate or Die," 484.

3. EDUCATION: REUNITING THE AIR-GROUND TEAM

1. Robert D. Heinl, *Soldiers from the Sea: The United States Marine Corps, 1775–1962* (Baltimore, MD: Nautical & Aviation Publishing Company of America, 1991), 534.

2. Vernon E. Megee, "The Evolution of Marine Aviation," *Marine Corps Gazette* (October 1965): 45–46.

3. Lt. Gen. Louis E. Woods, USMC (Ret.), Oral History, 1968 (Bound Volumes, Marine Corps Oral History Division, Quantico, VA), 336–337.

4. Brig. Gen. Edward C. Dyer, USMC (Ret.), Oral History, 1973 (Bound Volumes, Marine Corps Oral History Division, Quantico, VA), 204.

5. Brig. Gen. Ronald D. Salmon, USMC (Ret.), Oral History, 1975 (Bound Volumes, Marine Corps Oral History Division, Quantico, VA), 156.

6. Lt. Gen. Donn Robertson, USMC (Ret.), Oral History, 1978 (Bound Volumes, Marine Corps Oral History Division, Quantico, VA), 184.

7. Robert D. Heinl, "USMC: Author of Amphibious Warfare," *Naval Institute Proceedings* (November 1947): 1311–1324.

8. Gen. Merrill B. Twining, USMC (Ret.), Oral History, 1975 (Bound Volumes, Marine Corps Oral History Division, Quantico, VA), 243.

9. Lewis Walt, "The Closer the Better," *Marine Corps Gazette* (September 1946): 39.

10. Robert E. Cushman, "Amphibious Warfare: Naval Weapon of the Future," *Naval Institute Proceedings* (March 1948): 299–307.

11. James R. Ray, "Marine Air-Infantry School," *Marine Corps Gazette* (March 1946): 9–11.

12. Interview with Capt. Edward P. Stamford, Forward Air Controller, ANGLICO Team, 16 March 1961 (U.S. Marine Corps Archives, Quantico, VA, box 144), 3–4.

13. Vernon E. Megee, "Control of Supporting Aircraft," *Marine Corps Gazette* (January 1948): 8–12.

14. Maj. Gen. Norman J. Anderson, USMC, Oral History (U.S. Marine Corps Archives, Quantico, VA, box 3), 84–87.

15. Leo B. Shin, "Stop Fighting the Japs," *Marine Corps Gazette* (August 1946): 24.

4. DOCTRINE

1. Alexander A. Vandegrift, "The Marine Corps in 1948," *Naval Institute Proceedings* (February 1948): 135–143.

2. Clifton La Bree, *The Gentle Warrior: General Oliver Prince Smith, USMC* (Kent, OH: Kent State University Press, 2001), 94.

3. Alexander A. Vandegrift, *Once a Marine: The Memoirs of General A. A. Vandegrift, Commandant of the U.S. Marines in WW II* (New York: Marine Corps Association, 1964), 319–320.

4. Robert D. Heinl, *Soldiers of the Sea: The United States Marine Corps, 1775–1962* (Annapolis, MD: Nautical & Aviation Publishing Company of America, 1991), 359.

5. Ibid., 386–387.

6. Vernon E. Megee, "The Evolution of Marine Air," *Marine Corps Gazette* (October 1965): 46.

7. John DeChant, "Devil Birds: With the Fast Carrier Task Forces," *Marine Corps Gazette* (September 1947): 39.

8. Condon, John Pomeroy, *Corsairs and Flattops: Marine Carrier Air Warfare, 1944–1945* (Annapolis, MD: U.S. Naval Institute Press, 1998), 5.

9. John DeChant, "Devil Birds: Operation Victory," *Marine Corps Gazette* (November 1947): 32–34.

10. Heinl, *Soldiers of the Sea,* 502–503.

11. Ibid., 477.

12. Fred H. Allison, "The Black Sheep Squadron: A Case Study in US Marine Corps Innovations in Close Air Support" (PhD dissertation, Texas Tech University, 2003), 327.

13. Ibid., 326.

14. Ibid., 334.

15. Ibid., 329–333.

16. Keith B. McCutcheon, "Air Support Techniques," *Marine Corps Gazette* (April 1946): 23–25.

17. Ibid., 23–25.

18. Amphibious Instructions to Landing Forces, USF-63 (NAVMC-4247), Chapter XI, Air Support.

19. PHIB 12 Amphibious Operations—Air Operations 1946 (Historical Amphibious Files, Marine Corps Archives, Quantico, VA, HAF 228), 39–44; PHIB 12 Amphibious Operations—Air Operations 1948 (Historical Amphibious Files, Marine Corps Archives, Quantico, VA, HAF 229).

20. CMC letter to Commandant of Marine Corps Schools, Quantico, Virginia, 19 December 1946 (Historical Amphibious Files, Marine Corps Archives, Quantico, VA, box 41, HAF 744), 1.

21. Brig. Gen. Edward C. Dyer, USMC (Ret.), Oral History, 1973 (Bound Volumes, Marine Corps Oral History Division, Quantico, VA), 196–197.

22. Eugene W. Rawlins, *Marines and Helicopters, 1946–1962* (Washington, DC: History and Museums Division, Headquarters, U.S. Marine Corps, 1976), 41.

23. Ibid., 1.

24. Ibid., 24–25.

25. Marine Helicopter Squadron 1 (HMX-1), Amphibious Command Post Exercise, 10–26 May 1948 (Historical Amphibious Files, Marine Corps Archives, Quantico, VA, box 13, HAF 284), III-2.

26. Roy L. Anderson, "The Marine Corps and the Helicopter," *Marine Corps Gazette* (August 1949): 13.

27. Gen. Vernon E. Megee, USMC (Ret.), Oral History (Bound Volumes, Marine Corps Oral History Division, Quantico, VA), 129–130.

28. Dyer, Oral History, 201.

29. Robert A. Streiby, "Employment of the Small Helicopter," *Marine Corps Gazette* (June 1950): 14–19.

30. Brig. Gen. Samuel G. Taxis, USMC (Ret.), Oral History, 1984 (Bound Volumes, Marine Corps Oral History Division, Quantico, VA), 197–202.

31. Anonymous, "Coordination of Supporting Fires," *Marine Corps Gazette* (October 1946), 37.

32. Harry H. Reichner, "FSCC: Another Empire?" *Marine Corps Gazette* (June 1950): 34.

33. Thomas N. Greene, "Greater Coordination of Supporting Fires," *Marine Corps Gazette* (April 1947): 40–42.

34. Amphibious Manual 6, The Battalion Landing Team, 1949 (Landing Force Manuals, Marine Corps Archives, Quantico, VA), 2–11.

35. James A. Pounds, "The Target Grid System," *Marine Corps Gazette* (October 1949): 34.

36. Ransom M. Wood, "Artillery Support for the Brigade in Korea," *Marine Corps Gazette* (June 1951): 16–24.

37. Arthur J. Stuart, "We Must Learn to Stop Tanks," *Marine Corps Gazette* (October 1947): 20.

38. Ibid.

39. Anonymous, "MAG-12 Makes a Landing," *Marine Corps Gazette* (February 1949): 32.

5. POST–WORLD WAR II ORGANIZATION

1. Staff, "Statement by General Alexander A. Vandegrift, USMC, before the Senate Naval Affairs Committee Hearings on S. 2044," *Marine Corps Gazette* (July 1946): 1A.

2. J-Series Tables of Organization, approved 5 March 1948 (Visual Information Repository, Marine Corps Archives, Quantico, VA, boxes 1828 and 1829).

3. Anonymous, "Staffing the Peacetime Marine Division," *Marine Corps Gazette* (October 1947): 37–45.

4. Ibid., 38.

5. Anonymous, "New Developments," *Marine Corps Gazette* (August 1947), 55.

6. Anonymous, "The Peacetime Marine Brigade," *Marine Corps Gazette* (October 1947): 45.

7. Gen. Oliver P. Smith, USMC (Ret.), Oral History, 1975 (Bound Volumes, Marine Corps Oral History Division, Quantico, VA), 178.

8. FMFWESTPAC Organization—Ground (Visual Information Repository, Marine Corps Archives, Quantico, VA, box 1828).

9. Edward A. Craig, *Incidents of Service* (unpublished manuscript), 147.

10. Historical Branch, U.S. Marine Corps, *A Brief History of the Fifth Marines* (Washington, DC: Historical Branch, USMC, 1963), 61.

11. Marine Corps Board Report on Organization of the Fleet Marine Force in Peace and War, 1 December 1948 (National Archives and Research Administration, College Park, MD, Records Group 127, U.S. Marine Corps, stack location: 370/C/81/05–C/81/07, box 5, folder 5).

12. In peacetime all corps troops, including the corps headquarters itself, were in cadre status with the exception of one company of amphibious tractors, one platoon of amphibious trucks, a combat support group, and a fumigation bath platoon.

13. K-Series Tables of Organization, dated 31 May 1949 (Visual Information Repository, Marine Corps Archives, Quantico, VA, boxes 1832 and 1833).

14. Interview with Lt. Col. George R. Newton, 5 March 1951 (National Archives and Research Administration, College Park, MD, Records Group 127, U.S. Marine Corps, stack location 370/B/22/03, box 1, folder 6), 49.

15. A Report on the Activities of FMFPac from 25 June 1950 to the Amphibious Assault at Inchon, Headquarters, Fleet Marine Force, Pacific, 6 December 1940 (National

Archives and Research Administration, College Park, MD, Records Group 127, U.S. Marine Corps, stack location 370/B/24/06, box 19, folder 32-6), II-4.

16. Robert D. Taplett, *Dark Horse Six: A Memoir of the Korean War, 1950–1951* (Williamstown, NJ: Phillips Publications, 2002), 20.

17. Francis Fox Parry, *Three-War Marine: The Pacific—Korea—Vietnam* (Pacifica, CA: Jove, 1987), 143.

18. Lewis Meyers, "Developing the Fire Team," *Marine Corps Gazette* (February 1946): 59.

19. Ibid., 60.

20. Interview with Capt. Edward P. Stamford, Forward Air Controller, ANGLICO Team, 16 March 1951 (Oral History Files, box 144), 18–22.

21. Irvin C. Jacobsen, "School for Air Observers," *Leatherneck* (May 1946): 64.

22. Lt. Gen. John C. Munn, USMC (Ret.), Oral History, 1974 (Bound Volumes, Marine Corps Oral History Division, Quantico, VA), 94.

23. James M. Johnson, "The MAG Needs Reorganizing," *Marine Corps Gazette* (November 1949): 32–36.

24. Marine Corps Board Report on Organization of the Fleet Marine Force in Peace and War, 36, 46–47.

25. Ibid., 44.

26. Ibid., 7.

6. TRAINING

1. Joseph C. Goulden, *Korea: The Untold Story of the Korean War* (NY: Random House, 1982), 175.

2. Victor H. Krulak, interview with author, 17 June 2005.

3. Maj. Gen. Kenneth J. Houghton, USMC (Ret.), Oral History, 1973 (Bound Volumes, Marine Corps Oral History Division, Quantico, VA), 36.

4. Capt. Francis I. Fenton, USMC, interview conducted 6–9 November 1950 (Oral History Files, box 55), 1.

5. Robert Clement, letter to Dale E. Robinson, 1 October 1993 (U.S. Army Military History Institute, Carlisle Barracks, PA, Uzal Ent Papers, box 16, folder 1).

6. Richard T. Spooner, interview with author, 13 February 2007.

7. A Report on the Activities of FMFPac from 25 June 1950 to the Amphibious Assault at Inchon, Headquarters, Fleet Marine Force, Pacific, 6 December 1940 (National Archives and Research Administration, College Park, MD, Records Group 127, U.S. Marine Corps, stack location 370/B/24/06, box 19, folder 32-6), I-2–4.

8. FY 1950 Training Directive from Commandant of the Marine Corps to Commander Generals FMFLant, FMFPac, and Marine Corps Schools, 27 May 1949 (National Archives and Research Administration, College Park, MD, Records Group 127, U.S. Marine Corps, stack location 370/B/24/04, box 21, folder 3).

9. Brig. Gen. Frederick P. Henderson, USMC (Ret.), Oral History, 1976 (Bound Volumes, Marine Corps Oral History Division, Quantico, VA), 474–476.

10. Ibid., 477.

11. Ibid., 478.

12. Ibid., 479–481.

13. Lt. Col. Francis F. Parry, USMC (Oral History Files, box 122), 3.

14. Ibid., 21.

15. Tom Gibson, letter to Uzal Ent (U.S. Army Military History Institute, Carlisle Barracks, PA, Uzal Ent Papers, box 18, folder 11).

16. Donald R. Gagnon, letter to Uzal Ent (U.S. Army Military History Institute, Carlisle Barracks, PA, Uzal Ent Papers, box 18, folder 12).

17. Commandant of the Marine Corps letter to Quartermaster General of the Marine Corps, 13 May 1948 (National Archives and Research Administration, College Park, MD, Records Group 127, U.S. Marine Corps, stack location 370/24/22, box 22, folder 2).

18. Interview with Lt. Col. George R. Newton, 5 March 1951 (National Archives and Research Administration, College Park, MD, Records Group 127, U.S. Marine Corps, stack location 370/B/22/03, box 1, folder 6), 8.

19. Ibid., 4.

20. Robert D. Taplett, *Dark Horse Six: A Memoir of the Korean War, 1950–1951* (Williamstown, NJ: Phillips Publications, 2002), 4.

21. Robert D. Bohn letter to Uzal Ent (U.S. Army Military History Institute, Carlisle Barracks, PA, Uzal Ent Papers, box 18, folder 12).

22. Taplett, *Dark Horse Six,* 28.

23. A Report on the Activities of FMFPac from 25 June 1950 to the Amphibious Assault at Inchon, I-3–4.

24. Robert D. Bohn, "The Approach March in Korea," *Marine Corps Gazette* (October 1951): 18–22.

25. A Report on the Activities of FMFPac from 25 June 1950 to the Amphibious Assault at Inchon, VIII-7.

26. Uzal W. Ent, *Fighting on the Brink: Defense of the Pusan Perimeter* (Paducah, KY: Turner Publishing Company, 1998), 132.

27. Maj. Gen. Norman J. Anderson, USMC (Oral History Files, box 3), 94.

28. 1st Provisional Marine Brigade, FMF Special Action Report, 2 August–6 September 1950, Annex H, 2.

29. John D. Manza, "The First Provisional Marine Brigade in Korea: Part I," *Marine Corps Gazette* (July 2000): 67.

30. Capt. Joseph C. Fegan Jr., USMC (Oral History Files, box 55), 93.

31. Allan R. Millett, *Semper Fidelis: The History of the United States Marine Corps* (New York: Free Press, 1980), 465–466.

32. John C. Chapin, *The Fire Brigade: U.S. Marines in the Pusan Perimeter* (Washington, DC: History and Museums Division, Headquarters, U.S. Marine Corps, 2000), 4.

33. Allan C. Bevilacqua, "Send in the Fire Brigade," *Leatherneck* (July 2000): 14–16.

34. Gerald R. Pitzl, *A History of Marine Fighter Attack Squadron 323* (Washington, DC: History and Museums Division, Headquarters, U.S. Marine Corps, 1987), 10.

35. Fred H. Allison, "The Black Sheep Squadron: A Case Study in US Marine Corps Innovations in Close Air Support" (PhD dissertation, Texas Tech University, 2003), 359.

36. A Report on the Activities of FMFPac from 25 June 1950 to the Amphibious Assault at Inchon, I-4.

37. Interview with Maj. Warren P. Nichols, Operations Officer, VMF-323, 30 July 1951 (National Archives and Research Administration, College Park, MD, Records Group 127, U.S. Marine Corps, stack location 370/B/22/03, box 1, folder 5), 4.

38. Pitzl, *A History of Marine Fighter Attack Squadron 323,* 10–11.

39. Brig. Gen. Edward C. Dyer, USMC (Ret.), Oral History, 1973 (Bound Volumes, Marine Corps Oral History Division, Quantico, VA), 238–239.

40. Allison, "The Black Sheep Squadron," 355–356.

41. Interview with Capt. Edward P. Stamford, Forward Air Controller, ANGLICO Team, 16 March 1951 (Oral History Files, box 144), 8.

42. Gary W. Parker and Frank J. Batha, *A History of Marine Observation Squadron Six* (Washington, DC: History and Museums Division, Headquarters, U.S. Marine Corps, 1982), 12–13.

43. Eugene W. Rawlins, *Marines and Helicopters 1946–1962* (Washington, DC: History and Museums Division, Headquarters, U.S. Marine Corps, 1976), 29.

44. Ernest H. Giusti, "Marine Air over the Pusan Perimeter," *Marine Corps Gazette* (May 1952): 18.

7. LEADERSHIP

1. Historical Branch, U.S. Marine Corps, *A Brief History of the Fifth Marines* (Washington, DC: Historical Branch, USMC, 1963), 61.

2. Lynn Montross and Nicholas A. Canzona, *U.S. Marine Operations in Korea, 1950–1953, Volume I: The Pusan Permimeter* (Washington, DC: Historical Branch, U.S. Marine Corps, 1954), 54.

3. Donald Knox, *The Korean War: Pusan to Chosin, an Oral History* (New York: Houghton Mifflin Harcourt, 1985), 84.

4. Andrew Geer, *The New Breed: The Story of the U.S. Marines in Korea* (Nashville, TN: Battery Press, 1989), 4.

5. Allan C. Bevilacqua, "Send in the Fire Brigade," *Leatherneck* (July 2000): 15.

6. Bruce Norton and Maurice Jacques, *Sergeant Major, U.S. Marines: The Biography of Sergeant Major Maurice J. Jacques, USMC (Ret.)* (New York: Ballantine, 1995), 36–37.

7. Dick Camp, *Leatherneck Legends: Conversations with the Old Breed* (St. Paul, MN: Zenith Press, 2006), 63.

8. *Battle Cry* is Leon Uris's first novel. It was based on his experiences as an enlisted marine in World War II, which included serving in Murray's battalion.

9. Col. Lawrence C. Hays Jr., HQMC Official Biography, 1 September 1957 (Document Section, Marine Corps Historical Division, Quantico, VA).

10. Col. George R. Newton, Personnel File, 21 July 1958 (Document Section, Marine Corps Historical Division, Quantico, VA).

11. Col. Harold S. Roise, HQMC Official Biography, 1 June 1965 (Document Section, Marine Corps Historical Division, Quantico, VA).

12. Brig. Gen. Frederick P. Henderson, USMC (Ret.), Oral History, 1976 (Bound Volumes, Marine Corps Oral History Division, Quantico, VA), 484.

13. Robert D. Taplett, Personnel File, 31 July 1958 (Document section, Marine Corps Historical Division, Quantico, VA).

14. 1st Provisional Marine Brigade, FMF Special Action Report (SAR), 2 August–6 September 1950 (Marine Corps Archives, Gray Research Center, Quantico, VA), Annex H; 3rd Battalion, 5th Marines, Special Action Report (Marine Corps Archives, Gray Research Center, Quantico, VA), Annex C, 1.

15. Ransom M. Wood, Personnel File (Document Section, Marine Corps Historical Division, Quantico, VA).

16. 1st Provisional Marine Brigade SAR, Annex I.

17. Merlin R. Olson, Personnel File (Document Section, Marine Corps Historical Division, Quantico, VA).

18. John W. Stevens, Personnel File (Document Section, Marine Corps Historical Division, Quantico, VA).

19. John J. Canney, Personnel File (Document Section, Marine Corps Historical Division, Quantico, VA).

20. Robert D. Bohn, Official Biography, undated.

21. Lt. Gen. Joseph C. Fegan Jr., HQMC Official Biography, undated (Document Section, Marine Corps Historical Division, Quantico, VA).

22. There is no complete file of personnel records. These figures were compiled by examining Marine Corps personnel records held at the Historical Division in Quantico, VA; interview forms from Brig. Gen. Uzal Ent's collection at the U.S. Army Military History Institute in Carlisle Barracks, PA; and various personal accounts of participants.

23. Donald R. Gagnon, letter to Uzal Ent (U.S. Army Military History Institute, Carlisle Barracks, PA, Uzal Ent Papers, box 18, folder 12).

24. Provisional Brigade G-1 Journal, 7 July–9 August 1950 (National Archives and Research Administration, College Park, MD, Records Group 127, U.S. Marine corps, stack location 370/C/81/05–C/81/07, box 6).

25. Korean War Educator, "Veterans' Memoirs: Richard A. Olson," http://koreanwar -educator.org/memoirs/olson_richard (accessed 17 July 2007).

26. Ibid..

27. Korean War Educator, "Veterans' Memoirs: Gene Dixon," http://koreanwar -educator.org/memoirs/dixon_gene (accessed 17 July 2007).

28. Korean War Educator, "Veterans' Memoirs: Clarence Hagan Vittitoe," http:// koreanwar-educator.org/memoirs/vittitoe_c_hagan (accessed 17 July 2007).

29. Norton and Jacques, *Sergeant Major,* 41–45.

30. James A. Pounds, "Training the Barracks Detachment," *Marine Corps Gazette* (December 1948): 22.

31. Brig. Gen. Edward C. Dyer, USMC (Ret.), Oral History, 1973 (Bound Volumes, Marine Corps Oral History Division, Quantico, VA), 238.

32. 1st Provisional Marine Brigade SAR; Marine Air Group 33 Special Action Report, 5 July to 6 Sept 1950 (Marine Corps Archives, Quantico, VA), 2.

33. Col. Hunter Reinburg, USMC, Discussion of night course air operations in support of the First Marine Brigade (Oral History Files, box 122), 3.

34. John C. Chapin, *The Fire Brigade: U.S. Marines in the Pusan Perimeter* (Washington, DC: History and Museums Division, Headquarters, U.S. Marine Corps, 2000), 8.

8. MOBILIZING AND EMBARKING THE BRIGADE

1. 1st Provisional Marine Brigade, FMF Special Action Report (SAR), 2 August– 6 September 1950 (Marine Corps Archives, Gray Research Center, Quantico, VA), 1.

2. John C. Chapin, *The Fire Brigade: U.S. Marines in the Pusan Perimeter* (Washington, DC: History and Museums Division, Headquarters, U.S. Marine Corps, 2000), 5.

3. Marine Corps Board Study: An Evaluation of the Influence of Marine Corps Forces on the Course of the Korean War (4 August 1950–15 December 1950) (National Archives and Research Administration, College Park, MD, Records Group 127, U.S. Marine Corps, stack location 370/B/24/06, box 19, folder 48-6), IV-A-2–3.

4. Gen. Lemuel C. Shepherd, USMC (Ret.), Oral History, 1976 (Bound Volumes, Marine Corps Oral History Division, Quantico, VA), 127–131.

5. Ibid., 131.

6. See ibid.; see also Lt. Gen. Victor H. Krulak, USMC (Ret.), Oral History, 1973, and Brig. Gen. Frederick P. Henderson, USMC (Ret.), Oral History, 1976 (Bound Volumes, Marine Corps Oral History Division, Quantico, VA).

7. Krulak, Oral History, 140.

8. 1st Provisional Marine Brigade SAR.

9. Ibid., Appendix 3, Annex C, Headquarters, 1st Marine Division, FMF Activation of Command, 6 July 1950.

10. Lt. Gen. Edward A. Craig, USMC (Ret.), Oral History, 1967 (Bound Volumes, Marine Corps Oral History Division, Quantico, VA), 159–160.

11. Shepherd, Oral History, 134.

12. Lemuel C. Shepherd, *Korean War Diary Covering Period 2 July to 7 December 1950* (unpublished manuscript), 4–5.

13. Allan R. Millett, *Semper Fidelis: The History of the United States Marine Corps* (New York: Free Press, 1980), 479.

14. Edward A. Craig, *Incidents of Service, 1917–1951* (unpublished manuscript), 153.

15. Ibid.

16. Craig, Oral History, 159.

17. Ibid., 160.

18. 1st Provisional Marine Brigade SAR, 3.

19. A Report on the Activities of FMFPAC from 25 June 1950 to the Amphibious Assault at Inchon, Headquarters, Fleet Marine Force, Pacific. 6 December 1940 (National Archives and Research Administration, College Park, MD, Records Group 127, U.S. Marine Corps, stack location 370/B/24/06, box 19 folder 32-6), I-1.

20. Headquarters, 1st Marine Division, FMF Activation of Command.

21. 1st Provisional Marine Brigade SAR, Annex J, 1–5.

22. Ibid., Annex K, 1–2.

23. Ibid., Annex R, 1–2.

24. Ibid., Annex E, 1–2.

25. Ibid., Annex E, Appendix 2, 1–2.

26. Ibid., Annex T, 1.

27. Ibid., Annex T, 2.

28. Craig, Oral History, 160.

29. Ibid., 161.

30. Henderson, Oral History, 507.

31. Provisional Brigade G-1 Journal, 7 July–9 August 1950 (National Archives and Research Administration, College Park, MD, Records Group 127, U.S. Marine Corps, stack location 370/C/81/05- C/81/07, box 6).

32. Ronald J. Brown, *A Few Good Men: The Fighting Fifth Marines: A History of the USMC's Most Decorated Regiment* (Novato, CA: Presidio Press, 2001), 206.

33. Robert D. Taplett, *Dark Horse Six: A Memoir of the Korean War, 1950–1951* (Williamstown, NJ: Phillips Publications, 2002), 7.

34. Ibid., 20–21.

35. Robert D. Bohn letter to Uzal Ent, 14 February 1994 (U.S. Army Military History Institute, Carlisle Barracks, PA, Uzal Ent Papers, box 17, folder 8).

36. Capt. Joseph C. Fegan Jr., USMC (Marine Corps Archives, Quantico, VA, Oral History Files, box 55), 94.

37. Lynn Montross, "The Pusan Perimeter: Fight for a Foothold," *Marine Corps Gazette* (June 1951): 31.

38. Capt. Francis I. Fenton Jr., Interview conducted 6–9 November 1950 (Marine Corps Archives, Quantico, VA, Oral History Files, box 55), 3–4. The field equipment issued to each marine is known as 782 equipment (after the number of the form the marine signs to take possession).

39. Francis W. Muetzel letter to Uzal W. Ent (U.S. Army Military History Institute, Carlisle Barracks, PA, Uzal Ent Papers, box 17, folder 9).

40. Korean War Educator, "Veterans' Memoirs: Clarence Hagan Vittitoe," http://koreanwar-educator.org/memoirs//vittitoe_c_hagan (accessed 17 July 2007).

41. 1st Provisional Marine Brigade SAR, 2.

42. Ransom M. Wood, "Artillery Support for the Brigade in Korea," *Marine Corps Gazette* (June 1951): 16.

43. A Report on the Activities of FMFPAC from 25 June 1950 to the Amphibious Assault at Inchon, II-5.

44. Interview with Lt. Col. George R. Newton, USMC, 5 March 1951 (Marine Corps Archives, Quantico, VA, Oral History Files, box 122).

45. 1st Provisional Marine Brigade SAR, Annex H, Annex A, 2.

46. Ibid., Annex H, 2.

47. Ibid., Annex H, Annex A, 1.

48. Ibid., Annex H, Annex B, 1.

49. Oscar Gilbert, *Marine Corps Tank Battles in Korea* (Havertown, PA: Casemate, 2003), 15.

50. 1st Provisional Marine Brigade SAR, Annex H, Annex F, 1.

51. Marine Corps Board Study, iv-a–11–12.

52. 1st MAW Operations Order 1-50, 12 July 1950, 1.

53. 1st Marine Air Wing Historical Record, July to September 1950 (Marine Corps Archives, Gray Research Center, Quantico, VA), 3.

54. Ibid., 4.

55. 1st MAW Operations Order 1-50, Appendix I, 1.

56. MAG 33 Unit Diary, July 1950, 3.

57. MAG 33 Special Action Report (SAR) for period ending 6 September 1950 (Marine Corps Archives, Quantico, VA), Annex A, 1.

58. John Pomeroy Condon and Peter B. Mersky, *Corsairs to Panthers: U.S. Marine Aviation in Korea* (Washington, DC: Diane Publishing, 2003), 4.

59. MAG 33 SAR, Annex A, 1.

60. MAG 33 Unit Diary, July 1950, 3–4.

61. Condon and Mersky, *Corsairs to Panthers,* 4.

62. Interview with Maj. Warren F. Nichols, Operations Officer VMF 323, 30 July

1951 (National Archives and Research Administration, College Park, MD, Records Group 127, U.S. Marine Corps, stack location 370/B/22/03, box 1, folder 5), 7.

63. MAG 33 SAR, Annex A, 2.

64. Ibid., Annex D, 1.

65. Ibid.

66. FMFPac Operation Plan 1-50, 3.

67. MAG 33 SAR, Annex F, 2.

68. Ibid., Annex D, 1.

69. Ibid., Annex J, 1.

70. Ibid., Annex E, 1.

71. Ibid., Annex K, 1.

72. Chapin, *The Fire Brigade,* 28.

73. Gary W. Parker and Frank M. Batha Jr., *A History of Marine Observation Squadron Six* (Washington, DC: Diane Publishing, 1982), 14.

74. Shepherd, *Korean War Diary,* 6.

75. Craig, Oral History, 161.

76. Heinl, *Soldiers of the Sea: The United States Marine Corps, 1775–1962* (Baltimore, MD: Nautical & Aviation Publishing Company of America, 1991), 539.

77. Chapin, *The Fire Brigade,* 9–10.

78. 1st Provisional Marine Brigade SAR, 4.

79. Craig, Oral History, 161–162.

80. Craig, *Incidents of Service,* 156–157.

81. Craig, Oral History, 165.

82. 1st Provisional Marine Brigade SAR, Annex H, Appendix F, II.

83. COMPHIBPAC to CINPACFLT 150227Z July 1950, Provisional Brigade G-1 Journal.

84. 1st Provisional Marine Brigade SAR, 3.

85. Fenton, Interview, 6.

86. Ibid., 7–8.

87. Korean War Educator, "Veterans' Memoirs: Gene Dixon," http://koreanwar -educator.org/memoirs/dixon_gene (accessed 17 July 2007).

88. Korean War Educator, "Veterans' Memoirs: Vittitoe."

89. Korean War Educator, "Veterans' Memoirs: Richard A. Olson," http://koreanwar -educator.org/memoirs/olson_richard (accessed 17 July 2007).

9. THE SACHON OFFENSIVE

1. 1st Provisional Marine Brigade, FMF Special Action Report (SAR), 2 August– 6 September 1950 (Marine Corps Archives, Gray Research Center, Quantico, VA), 7.

2. Ibid.

3. Col. Hunter Reinburg, USMC, Discussion of night course air operations in support of the First Marine Brigade Oral History (Marine Corps Archives, Oral History Files, box 122), 3.

4. MAG 33 Special Action Report (SAR) for period ending 6 September 1950 (Marine Corps Archives, Quantico, VA), Annex Q, 1.

5. Lynn Montross and Nicholas A. Canzona, *U.S. Marine Operations in Korea,*

1950–1953, Volume I: The Pusan Perimeter (Washington, DC: Historical Branch, U.S. Marine Corps, 1954), 90.

6. John C. Chapin, *The Fire Brigade: U.S. Marines in the Pusan Perimeter* (Washington, DC: History and Museums Division, Headquarters, U.S. Marine Corps, 2000), 12.

7. Andrew Geer, *The New Breed: The Story of the U.S. Marines in Korea* (Nashville, TN: Battery Press, 1989), 12.

8. MAG 33 SAR, Annex C, 2.

9. VMF 214 Summary of monthly operations, August 1950 (Marine Corps Archives, Quantico, VA), 5.

10. VMF 323 Report of the Evaluations of Operations Conducted 3 August 1950 to 6 September 1950 (Marine Corps Archives, Quantico, VA), 5.

11. Fred H. Allison, "The Black Sheep Squadron: A Case Study in US Marine Corps Innovations in Close Air Support" (PhD dissertation, Texas Tech University, 2003), 410.

12. Reinburg, Discussion, 7.

13. Ibid., 14–15.

14. MAG 33 SAR, Annex Q, 1–2.

15. Ibid., 3–6.

16. Lt. Gen. Edward A. Craig, USMC (Ret.), Oral History, 1967 (Bound Volumes, Marine Corps Oral History Division, Quantico, VA), 165.

17. 1st Provisional Marine Brigade SAR, 8.

18. Marine Corps Board Study: An Evaluation of the Influence of Marine Corps Forces on the Course of the Korean War (4 August 1950–15 December 1950) (National Archives and Research Administration, College Park, MD, Records Group 127, U.S. Marine Corps, stack location 370/B/24/06, box 19, folder 48-6), II-A-6.

19. Donald Knox, *The Korean War: Pusan to Chosin, an Oral History* (New York: Houghton Mifflin Harcourt, 1985), 84–85.

20. Montross and Canzona, *U.S. Marine Operations in Korea,* 92.

21. 1st Provisional Marine Brigade SAR, 8.

22. Capt. Joseph C. Fegan Jr., USMC (Marine Corps Archives, Oral History Files, box 55), 95.

23. Chapin, *The Fire Brigade,* 15.

24. Craig, Oral History, 168–169.

25. Robert D. Taplett, *Dark Horse Six: A Memoir of the Korean War, 1950–1951* (Williamstown, NJ: Phillips Publications, 2002), 25.

26. Craig, Oral History, 168.

27. Ibid., 66.

28. 1st Provisional Marine Brigade SAR, Annex E, 17.

29. MAG 33 SAR, Annex R, 7.

30. Chapin, *The Fire Brigade,* 18.

31. Report from the Secretary of Defense to the President of the United States on Operations in Korea During the Period 25 June 1950 to 8 July 1951 (National Archives and Research Administration, College Park, MD, Records Group 127, U.S. Marine Corps, stack location 370/B/22/03, box 7, folder 7), III-12.

32. Ransom M. Wood, "Artillery Support for the Brigade in Korea," *Marine Corps Gazette* (June 1951): 16.

33. Taplett, *Dark Horse Six,* 31.

34. Montross and Canzona, *U.S. Marine Operations in Korea,* 108.

35. Allan C. Bevilacqua, "Send in the Fire Brigade," *Leatherneck* (July 2000): 15.

36. Uzal W. Ent, *Fighting on the Brink: Defense of the Pusan Perimeter* (Paducah, KY: Turner Publishing Company, 1998), 137.

37. Chapin, *The Fire Brigade,* 19.

38. Bevilacqua, "Send in the Fire Brigade," 15.

39. Montross and Canzona, *U.S. Marine Operations in Korea,* 21.

40. Knox, *The Korean War,* 100.

41. 1st Provisional Marine Brigade SAR, Annex I, 1.

42. Robert Emmett, *A Brief History of the 11th Marines* (Washington, DC: Historical Branch, U.S. Marine Corps, 1968), 31–33.

43. 1st Provisional Marine Brigade SAR, Annex I.

44. Montross and Canzona, *U.S. Marine Operations in Korea,* 109.

45. Edward A. Craig, *Incidents of Service, 1917–1951* (unpublished manuscript), 158–159.

46. Wood, "Artillery Support for the Brigade in Korea," 17.

47. Craig, Oral History, 170.

48. VMF 214 Historical Diary August 1950 (Marine Corps Archives, Quantico, VA), 6–19.

49. VMF 323 Unit Diary August 1950 (Marine Corps Archives, Quantico, VA), 2–16.

50. Ernest H. Giusti, "Marine Air over the Pusan Perimeter," *Marine Corps Gazette* (May 1952): 19.

51. 1st Provisional Marine Brigade SAR, Annex E, 3.

52. Chapin, *The Fire Brigade,* 21.

53. Frank Smyth, "Night Support," *Marine Corps Gazette* (November 1951): 16–20.

54. MAG 33 SAR, Annex Q, 5–19.

55. 1st Provisional Marine Brigade SAR, Annex E, 12.

56. R. E. Sullivan, Colonel, USMC (Ret.), "An Interesting Life: Boot Camp to Eagles, Wars to Sail—the Rocks and Shoals," "Chindong-ni," www.kmike.com/Sully/Sully3.htm (accessed 7 January 2008).

57. Ent, *Fighting on the Brink,* 140.

58. Chapin, *The Fire Brigade*, 22.

59. 1st Provisional Marine Brigade SAR, Annex J, 3.

60. Paul Santiago letter to Uzal Ent (U.S. Army Military History Institute, Carlisle Barracks, PA, Uzal Ent Papers), Box 12.

61. Capt. Francis I. Fenton Jr., USMC, Interview conducted 6–9 November 1950 (Marine Corps Archives, Quantico, VA, Oral History Files), 14.

62. Ibid., 15.

63. 1st Provisional Marine Brigade SAR, Annex E, 5.

64. Ent, *Fighting on the Brink,* 142.

65. Taplett, *Dark Horse Six,* 40–42.

66. 1st Provisional Marine Brigade SAR, Annex I, 2.

67. Ent, *Fighting on the Brink,* 146.

68. Taplett, *Dark Horse Six,* 48.

69. Craig, *Incidents of Service,* 160.

70. Taplett, *Dark Horse Six,* 51.

71. 1st Provisional Marine Brigade SAR, Annex S, 2.

72. Ibid., Annex D, 4.

73. Giusti, "Marine Air over the Pusan Perimeter," 20.

74. Craig, Oral History, 171.

75. Ent, *Fighting on the Brink*, 148.

76. Official Marine Corps History refers to this as the Changchon Ambush. See Montross and Canzona, *U.S. Marine Operations in Korea,* Ch 8.

77. Francis I. Fenton Jr., "Changallon Valley," *Marine Corps Gazette* (November 1951): 49.

78. Fenton, Oral History, 38.

79. Fenton, "Changallon Valley," 50.

80. Ibid., 51.

81. Statement of Lt. Col. Robert D. Taplett, USMC, to Marine Corps Board (Marine Corps Archives, Quantico, VA, Oral History Files, box 144), 3.

82. Fenton, "Changallon Valley," 52.

83. 1st Provisional Marine Brigade SAR, Annex Sugar.

84. Ibid., 5.

85. Chapin, *The Fire Brigade,* 31.

86. 1st Provisional Marine Brigade SAR, Annex F, 3.

87. Ibid., Annex G, 2.

88. Knox, *The Korean War,* 112.

89. Chapin, *The Fire Brigade,* 35–36.

10. THE FIRST BATTLE OF THE NAKTONG BULGE

1. John C. Chapin, *The Fire Brigade: U.S. Marines in the Pusan Perimeter* (Washington, DC: History and Museums Division, Headquarters, U.S. Marine Corps, 2000), 38.

2. Ibid.

3. Interview with Maj. Warren F. Nichols, Operations Officer VMF-323, 30 July 1951 (National Archives and Research Administration, College Park, MD, Records Group 127, U.S. Marine Corps, stack location 370/B/22/03. box 1, folder 5), 17.

4. 1st Provisional Marine Brigade, FMF Special Action Report (SAR), 2 August–6 September 1950 (Marine Corps Archives, Gray Research Center, Quantico, VA), 12.

5. Ibid., Annex K, 4.

6. Ibid., Annex H, 08.

7. Ransom M. Wood, "Artillery Support for the Brigade in Korea," *Marine Corps Gazette* (June 1951): 19.

8. Ernest H. Giusti, "Marine Air over the Pusan Perimeter," *Marine Corps Gazette* (May 1952): 432.

9. Marine Corps Board Study: An Evaluation of the Influence of Marine Corps Forces on the Course of the Korean War (4 August 1950–15 December 1950) (National Archives and Research Administration, College Park, MD, Records Group 127, U.S. Marine Corps, stack location 370/B/24/06, box 19, folder 48-6), II-A-21.

10. 1st Provisional Marine Brigade SAR, Annex H, 8.

11. Ibid., Annex H, 3.

12. Uzal W. Ent, *Fighting on the Brink: Defense of the Pusan Perimeter* (Paducah, KY: Turner Publishing Company, 1997), 191; and Chapin, *The Fire Brigade,* 39.

13. Ent, *Fighting on the Brink,* 192.

14. Paul DiNito letter to Brig. Gen. Uzal Ent (U.S. Army Military History Institute, Carlisle Barracks, PA, Uzal Ent Papers, box 18, folder 12).

15. Ent, *Fighting on the Brink,* 193.

16. Lt. Gen. Edward A. Craig, USMC (Ret.), Oral History, 1967 (Bound Volumes, Marine Corps Oral History Division, Quantico, VA), 176.

17. 1st Provisional Marine Brigade SAR, Annex H, 9.

18. Donald Knox, *The Korean War: Pusan to Chosin, an Oral History* (New York: Houghton Mifflin Harcourt, 1985), 141.

19. Francis I. Fenton letter to Brig. Gen. Uzal Ent (U.S. Army Military History Institute, Carlisle Barracks, PA, Uzal Ent Papers, box 16, folder 2).

20. Korean War Educator, "Veterans' Memoirs: Ted Heckelman," http://koreanwar-educator.org/memoirs/heckelman (accessed 17 July 2007).

21. Capt. Francis I. Fenton, USMC, Interview conducted 6–9 November 1950 (Marine Corps Archives, Quantico, VA, Oral History Files), 48–49.

22. 1st Provisional Marine Brigade SAR, Annex H, 14–15.

23. Chapin, *The Fire Brigade,* 45.

24. Fenton, Interview, 50.

25. Fred H. Allison, "The Black Sheep Squadron: A Case Study in US Marine Corps Innovations in Close Air Support" (PhD dissertation, Texas Tech University, 2003), 439–440.

26. Fenton, Interview, 52.

27. Interview with Lt. Col. George R. Newton, 5 March 1951 (Marine Corps Archives, Quantico, VA, Oral History Files, box 122).

28. Fenton letter to Ent.

29. Marine Corps Board Study, II-A-27.

30. 1st Provisional Marine Brigade SAR, Annex O, 4.

31. VMF 214 Summary of monthly operations, August 1950 (Marine Corps Archives, Quantico, VA), 17.

32. Richard P. Hallion, *The Naval Air War in Korea* (Baltimore, MD: Nautical & Aviation Publishing Company of America, 1986), 46–47; William T. Y'Blood, *Down in the Weeds: Close Air Support in Korea* (Washington, DC: Air Force Museums and History Program), 5–3. Y'Blood reported that an F-80 flying from Japan had only about 10 minutes on station time. The Black Sheep squadron dropped 14,500 pounds of bombs that day, whereas Hallion reported that an F-80 squadron dropped 7,500 pounds in 17 days.

11. THE SECOND BATTLE OF THE NAKTONG BULGE

1. Capt. Francis I. Fenton Jr., USMC, Interview conducted 6–9 November 1950 (Oral History, Bound Volumes, Marine Corps Oral History Division, Quantico, VA, box 55), 62.

2. Ransom M. Wood, "Artillery Support to the Brigade in Korea," *Marine Corps Gazette* (June 1951): 21.

3. Personnel Periodic Report No 4 from 191800K August–261800K August, 1st Provisional Marine Brigade, FMF Special Action Report (SAR), 2 Aug–6 Sep 1950, Annex A, Appendix 3.

4. A Report on the Activities of FMFPAC from 25 June 1950 to the Amphibious Assault at Inchon, Headquarters, Fleet Marine Force, Pacific. 6 December 1940 (National Archives and Research Administration, College Park, MD, Records Group 127, U.S. Marine Corps, stack location 370/B/22/03, box 19, folder 32-6), II-9–10.

5. Paul DiNoto letter to Brig. Gen. Uzal Ent (U.S. Army Military History Institute, Carlisle Barracks, PA, Uzal Ent Papers, box 18, folder 12).

6. Fred Allison, "The Black Sheep Squadron" (PhD dissertation, Texas Tech University, 2003), 448–449.

7. 1st Provisional Marine Brigade SAR, Annex I, 4.

8. Korean War Educator, "Veterans' Memoirs: William James Fisher," http:// koreanwar-educator.org/memoirs/ fisher_william (accessed 17 July 2007).

9. Robert D. Taplett, *Dark Horse Six: A Memoir of the Korean War, 1950–1951* (Williamstown, NJ: Phillips Publications, 2002), 80–81.

10. John C. Chapin, *The Fire Brigade: U.S. Marines in the Pusan Perimeter* (Washington, DC: History and Museums Division, Headquarters, U.S. Marine Corps, 2000), 50.

11. Lt. Gen. Edward A. Craig, USMC (Ret.), Oral History, 1967 (Bound Volumes, Marine Corps Oral History Division, Quantico, VA), 175.

12. Marine Corps Board Study: An Evaluation of the Influence of Marine Corps Forces on the Course of the Korean War (4 August 1950–15 December 1950) (National Archives and Research Administration, College Park, MD, Records Group 127, U.S. Marine Corps, stack location 370/B/24/06, box 19, folder 48-6), II-A-31.

13. MAG 33 Special Action Report for period ending 6 September 1950 (Marine Corps Archives, Quantico, VA) states that from 3 to 5 September the two squadrons combined flew only seventy-five strikes, or less than half the number normally flown from the carriers.

14. 1st Provisional Marine Brigade SAR, 10.

15. Ibid., Annex H, 3.

16. Ibid., 4.

17. Ibid., Annex E, 15.

18. Letter from Maj. Gen. O. P. Smith to Commandant of the Marine Corps, 7 September 1950 (National Archives and Research Administration, College Park, MD, Records Group 127, U.S. Marine Corps, stack location 370/C/81/05- C/81/07, box 1 folder 29), 3.

19. Taplett, *Dark Horse Six,* 102.

20. Chapin, *The Fire Brigade,* 58.

21. Fenton, Oral History, 72.

22. 1stProvMarBde SAR 2 Aug—6 Sep 1950, Annex E, 16.

23. 1st Provisional Marine Brigade SAR, Annex I, 5.

24. Fenton, Oral History, pp. 79–80.

25. Uzal W. Ent, *Fighting on the Brink: Defense of the Pusan Perimeter.* Paducah, KY: Turner Publishing Company, 1998), 307.

26. Robert Emmett, *A Brief History of the 11th Marines* (Washington, DC: Historical Branch, U.S. Marine Corps, 1968), 32.

27. Ibid., 33.

28. 1st Provisional Marine Brigade SAR, Annex A, Appendix 8, 1.

29. Marine Corps Board Study, Annex A.

30. Chapin, *The Fire Brigade,* 63.

31. Taplett *Dark Horse Six,* 102.

32. Commanding general 1st Marine Division message to commanding general, FMFPac dtg 100802Z, Historical Diary, 1st ProvMarBde (Rein) for the Month of Sept, Enclosure 1.

33. Lynn Montross and Nicholas Canzona, *U.S. Marine Operations in Korea, Volume I: The Pusan Perimeter* (Washington, DC: Historical Branch, U.S. Marine Corps, 1954), 239.

34. R. J. Speights, *Roster of the 1st Provisional Marine Brigade, Reinforced for August and September 1950 While in Action in Korea* (Austin, TX: n.p., 1990), 53–160.

12. WHY DID THEY WIN?

1. A Report on the Activities of FMFPAC from 25 June 1950 to the Amphibious Assault at Inchon, Headquarters, Fleet Marine Force, Pacific. 6 December 1940 (National Archives and Research Administration, College Park, MD, Records Group 127, U.S. Marine Corps, stack location 370/B/22/03, box 19, folder 32-6), VIII-2.

2. Ibid., II-1.

3. John C. Chapin, *The Fire Brigade: U.S. Marines in the Pusan Perimeter* (Washington, DC: History and Museums Division, Headquarters, U.S. Marine Corps, 2000), 22.

4. Personnel Periodic Report No 4 from 191800K August–261800K August, 1st Provisional Marine Brigade, FMF Special Action Report (SAR), 2 August–6 September 1950, Annex D, 6.

5. Craig Cameron, *American Samurai: Myth, Imagination, and the Conduct of Battle in the First Marine Division, 1941–1951* (Cambridge: Cambridge University Press, 1994), 54.

6. Robert D. Heinl Jr., "The Marine Corps—Here to Stay," *Naval Institute Proceedings* (October 1950): 1088.

7. Interview with Lt. Col. George R. Newton, 5 March 1951 (Marine Corps Archives, Quantico, VA, Oral History Files, box 122), 17.

8. Lt. Gen. Edward A. Craig, USMC (Ret.), Oral History, 1967 (Bound Volumes, Marine Corps Oral History Division, Quantico, VA), 165.

9. John G. Westover, *Combat Support in Korea* (Washington, DC: Combat Forces Press, 1955), 109.

10. Ransom M. Wood, "Artillery Support for the Brigade in Korea," *Marine Corps Gazette* (June 1951): 24.

11. Gen. Oliver P. Smith, USMC (Ret.), Oral History, 1975 (Bound Volumes, Marine Corps Oral History Division, Quantico, VA), 178.

12. FMFWESTPAC Organization—Ground (Visual Information Repository, Marine Corps Archives, Quantico, VA, box 1828).

13. Robert Emmett, *A Brief History of the 5th Marines* (Washington, DC: Historical Branch, U.S. Marine Corps, 1963), 61.

14. Fred H. Allison, "The Black Sheep Squadron: A Case Study in US Marine Corps Innovations in Close Air Support" (PhD dissertation, Texas Tech University, 2003), 348.

15. Malcolm W. Cagle and Frank A. Manson, *The Sea War in Korea* (Annapolis, MD: Naval Institute Press, 1957), 51.

16. Allison, "The Black Sheep Squadron," 469.

17. Ibid., 470.

18. Ibid., 471.

19. Michael Lewis, *Lt Gen Ned Almond, USA: A Ground Commander's Conflicting View with Airmen over CAS Doctrine and Employment* (Maxwell Air Force Base, AL, 1997), 58.

20. Ibid.

21. Max Hastings, *The Korean War* (New York: Simon & Schuster, 1987), 255.

22. Lt. Col. Francis Fox Parry, USMC, Oral History (Marine Corps Archives, Quantico, VA, Oral History Files, box 122), 20.

23. 1st Provisional Marine Brigade SAR, Annex E, 15.

24. Allison, "The Black Sheep Squadron," 469.

25. Ibid., 469.

26. Daniel W. Boose Jr., "The Army View of Close Air Support in the Korean War," in Jacob Neufeld and George M. Mason Jr., eds., *Coalition Air Warfare in the Korean War, 1950–1953* (Washington, DC: US Air Force History and Museum Program, 2005), 104.

27. Robert D. Heinl Jr., *Soldiers of the Sea: The United States Marine Corps, 1775–1962* (Baltimore, MD: Nautical & Aviation Publishing Company of America, 1990), 588–589.

28. Marine Corps Schools, "Qualifications for Air Observers" (Quantico, VA, 1950), 25.

29. Gray Library Landing Force Manual 25, The Tactical Air Control Party, 1955 (Landing Force Manuals, Marine Corps Archives, Quantico, VA).

30. HAF 679, Extracts from CMC Decisions on Recommendations of the Harris Board, December 1951 (Historical Amphibious Files, Marine Corps Archives, Quantico, VA), 2.

31. Martin Van Creveld, *The Changing Face of War: Lessons of Combat, from the Marne to Iraq* (New York: Presidio Press, 2006), 105.

32. Brig. Gen. Ronald D. Salmon, USMC (Ret.), Oral History, 1975 (Bound Volumes, Marine Corps Oral History Division, Quantico, VA), 159.

33. Terry Terriff, "Innovate or Die: Organizational Culture and the Origins of Maneuver Warfare in the United States Marine Corps," *Journal of Strategic Studies* (June 2006): 483.

34. T. R. Fehrenbach, *This Kind of War: A Study in Unpreparedness* (New York: Macmillan, 1963), 188–189.

Bibliography

ARCHIVAL SOURCES

U.S. Army Military History Institute, Carlisle Barracks, PA
Uzal Ent Papers, Boxes 1–19

National Archives and Research Administration, College Park, MD,
Records Group 127, U.S. Marine Corps

Stack location 370/C/81/05–C/81/07
Box 6: Provisional Brigade G-1 Journal, 7 July–9 August 1950
Box 6: Provisional Brigade G-2 Journals 10 Ju1–10 August 1950
Box 7: Provisional Brigade G-2 Journals, 10–30 August 1950
Box 8: Provisional Brigade G-2 Journal, 31 August–9 September 1950

Stack location 370/B/22/03
Box 1, Folder 5: Interview with Maj. Warren P. Nichols, Operations Officer VMF-323, 30
    July 1951
Box 1, Folder 6: Interview with Lt. Col. George R. Newton, 5 March 1951
Box 1, Folder 11: Captain Osberne's Notes on Brigadier General Craig Comments, 26
    August 1950
Box 1, Folder 29: Copy of letter received by Gen. H. M. Smith from Marine Officer "Olin,"
    written in Korea, 24 December 1950
Box 1, Folder 29: Letter from Maj. Gen. O. P. Smith to Commandant of the Marine Corps,
    7 September 1950
Box 1, Folder 30: CINPACFLT Unclassified Summary Report of the Korean War to 1
    January 1951
Box 5, Folder 5: Marine Corps Board Report on Organization of the Fleet Marine Force in
    Peace and War, 1 December 1948
Box 7, Folder 7: Report from the Secretary of Defense to the President of the United States
    on Operations in Korea During the Period 25 June 1950 to 8 July 1951

Stack location 370/B/24/04
Box 6, Folder 23-2: Statement of General A. A. Vandegrift USMC (Ret.), Delivered Before the HASC Investigating the B-36 and Related Matters
Box 6, Folder 23-3: Statement of Clifton B. Cates, General, USMC, Commandant, USMC, Before the HASC Investigating the B-36 and Related Matters

Stack location 370/B/24/06
Box 19, Folder 32-6: A Report on the Activities of FMFPac from 25 June 1950 to the Amphibious Assault at Inchon, Headquarters, Fleet Marine Force, Pacific. 6 December 1950
Box 19, Folder 48-6: Marine Corps Board Study: An Evaluation of the Influence of Marine Corps Forces on the Course of the Korean War (4 August 1950–15 December 1950)

Stack location 370/24/22
Box 21, Folder 3: FY 1950 Training Directive from Commandant of the Marine Corps to Commander Generals FMFLant, FMFPac, and Marine Corps Schools, 27 May 1949
Box 22, Folder 2: Letter from Commandant of the Marine Corps to the Quartermaster General of the Marine Corps, 13 May 1948

National Archives and Research Administration, College Park, MD,
Records Group 319, U.S. Army

Stack location 631-32-09
Box 121: Letter from Brig. Gen. W. L. Roberts, Chief of U.S. Military Advisory Group to the Republic of Korea, to MG C. L. Bolts, G-3 U.S. Army, 8 Mar 1950

Marine Corps Archives, Gray Research Center, Quantico, VA
1st Marine Air Wing Historical Record, July to September 1950
1st Provisional Marine Brigade, FMF Special Action Report, 2 August–6 September 1950

Document Section, Marine Corps Historical Division, Quantico, VA
HQMC Official Biography, Bonn, Robert D., undated
HQMC Official Biography, Fegan, Joseph C., Lieutenant General, undated
HQMC Official Biography, Hays, Lawrence C., Jr., Colonel, 1 September 1957
HQMC Official Biography, Roise, Harold S., Colonel, 1 June 1965
HQMC Official Biography, Taplett, Robert D., Colonel, 31 July 1958
HQMC Official Biography, Wood, Ransom M., Colonel, undated
Personnel File, John J. Canney
Personnel File, Newton, George R., Colonel, 21 July 1958
Personnel File, Olson, Merlin R.
Personnel File, Stevens, John W.
Personnel File, Taplett, Robert D., 31 July 1958
Personnel File, Wood, Ransom M.

Historical Amphibious Files, Marine Corps Archives, Quantico, VA
Box 10: HAF 228 PHIB 12 Amphibious Operations—Air Operations 1946
Box 10: HAF 229 PHIB 12 Amphibious Operations—Air Operations 1948

Box 11B: HAF 255 COMINCH P-0012 Amphibious Operations Capture of Iwo Jima, 16 February to 16 March 1945

Box 13: HAF 284 Marine Helicopter Squadron One (HMX-1), Amphibious Command Post Exercise, 10–26 May 1948

Box 15: HAF 328 The Defense of Advanced Naval Bases 1948

Box 38: HAF 678 Extracts from the Marine Corps Board Report on Organization of the Fleet Marine Force, War and Peace, Dated 1 December 1948 (Hogaboom Board)

Box 38: HAF 679 Extracts from CMC Decisions on Recommendations of the HARRIS Board Dec 1951.

Box 41: HAF 742 STAFF STUDY The Establishment of a Balanced FMF Air Ground Force in the Western Pacific, HQS, FMFPAC, 19 October 1950

Box 41: HAF 744 CMC letter to Commandant of Marine Corps Schools, Quantico, Virginia, 19 December 1946

Box 47: HAF 787 Close Air Support of 1sy MARDIV—Letter and Extracts Supporting CMC Presentation to JCS Through CNO

Landing Force Manuals, Marine Corps Archives, Quantico, VA

Box 4: Amphibious Manual 6, The Battalion Landing Team 1949

Box 4: Amphibious Manual 5, The Regimental Combat Team 1951

Gray Library: Landing Force Manual 22, Coordination of Supporting Arms. 1954

Gray Library: Landing Force Manual 25, The Tactical Air Control Party, 1955

Gray Library: Tactical and Gunnery Air Observation, 1950

Gray Library: The Battalion Landing Team, 1949

Gray Library: The Regimental Combat Team 1951

MAG 33 Special Action Report for period ending 6 September 1950

Marine Corps Schools

Box 2: Amphibious Warfare School, Senior Course Syllabus, 1946

Box 2: Amphibious Warfare School, Senior Course Syllabus, 1949

Box 2: Marine Corps Schools, Qualifications for Air Observers, 1950

Box 7: Tactical and Gunnery Manual for Aerial Observers, 1948

Box 7: Tactical and Gunnery Manual for Aerial Observers, 1950

Visual Information Repository, Marine Corps Archives, Quantico, VA

Boxes 1828 and 1829: J-Series Tables of Organization, approved 5 March 1948, FMFWESTPAC Organization—Ground

Boxes 1832 and 1833: K-Series Tables of Organization, 31 May 1949, MTACS 2 Historical Diary, August 1950

Marine Corps Archives, Quantico, VA, Oral History Files

Box 3: Maj. Gen. Norman J. Anderson, USMC

Box 55: Capt. Joseph C. Fegan Jr., USMC

Box 55: Capt. Francis I. Fenton Jr., USMC, Interview conducted 6–9 November 1950

Box 77: Maj. Robert Hall, USMC

Box 122: Lt. Col. John H. Partridge, USMC

Box 122: Lt. Col. Francis Fox Parry, USMC

Box 122: Interview with Lt. Col. George R. Newton, USMC, 5 March 1951
Box 122: Col. Hunter Reinburg, USMC, Discussion of night course air operations in support of the First Marine Brigade
Box 144: Statement of Lt. Col. Robert D. Taplett, USMC, to Marine Corps Board
Box 144: Interview with Capt. Edward P. Stamford, Forward Air Controller, ANGLICO Team, 16 March 1951

Bound Volumes, Marine Corps Oral History Division, Quantico, VA
Maj. Gen. Robert Blake, USMC (Ret.), 1973
Lt. Gen. Edward A. Craig, USMC (Ret.), 1967
Lt. Gen. Edward A. Craig, USMC, Pusan Perimeter to Pohang, 8 May 1950
Gen. Clifton B. Cates, USMC (Ret.), 1973
Gen. Raymond G. Davis, USMC (Ret.), 1978
Lt. Gen. George F. Good, USMC (Ret.), 1974
Brig. Gen. Edward C. Dyer, USMC (Ret.), 1973
Lt. Gen. George F. Good Jr., USMC (Ret.), 1974
Brig. Gen. Frederick P. Henderson, USMC (Ret.), 1976
Brig. Gen. Bankston T. Holcomb, USMC (Ret.), 1974
Maj. Gen. Kenneth J. Houghton, USMC (Ret.), 1973
Lt. Gen. Victor H. Krulak, USMC (Ret.), 1973
Lt. Gen. Robert B. Luckey, USMC (Ret.), 1973
Gen. Vernon E. Megee, USMC (Ret.), 1973
Lt. Gen. John C. Munn, USMC (Ret.), 1974
Maj. Gen. Raymond Murray, USMC (Ret.), undated
Lt. Gen. Carson A. Roberts, USMC (Ret.), 1971
Lt. Gen. Donn J. Robertson, USMC (Ret.), 1978
Brig. Gen. Ronald D. Salmon, USMC (Ret.), 1975
Lt. Gen. Alan Shapley, USMC (Ret.), 1976
Gen. Lemuel C. Shepherd, USMC (Ret.), 1976
Lt. Gen. Merwin H. Silverthorn, USMC (Ret.), 1973
Lt. Gen. Ormond R. Simpson, USMC (Ret.), undated
Gen. Oliver P. Smith, USMC (Ret.), 1975
Lt. Gen. Edward W. Snedeker, USMC (Ret.), 1973
Brig. Gen. Joseph L. Stewart, USMC (Ret.), undated
Brig. Gen. Samuel G. Taxis, USMC (Ret.), 1984
Gen. Merrill B. Twining, USMC (Ret.), 1975
Lt. Gen. William J. Van Ryzin, USMC (Ret.), 1976
Lt. Gen. William J. Wallace, USMC (Ret.), 1967
Maj. Gen. Donald M. Weller, USMC (Ret.), 1989
Lt. Gen. Louis E. Woods, USMC (Ret.), 1968
MAG 33 Unit Diary, July 1950
VMF 214 Historical Diary, August 1950
VMF 214 Summary of Monthly Operations, August 1950
VMF 323 Unit Diary, August 1950
VMF 323 Report of the Evaluations of Operations Conducted 3 August 1950 to 6 September 1950

PUBLISHED SOURCES

Anderson, Roy L. "The Marine Corps and the Helicopter." *Marine Corps Gazette* (August 1949): 13–15.

Anonymous. "Coordination of Supporting Fires." *Marine Corps Gazette* (October 1946): 37–39.

——. "MAG-12 Makes a Landing." *Marine Corps Gazette* (February 1949): 32.

——. "New Developments." *Marine Corps Gazette* (January 1947): 56.

——. "New Developments." *Marine Corps Gazette* (February 1947): 56.

——. "New Developments." *Marine Corps Gazette* (August 1947), 55.

——. "The Peacetime Marine Brigade." *Marine Corps Gazette* (October 1947): 45.

——. "Staffing the Peacetime Marine Division." *Marine Corps Gazette* (October 1947): 37–45.

Appleman, Roy E. *South to the Naktong, North to the Yalu (June–November 1950).* Washington, DC: U.S. Government Printing Office, 1960.

Averill, Gerald P. *Mustang: A Combat Marine.* Novato, CA: Presidio Press, 1987.

Banks, Charles L. "Are You Fit?" *Marine Corps Gazette* (April 1949): 38–40.

Barlow, Jeffrey G. *Revolt of the Admirals: The Fight for Naval Aviation, 1945–1950.* Washington, DC: U.S. Government Printing Office, 1994.

Bartlett, Merrill L. *Assault from the Sea: Essays on the History of Amphibious Warfare.* Annapolis, MD: Naval Institute Press, 1983.

Bevilacqua, Allan C. "Send in the Fire Brigade." *Leatherneck* (July 2000): 14–21.

Bevin, Alexander. *Korea: The First War We Lost.* New York: Hippocrene Books, 1986.

Biddle, Stephen. *Military Power: Explaining Victory and Defeat in Modern Battle.* Princeton, NJ: Princeton University Press, 2004.

Boggs, Charles W. *Marine Aviation in the Philippines.* Washington, DC: Historical Branch, U.S. Marine Corps, 1951.

Bohn, Robert D. "The Approach March in Korea." *Marine Corps Gazette* (October 1951): 19–21.

Brady, James. *Why Marines Fight.* New York: Thomas Dunne Books, 2007.

Brown, Ronald J. *A Few Good Men: The Fighting Fifth Marines: A History of the USMC's Most Decorated Regiment.* Novato, CA: Presidio Press, 2001.

——. *Whirlybirds: US Marine Helicopters in Korea* (Washington, DC: Diane Publishing, 2000).

Burns, Milton. "Air Doubletalk." *Marine Corps Gazette* (January 1946): 67–69.

Cagle, Malcolm, and Frank Manson. *The Sea War in Korea.* Annapolis, MD: Naval Institute Press, 2000.

Cameron, Craig M. *American Samurai: Myth, Imagination, and the Conduct of Battle in the First Marine Division, 1941–1951.* Cambridge: Cambridge University Press, 1994.

Camp, Dick. *Leatherneck Legends: Conversations with the Old Breed.* St. Paul, MN: Zenith Press, 2006.

Caputo, Philip. *A Rumor of War.* New York: HRW, 1977.

Carr, Robert A. "A Job for Dive and Torpedo Bomber Pilots." *Marine Corps Gazette* (September 1949): 44.

Chapin, John C. *The Fire Brigade: U.S. Marines in the Pusan Perimeter.* Washington, DC: History and Museums Division, Headquarters, U.S. Marine Corps, 2000.

Clancy, Tom, with General Tony Zinni and Tony Koltz. *Battle Ready.* New York: Putnam, 2004.

Clausewitz, Carl von. *On War.* Ed. and transl. by Michael Howard and Peter Paret. Princeton, NJ: Princeton University Press, 1976.

Clay, Blair. *The Forgotten War: America in Korea, 1950–1953.* New York: Doubleday, 1989.

Condon, John Pomeroy, and Peter B. Mersky. *Corsairs and Flattops: Marine Carrier Air Warfare, 1944–1945.* Annapolis, MD: U.S. Naval Institute Press, 1998.

——. *Corsairs to Panthers: U.S. Marine Aviation in Korea.* Washington, DC: Diane Publishing, 2003.

Corbin, John. "The Thin Line of Tradition." *Marine Corps Gazette* (April 1948): 8–11.

Craig, Berry. *The Chosin Few: North Korea, November–December 1950.* Paducah, KY: Turner Publishing Company, 1989.

Cushman, Robert E. "Amphibious Warfare: Naval Weapon of the Future." *Naval Institute Proceedings* (March 1948): 299–307.

——. "Battle Replacements." *Marine Corps Gazette* (November 1947): 46–49.

Danelo, David J. *Blood Stripes: The Grunt's View of the War in Iraq.* Mechanicsburg, PA: Stackpole Books, 2006.

DeChant, John. "Devil Birds." *Marine Corps Gazette* (July 1947): 52–56.

——. "Devil Birds: The Battle for Okinawa." *Marine Corps Gazette* (October 1947): 46–53.

——. "Devil Birds: Operation Victory." *Marine Corps Gazette* (November 1947): 32–34.

——. "Devil Birds: With the Fast Carrier Task Forces." *Marine Corps Gazette* (September 1947): 36–45.

——. "Marine Aviation Observers in Africa and Europe." *Marine Corps Gazette* (July 1946): 21–23.

Eickelman, Dale F. "Culture and Identity: How They Influence Governance and Governability." Prepared for the National Defense University seminar Trends and Shocks, Columbia, MD, 25–26 September 2007.

Emmett, Robert. *A Brief History of the 11th Marines.* Washington, DC: Historical Branch, U.S. Marine Corps, 1968.

——. *A Brief History of the Fifth Marines.* Washington, DC: Historical Branch, U.S. Marine Corps, 1963.

Ent, Uzal W. *Fighting on the Brink: Defense of the Pusan Perimeter.* Paducah, KY: Turner Publishing Company, 1998.

Fehrenbach, T. R. *This Kind of War: A Study in Unpreparedness.* New York: Macmillan, 1963.

Fenton, Francis I., Jr. "Changallon Valley." *Marine Corps Gazette* (November 1951): 48–52.

Fick, Nathaniel. *One Bullet Away: The Making of a Marine Officer.* New York: Houghton Mifflin Harcourt, 2005.

Field, James A., Jr. *History of United States Naval Operations in Korea.* Washington, DC: U.S. Government Printing Office, 1962.

Futrell, Robert F. *The United States Air Force in Korea, 1950–1953,* rev. ed. Washington, DC: Office of Air Force History, 1983.

Geer, Andrew. *The New Breed: The Story of the U.S. Marines in Korea.* Nashville, TN: Battery Press, 1989.

Gilbert, Oscar. *Marine Corps Tank Battles in Korea*. Havertown, PA: Casemate, 2003.

Giusti, Ernest H. "Marine Air over the Pusan Perimeter." *Marine Corps Gazette* (May 1952): 18–25.

Godbold, Bryghte D. "Origin of the New Personnel System." *Marine Corps Gazette* (November 1949): 48–51.

Goulden, Joseph C. *Korea: The Untold Story of the Korean War*. New York: Random House, 1982.

Greene, Thomas N. "Greater Coordination of Supporting Fires." *Marine Corps Gazette* (April 1947): 40–42.

Griffitts, Lynn W. "Aviators Should Fly." *Marine Corps Gazette* (February 1950): 28–29.

Hallion, Richard P. *The Naval Air War in Korea*. Baltimore, MD: Nautical & Aviation Publishing Company of America, 1986.

Hanson, Victor D. *The Western Way of War: Infantry Battle in Classical Greece*. Berkeley: University of California Press, 2009.

Harnsborough, John W. "The Air-Ground Problem." *Marine Corps Gazette* (November 1946): 59–61.

Hashim, Ahmed. *Development of the Rifle Squad: A Historical Analysis*. Alexandria, VA: Center for Naval Analyses, 2000.

Hastings, Max. *The Korean War*. New York: Simon & Schuster, 1987.

Haynes, Fred E. "Marine Command of the Future." *Marine Corps Gazette* (November 1948): 38–43.

Heinl, Robert D. "The Marine Corps: Here to Stay." *Naval Institute Proceedings* (October 1950): 1085–1093.

——. *Soldiers of the Sea: The United States Marine Corps, 1775–1962*. Baltimore, MD: Nautical & Aviation Publishing Company of America, 1991.

——. "USMC: Author of Amphibious Warfare." *Naval Institute Proceedings* (November 1947): 1311–1324.

Higgins, Trumbull. *Korea and the Fall of MacArthur: A Précis in Limited War*. New York: Oxford University Press, 1960.

History and Museums Division. *The 1st Marine Division and Its Regiments*. Washington, DC: History and Museums Division, Headquarters, U.S. Marine Corps, 1981.

Hittle, J. A. "The Transport Helicopter: New Tool of Sea Power." *Marine Corps Gazette* (March 1950): 14–18.

Hodgson, Richard A. "The A-Bomb Comes into Focus." *Marine Corps Gazette* (October 1946): 22–27.

——. "The Atomic Bomb Tests and the Marine Corps." *Marine Corps Gazette* (July 1946): 25–29.

Hoffman, Carl W. "Concerning Bazookas." *Marine Corps Gazette* (July 1946): 31–32.

Hoffman, Frank. "The Marines: Premier Expeditionary Warriors." Foreign Policy Research Center, November 2007, www.fpri.org/enotes/200711.hoffman.marinesexpeditionarywarriors.html, accessed March 2008.

Hoyt, Edwin P. *The Pusan Perimeter: Korea 1950*. New York: Military Heritage Press, 1984.

Isley, Jeter A., and Philip A. Crowl. *The U.S. Marines and Amphibious War: Its Theory, and Its Practice in the Pacific*. Princeton, NJ: Princeton University Press, 1951.

Jacobsen, Irvin C. "School for Air Observers." *Leatherneck* (May 1946): 64.

Johnson, James M. "The MAG Needs Reorganizing." *Marine Corps Gazette* (November 1949): 32–36.

Jones, Brett A. *A History of Marine Attack Squadron 223*. Washington, DC: History and Museums Division, Headquarters, U.S. Marine Corps, 1978.

Keegan, John. *Mask of Command*. London: Penguin, 1988.

Keiser, Gordon W. *The Marine Corps and Defense Unification, 1944–47*. Baltimore, MD: Nautical & Aviation Publishing Company of America, 1996.

Kessler, Woodrow M. "Here's Your Recruit." *Marine Corps Gazette* (November 1948): 20–21.

Kier, Elizabeth. *Imagining War: French and British Military Doctrine Between the Wars*. Princeton, NJ: Princeton University Press, 1997.

Kintner, William R. "Panic: Discipline and Training." *Marine Corps Gazette* (September 1947): 30–33.

Kirkland, Faris R. "Soldiers and Marines at Chosin Reservoir: Criteria for Assignment to Combat Command." *Armed Forces and Society* (Winter 1995–1996): 257–274.

Knox, Donald. *The Korean War: Pusan to Chosin, an Oral History*. New York: Houghton Mifflin Harcourt, 1985.

Krulak, Victor H. *First to Fight: An Inside View of the U.S. Marine Corps*. Annapolis, MD: U.S. Naval Institute Press, 1984.

La Bree, Clifton. *The Gentle Warrior: General Oliver Prince Smith, USMC*. Kent, OH: Kent State University Press, 2001.

Leckie, Robert. *The Korean War*. London: Pall Mall Press, 1962.

Lewis, Michael. *Lt Gen Ned Almond, USA: A Ground Commander's Conflicting View with Airmen over CAS Doctrine and Employment*. Maxwell Air Force Base, AL, 1997.

Lubin, David. "Combat Air Observation." *Marine Corps Gazette* (June 1946): 39–43.

Lynn, John A. *Battle: A History of Combat and Culture*. New York: Basic Books, 2003.

Manza, John D. "The First Provisional Marine Brigade in Korea: Part I." *Marine Corps Gazette* (July 2000): 66–72.

——."The First Provisional Marine Brigade in Korea: Part II." *Marine Corps Gazette* (August 2000): 64–72.

Marshall, S. L. A. *Men Against Fire: The Problem of Battle Command in Future War*. Washington, DC: William Morrow, 1947.

Marutollo, Frank. *Organizational Behavior in the Marine Corps: Three Interpretations*. New York: Praeger Publishers, 1990.

McCutcheon, Keith B. "Air Support Techniques." *Marine Corps Gazette* (April 1946): 23–24.

McGlashan, Robert C. "The Bottom of the Barrel." *Marine Corps Gazette* (July 1949): 10–13.

McGuire, John D. "Marine Battalion Commanders, 1942–1988." Marine Corps Command and Staff College, 15 May 1989.

Megee, Vernon E. "The Evolution of Marine Aviation." *Marine Corps Gazette* (October 1965): 45–49.

——. "Control of Supporting Aircraft." *Marine Corps Gazette* (January 1948): 8–12.

Mersky, Peter B. *US Marine Corps Aviation: 1912 to the Present*. Baltimore, MD: Nautical & Aviation Publishing Company of America, 1983.

Meyers, Lewis. "Developing the Fire Team." *Marine Corps Gazette* (February 1946): 59–60.

Millett, Allan R. *Semper Fidelis: The History of the United States Marine Corps*. New York: Free Press, 1980.

———. *The War for Korea, 1945–1950: A House Burning.* Lawrence: University Press of Kansas, 2005.

Montross, Lynn. *Cavalry of the Sky: The Story of the US Marine Combat Helicopters.* New York: Harper & Brothers, 1954.

———. "The Pusan Perimeter: Fight for a Foothold." *Marine Corps Gazette* (June 1951): 30–40.

Montross, Lynn, and Nicholas Canzona. *U.S. Marine Operations in Korea, 1950–1953, Volume I: The Pusan Perimeter.* Washington, DC: Historical Branch, U.S. Marine Corps, 1954.

———. *US Marine Operations in Korea, 1950–1953,* commemorative edition CD. Washington, DC: History and Museums Division, Headquarters, U.S. Marine Corps, 2000.

Murray, Raymond L. "The First Naktong." *Marine Corps Gazette* (November 1965): 84–86.

Neufeld, Jacob, and George M. Watson, eds. *Coalition Air Warfare in the Korean War, 1950–1953.* Washington, DC: US Air Force History and Museum Program, 2005.

Norton, Bruce, and Maurice Jacques. *Sergeant Major, U.S. Marines: The Biography of Sergeant Major Maurice J. Jacques, USMC (Ret.).* New York: Ballantine, 1995.

Parker, Gary W., and Frank M. Batha Jr. *A History of Marine Observation Squadron Six.* Washington, DC: Diane Publishing, 1982.

Parry, Francis Fox. *Three-War Marine: The Pacific—Korea—Vietnam.* Pacifica, CA: Jove, 1987.

Pierce, Philip N., and Frank O. Hough. *The Compact History of the United States Marine Corps.* New York: Hawthorn Books, 1960.

Pitzl, Gerald R. *A History of Marine Fighter Attack Squadron 323.* Washington, DC: History and Museums Division, Headquarters, U.S. Marine Corps, 1987.

Pounds, James A. "The Target Grid System." *Marine Corps Gazette* (October 1949): 32–35.

———. "Training the Barracks Detachment." *Marine Corps Gazette* (December 1948): 22–24.

Rawlins, Eugene W. *Marines and Helicopters 1946–1962.* Washington, DC: History and Museums Division, Headquarters, U.S. Marine Corps, 1976.

Ray, James R. "Marine Air-Infantry School." *Marine Corps Gazette* (March 1946): 9–11.

Reichner, Henry H. "FSCC: Another Empire?" *Marine Corps Gazette* (June 1950): 32–36.

Ricks, Thomas E. *Making the Corps.* New York: Scribner, 1997.

Ridgway, Matthew B. *The Korean War.* Garden City, NY: Doubleday, 1967.

Robertson, Dr. William G. *Counterattack on the Naktong, 1950.* Fort Leavenworth, KS: Combat Studies Institute, U.S. Army Command and General Staff College, 1985.

Rose, Arthur. "Training Our New Reserve." *Marine Corps Gazette* (January 1946): 30–31.

Rush, Robert Sterling. *Hell in Hürtgen Forest: The Ordeal and Triumph of an American Infantry Regiment.* Lawrence: University Press of Kansas, 2004.

Sambito, William J. *A History of Marine Fighter Attack Squadron 312.* Washington, DC: History and Museums Division, Headquarters, U.S. Marine Corps, 1978.

Saxon, T. J. "Reply to Aviators Should Fly." *Marine Corps Gazette* (June 1951): 24–25.

Schuon, Karl. *U.S. Marine Corps Biographical Dictionary.* New York: Watts, 1963.

Shin, Leo B. "Stop Fighting the Japs." *Marine Corps Gazette* (August 1946): 23–25.

Sledge, Eugene B. *With the Old Breed*. New York: Presidio Press, 1981.

Smyth, Frank. "Night Support." *Marine Corps Gazette* (November 1951): 16–20.

Spector, Ronald H. *At War at Sea: Sailors and Naval Combat in the Twentieth Century*. New York: Viking, 2001.

Speights, Richard J. *Roster of the 1st Provisional Marine Brigade, Reinforced for August and September 1950 While in Action in Korea*. Austin, TX: n.p., 1990.

Staff. "Air Wing." *Marine Corps Gazette* (October 1946): 69.

——. "Coordination of Supporting Fires." *Marine Corps Gazette* (October 1946): 37.

——. "In Brief." *Marine Corps Gazette* (December 1949): 26.

——. "The Peacetime Marine Brigade." *Marine Corps Gazette* (October 1947): 45.

——. "Statement by General Alexander A. Vandegrift, USMC, Before the Senate Naval Affairs Committee Hearings on S. 2044." *Marine Corps Gazette* (July 1946): 1A.

——. "Summary of the Marine Corps Position." *Marine Corps Gazette* (December 1949): 17–19.

Streiby, Robert A. "Employment of the Small Helicopter." *Marine Corps Gazette* (June 1950): 14–19.

Strope, Walmer. "The Navy and the Atomic Bomb." *Naval Institute Proceedings* (October 1947): 1221–1228.

Stuart, Arthur J. "We Must Learn to Stop Tanks." *Marine Corps Gazette* (October 1947): 18–25.

Suh, Dae-Sook. *Kim Il Sung: The North Korean Leader*. New York: Columbia University Press, 1988.

Taplett, Robert D. *Dark Horse Six: A Memoir of the Korean War, 1950–1951*. Williamstown, NJ: Phillips Publications, 2002.

Terriff, Terry. "Innovate or Die: Organizational Culture and the Origins of Maneuver Warfare in the United States Marine Corps." *Journal of Strategic Studies* (June 2006): 475–503.

——. "Of Romans and Dragons: Preparing the US Marine Corps for Future Warfare." *Contemporary Security Policy* (April 2007): 143–162.

——. "Warriors and Innovators: Military Change and Organizational Culture in the US Marine Corps." *Defence Studies* (June 2006): 215–247.

Terry, Addison. *The Battle for Pusan: A Korean War Memoir*. Novato, CA: Presidio Press, 2000.

Thomason, John W. *Fix Bayonets! And Other Stories*. Washington, DC: MCA Heritage, 1980.

Toland, John. *In Mortal Combat: Korea, 1950–1953*. New York: William Morrow, 1991.

Van Creveld, Martin. *The Changing Face of War: Lessons of Combat, from the Marne to Iraq*. New York: Presidio Press, 2006.

——. *Fighting Power: German and US Army Performance 1939–1945*. Westport, CT: Greenwood Press, 1982.

Vandegrift, Alexander A. "The Marine Corps in 1948." *Naval Institute Proceedings* (February 1948): 135–143.

——. *Once a Marine: The Memoirs of General A. A. Vandegrift, Commandant of the U.S. Marines in WW II*. New York: Marine Corps Association, 1964.

Walt, Lewis W. "The Closer the Better." *Marine Corps Gazette* (September 1946): 38–40.

Warren, James A. *American Spartans: The U.S. Marines: A Combat History from Iwo Jima to Iraq.* New York: Free Press, 2005.

Weigley, Russell. *The American Way of War: A History of US Military Strategy and Policy.* Bloomington: Indiana University Press, 1977.

Westover, John G. *Combat Support in Korea.* Washington, DC: Combat Forces Press, 1955.

Whelan, Richard. *Drawing the Line: The Korean War, 1950–1953.* Boston, MA: Little, Brown, 1990.

Wiersema, Richard E. *No More Bad Force Myths: A Tactical Study of Regimental Combat in Korea.* Fort Leavenworth, KS: Army Command and General Staff College School of Advanced Warfighting, 1998.

Wilson, Peter H. "Defining Military Culture." *Journal of Military History* (January 2008): 11–41.

Wood, Ransom M. "Artillery Support for the Brigade in Korea." *Marine Corps Gazette* (June 1951): 16–24.

Y'Blood, William T. *Down in the Weeds: Close Air Support in Korea.* Washington, DC: Air Force Museums and History Program, 2002.

Zimmerman, John L. "Marine Corps Training." *Naval Institute Proceedings* (March 1948): 786–791.

———. "Stand, Gentlemen." *Naval Institute Proceedings* (March 1949): 289–293.

UNPUBLISHED MANUSCRIPTS

Allison, Fred H. "The Black Sheep Squadron: A Case Study in US Marine Corps Innovations in Close Air Support." PhD dissertation, Texas Tech University, 2003.

Craig, Edward A. *Incidents of Service 1917–1951.*

Shepherd, Lemuel C., Jr. *Korean War Diary Covering Period 2 July to 7 December 1950.*

ONLINE SOURCES

Highlands, Robert. "Korean War Memoirs of Robert Highlands, Co E, 2/5," http://members.aol.com/famjustin/Highlandbio.html, accessed 20 August 2007.

Korean War Educator, http://koreanwar-educator.org/memoirs
    Jack Burkett, accessed 20 August 2007.
    Charlie Carmin, accessed 14 August 2007.
    Joseph Alfred Crivello, Jr., accessed 17 July 2007.
    Frank Paul Czyscon, accessed 20 August 2007.
    Edwin Anthony DeDeaux, accessed 20 August 2007.
    Wilfred "Will" Diaz, accessed 17 July 2007.
    Gene Dixon, accessed 17 July 2007.
    William James Fisher, accessed 17 July 2007.
    Ted Heckelman, accessed 17 July 2007.
    Richard A. Olson, accessed 17 July 2007.
    Dean F. Servais, accessed 17 July 2007.

Albert H. Styles, accessed 17 August 2007.

Clarence Hagan Vittitoe, accessed 17 July 2007.

Ray L. Walker, accessed 17 July 2007.

Sullivan, Robert E. "An Interesting Life: Boot Camp to Eagles, Wars to Sail—the Rocks and Shoals," www.kmike.com/Sully/Sully2.htm, accessed 20 August 2007.

VMF(N)-513 "Flying Nightmares" (1951–1954). "How It Was: Kunsan Airbase," www.kalaniosullivan.com/KunsanAB/VMF513/Howitwasa1aa.html, accessed 20 January 2008.

PERSONAL INTERVIEWS

Krulak, Victor H., 17 June 2005.

Speights, Robert, 13 February 2007.

Spooner, Richard, 12 February 2007.

Index